PO 1695

£38

Mediation, Information, and Communication

Editorial Board

Mediation, Information, and Communication

Information and Behavior

Volume 3

Edited by

Brent D. Ruben

and

Leah A. Lievrouw

Transaction Publishers
New Brunswick (U.S.A.) and London (U.K.)

Copyright © 1990 by Transaction Publishers,
New Brunswick, New Jersey 08903

Library of Congress Catalog Number: 88-29598
ISBN: 0-88738-278-9
Printed in the United States of America

Library of Congress Cataloging-in-Publication Data

Information and behavior.

    Includes index.
    Contents:—v.   3. Mediation, information, and communication.
    1. Communication.   2. Information science.   I. Ruben, Brent D.
P90.1477   1989   001.51   88-29598
ISBN 0-88738-278-9 (v. 3)
ISSN: 0740-5502

Contents

List of Figures   viii

List of Tables   ix

Preface   xi
    Brent D. Ruben and Leah A. Lievrouw

Acknowledgments   xiv

Guidelines for Manuscript Preparation and Submission   xv

**PART I   Theories of Mediation: Views of the Communication
             Process**

Introduction   3
    Leah A. Lievrouw and Brent D. Ruben

1. The Critical Importance of Mass Communication as a Concept   9
    Joseph Turow

2. A Theory of Mediation   21
    Gary Gumpert and Robert Cathcart

3. Identifying the Common Dimensions of Communication: The
   Communication Systems Model   37
    Leah A. Lievrouw and T. Andrew Finn

4. Using Contextual Analysis to Bridge the Study of Mediated
   and Unmediated Behavior   67
    Joshua Meyrowitz

5. A Sequel to the "False Dichotomy" Perspective: Applications
   to the Challenge of Teaching Children about AIDS   95
    Kathleen Kelley Reardon

6. The Death of Intellectual History and the Birth of the
   Transient Past   117
    Sari Thomas and Michael Krippendorf

7. Interacting with Media: Para-Social Interaction and Real
   Interaction   125
   Sheizaf Rafaeli

**PART II   Information Societies: Developments in Research and
Policy**

Selected papers from a research forum sponsored by the
Annenberg Washington Program in Communication Policy
Studies, Washington, D.C., December 1984   184
   Convener. Everett M. Rogers
8. Introduction: The Emergence of Information Societies   185
   Everett M. Rogers

A.   Information Societies-in-Progress

9. Silicon Valley: A Scenario for the Information Society of
   Tomorrow   193
   Judith K. Larsen
10. The Research Triangle of North Carolina: Its History and
    Influence as an Information Society Component   205
    Quentin W. Lindsey
11. High Technology Development in Brazil   211
    Luiz Fonseca
12. Government Policies and High Technology in Japan   227
    Ryuzo Ogasawara
13. Telecommunications and International Financial Centers   239
    Mitchell L. Moss

**B.   Social Theory and the Emergence of Information
Societies**

14. Marketplace vs. Public Utility Models for Developing
    Telecommunications and Information Industries   253
    Jerry L. Salvaggio and Richard A. Nelson
15. University-Industry Technology Transfer in the Information
    Society   267
    Everett M. Rogers and James W. Dearing
16. The Communications Revolution Revisited   285
    Frederick Williams
17. The Information Society: Recurring Questions   295
    Rolf T. Wigand

**PART III   Current Reflections on Information and Communication
            Theory**

18. Tropes and Things   323
      Lee Thayer
19. Resonance and the Energy of Intelligence   349
      Gordon L. Miller
20. Thinking in Museums: Reflections among Masks   365
      David Carr
21. Information as an Economic Good: A Reevaluation of
      Theoretical Approaches   379
      Benjamin J. Bates
22. A Time-Line of Information Technology   395
      Jorge Reina Schement and Daniel A. Stout, Jr.

    About the Contributors   425
    Subject/Citation Index   431
      Gary P. Radford and James D. Anderson

List of Figures

Figure 3.1   Dimensions of Communication Behavior   51
Figure 3.2   Face-to-Face Communication within Dimensions of
  Communication Behavior   52
Figure 3.3   Communication Systems Arrayed within Dimensions
  of Communication Behavior   53
Figure 3.4   Communication Systems Arrayed within Dimensions
  of Communication Behavior   54
Figure 3.5   The Social Context of Communication   56
Figure 3.6   The Communication Systems Model   57
Figure 7.1   PSI as a Condition   141
Figure 7.2   Temporal Assymetry: PSI as a Path   142
Figure 13.1   Pacific Rim Cables   246
Figure 13.2   U.S. Pacific Rim: Trade and Communication   247
Figure 13.3   Pacific Rim: Concentration of GDP, Telephones, and
  Population   249
Figure 14.1   Marketplace Model   257
Figure 14.2   Public Utility Model   259
Figure 19.1   The Concept of Structure   357
Figure 19.2   Ratio and Rationality   358
Time Line of Information Technology   403

List of Tables

Table 7.1   Interacting with Print Mass Media, Percentages of
Interactants and Noninteractants   150
Table 7.2   Interacting with Electronic Mass Media, Percentages of
Interactants and Noninteractants   151
Table 7.3   Demographic Characteristics of Writers and
Nonwriters, by Group, in Percentages (1972, 1976, 1985)   153
Table 7.4   Distribution of Responses to Para-Social Interaction
Items   154
Table 7.5   Univariate and Bivariate Statistics for Scales Used in
Tables 7.6 and 7.8   155
Table 7.6   Hierarchical Regression of Television Use, by
Sociability and PSI   156
Table 7.7   Interaction Pattern and Cross-Tabulation for Television
Use, by Para-Social Interaction, and Sociability   158
Table 7.8   A Path Model of Sociability Effects on PSI and
Television Use   159
Table 7.9   Univariate Statistics and Intercorrelations for Scales
Used in Tables 7.10–7.12, 7.16–7.18   160
Table 7.10   Hierarchical Regression of Newspaper Use, by
Situational Sociability and Letter Writing   162
Table 7.11   Interaction Pattern, Cross-Tabulation for Newspaper
Use, by Letter Writing and Situational Sociability   163
Table 7.12   A Path Model of Situational Sociability Effects on
Real Interaction and Newspaper Use   164
Table 7.13   Hierarchical Regression of Newspaper Use by
Sociability and Letter Writing   165
Table 7.14   Interaction Pattern and Cross-tabulation for
Newspaper Use, by Letter Writing and Sociability   166

Table 7.15   A Path Model of Sociability Effects on Real
Interaction and Newspaper Use   167
Table 7.16   Hierarchical Regression of Newspaper Use by
Sociability Disposition and Letter Writing   168
Table 7.17   Interaction Pattern, Cross-Tabulation for Newspaper
Use, by Letter Writing and Disposition toward Sociability   169
Table 7.18   A Path Model of Sociability Disposition Effects on
Real Interaction and Newspaper Use   170
Table 13.1   Location of Largest 15 U.S. Law Firms in the Pacific
Rim   243
Table 14.1   High Technology Sales   261

Preface

Brent D. Ruben and Leah A. Lievrouw

When the idea for the *Information and Behavior* series was developed in 1983, one could be only partially aware of the significance that the relationship between the concepts of "information" and "behavior" would come to have five years later. The emerging popularity of the term "information" and phrases like "the information age" and "the information society" were hard to miss. But it was the view of the editor and members of the editorial board that beyond the faddish preoccupation with the newspeak of "information age," there were important issues of substance for scholars from a wide range of fields.

It was noted in the introduction to *Information and Behavior: Volume 1* that the relationship between information and behavior was a fundamental one (Ruben, 1985). Information processing was defined as one of two primary means through which living organisms adapt to their physical and social environments. It was also suggested that information and information processing play an indispensable role in physiological self-regulation, mating, reproduction, parent-offspring relations and socialization, locomotion, and the establishment and maintenance of territory. Moreover, information and information processes were acknowledged as being essential to higher-level processes including perception, cognition, personality development, and other forms of complex individual behavior. Information and information processes were considered to be of fundamental importance at the interpersonal, social, and cultural levels of analysis and were basic to the establishment and maintenance of relationships, groups, organizations and societies, and to the cultures, normative realities, rules, and roles of each. Finally, it was observed that the central role of concepts of information in generic theories such as system theory, cybernetics, information theories, and in disciplines such as communication, media studies, information science, computer science, and cognitive psychology pointed in the direction of heightening interdisciplinary interest and significance for the information concept (Ruben, 1985).

It was difficult to envision how broadly based the preoccupation with "information" would become, and to appreciate fully the potential for emerging concepts of information to link and further scholarship in a variety of fields. In many ways we have only begun to realize this later challenge and continue to search for the best ways to assist in the quest. In what may well become a tradition for *Information and Behavior: Volume 3* includes sections with chapters focused on selected issues that seem of particular importance to furthering our understanding of the information concept and its relationship to human behavior. Part I is concerned with *mediation*—the role of technology in communication and human information processes—and the nature of the relationship between mass and interpersonal communication processes. Part II provides a broad examination of *information societies,* drawing on contributions to a special Annenberg conference on the topic. Part III includes essays addressing a variety of topics related to information and communication theory.

As we offer the third volume in the annual series to readers, we would like to emphasize several points that have come to characterize *Information and Behavior.*

First, this volume, as others in the past have been, and as we hope volumes to come will be, is centered around conceptual or theoretical issues. This focus is essential to the continued vitality of research in both information science and communication research. In the past, both fields have been occasionally criticized for the weakness of their theoretical foundations (some take the extreme view, with which we strongly disagree, that studies of information and communication have been virtually atheoretical). We therefore submit *Information and Behavior* as a regular forum for the exploration of new models and theories in this area. As an annual, we believe it is uniquely suited for the presentation of theoretical research, instead of shorter-term empirical studies that may have temporary or limited applicability.

Second, we continue our strong commitment to the belief that the fields of communication research and information science are close allies in the search for understanding the communication basis of human social behavior. In recent years "information" has taken on a certain technological connotation, which is understandable, given the concurrent rise of computing and other new technologies that have been employed as communication media. However, information—and its "cousins" knowledge, belief, understanding, culture, wisdom—reflects human communication behavior within specific social contexts. Information science and communication, therefore, are seen here as being cut essentially from the same cloth, even though their patterns may differ.

Third, we want *Information and Behavior* to encourage scholars from more conventional subfields—mass media studies, interpersonal communication and speech, or telecommunications, for example, to reexamine their common concerns. A number of the contributors to this volume— Everett Rogers, Kathleen Reardon, Lee Thayer, Joseph Turow, Frederick Williams, David Carr, Mitchell Moss, and Joshua Meyrowitz, for example—all have well-earned reputations in their various subfields of specialization within communication and information science. However, their interests and questions tend to range far beyond those narrow disciplinary boundaries. Their pioneering efforts to find convergent threads or themes among their disparate specialties is the special concern of *Information and Behavior* as a research forum. While we may never really find a unified field theory of information and communication, it is at least helpful to begin by having a "unified field series." Therefore we want to stand at the intersections of several conceptual borderlines, where we believe the most interesting research is being done. We have looked for studies that are a bit more on the "fringe" than most of mainstream communication-information science research, and we have found an enormous source of creativity and scholarly vitality among the scholars represented here. We hope that the contributions to this volume are as provocative and enjoyable to read as they were to gather together.

References

Ruben, B. D. (1985). *Information and Behavior: Volume 1*. New Brunswick, N.J.: Transaction.

Acknowledgments

Many people have contributed to the development of the *Information and Behavior* Series, and in particular to *Volume 3*. We are particularly grateful to Associate Editors Jim Anderson and Dick Hixson, and Assistant Editor Gary Radford. Special thanks also to each member of the Editorial Board, whose valued guidance has been essential to the advancement of the Series.

We want to thank Irving Louis Horowitz, Scott Bramson, Mary Curtis, and Esther Luckett of Transaction for their encouragement and insight, and Joan Chabrak for her helpfulness at all stages of the manuscript preparation and review process. Finally, a note of appreciation to Rutgers University and the School of Communication, Information and Library Studies for continuing support.

Guidelines for Manuscript Preparation and Submission

Manuscripts are encouraged that address topics of information, communication processes, and technology, including: the information concept, applications and impact of information and information-processing technology, communication and information policy; information networks; cognitive information processing; information systems; information organization; information storage and retrieval; information management; economics of information; scientific communication; information forms; information media; artificial intelligence; and individual, social, and cultural functions of communication and information.

Articles may be philosophical, qualitative, quantitative, or policy-oriented in perspective. Preference will be given to manuscripts that address issues in a manner that will be of interest to an interdisciplinary audience.

Manuscripts to be considered for publication should be submitted in triplicate, following American Psychological Association style, to Brent D. Ruben, Professor and Director, Ph.D. Program, School of Communication, Information and Library Studies, 4 Huntington Street, Rutgers University, New Brunswick, New Jersey 08903. A style summary sheet is available from the editor.

PART I
THEORIES OF MEDIATION:
VIEWS OF THE COMMUNICATION
PROCESS

Introduction

Leah A. Lievrouw and Brent D. Ruben

In the last few years there has been a growing dissatisfaction among communication scholars with the gap that exists between the subfields of interpersonal communication theory and mass media theory. For scholars considering the social impacts of new telecommunications technologies, the dissatisfaction presents itself as struggles to define "mediated interpersonal"—but not mass—channels such as telephone, videotex, facsimile, or electronic mail. For students of popular culture it is expressed in debates over the nature of "mass audiences," if indeed such groups exist. In information science there is a contradiction between models of information needs (which emphasize meaning) and models of information delivery (which emphasize document retrieval). Among mass media scholars, debates continue over "effects" theories and the differences between mass communication and mass media. In the interpersonal area there is a growing sense that some channels that are not face-to-face per se (such as the telephone) may nonetheless provide a rich context for interaction.

Some scholars have explored the gray area where theories of interpersonal and mass communication intersect (Gumpert & Cathcart, 1979; 1982; 1986; Hawkins, Wiemann, & Pingree, 1988; Miller, 1988; Ruben, 1975; Thayer, 1968). Others have demonstrated the blurred line between interpersonal and mass communication experiences for individuals in developed societies. For example, Meyrowitz (1985) argues that mass-mediated content sacrifices individuals' regional or local geographic identities in favor of mass-market segmentation, leaving audiences with "no sense of place." In a similar vein, Beniger (1987) links the mass media with the creation of individually experienced pseudo-communities. Rafaeli (1988)

3

notes that the concept of "interactivity" as applied to newer telecommunications media is gradually being recognized as a technologically loaded euphemism for ordinary human communication behavior.

These are by no means the only examples that provide evidence for the shifting theoretical sensibilities among communication researchers. However, they are representative of work that has laid the foundation for the papers collected in the following section. We invite readers to consider several questions, which we believe provide a general framework for considering the articles as a collection.

What constitutes mediation or mediated communication? Do the media provide a genuinely different communication experience from face-to-face interaction, and if so, how? Are media merely "extensions" of our senses in a McLuhanesque sense? This point of view may suggest that all communication is mediated, whether by light, air, human senses and cognitive-emotional perceptions, or by complex electronic systems, or a combination of both, as Lievrouw and Finn suggest in their study in the present volume. Gumpert and Cathcart argue that it is important to preserve the concept of mediation because it represents the line between differing experiences of technology in the communication context. Another issue that bears examination is the various subcategories of mediation, for example, by time vs. distance, or whether these subcategories overlap. The essay by Sari Thomas on the impacts of different media used by writers on the subsequent historical records of their work brings the time element into sharp focus. Where does the line between interpersonal and mediated communication behavior lie?

What are the current differences between interpersonal and mass communication theory, and in what directions are these subfields headed? A principal issue is whether the two subfields consider human action as essentially different in face-to-face vs. mediated communication contexts. Mass communication theory, in the form of uses and gratifications or sense-making theory, seems to account better for individual differences in perception and participation than do older "bullet" or "hypodermic" theories of the media. Conversely, interpersonal theory is attending more to the social/media environment of dyadic and small-group interaction, and to the impact of technology in relationship formation and evolution. In the present volume, Reardon looks at the persuasive power of a combination of interpersonal and mass-mediated channels for informing children about their health risks for AIDS. Turow argues for the preservation of the "mass media" concept on the grounds that what is important is the ways in which mass media content is *produced* rather than how it is perceived—i.e., mass media is analogous with mass production in the industrial sense. From another perspective, Rafaeli examines "interactivity" as a construct that traditionally has been used by communication scholars to demarcate the dividing line between interpersonal and mass communication. In his study, Rafaeli finds that we may be able to distinguish between real (i.e., interpersonal, face-to-face, in real time) interaction, which he refers to as "ortho-social" interaction, and the sensation of interaction that is afforded by certain mediated channels such as video-games or computer data bases. This latter type of interaction is referred to by Rafaeli as "para-social" interaction. His scheme thus calls into question a term that many researchers have taken for granted.

Is the unmediated-/mediated-communication dichotomy in communication studies theoretically helpful, or does it prevent us from seeing new ways to conceptualize human interaction? Are there new theories of mediation emerging that might eclipse these differences? A growing group of scholars, several of whom are represented in the present volume (Ball-Rokeach & Reardon, 1988; Rogers, 1986; Rogers & Kincaid, 1981; Ruben, 1975) have argued that the divisions between interpersonal and mass theories owe more to the history and institutional constraints faced by communication research as a field than to any intrinsic differences in human behavior peculiar to one subfield or another. Bridges between the subfields, they argue, can only help illuminate the processes common to each, and possibly open the way for a contemporary general field theory of communication to emerge. Likewise, and in a way that echoes Rafaeli's efforts to call some given terms into question, Meyrowitz considers "context" or "situation" as a term that has been taken for granted but which is far from being unproblematic when we examine most individuals' actual communication behavior. Contexts are quite complex, but Meyrowitz suggests that the context or situation may serve as a new level of analysis for considering interpersonal and mass-mediated communication behavior simultaneously.

Is mass media/mass communication "dead" as an area of study? This is a hotly debated question, considering how much of the core of communication research has been founded on assumptions of mass social behavior affected by mass-mediated messages that reach huge segments of a population almost simultaneously (for example, studies on propaganda and persuasion, political campaigns, and even the early Paine Fund studies of motion pictures). In the present collection, Turow as well as Gumpert and Cathcart argue strongly that theories of mass communication are far from moribund, and continue to inform and enrich new theory. Turow explains his support of "mass communication" as a construct; he believes that mass media research has been misled to some extent by a mistaken emphasis on the effects of mediated messages on receivers—individuals—at the expense of looking at how the content itself is mass produced.

Should our notions of media structures be revised to encompass insti-tutions, transportation, and popular culture as well as the traditional electronic and print message channels? Perhaps the focus on "media" as large information-processing institutions based on print or electronic tech-nological infrastructures is too restricting (cf. Budd & Ruben, 1988). Perhaps fashion, mass retailing and marketing, and the shift from land-based to air transportation have all played a role in shaping our mediated and face-to-face symbolic environments. Turow's essay addresses this issue by suggesting that not enough attention has been paid to the roles of public relations, program syndication, and artist management firms, for example, as social structures that reflect the mass-produced nature of media content.

Would thorough social histories of all types of mediated channels—from the post, to print, to the telephone, to television, computers, and other electronic media—help inform this reassessment? Sari Thomas's essay traces this issue in the literary arena: what impact do the telephone, travel, and computers have on the primary historical materials writers (or other creative artists) leave behind about their intellectual or creative work processes and interpersonal interactions? Social histories of particular media technologies (e.g., the history of the typewriter as detailed by Jensen [1988]) may help observers identify previously unseen parallels among apparently differing systems.

The studies in this section cannot provide comprehensive answers for such a wide range of questions. But they do contribute substantially to the dialogue that is currently underway in the field. We believe that this conceptual area is of vital importance to the future course that communi-cation researchers and their students may take as they begin to cross the real and perceived boundaries that have divided interpersonal and mass communication theory and research.

References

Ball-Rokeach, S. J., & Reardon, K. K. (1988). Monologue, dialogue and telelog: Comparing an emergent form of communication with traditional forms. In R. P. Hawkins, J. M. Wiemann, & S. Pingree (Eds.), *Advancing communication science: Merging mass and interpersonal processes*. Newbury Park, CA: Sage.

Beniger, J. R. (1987). Personalization of mass media and the growth of pseudo-community. *Communication Research, 14*(3), 352–72.

Budd, R. W., & Ruben, B. D. (1988). *Beyond media: New approaches to mass communication* (2d ed.). New Brunswick, NJ: Transaction.

Gumpert, G., & Cathcart, R. (1979). *Inter/media: Interpersonal communication in a media world*. New York: Oxford University Press.

Gumpert, G., & Cathcart, R. (1982). *Inter/media: Interpersonal communication in a media world* (2d ed.). New York: Oxford University Press.

Gumpert, G., & Cathcart, R. (1986) *Inter/media: Interpersonal communication in a media world* (3d ed.). New York: Oxford University Press.

Hawkins, R. P., Wiemann, J. M., & Pingree, S. (Eds.) (1988). *Advancing communication science: Merging mass and interpersonal processes*. Newbury Park, CA: Sage.

Jensen, J. (1988). Using the typewriter: Secretaries, reporters, and authors, 1880–1930. *Technology in Society, 10*(2), 267–80.

Meyrowitz, J. (1985). *No sense of place: The impact of electronic media on social behavior*. New York: Oxford University Press.

Miller, G. R. (1988). Media messages and information processing in interpersonal communication: "Generally speaking." In B. D. Ruben (Ed.), *Information and Behavior: Volume 2*. New Brunswick, NJ: Transaction.

Rafaeli, S. (1988). Interactivity: From new media to communication. In R. P. Hawkins, J. M. Wiemann, and S. Pingree (Eds.), *Advancing communication science: Merging mass and interpersonal processes*. Newbury Park, CA: Sage.

Rogers, E. M. (1986). *Communication technology: The new media in society*. New York: Free Press.

Rogers, E. M., & Kincaid, L. (1981). *Communication networks: A new paradigm for research*. New York: Free Press.

Ruben, B. D. (1975). Intrapersonal, interpersonal, and mass communication processes in individual and multi-person systems. In B. D. Ruben, & J. Y. Kim (Eds.), *General system theory and human communication*. Rochelle Park, NJ: Hayden.

Thayer, L. (1968). *Communication and communication systems*. Homewood, IL: Irwin.

1

The Critical Importance of Mass Communication as a Concept

Joseph Turow

Some media scholars have argued recently that mass communication has outlived its usefulness as a concept. The present article reviews the term's history and suggests that this attitude comes from ignoring an entire intellectual tradition relating to it. It further argues that academics who denigrate the relevance of mass communication are, in effect, asking researchers to ignore many key questions about the relationship between power, society, and media. The article shows how a revitalized conception of mass communication can help illuminate a number of key developments central to late twentieth-century life.

During the past several years the rise of new information and communication technologies in the home, office, and elsewhere has sparked a fresh dialogue among communication researchers. A raft of questions centers on the best perspectives to use in examining these phenomena and their relationship to more traditional modes of human interaction.

One term that has drawn a lot of heat in some quarters is "mass communication." A few years ago the Eastern Communication Association even held a panel debate on whether the term should be abolished. At least a few people at the session agreed that the concept has outlived its usefulness. The gist of their argument was that mass communication means sending messages to huge numbers of individuals who have little in common. The conventional mass media—television, radio, newspapers—have been the vehicles through which mass communication has taken place. But, the argument continues, these vehicles have been undergoing revolutionary changes that have made their characterization as mass media increasingly anachronistic. The rise of cable television and videocassette recorders; the maturing of FM radio and the portability of audiocassette players; the competition that suburban newspapers, "shoppers," and other print vehicles have brought to the entrenched urban dailies—these and other evidence of fragmented channels have been slicing audiences into smaller and smaller groups. Moreover, the trend in audience and market research has been to utilize the latest telecommunication technologies so that media executives can selectively target particular messages to small numbers of consumers even when channels do reach large audiences.

With channel fragmentation and audience selectability seen as waves of the future, the idea of calling television, radio, and newspapers "mass media"—that is, vehicles that reach huge numbers of disconnected individuals—becomes more and more suspect to the term's critics. So, by extension, does the term mass communication. The critics urge that the process of mass communication be considered a fading historical stage in the development of more sophisticated technologies that mediate person-to-person communication. By making mass communication obsolete as a description of contemporary phenomena, the critics hope to focus research attention away from the "mass audience" to what they generally consider most important about media—the way persons use them to cope with themselves and others in everyday life.

The subject of coping is indeed important, and its exploration ought to be encouraged. At the same time, justifying research on media and the individual by denying the viability of mass communication as a concept in contemporary scholarly discourse is misguided. This article uses the debate about the term as a jumping point for arguing that it still holds valuable implications for researchers. I suggest that calls for its abolition (if only to make an intellectual point) perpetuate a tradition that ignores the special societal importance of mass communication. That special importance is rooted in the industrialized context of message creation as well as in the ability to have millions of people share the messages publicly throughout the society. From this perspective, a revitalized conception of mass communication helps to illuminate a number of developments that are central to late twentieth-century media.

Roots of the Problem

The tradition that stands in the way of a better contemporary understanding of the society-wide implications of mass communication has its roots in a perspective that, ironically, initially emphasized the society-wide importance of new mediating technologies. The perspective harks to nineteenth-century Europe. Early sociologists, followers of Auguste Comte, were trying to make sense of the cauldron of changes that were all around them—most prominently the lurching toward democracy, the industrial revolution, and rapid urbanization (Gouldner, 1970). In their view, a key to understanding what was going on lay in examining the increasingly evident phenomenon of the crowd, or mass.

To these observers, the prominence of the mass was part of a twofold change in the connection of the individual to society. On the one hand, increased urbanization and occupational specialization has sharpened an individual's disconnectedness by fragmenting the traditional communal bonds (what Ferdinand Tonnies called *gemeinschaft*) that had marked the society in earlier centuries. On the other hand, the new environment seemed to be encouraging people to periodically submerge their individuality in masses or crowds that, like organisms, seemed to take on a power of their own.

To Karl Marx and other observers, the rise of the mass indicated the potential power of the proletariat to exert favorable upheavals in society. To less radical thinkers, the violence and agitation of the masses were warnings that remedial actions had to be taken to solve the problems of industrialization and urbanization if additional turmoil were to be avoided. To conservative intellectuals, the power of the masses was part of a decline of civilization that had to be stopped.

Gustave Le Bon's (1896) book *The Crowd* was the most popular exponent of the conservative viewpoint. Le Bon wrote that "the substitution of the unconscious action of crowds for the conscious action of individuals is one of the principal characteristics of the present age" (p. 6). He also wrote that "crowds are only powerful for destruction" and added that "we are bound to resign ourselves to the reign of the masses, since want of foresight has in succession overthrown all the barriers that might have kept the crowd in check" (p. 18). Le Bon's description of the mass made a powerful impression in Europe and the United States. Significantly, discussion of the concept tended to shift between the two senses of the individual's connection to society that had developed in the previous century (Williams, 1976). While mass indicated (both favorably and unfavorably) the organic unity (i.e., aggregate) that Le Bon and others had emphasized, it also conjured up a very large number of dispersed individuals who had few, if any, communal bonds.

In the United States at the turn of the century, both meanings alerted American intellectuals to startling changes in the nature of the nation's communication media and in the audience for them. For the first time millions were reading issues of daily newspapers and weekly magazines. Also, millions were listening to phonograph records and watching motion pictures. Moreover, the novel elements that comprised the audience were drawing at least as much attention as its size. Children and illiterate adults were among the multitudes drawn to records and movies, which required no reading ability. And the immigrants who were then flooding the United States from eastern and southern Europe were attracted not only to the movies (which, soundless, required little knowledge of English) but to records and a burgeoning foreign-language press.

It was around these populations which until then had been marginally connected to communication technology that the most nervous discussions about the implications of the growth in that technology tended to coalesce. Emphasis on one or the other sense of "the mass," though, tended to highlight different problems for social thinkers and suggest different solutions. One branch of the academic discussion asked how individuals (usually children or criminals) react to particular messages. The other delved into how patterns of messages were influencing large social aggregates (Jowett, 1976).

It is this second branch that has been ignored in much mass communication research of the post–World War II era, and it is this branch and its philosophical offshoots that is ignored among those who argue that mass communication ought to be expunged from the contemporary researcher's vocabulary. During the first third of the twentieth century, though, the perspective that emphasized patterns of messages and their consequences for large social aggregates was espoused at what was then the center of American sociology, the University of Chicago.

There, John Dewey, Charles Horton Cooley, Robert E. Park, W. I. Thomas, and Florence Zaniecki found it critical to examine the role that mass media played in the society as a whole (Czitrom, 1982). In an important way they were responding to their immediate environment. They saw Chicago bursting with the benefits and costs of America's urban and industrial expansion. They saw it teeming with recent immigrants and brimming with vociferous debates about the need to "Americanize" the foreigners. Wistful for a return to the small town democracy of earlier decades, they looked to new media technologies for the vehicles through which a *gemeinschaft* life style could be encouraged in the new metropolitan age.

Robert E. Park was particularly concerned with this issue. An experienced reporter, he had studied "collective psychology" in Germany for his work toward a Ph.D. His dissertation, "The Crowd and the Public," was an attempt to move the perspectives of Le Bon and other conservative European social theorists in a somewhat optimistic direction (Czitrom,

1982). Adopting their notion that the crowd or mass was a negative social force, Park proposed the possibility of a "public" as a more favorable form of collective behavior. Park was suggesting, to quote Daniel Czitrom, that "the modern world offered more than the crowd as an alternative to traditional community" (Park, 1922). He posited that whereas the crowd was energized by feeling, empathy, and instinct, the public was motivated by thinking and reason. The great promise of modern media of communication, he argued, was their potential to defuse the possibility for crowd activity and, instead, create huge publics that shared a common sense of national heritage and concern for democratic values.

Park applied this perspective to the immigrant press that was growing throughout the country. Conclusions from his research countered those who argued that foreign-language newspapers ought to be suppressed because they were inhibiting large numbers of people from becoming true Americans. In fact, said Park, the immigrant press was typically creating publics with shared knowledge about how best to assimilate into their new country. Foreign-language newspapers, he said, served to "breed new loyalties from the old heritages," easing immigrants into American life.

In these and other writings, Park's emphasis was on the mass media's ability to energize populations (and create either masses or publics) by establishing shared knowledge. His unit of analysis was the society or social aggregate, not the individual. He inferred the societal role that newspapers were playing in two ways—by examining their content for recurring themes that were being shared by the audience, and by exploring the context of their production in order to understand the considerations that were leading to continuity and change in those themes.

In this respect, Park proved to be out of step with evolving academic interests in what was increasingly being called mass communication. From the standpoint of the dual sense of the mass, the stress on discussing individuals rather than organic aggregation gained dominance. During the 1930s and 1940s it became clear that the thrust of research on modern media lay in making the individual, rather than the society, the essential unit of analysis. Questions about the ability of particular movies to incite a child to juvenile delinquency (Charters, 1933), the ability of radio programs to induce a listener to panic (Cantril, 1939), the relative influence of interpersonal and media factors to encourage voting (Lazarsfeld, Berelson, & Gaudet, 1948), and the power of propaganda to change individual opinions (Hovland, Janis, & Kelly, 1953)—these became the central issues around which the field of mass communication research evolved.

The projects encouraging scholars in that direction came from Ohio State University, Princeton, Columbia, and Yale. When it came to grappling with, and extending, the meaning of "mass" that was implicit in their approach to mass communication, however, researchers turned to Herbert Blumer, a University of Chicago theorist. In a number of writings about collective behavior, Blumer had gone beyond Park's terminology to distinguish between a crowd, a mass, and a public (Blumer, 1956). By doing that, Blumer diverged from Park subtly though significantly. Unlike Park, he posited that a crowd and a public were both created not via the media but only through direct interactions among the people involved (the first on emotional, the second on rational, grounds). He added, also unlike Park, that a mass was not a product of interpersonal interaction.

Consequently, while crowds and publics were actual groupings, a mass could never become one. Instead, it was an indefinite, "elementary and spontaneous," array of dispersed individuals, anonymous to one another, with no leadership, who shared an interest in an event. The actions of individuals in the mass could have major implications for large-scale action in society, if all the individuals responded to the event similarly. The key question was, when and why did people respond in similar ways. To Blumer, this approach to the mass was the logical description of the audience for mass communication. Other researchers in the 1940s and 1950s seemed to agree with his individualistic tack but chafed at his notion of mass for its implication that the individuals in an audience do not interact.

That tension is reflected in a well-known 1953 *American Sociological Review* article titled "Communication Research and the Concept of the Mass," by Elliot Friedson (Friedson, 1956). Friedson tried to place Blumer's approach in synch with the contemporary emphasis on the role that interpersonal interaction played in people's responses to messages. Friedson accepted Blumer's individualistic orientation toward the mass but cautioned that, on a local level at least, the concept must account for the fact that people may use the mass media to reach other individuals.

Despite this attempt to update the individualistic slant on the mass, the sense of the concept as picturing an unrealistic notion of the audiences for television, newspapers, magazines and movies (and, later, cable television and videocassettes) has persisted. Researchers who focus on the interpersonal context in which these technologies operate are fond of insisting that the term is an incorrect characterization of individual behavior. The second slant on the term, the one that evokes large social aggregates that share messages, is not discussed much among contemporary communication researchers. Still, the approach is often implicit in Marxist and other critical perspectives that discuss the relationship between the media and social power. At the same time, this sense of the mass is underdeveloped and often not well understood.

Its emphasis on large-scale societal processes often has been associated with what is called a "mass society perspective." That view, in turn, has taken on a decidedly pejorative cast among even critical researchers during the past several years. In addition to evoking an audience of disconnected, faceless individuals, the mass society perspective often has been identified with a discredited "stimulus-response" understanding of media effects, which assumed that individual messages would have the same effect on everyone. One result is that not many people have come to the defense of mass communication as a viable concept for studying today's media environment.

The Concept's Contemporary Significance

The situation described above is unfortunate, because certain key developments in late twentieth-century Western society may be overlooked if television, radio, newspapers, billboards, comic books, and other such technologies are placed into the same category of "mediated communication" as the telephone or closed-circuit television. Moreover, the term's development should not be hindered by stereotyped images of a mass society. There is no reason to associate an insistence on the importance of shared media messages with a simplistic view of people's interpretive powers.

As researchers as diverse as George Gerbner, Elisabeth Noelle-Neumann, and Steven Chaffee have argued, it is perfectly compatible with an emphasis on message sharing to realize that not everyone in the audience may accept media presentations in the same way (Gerbner, Gross, Morgan, & Signiorelli, 1986; Noelle-Neumann, 1981; and Chaffee, 1981). For some, the media images may provoke discontent and underscore the importance of controlling the mediated cultural models. Others may accept the depictions as the way it is for others, though not for them.

This slant on mass communication does posit, however, that, whatever their particular interpretations, the dissemination of messages through mass media provides a unique potential for large numbers of otherwise different and unrelated people to orient around the same (or similar) images of the world. The potential comes not from the technologies of communication alone. Scholars as diverse as Karl Marx, Max Weber, and Robert E. Park understood that it comes from the use of those instruments by large-scale organizations as they apply standards of mass production to the creation and dissemination of news and entertainment.

With this orientation in mind, it becomes useful to refocus the conception of mass communication in order to separate it from visions of mass society and to make its relevance to contemporary society clear. Accordingly, mass communication is best viewed as the industrialized (mass) production, reproduction, and multiple distribution of messages through technological devices.

The word "industrialized" means that the process is carried out by mass media complexes or industries, that is, by conglomerations of organizations that interact regularly in the process of producing and distributing messages. Industrialized also implies the use of technology that provides the potential for reaching large, separated, diverse groups of people. Note that in shifting the primary focus of the word "mass" from the nature of the audience to the nature of the process, we avoid setting forth requirements about the number and nature of the people attending to the messages. Whether and how the production process influences, or is influenced by, the size and characteristics of the audience should be a matter of discussion and empirical examination.

Such definition implies other research directions. It urges exploration of the way that shared portrayals of the society and its institutions—the models of cultural authority they present and the issues they raise—get established, reinforced, and changed. It points to the usefulness of charting the common denominators that large segments of society share. And it implies the importance of learning more about the social aggregates that may be created when news and entertainment reach large numbers of diverse individuals—individuals who may broaden the audience for shared messages even further by discussing them with other people.

For the purpose of this paper, as a response to those who question the relevance of mass communication in the face of channel fractionalization, it will be useful to show how this reconstituted perspective on the term can encourage looking at the fractionalization trend in ways that are typically ignored in the communication literature. A point that the orientation encourages from the start is not to dismiss the importance of message sharing so easily. Whenever there exists the industrialized production and multiple distribution of symbolic materials through technological devices, there is likely to be significant social orientation around certain ideas. Of course, the size of the aggregate, or "public," so created may be an important issue. As noted earlier, much of the current literature projects that the publics for media materials are becoming progressively and inexorably smaller.

But taking a mass communication perspective on this phenomenon can encourage scholars to see it in a different light. Traditionally, academics interested in mass media have focused on particular industries that revolve around certain technologies—the broadcast television industry, the newspaper industry, the cable television industry, and the like. Researchers who attend to process of producing and distributing news and entertainment know that during the past few decades the lines between mass media industries have become increasingly blurred as producers long involved in one industry convey their material to other symbol-producing and distributing domains. So, for example, products created by the movie industry typically run through a gauntlet of distribution "windows" in different industries, starting with theaters, moving through pay cable and home video, and ending up in television syndication.

The cross-fertilization of production and distribution channels points to the idea that while the sharing of messages may be declining for any particular medium or media channel, that sharing may not be diminishing nearly as much, or hardly at all, if one takes into consideration the movement of news and entertainment across media boundaries. Through one form or another, and through one forum or another, the publics for particular depictions of the world may snowball tremendously. Even people who do not see a movie, for example, may share public statements about its basic themes by reading ads, hearing reviews on the radio, or seeing interviews with its stars on television magazine programs.

This shows the importance of a variety of organizations that have hardly gotten sociological attention for their cross-media roles. Public relations firms, syndication and creative rights companies, talent agencies, the press services, and advertising agencies are often active bridges between distribution channels. So are media conglomerates, corporations with financial holdings in several media industries. Not only might these firms be interested in exposing people and ideas in different media, they may also find it essential to do that financially. The reason for that has to do with an aspect of the current channel fractionalization that is rarely considered by communication researchers, namely, the inability of many producers and distributors to recoup their funds by exhibiting their material through one vehicle. The money squeeze forces them to find multiple ways to create huge audiences. If they cannot do it through one medium, they will do it through several (Turow, 1983).

The mass communication perspective, then, stresses close understanding of the production and distribution processes as a prerequisite for discerning opportunities for the widest sharing of messages. Fitting nicely with this approach is a strong research tradition on the considerations that shape news and entertainment. It emphasizes that the patterned approaches that lead to similar cultural models across stories are at least as important as individual stories (Turow, 1984). In other words, even when the specific subjects media carry are not the same, the similiarity with which creators approach the world can still yield similar perspectives. So, for example, when local television stations across the country daily fill their 7:25 AM newscasts with tales of overnight murders, robberies, and accidents, the general knowledge and world view that can be gleaned from those patterns might be the same, even though individual stories might not be. It is fascinating to consider what collective notions about everyday life Americans share as a result of such broadcasts.

Investigating the implications of these and other mass communication processes often means dealing with enduring questions about the models of society that people share through the media, the cultural argumentation that takes place as a result of media depictions, and the control over images that organizations and individual may attempt to exert. Another long-standing research concern is the ability of media organizations to provide publics with windows on certain issues relating to key areas of life while they turn people's collective attention away from other concerns. The study of media processes may also highlight the way in which forces in society at large use mass media as one among many instruments for accomplishing certain cultural goals and extending the groups' cultural power. In the end, the issues raised extend to the production and repro-duction of society itself (Turow, in 1989).

The ramifications of sharing messages, and patterns of messages, through society may be profound. By signaling the importance of studying such phenomena for the creation and sustenance of large social aggregates, the mass communication perspective encourages a slant on the role of media technology that is quite different from the slant that people who emphasize "mediated communication" use. When researchers interested in the role that media play in the lives of individuals urge academics to abandon the term "mass communication," they are, in effect, asking the field to ignore many questions of power and society that hinge on perceiv-ing the unique societal contributions that certain mediated communication processes make. In an era that is seeing major industrial as well as technological changes relating to media, we need a mass communication perspective to illuminate a range of societal issues and options that might otherwise be ignored. Far from having outlived its usefulness, the concept of mass communication ought to stand as an important signpost for a critical process in contemporary society.

References

Blumer, H. (1956). The crowd, the public and the mass. In W. Schramm (Ed.), *The process and effects of mass communication*. Urbana, Il: University of Illinois Press. (Original work published 1946).

Cantril, H. (1939). *The invasion from Mars*. Princeton, NJ: Princeton University Press.

Chaffee, S. (1981). Mass media in political campaigns: An expanding role. In R. Rice and W. Paisley (Eds.), *Public communication campaigns*. Beverly Hills, CA: Sage.

Charters, W. W. (1933). *Motion pictures and youth*. New York: Macmillan.

Czitrom, D. (1982). *Media and the American mind*. Chapel Hill, NC: University of North Carolina Press.

Friedson, E. (1956). Communication research and the concept of the mass. IN W. Schramm (Ed.), *The process and effects of mass communication*. Urbana, Il: University of Illinois Press.

Gerbner, G., Gross, L., Morgan, M. & Signiorelli, N. (1986). Living with television: The dynamics of the cultivation process. In J. Bryant and D. Zillman (Eds.), *Perspectives on media effects*. Hillsdale, NJ: L. Erlbaum.

Gouldner, A. (1970). *The coming crisis in western sociology*. New York: Basic Books.

Hovland, C., Janis, I., & Kelley, H. (1953). *Communication and persuasion*. New Haven: Yale University Press.

Jowett, G. (1976). *Film: The democratic art*. New York: Little Brown.

Lazarsfeld, P. F., Berelson, B., & Gaudet, H. (1948). *The people's choice*. New York: Columbia University Press.

Le Bon, G. (1896). *The Crowd*. London, UK: E. Benn.

Noelle-Neumann, E. (1981). Mass media and social change in advanced societies. In E. Katz and T. Szecsko (Eds.), *Mass media and social change*. Beverly Hills, CA: Sage.

Park, R. E. (1922). *The immigrant press and its control*. New York: Harper & Brothers.

Turow, J. (1983). Corporate planning and media culture. In R. Bostrom (Ed.), *Communication Yearbook 7*. Beverly Hills: CA: Sage.

Turow, J. (1984). *Media industries: The production of news and entertainment*. New York: Longman.

Turow, J. (1985). Cultural argumentation and the mass media: A perspective for research. *Communication, 8*(2), 139–64.

Turow, J. (1989). Television and institutional power: The case of medicine. In B. Dervin, L. Grossberg, and E. Wartella (Eds.), *Paradigm dialogues*. Beverly Hills, CA: Sage.

Williams, R. (1976). *Keywords*. New York: Oxford University Press.

2

A Theory of Mediation

Gary Gumpert and Robert Cathcart

This essay takes the position that the concept of mediation includes more than the channels that carry information, more than awareness of the producers of media messages, and more than the effects of the content of such messages. The study of mediation requires an awareness and understanding of the ways that all media technology produce unique forms of information which in turn have potent effects on producers, programmers, messages, receivers and the social construction of reality. The study of mediation cannot be limited to so-called mass distributors of information, but must include all media technology—cave paintings, hieroglyphics, script writing, print, telegraphy, telephone, radio, photography, film, and television. No technological medium of communication operates in isolation. Media technologies continually interface, redefining the older technologies, producing new forms and uses of mediated information. The presence of mediated communication influences even those acts in which mediation is absent. No one can function independently of the existing communication media. Our self-identity and cultural consciousness are inextricably intertwined with the media of communication.

> There was a clear fountain with water like silver
> to which the shepherds never drove their flocks,
> nor the mountain goats resorted, nor any of the
> beasts of the forest, neither was it defaced with
> fallen leaves or branches; but the grass grew
> fresh around it, and the rocks sheltered it from

21

the sun. Hither came one day the youth [Narcissus] fatigued with hunting, heated and thirsty. He stooped down to drink, and saw his own image in the water; he thought it was some beautiful water-spirit living in the fountain. He stood gazing with admiration at those bright eyes, those locks curled like the locks of Bacchus or Apollo, the rounded cheeks, the ivory neck, the parted lips, and the glow of health and exercise over all. He fell in love with himself. He brought his lips near to take a kiss; he plunged his arms in to embrace the beloved object. It fled at the touch, but returned again after a moment and renewed the fascination. He could not tear himself away; he lost all thought of food or rest, while he hovered over the brink of the fountain gazing at his own image. He talked with the supposed spirit: 'Why, beautiful being, do you shun me? Surely my face is not one to repel you. The nymphs love me and you yourself look not indifferent upon me. When I stretch forth my arms you do the same; and you smile upon me and answer my beckonings with the like.' His tears fell into the water and disturbed the image. As he saw it depart, he exclaimed, 'Stay, I entreat you! Let me at least gaze upon you, if I may not touch you'.
—Bullfinch, *Mythology*

Introduction

Narcissus became entranced with his self-image because he could not distinguish one state of reality from another, because his reflection was absorbed into the very process of ratiocination. The plight of Narcissus serves us today as a guiding metaphor for a thesis that the process of mediation has been infused into the very fabric of contemporary human activity; that all mechanical/electronic extensions of human interaction have been absorbed into the human cognitive and affective domains.

Every new media technology extends the reach of human communication, and, more important, it alters the ways in which humans relate to information and to each other. What we call "mediation" refers to something more than human communication via neutral electro/mechanical channels of transmission. The mediation of human communication involves forces that influence human information processing and shapes social interaction. Unfortunately, there exists a tendency to view a technological medium of communication as a mere mechanistic transmission device; as something which stands, as it were, between a sender and a receiver, in the middle, like a rock between two sides of a stream, integral neither to the sides of the stream nor to the person crossing over by means of it.[1] Such a view must be replaced with an awareness that humans, when employing a technological communications media for self-expression, are making "an extension of themselves" (McLuhan, 1964; Rogers, 1986). The medium becomes not only a part of the message, but also an extension of senders and receivers. The notion of mechanical tools as an extension of the physical self and communication as an extension of the psychological self has long been accepted, but not until the seminal works of Innis (1951) and McLuhan (1964) was it recognized that communication media were also an extension of the human self. Carey (1968), in summarizing the Innis-McLuhan position, explains;

> There are presumably two reasons for the centrality of communications technology—one logical, one historical. Innis assumes that man stands in a unique, symbiotic relationship to his technology. In McLuhan's phrase, technology is literally an extension of man, as the axe is an extension of the hand, the wheel of the foot. Most instruments are attempts to extend man's physical capacity, a capacity shared with other animals. Communications technology, on the other hand, is an extension of thought, of consciousness, of man's unique perceptual capacities. Thus communications media, broadly used to include all modes of symbolic representation, are literally extensions of mind. (P. 273)

Basic human feelings and thoughts have remained unchanged, but the rationality with which they are recognized, the manner in which they are expressed, and the environment in which they are interpreted are all dictated by the nature of the communications media that provide for their expression (Ong, 1977). Thus, media become inseparable from the human communication process.

Most human beings like to believe that they are generally in control of their fate; that their options are not predetermined. Likewise, they tend to believe that they are masters of the tools and technologies that surround them; that humans can use these technologies as they please and discard them at will. Self-determination, however, can never be realized in a true sense. Humans can never be fully free to determine their own ends nor can they escape the determining consequences of their technologies; witness the effects on human destiny of the early invention of the wheel and its later extension—the automobile. Of even greater consequence in determining the direction of human history was the development of imprinting technologies and the alphabet. Ellul (1964) in examining the question of media determinism makes this important claim:

> Individual decisions are always made within the framework of . . . sociological reality, itself pre-existent and more or less determinative. . . . I do not maintain that the individual is more determined today than he has been in the past; rather, that he is differently determined. Primitive man, hemmed in by prohibi-

tions, taboos, and rites, was, of course, socially determined. . . . Today, we are conditioned by something new, technological civilization. . . . Keeping in mind that sociological mechanisms are always significant determinants . . . for the individual, I would maintain that we have moved from one set of determinants to another. (Pp. xxvii–xxix)

There are always forces outside ourselves that limit or change our alternatives. Part of these forces are the technologies we have become dependent on. Mass communications technologies, for example, have created dependencies that shape our ways of thinking and behaving. Ball-Rokeach and DeFleur (1975) reveal some of the deterministic powers of media in their "dependency model of mass media effects":

> [Our] conceptualization stresses as a central issue the *dependency* of audiences on media information resources—a dependency that leads to modifications in both personal and social processes. . . . Dependency on media information resources is an ubiquitous condition in modern society. . . . There are numerous ways in which people are dependent on media to satisfy information needs. For example, one form of dependency is based on the need to understand one's social world; another type of dependency arises from the need to act meaningfully and effectively in the world; still a third type of dependency is based on the need for fantasy-escape from daily problems and tensions. The greater the need and consequently the stronger the dependency in such matters, the greater the likelihood that the information supplied will alter various forms of audience cognition, feelings, and behavior. (Pp. 240–41)

The claim that we are media dependent is often met with resistance, probably because a communications medium is seen by most as merely a mechanistic tool serving human communication rather than as a unique symbol system that defines, in part, the nature of human will. No one today can operate apart from the influences of mediation, because our functional, cultural, social, and psychological identities are, in large part, dependent on the instrumentalities of media.

A Theory of Mediation

First, There Was a Medium

No theory of mediation can be postulated without some agreement about the nature of its central term—a medium. A definition of "medium" must begin with the awareness that *a medium is a channel of communication interfacing with any two points in time and/or space.* Functionally, such electro/mechanical channels disseminate, preserve, and retrieve information. *A channel refers to that part of a medium which carries electro/*

mechanical signal information dedicated to a sense modality. Thus, a medium consists of one or more channels, carrying signals that are sensed through a variety of human sensing modalities, and primarily functions to connect points in time and space (Chesebro, 1986). There is nothing intrinsic to a communications medium which stipulates the motives of senders and receivers, or stipulates the size of audience. Nor can a definition of communications media be limited to those media which have broadcast or mass audience potential.

Media and Mass Media

The popular conceptualization of "media" as mass communication incorporates properties *extrinsic* to those characteristics that define any specific communication medium. Much research has focused on extrinsic factors, such as the ways individuals and groups depend upon, utilize, are gratified by, and linked by the communication media and the infrastructure upon which they depend. Investigation of the effect of mass media has tended to overlook the interface of personal communication and media, where the media are utilized for non–mass communication, such as the telephone or the ordinary postal letter (Gumpert & Cathcart, 1986). Mass communication refers to relatively immediate communication over time and space to large, heterogeneous groups, but no technological medium of communication is restricted to a mass communication function. The broadcasting media have an intrinsic bias toward instantaneous communication with large numbers of individuals, but there is no inherent limitation preventing its use as point to point communication; nor is there any inherent limitation on the use of the telephone or the postal letter for reaching a mass audience. A study of media should focus not only on the connection of the mass media with society, it should also examine any situation in which a technological medium is interposed between two communicating parties. Human interaction is altered not only by the interposition of mass media but by any medium that extends the scope of human communication. The process of writing and sending a letter to another person and the process of transmitting the human image instantaneously to thousands of receivers have something in common—they both approximate the interpersonal communicative act and extend it through time and space (Cathcart & Gumpert, 1983).

A symbiotic relationship exists between any medium of communication—mass or micro media—and interpersonal relationships. Thayer (1979) has addressed this issue and makes these particularly cogent remarks:

A much more important distinction, theoretically, is that between a communication network and a mass communication network. A communication network emerges from people talking to each other about matters that make a difference to them. . . . A mass communication network is superimposed or overlaid on existing communication networks (*viz.,* social structure) to the extent made possible by the available technology. . . . *What is* and *what matters*—indeed, all human reality, all human values—are products of communication networks. . . . The basic dynamic in the phenomena of mass communication, the pivotal mechanism out of which all else evolves, is not the technology, awesome as that has become. Nor is it the "message," or the implicit culture imparted in the "content" of the media. Nor is it the "effects" which the media are purported to have. The basic mechanism inheres in the *social and personal uses* to which people put the media and their fare. It is this basic dynamic which any relevant theory of mass communication will have to be based upon. (Pp. 60–63)

The contemporary focus on mass communication, to the exclusion of other forms of mediated human communication, has created an understandable bias that connects media technology with the industrial revolution and mass production. This bias toward mass communication with its implications for an industrialized-urbanized society has resulted in a limited concept of mediation that ignores several millennia of technological development and influence. Since the beginning of recorded history, and even before, human communication has been extended through such media as cave paintings, drawings, carvings, clay tablets, papyrus and architecture (Ong, 1977). A theory of mediation should reconcile the current bias by stressing the development and continuity of media technology and its effects. The defining rubric must be "medium," not "mass media," and must include all analogical communication technologies of print (pre-Gutenberg to post-Gutenberg); sound technologies, including the telephone and all forms of auditory recording; iconic media, including painting, still photography, film, television, all display media; and those media interfacing with the computer.

Media Context

A technological medium of communication functions in a cultural, social, and political environment and in that setting is operationalized through established organizations and institutions following accepted community patterns. Although the institutions that operationalize media in a specific society are extremely important, they should not be confused with those characteristic properties that define a medium. They are not inherent in any specific medium. In some societies radio, motion picture, television, and newspapers are governmentally controlled. In others they are privately owned but carefully regulated by government; and in still others radio and television programming is governmentally produced and distributed while newspapers and motion pictures are privately produced and distributed. None of these systems of operationalizing communications media are inherent in the media technology, nor do they alter the basic structure of the channel and the form of its language.

Ultimately, the study of media becomes the study of humans, because it is, by implication, the study of those human impulses that lead people to filter ideas through mechanical devices. The impulse to extend and replicate personal experiences, and to distort them creatively, in ways that reflect not only fact and feeling but extend them over time and space, is at the heart of media technology. It is this notion of the medium as an extension of humans, and as determiner of the kind of message to be delivered that forms the basis for our theory of mediation.

Media: Mechanical and Communicative

To further our exploration of a theory of mediation let us consider the relationship of mechanical media to communicative media. Mechanical media, in this context, are those that extend the physical being. Hence, to borrow from McLuhan, eyeglasses are an extension of the eye, a hammer or a pair of scissors is an extension of the hand, a car is an extension of walking legs. Communications media, on the other hand, are those that extend psychological processes.

No communication medium is totally a psychological extension of humans. Conversely, no mechanical medium is totally without communicative significance. Although all communications media reflect human thought processes, all of them also serve a physical function, namely, that of transmission of information. On the physical level, for example, the printing press is both an extension of the hand that writes, and an indirect means of transmitting the voice. On the psychological level print, to the degree that it aids in the expression of emotions and ideas, is also an extension of the self. The personal letter, while a mechanical extension of the human voice, projects an image of the sender, hence the concern for handwriting style, margins, salutations, etc. Likewise, most mechanical objects have a communicative function. Automobile manufacturers understand this communicative function and change car models year after year. A hand gun may be viewed as a mechanical extension of the fist, but everyone recognizes a gun's communicative significance. Thus, the distinction between mechanical extensions and communicative extensions is an important one but never an absolute one. The two functions continually overlap, and at times are almost inseparable. A computer, for example, performs physical, mechanical functions by storing and retrieving information, but it also performs communicative functions by duplicating human mental processes, indirectly transmitting information from the programmer to the person who uses the computer. In all these examples, transmission and expression are always bonded.

Any communication medium is an extension not only of the communicator but also of the auditor or receiver, both physically and psychologically. Phonetic writing, for example, extends not only the voice of the communicator but also the ear, perceptive processes, and emotions of the reader. When the president addresses the nation via radio and television, the medium is acting not only as an extension of the communicator's mental and physical presence but also of the mental and physical presences of those who choose to listen.

Finally, a medium becomes communicative only when some level of symbolization or signification is involved. This is easy to see in the symbolization of written and spoken language. With newer media, however, the situation is different. Film, for example (while always communicative in that no one ever mistakes a film for the real, in-the-flesh event), is not a medium of mere recording and transmission because it uses forms of symbolization or signification (such as montage) that exist only within the context of film grammar. All media are communicative in this sense, because (1) there is a set of codes and conventions integral to each medium; (2) such codes and conventions constitute part of our media consciousness; (3) the information processing made possible through these various grammars influence our perceptions and values; and (4) the order of acquisition of media literacy will produce a particular world perspective which relates and separates persons accordingly (Gumpert & Cathcart, 1985, p. 24).

A medium of communication is not a neutral instrument (mechanical tool) which can be manipulated and orchestrated at will, but is rather a potent system of symbols that transfers data and information and simultaneously alters the way human beings conceive reality and perceive others. Thus, language and medium represent coexisting and reciprocal means of communication.

The Pervasiveness of Media

Once a medium of communication is integrated into the human information processing system the presence of mediation influences thoughts and acts even when mediation is absent. The photograph serves as an excellent example of a medium so integrated into our consciousness that its presence, as opposed to actual use, influences how we perceive ourselves and others. The camera eye has become integrated into the process of perception and into the process of self-image.

> The photograph by its nature as a physical object makes possible the distance necessary to view ourselves as the "I"—the actor. The photographic images give the "me" something substantial and performative with which to react. The "me" can determine if the image embodies those attributes that peers and society value. The image in the photo evokes the "generalized other." We eagerly seek the photographic image because it helps give us the psychic distance necessary to the internal dialogue through which we maintain our self image. (Cathcart & Gumpert, 1986, p. 95)

Further, we recognize there is a grammar for each medium based upon the physical-electronic properties which constitute that medium. People acquire grammars, usually informally, of all the media existent in the world at the time they are born. As new media technologies are introduced, persons acquire the new media grammars and become literate in those also, but they never fully or completely replace the world perspective concomitant with the media grammars first acquired.

Growing up literate in a contemporary society means that we must adopt the accouterments of language, written and iconic as well as verbal. A medium is not only a channel or channels of communication, but is also a learned, shared, and arbitrary system of symbols. That is, it is one of the languages through which human beings interact and communicate in terms of their common cultural experiences and expectations.

One of the difficulties of dealing with contemporary literacy is that it is difficult to define in light of the development of filmic and electronic technologies. The traditional view of literacy excludes the iconic and limits the text to a verbal linguistic symbol system. The critic Roland Barthes (1967) has attempted to deal with this problem by using metalanguage to analyze text. Barthes gives the example of the fashion magazine. One cannot submit a fashion magazine to linguistic analysis only, because the unique nature of the fashion magazine is to create meaning through a highly developed interrelationship among the text, the drawn illustrations, and the photographed pictures. All of which, when juxtaposed and united, form the magazine's metalanguage. Most contemporary communications media combine linguistic elements that are separately expressive. A film seen without its musical score is still using the language of film, just as the score alone still uses musical language.[2] When the two are joined, however, metalinguistic levels of connotation are achieved. Most modern communication systems are mixed-media systems, and metalinguistics might therefore be considered, in this context, the study of mixed media.

The implications of this are most meaningful for a theory of mediation.

Structuralist philosophers and critics see linguistic analysis as a prime means of getting at human rationality. Yet for a world which has gone beyond a singular language into metalanguage for the structure of meaning, there exists few well-defined means of metalinguistic analysis. This may account, in part, for our failure to develop a theory of mediation. We are not sure what is/(are) the language(s) of contemporary media and how meaning is structured and interpreted when its main form is metalinguistic.

To summarize our mechanical-communicative distinction, all media are extensions of humans that extend both the physical being and the mental being. Media communicate only when they serve as an extension of both the communicator and the auditor or receiver. Media technology create symbol systems that express ideas and feelings that transcend their mere physical existence.

Media: Reflective and Projective

Media are not only extensions of communicators and receivers, they reflect social values and belief systems, and more important, they project social realities and idiosyncratic values. Projection involves the notion that media, the mass media in particular, not only mirror world views of people, but also create social reality (Loevinger, 1968). In mechanical media, for example, reflection occurs to the extent that a mechanical extension imitates a previous human process. Thus a scissors imitates the process of a person's tearing with one's fingers. A form of projection occurs here in that the use of scissors creates a desire for objects cut into intricate patterns with sharp, clean edges. This projection can lead to placing a higher value on scissor tearing.

Similarly, the concepts of reflection and projection may be applied to communications media. Media reflect thought processes, yet in the process of communication thought processes revised or distorted. Hence, in responding to these altered reflections we project and perceive new realities. The medium used, therefore, is likely to dictate the type of projection, based on revised reflection which is likely to occur when a new medium is employed. Yet, no medium is purely reflective. A story presented in the verbal symbol system of the printed novel is quite different from that same story presented by the signifying system of film. The sensory channels of each medium and the information they encode makes it impossible for them to transmit identical ideas and feelings. The process of transmission, which, while essentially a mechanical (and reflective) process, can rarely be totally devoid of projected expressiveness in its own right. (A standard example of this is the subtle set of differences between seeing a movie on television and in a theater.)

Media Evolution

To the extent that human's mental processes allow them to make complex and varied extensions of themselves, one might see the development of media technology, in the loosest sense, as a form of biological development. We may infer that the principles of biological evolution can be used to explain media evolution.[3] We could call this a biotechnological explanation of mediation.[4]

There are five basic ideas that support this biotechnological explanation: (1) that media exist in varying degrees of complexity, adaptation, and specialization; (2) that media and their environment are interrelated and cannot accurately be talked about separately; (3) that any form of development (evolution) is two sided and must be attributed both to changes in environment and to mutations; (4) that there are two forms of adaptive success—success in terms of geographic extent and success in terms of the longevity of the species—which in media directly parallel Innis's concept of time-bias and space-bias; and (5) that the two types of relationships in an ecological system are competition and symbiosis, a concept that holds true for media systems as well.

Complexity, Adaptation, and Specialization

Biological organisms exist in varying degrees of complexity, adaptability, and specialization. And so do media, both mechanical and communicative. The wheelbarrow is a comparatively simple, stable, unchangeable, and unspecialized extension of a person. The truck, on the other hand, while descendent from the wheelbarrow, exists, almost like a higher form of life, in numerous forms, with a high degree of complexity, adaptation, and specialization. Communications media, on the other hand, have at their one extreme speech, which, while existent in many forms, is nonetheless limited by the number of phonemes that can be physiologically produced. At the other extreme there are elaborate communications systems such as magazines. A magazine contains various organs and systems that divide its labors. Individual magazines can reach a degree of specialization that reveals a high level of adaptation to a very specific environment. Yet, as is true in the biological realm, overspecialization can lead to extinction, so that a species of magazine like *Hot Rod* can expect to live only so long as hot-rodding remains a popular sport. The death of a magazine like *The Saturday Evening Post* becomes, therefore, particularly noteworthy, because it signals a change of environment.

Interrelation of Organisms and Environment

The issue of environment is essential in any theory of mediation. Just as one cannot study biology without touching on geology and oceanography, one cannot study communication systems without studying the political, cultural, and societal environments in which they operate. Just as it is important to recognize the social, cultural, and political conditions that enable communications to expand and progress, reflecting the society around them, we must recognize the changes which new forms of communication make on a society, in a projective function.

Two-sided Evolution

One of the principles of evolution is that it is two sided. On the one hand, a geological or environmental change, like an ice age, can wipe out an entire species. On the other hand, a species can develop by mutation into a new species, and thereby either fill an ecological niche which has recently been created, or else compete with other species for another already inhabited environment.[5] So it is with communications media. A change in political or social environment can limit the need for certain forms of communication and create the need for others. During the Middle Ages, for example, elaborate Roman systems of communication fell into disuse, while the need to preserve Roman culture rose and was filled by the use of the codex in monastic libraries. On the other hand, the mutation of a communication system, such as occurred with the development of the printing press (producing a new form of writing), can be like the development of a new, successful species of animal. Not only did the printing press, to continue that example, fill niches in the communication ecology which had previously gone uninhabited, it also competed successfully with methods of communication which had been successful up to that time.

In the present, because of the complexity of our communications systems, both major and minor mutations occur more frequently. The silent film, for example, mutated so quickly into the talkie that it takes up what is perhaps a disproportionately small period in the history of communications for a medium so widespread and popular. Other mutants, such as 3-D movies or Smell-O-Vision, have failed to adapt to the environment. One might expect most of these new mutants to be short-lived, arguing that long traditions behind older forms of media are a sign of a high degree of environmental adaptation. New media will have to be extraordinarily well suited to people's needs and to the environment if traditional forms are to be replaced.

Two Kinds of Success

The success of a biological organism's ability to fit its environment is measured in two ways: first, by the geographic range of the organism, that is, the extent of the territory it is able to cover; and second, by the length of time the organism thrives. Many organisms are extraordinarily widespread for historically brief periods of time. Others, having adapted to a specialized environment, are comparatively isolated geographically, but can continue to exist for extended lengths of time. This biological situation is comparable to Innis's notion of time-bias and space-bias when applied to communications. A time-biased communication organism would be one with small geographic extent, but with great survival power; the space-biased organism, on the other hand, while widely spread out geographically, runs greater risks of being able to adapt neither to localized nor to worldwide environmental changes.

Two Kinds of Coexistence

The success of one biological organism almost invariably is accompanied by a degree of success or failure of some related organism. Similarly, media are interrelated either competitively or symbiotically. "Symbiosis" is an important concept for a theory of mediation. While media can vie with each other to be the dominating factors in a given society, the recognized dominance of one medium in an area can often bring about a change of function for another medium, making the two mutually dependent. Innis (1972), in talking about communication monopolies, emphasizes the competitive aspect of media, at the expense of the symbiotic side. By describing what he called "empire" only in terms of the achievement or balance between competing time-biased and space-biased media, Innis passes over the possibility that the time-biased functions of a civilization might be performed by one medium and the space-biased by another, and that the upsetting of empire comes not because of competition between the time-biased and the space-biased but between two time-biased or space-biased organisms competing for an identical function within the society, and thereby weakening it.

It is this quality of symbiosis that seems to characterize modern media of communications. Innis's notion of competition would be correct, for example, if television had completely replaced all other forms of communication, but it hasn't. Literacy is higher in the United States than it ever has been, and no doubt people are reading more books and magazines than ever before, but the function of reading in our society has changed.

Nor has television replaced radio. Television's monopoly exists only in selected areas and with particular segments of the population.

Symbiotic coexistence between media, on the other hand, has produced forms of social organization and development quite different from what we experienced several decades ago. Today one can extend her/his social identity not only geographically—by reading and identifying with a national magazine and newspaper—but also by feeling linked to various groups of mutual interest, be that interest in health foods or horse racing (Gumpert, 1987). In addition, media often enhance each other. A novelist is likely to have more people read a book if it is made into a successful movie than if not. Rather than destroy the novel, the motion picture has merely changed its function and extended its influence, just as photography, as so many have pointed out, changed the nature of painting.

Obviously, not all media can coexist peacefully, and competition among media is still a vital part of our society. However, what might be called "monomedia" ages are now nearly over, and there is a multiplicity of media options available.

Conclusion

Media, in particular, have been subjected to quantitative studies that treat them as mechanical extensions of man, and to qualitative criticism that treats them as communicative extensions, which is rather like trying to study physiology without psychology or psychology without physiology. A way must be found to unite the two. The main purpose of developing a theory of mediation is to establish an intellectual perspective that facilitates the successful study of media.

> A theory is a set of interrelated constructs (concepts), definitions, and propositions that present a systematic view of phenomena by specifying relations among variables, with the purpose of explaining and predicting the phenomena. (Kerlinger, 1973, p. 8)

We have attempted to establish a foundation which will support a theory (or theories) of mediation—a series of postulates upon which any theory of mediation must rest. The development of a theory requires a series of supporting interrelating assertions to support the model inherent in the theory.

A theory of mediation must, according to our bent, recognize the supporting premises that we have attempted to establish: (1) that communication media are extensions of the psychological and physical self; (2) that the primary function and capability of any medium is to transcend either time and/or space; (3) that media institutions and the intrinsic properties that define a communication medium are separate and distinct; (4) that the grammar of each communication medium is unique; (5) that media dependency determines individual and social expression; (6) that all communication media are historically interdependent; and (7) that all communication media are both reflective and projective.

Human and media development are intertwined in an helixlike embrace. It is human nature to seek to transcend the limits of time and place by utilizing a media technology for that purpose. In the process of communication, the perception of self and the impact of person on environment has been altered and transformed. Yet, the connection among medium, person, and affects has hardly been understood, primarily because no unifying theory of media technology has existed to facilitate prediction of impact and consequence. Part of the problem is the common perception of media as nonreflexive tools of human needs. Another is the result of a popular and scholarly preoccupation with only those media of spectacular social impact (e.g., television) and the desire to establish direct causality between a medium and a problem (e.g., television and violence). We are proposing that future research and analysis be predicated upon an evolutionary relationship of media and person, and we have ventured to establish the framework for a theory of mediation.

Notes

1. Everett Rogers (1986) says this very succinctly: "It is an oversimplification to think of technology as an autonomous, isolated force that is disconnected from the rest of society" (p. 1).
2. This is suggested, in part, by Alan Miller Thomas's provocative analysis of the effects of broadcasting on music and speech. See Alan Miller Thomas, "A Concept of the Audience: An Examination of the Work of Harold A. Innis with Respect to Its Application to the Development of Broadcasting." Ph.D. diss., Columbia University, 1964. Available from University Microfilms, Ann Arbor, Michigan, pp. 199–229.
3. Evolutionary theories of social organization are obviously not new. Auguste Comte's concept of society as an organism, with his emphasis on socialization and diversification of labor, employs principles similar to those outlined in the following pages. Likewise, Herbert Spencer's laws of evolution, as he applied them to society, are at least analogous to our own in general ways. Although no conscious extension of Comte and Spencer was attempted in this paper, the lineage cannot help but be apparent, particularly to the extent that Darwin was influenced by the latter. Both Comte and Spencer are cited in Melvin L. DeFluer, *Theories of Mass Communication*. New York: D. McKay, 1966, pp. 99–104.
4. The term "biotechnology" originates with Raoul France, who, in studying what he called "biotechnics," saw nature as a prime model for the inventor and the engineer. This notion is quite congruent with our own seeing of media-machines

as extensions of man's very biological and psychological self. France is cited and quoted in Laszlo Moholy-Nagy, *The New Vision and Abstract of an Artist*. New York: G. Wittenborn, 1947, p. 29.

5. Our use of the term "mutation" here coincides with that of the phrase "cultural mutation" used by certain French intellectuals who have been calling for new technological forms to usurp the power previously held by supposedly now-effete forms of culture, like the novel or painting. Pierre Schneider describes this in his article " 'Mutation' Marks Trend at Paris Biennial," *The New York Times*, 10 November 1969, p. 54.

References

Ball-Rokeach, S. J., & DeFleur, M. (1975). *Theories of mass communication* (4th ed.). New York: Longman.

Barthes, R. (1967). *Elements of semiology* (A. Lavers & C. Smith, Trans.). New York: Hill & Wang (Original work pub. 1964).

Bullfinch. (1974). *Bullfinch's mythology*. New York: Thomas Y. Crowell.

Carey, J. (1968). Harold Innis and Marshall McLuhan. In R. Rosenthal (Ed.), *McLuhan: Pro and Con*. Baltimore, MD: Pelican.

Cathcart, R., & Gumpert, G. (1983). Mediated interpersonal communication: Toward a new typology. *Quarterly Journal of Speech, 69*, 267–77.

Cathcart, R., & Gumpert, G. (1986). I am a camera: The mediated self. *Communication Quarterly, 34*, 89–102.

Chesebro, J. W. (1986). *Media transformations: Revolutionary challenges to the world's cultures. Part II*. Paper presented at the annual meeting of the Speech Communication Association of Puerto Rico, San Juan, Puerto Rico.

Gumpert, G. (1987). *Talking tombstones: And other talkes of the media age*. New York: Oxford University Press.

Gumpert, G., & Cathcart, R. (1985). Media grammars, generations, and media gaps. *Critical Studies in Mass Communication, 24*, 23–35.

Gumpert, G., & Cathcart, R. (Eds.) (1986). *Inter/Media: Interpersonal communication in a media world* (3d ed.). New York: Oxford University Press.

Innis, H. A. (1951). *The bias of communication*. Toronto: University of Toronto Press.

Innis, H.A. (1972). *Empire and communications*. Toronto: University of Toronto Press.

Kerlinger, F. N. (1973). *Foundations of behavioral research*. New York: Rinehart & Winston.

Loevinger, L. (1968). The ambiguous mirror: The reflective-projective theory of broadcasting and mass communications. *Journal of Broadcasting, 12*, 97–116.

McLuhan, M. H. (1964). *Understanding media: The extensions of man*. New York: McGraw-Hill.

Ong, W. J. (1977). *Interfaces of the word: Studies in the evolution of consciousness and culture*. Ithica, NY: Cornell University Press.

Rogers, E. M. (1986). *Communication technology: The new media in society*. New York: Free Press.

Thayer, L. (1979). On the mass media and mass communication: Notes toward a theory. In R. W. Budd, & B. D. Ruben (Eds.), *Beyond media: New approaches to mass communication*. Rochelle Park, NJ: Hayden.

3

Identifying the Common Dimensions of Communication: The Communication Systems Model

Leah A. Lievrouw and T. Andrew Finn

This paper presents a model of communication behavior in specific social contexts that has theoretical implications for telecommunications systems. Three primary dimensions common to all communication behavior are proposed: temporality, involvement, *and* control. *Temporality is the experience of time in a given communication situation; involvement is the degree to which cognitive, affective, and sensory capabilities are employed in a communication situation; and control is the degree to which communicators can exert influence in a given communication situation. Furthermore, the present model situates these dimensions within social context, which is comprised of the prevailing* culture, *the specific interpersonal* relationships *involved, and the specific* content *or meaning shared among communicators. The model is based on a review of the relevant literature on the social impact of communication technologies. The paper concludes with implications of the model in four traditional areas of communication research (media effects, media uses and gratifications, the study of group processes, and communication policy).*

Introduction

Communication scholars have studied all types of media at one time or another, yet one would be hard pressed to point to any theory or conceptual framework that specifically encompasses the remarkable array of communication systems and enhancements that have become available in the information age. Many current theoretical models such as theories of mass communication intentionally encompass only a subset of the communication media available today. Mass communication systems such as movies, large assemblies, television, radio, newspapers, books, and magazines have been available to U.S. residents most of their lives. In recent years these systems have been supplemented by cable television, satellite dishes, remotely printed newspapers, general interest information retrieval systems (e.g., Dow Jones News/Retrieval), and videocassette recorders (VCRs). In the realm of person-to-person communication, people have used for generations face-to-face communication, postal mail, telegraph service, and the telephone. More recently, these communication systems have been supplemented by overnight delivery services, enhanced capabilities for the telephone (e.g., answering machines, three-party calling, and call waiting), facsimile, CB radio, and computer-based messaging services and bulletin boards (e.g., The Source and CompuServe). In addition, members of large organizations frequently have the additional options of video- or audio-graphic-teleconferencing, electronic mail, voice mail, telex, and direct computer-to-computer communication. Such systems have been characterized as "conversational technologies" (Hunter, 1987).

The purpose of this paper is to examine the rich variety of human communication across these diverse systems and to derive a number of common dimensions shared by all communication behavior. These dimensions are used to construct a framework for understanding communication within a given social context. Along the way, our model is used as a vehicle for classifying and comparing different communication systems, as well as for drawing inferences and deriving specific, testable hypotheses about the process, use, and effects of human communication. Admittedly, these are ambitious goals. We introduce ideas and suggest relationships that cannot be fully explored in one paper. In the present paper we introduce certain essential elements of a model of communication which have strong implications for the study of telecommunications systems; however, we invite readers to join us in the process of development of the model. We feel that our preliminary steps have been necessary to develop the conceptual tools that are needed by researchers working in the area.

Assumptions and Foundations

Just as it is difficult to judge how well a house is built by simply examining the visible parts of the final structure, it is difficult to judge the usefulness of a theory without knowing its underlying assumptions. This section discusses the ideas that form the foundation of the model of the common dimensions of communications.

Preliminary Platitudes

The somewhat flippant title of this section was chosen since we want to set out several assumptions, which may strike some readers as so obvious as to require no formal statement, while striking others as simply incorrect. While they are not required to support the communication dimensions model presented later in the paper, these assumptions are derived from communication theory and general systems theory, and have become part of the working environment in which most of the recent studies of communication technologies have been conducted. (The order of items is not intended to imply priorities or causality among the assumptions.)

- Most human communication behavior is devoted to identifying and controlling uncertainty in the environment.
- Social organization is one mechanism by which individuals attempt to reduce uncertainty, but the act of organization itself has the effect of increasing the need for information and communication.
- Information is (and is perceived to be) an increasingly important commodity in modern society.
- The information-seeking behavior of individuals changes in response to changes in their social context.
- Individuals' sources of information and numbers of communication partners tend to increase.
- Communication links (networks) among individuals tend to persist even when they are not used.

The net effect of these processes or tendencies is to encourage the development of complex communication systems in response to contextually bound communicator needs.

This leads us to reject two additional assumptions that are implicit in the literature. First, the assumption that we refer to as the *bias toward maximizing channels*, that is, that communicators prefer (or should prefer) communication systems that most closely imitate face-to-face interactions (see Rogers, 1986, p. 212). Instead, we propose that communicators use channels selectively and strategically according to their situations and purposes. Second, we reject the assumption of efficiency in the selection of channels, that is, that systems are chosen primarily on the basis of their efficiency in conveying a message. We propose, instead, that systems are used efficiently or inefficiently according to communicators' personal preferences and purposes.

While this set of assumptions may be appropriate for a wide range of communication behaviors, the assumption of rationality inherent in this view precludes less purposive forms of communicating such as expressive (music, art) and even irrational communication. Thus, while we believe a great deal of communication behavior is rational, the communication systems model is intended to encompass communication acts that are essentially nonrational in nature.

Communication researchers have (unconsciously) adopted the rational assumptions of the engineers and inventors who design communication technologies. However (as we point out later) there is little correlation between the rationality designed into most communication technologies and the varying motives behind actual communication behavior, except insofar as inventors attempt to get communicators to adopt their systems (usually with little degree of success).

These assumptions have specific relevance to the study of electronic communication systems that have been created in the twentieth century, because whether explicitly stated or not, the assumptions have been powerful shapers of the ideas we have about the role of communication technologies in society.

Assumptions about the Communication Process

Our basic premise in formulating the present framework is that it is *communication behavior,* and not technology, that drives the evolution, implementation, and acceptance of communication systems which enhance, extend, or otherwise facilitate the sharing of meaning among individuals. The derivation of our thinking is basically inductive; like other analysts, we began by looking at the technologies themselves, but soon we concluded that what interests us about technologies is how people behave with and about them, not the technologies per se. Our premise is founded on several assumptions: (1) that individuals perceive the world around them in highly personal and individual ways; (2) that communication behavior exists in a social context that helps communicators to organize these perceptions; and (3) that people share these organized perceptions— communicate—in order to construct meaning, or make sense, of their world. Therefore, we view communication as a socially constructed activity. Our perspective is consistent with the constructivist approach to social behavior as articulated by Knorr-Cetina (1981), Restivo and Loughlin (1987), and Woolgar (1980). It is also similar to the convergence model of communication proposed by Rogers and Kincaid (1981), and the theory of the coordinated management of meaning set out by Pearce and Cronen (1980). For a review of the sense-making theory of communication see also Dervin (1983). In addition, we use the term "communication system" to describe any interacting set of social and technical structures that facilitates the sharing of meaning.

We also see more value in a focus on the *purpose* of communication, for example, viewing interpersonal communication in terms of relationships (Ruben, 1988) rather than in terms of the system used to accomplish the communication. Consistent with our belief in the importance of the social context of communication, the communication systems model described below defines the range a particular system occupies on specific dimensions; the precise placement of an individual communication act on these dimensions is determined by the participants, according to their own purposes, motives, and so on.

The Myth of Unmediated Communication

There is at least one more assumption about the communication process that strikes us as curious. Traditionally, communication scholars appear to have accepted a division of research into face-to-face (FtF) and mediated communication studies. This has led to the erection of boundaries between the subfields of interpersonal communication and mass communication, rather than a search to uncover the similarities between them. While such a delineation may help scholars select the particular communication systems they study, in our view this distinction is artificial. While FtF interaction clearly has some very special qualities found in no other communication system, these are traceable to the *potential* richness of the interaction, or the number of simultaneous channels of communication available to participants.

But it is inaccurate to maintain that FtF communication is not mediated. *All* communication is mediated, since even in FtF situations one or more of the five senses are required for two minds to share meaning. Without the senses, people have no channels for communicating and interacting in the physical world. So the distinction that should be made is that most FtF interactions (visual, auditory, and even olfactory cues) are mediated by the natural channels of light and air (leaving out the senses mediated by surface receptors for the present), while most other forms of communication are mediated by man-made channels.[1]

There are two fundamental ways that communication can be mediated: across distances and across time. Most scholars of interpersonal communication do not think of FtF communication as mediated because the descriptive phrase itself, "face-to-face," dismisses the dimension of space (distance) as important. Yet distance is a relevant variable in much of the interpersonal literature: studies of personal space, propinquity, and proximity attest to the relevance of distance in FtF communication. There are, in fact, two distinct aspects to the mediation of communication across distances. The first aspect is largely ignored as a subject for research today: the mediation of communication across distances where both the sender and the receivers are colocated (the plural form, "receivers," is used here since a key attribute of this form of mediation across distance is the attempt to reach a larger audience). Simple tools that enhance the mediation across distances for colocated communicators include a podium or stage; the emergence of electronically amplified communication systems in the twentieth century (microphones, electric guitars, or other musical instruments) has produced communication with much larger assemblies than were ever possible before.

In addition, most *telecommunication* systems are thought of as mediating across both time and space (for example, the ability for telecommunication to substitute for travel). Communication systems that mediate across *distances* employ either natural media (atmosphere and light), electronic media, or the physical transport of objects. Communication systems that mediate across time must employ some type of *storage* of symbols, either physical or electronic. Because storage is a key element in systems that mediate across time, these systems are usually good at mediation across distances as well (books are one of the oldest systems; compact disks are one of the newest). But this is not always true, e.g., cave drawings, or highway billboards.

Essentially, then, all communication is mediated. Because of the limited range of the human senses, FtF interactions are relatively poor at mediating communication across space and time. Our discipline clearly prefers focusing on the advantages of FtF interaction rather than its limitations (one rarely hears mention of them); and in the real world, communicators frequently forego the advantages of FtF for the advantages of mediation across larger segments of space and time.

We will return to these assumptions and some of the implications of the forms of mediation later, but first we examine the way that the concept of mediation has been treated in previous communication research. In the following overview we continue to use the term "mediated communication" to refer to communication that does not take place face-to-face. However, if we have achieved our aims, the distinction will seem unnecessary by the time the reader finishes this essay.

Literature Review

We first explore the issue of mediation as it pertains to three traditional areas of communication research (interpersonal, organizational, and mass), in order to consider whether the mediation concept has been theoretically as useful as is generally assumed. Second, we discuss the special case of electronically mediated communication systems, and review some of the efforts that have been made to conceptually organize the work in this area and offer an organizing scheme of our own. This review is by no means an exhaustive one; we have selected examples for review that are most representative of the major themes or directions in the area.

Communication Research and Mediation

Interpersonal communication. As the subfield of interpersonal communication research emerged from the rhetoric tradition in speech, general semantics, and humanistic psychology, it clearly focused on FtF interaction, usually in the dyad (Wilmot, 1979). Interpersonal communication apparently has become synonymous with FtF communication; studies of dyadic communication mediated by letters or the telephone are still viewed today as being on the fringe of interpersonal communication research. The dominant research interest in interpersonal studies is based on the richness of the FtF experience—the ability to communicate across multiple channels and with multiple senses.

Yet, this approach leaves us with certain difficult anomalies about human relationships; sharing a silent elevator ride with a stranger qualifies as interpersonal communication, while a long-term relationship carried out through letters or over the telephone does not. It is this dominant view equating FtF communication with interpersonal communication that has led to the neglect of important communication systems. For example, a communication system such as the telephone, for all its impact as recognized by sociologists and anthropologists, is not generally studied as a vehicle for interpersonal communication.[2]

Mass communication. The history of communication scholarship suggests an interesting dichotomy in the treatment of mediated communication: the study of mass communication is dominated by it and the study of interpersonal communication is devoid of it. Although mass communication research began with early work on movies and radio, heightened interest and explosive growth came from political interest in propaganda and its effects. While it could be argued that the most influential medium in history has been print, it took the advent of electronic media (specifically, radio) to focus scholarly attention on the mass effects of media. Mass communication scholars have focused on electronically mediated communication almost completely, ignoring, for the most part, the effects of large group assemblies (a communication system not ignored in speech and rhetoric). While this may be justified in view of the sheer numbers reached by electronically mediated mass communication, one never hears the argument raised that assemblies are important because of the quality or intensity of the interaction possible because of its FtF nature, an argument clearly present in discussions of FtF vs. mediated communication in interpersonal communication circles.

Another way to view this is that mass communication has focused on communication that mediates across distances, while essentially ignoring communication that mediates across time. Books, perhaps even the great religious books of history by themselves, have had a tremendous impact on society; yet they receive relatively little attention compared with radio and television. While such books may be read over and over, and affect individuals across the span of their lives, indeed, across generations, there is more appeal to studying the impact of a communication system that imparts its message to its receivers all at once. Although it is more difficult to study the impact of communication mediated across time, it is still true that such media are not given credit for having as much power as communication that mediates across distance. This bias (in lieu of definitive evidence it seems fair to call it a bias) carries over to our regulation of the mass media, which is filled with statutory restrictions on electronic media that do not apply to print; for example, the banning—voluntary or otherwise—of advertisements for cigarettes and distilled spirits from television and radio, while no such restrictions exist for the print media. The electronic mass media are simply viewed as more powerful (Finn & Strickland, 1982).[3] Music provides another example. Although home collections of recorded music probably have a major effect on listeners, more time is spent researching the music played on the radio and MTV. While good arguments can be mounted to defend this approach, it is also true that this emphasis again reflects the bias against research on time-mediated communication and toward research on distance-mediated communication.

Organizational communication.   Out of the first two traditions have come the more recent interests in the study of organizational communication. Following the lead of interpersonal scholars, organizational communication researchers have focused on FtF interactions and, for the most part, have overlooked tools of mediated communication such as the telephone. Yet the complex nature of organizations and their concomitant complex infrastructure of communication systems have led researchers in organizational communication toward the study of mediated communication in recent years. While mass communication and interpersonal communication have clearly delineated their stands on mediated communication, it strikes us that organizational communication, because it is faced with this infrastructure of communication systems, is still struggling with the relative importance of FtF and mediated communication.

Organizing Themes in Research on Electronically Mediated Communication Systems

There are literally hundreds of studies on the use of various electronic communication systems that implicitly accept the FtF/mediated dichotomy described above. Researchers examining the social impacts of new communication systems have frequently been criticized for operating in the absence of theory. By focusing on the communication systems themselves, and the technology that characterizes communication systems, researchers have built up a body of isolated research findings that have defied synthesis. In starker terms which we call "Dordick's Lament," these students of communication have simply been engaged in marketing research—studying when, where, and how people choose to use a particular system or selected feature of a system, rather than studying the process of communication itself (Dordick, 1987). We now review previous attempts to organize these studies.

Communication technology and the "new" media literature. In a book whose title has provided a convenient label for telecommunications technology research—*The New Media*—Rice and associates (1984) document the explosive growth of research in the area since the 1970s. They attribute this trend to three factors: (1) specific technological innovations in society (such as microcomputing, videogames, videotex, and the growth of cable), (2) the rise of particular research institutions (such as the Institute for Communication Research at Stanford University and the Annenberg School of Communications at the University of Southern California), and (3) the emergence of research interest groups in professional and scholarly organizations (such as the Human Communication Technology interest group of the International Communication Association and the American Society for Information Science). Rice advocates a conservative theoretical stance, that is, adopting traditional media theories and applying them to the new media. Accordingly, *The New Media* is organized along lines that are familiar to old media researchers: technological issues are divided according to the number of people involved in a given communication activity, into interpersonal/group, organizational, and institutional levels. Rice is specifically interested in the technologies and their attributes as a point of departure. Communication is considered solely within the framework of a technology-rich environment.

At first glance, Rice's framework seems appropriate: general theories of communication should be applicable to new technologies. But the apparent lack of fit between traditional theoretical distinctions and the reality of telecommunications technologies—the failure of such theoretical categories as "organizational communication," for example, in the telecommunications context—would seem to suggest that the distinctions are artifactual. The divisions among interpersonal, group, and mass communication, and the division of communication into mediated and unmediated forms are helpful, but ultimately do not explain all types of communication *behavior*, and therefore, all types of communication systems.

Another more recent scheme for organizing the literature is offered by Steinfield and Fulk (1987). As editors of a special issue of *Communication Research* dedicated to research on information technology in organizations, they, like Rice, invoke the familiar levels of analysis from communication research. The studies in their compilation are set firmly within the subfield of organizational communication, and as a collection they examine the ways that technologies have been transformed into communication media in specifically organizational settings. Steinfield and Fulk make helpful distinctions between what they call the "media characteristics perspective," which focuses on the technical features of specific technologies, and the social constructivist approach, which considers both the communication behavior and perceptions of individuals in organizations as well as the organizational structures that arise from those behaviors.

Both of these efforts to organize the new media literature provide interesting insights into current thinking about the social impacts of technology among communication researchers. Both works employ a number of concepts from conventional communication research. The distinction between "old media" and "new media" is clearly drawn; and the division of communication settings into traditional levels of measurement is used, from interpersonal, through small group, organizational, and institutional, to mass media. While these distinctions have the advantage of familiarity and are an attempt to extend previous models to new subjects, they reinforce the division of human communication into interpersonal vs. mediated forms, and into individual vs. mass levels of analysis. Interestingly, both efforts have appeared during a time when many communication scholars have called traditional media research into question and, indeed, have been struggling with new ways to categorize human communication behavior (*Ferment in the Field,* 1983).

The Rice and the Steinfield and Fulk efforts have attempted to lend structure to a scattered literature by using conventional structures borrowed from old media research, by relating the so-called new media to the traditional levels of analysis of communication research. We propose to organize the literature in yet another manner, by focusing on three themes that dominate communication technology studies: media characteristics, individual users, and social organizations. We have selected only the most representative examples from this literature, in order to point out briefly the importance of these themes. Our approach breaks down, rather than preserves, the traditional framework of communication research and allows us to see the more continuous nature of all types of systems.

Media characteristics. This perspective has a long tradition in the history of communication technologies research, reaching back at least to the immediate reward/delayed reward model, or the big media, little media dichotomy, both proposed by Schramm (1949; 1977). The central issue of that tradition, which extends forward through current telecommunications research, has been the specific effects of technological media on audiences and individuals. Its focus is on the technical features of electronic media, or on the artifacts of mediation.

Certainly, notions about mass media and their effects belong to this tradition (Schramm and Roberts, 1971; McLuhan, 1964; DeFleur & Ball-Rokeach, 1982), where individuals are seen to exist within, and react to, a technological environment over which they may have little or no control. While this perspective was originally formulated to describe the differences between interpersonal and mass-mediated communication, it has lately been reinterpreted to include intermediate-scale channels like the telephone as "telelogic communication," as opposed to "monologic" and "dialogic" forms (Ball-Rokeach & Reardon, 1988).

In addition, a number of descriptive studies have been conducted which compare the technical features and social applications of various telecommunications systems. These studies continue to contribute materially to discussions in telecommunication policy circles (e.g., Nilles, Carlson, Gray, & Hanneman [1976] on the telecommunications-transportation tradeoff; Short, Williams, & Christie [1976] on the social presence of telecommunication technologies; Johansen, Vallee, Spangler, & Shirts [1977], Johansen, Vallee, & Spangler [1979], and Svenning & Ruchinskas [1984] on teleconferencing; Dordick, Bradley, & Nanus [1987] on the increasing importance of value-added networks; Korzenny & Bauer (1981) on propinquity; and Dutton & Lievrouw [1982] on telecommunication technologies in education).

Individual users. If the media characteristics perspective is primarily interested in telecommunications technology artifacts, then the individual users perspective is primarily interested in the behavior of individuals in environments filled with those artifacts. Researchers have explored the attitudes (Phillips, 1982a, 1982b; Williams, Phillips, & Lum, 1982; Williams, Coulombe, & Lievrouw, 1983), emotions (Kiesler, Zubrow, Moses, & Geller, 1985; Sproull & Kiesler, 1986; Kiesler, Siegel, & McGuire, 1984), task performance or appropriateness (Hiltz & Turoff, 1986; Rice &

Case, 1983), satisfaction (Hiltz & Johnson, 1987; Wilkins & Plenge, 1981), productivity (Vallee & Gibbs, 1976), efficiency (Hiltz, 1978), interaction (Carey, 1981; Barefoot & Strickland, 1982; Siegel, Dubrovsky, Kiesler, & McGuire, 1986), and even the audience behavior (Nightingale & Webster, 1986) of communicators who use various telecommunications technologies. An additional and interesting subtext of this body of work is its openness to social constructivist or symbolic interactionist interpretations of technology use. The focus on individual perceptions and behavior here may tend to lead researchers toward this perspective (Steinfield & Fulk, 1987).

Social organizations.   Many new media researchers are fundamentally interested in the relationship between new communication technologies and the evolution of social structures. One of the most highly regarded researchers in this tradition is Rob Kling, whose "six perspectives" on computing in organizations have been widely adopted as a general model for understanding the role of technologies in organizations (Kling, 1980; Kling & Scacchi, 1980; see also Rice et al., 1984, pp. 76–79). The perspectives are contrasted primarily by the fact that three of them apply to organizations characterized by consensus, while others pertain to organizations where conflict is assumed or is the norm. To some extent Kling also integrates the individual users perspective with the social organizations perspective by drawing on the symbolic interactionist tradition (Kling & Gerson, 1978).

A principal theme in the social organization literature is the adoption of new telecommunications technologies. Adoption is considered to be dependent upon the technical features of the technology itself, on the readiness or ability of individual users, and especially on the organizational acceptance of the technology. Most adoption studies use individual users or organizations as their units of analysis. However, it is generally acknowledged that even the best system, implemented in a favorable organizational setting, depends on individuals who are willing and able to use it (Rogers & Agarwala-Rogers, 1976; Johnson & Rice, 1984). Both Rice et al. (1984) and Steinfield and Fulk (1987), as discussed above, are influential contributors to this research perspective. Other studies of the organizational impacts of specific technologies include Steinfield (1983) and Sproull & Kiesler (1986), who examine electronic mail in corporate and university environments, respectively, and Finn (1985) and Stewart & Finn (1985), who compare electronic mail and voice mail systems in a large corporate setting.

To summarize, there appear to be three main themes embodied in studies about telecommunications technologies in society: the media characteristics perspective, the individual users perspective, and the social organizations perspective. We believe that these categories have evolved not because of some inherent characteristics of the subject area itself, but because individual researchers (ourselves included) have approached the area from familiar theoretical backgrounds in communication, management, social psychology, political science, and computer science/engineering. The categories that we have suggested here are therefore the result of the various authors' collective preconceptions of the importance of new communications technologies in society. However, the key to understanding complex systems like telecommunications technologies may not lie in their arbitrary simplification, or in classifying systems according to preconceived disciplinary "turfs." Some effort should be made to analyze systems as elements in more complex social situations in which humans interact and communicate, using an abstract model as a guide.

The Common Dimensions of Communication

Our discussion up to this point illustrates that communication scholars have tended to study communication systems, especially the new media, according to more or less arbitrary structural criteria drawn from traditional communication research. The result has been a set of isolated findings that have not integrated behavior, systems, and their social context. In this section we propose a model which does integrate all of these elements.

The model is comprised of two major components: the dimensions of communication behavior and the social context of that behavior. Together, these components comprise an "ideal typical" model of communication. Again, we emphasize that these are dimensions of *behavior,* not dimensions of technological systems.

Let us restate our definitions: *communication* is human behavior that facilitates the sharing of meaning and takes place in a particular social context. Any interacting set of social and technical structures which facilitates the sharing of meaning among people is a *communication system.*

Dimensions of Communication Behavior

The most elemental aspect of the proposed model is communication behavior itself. Considered abstractly, any communicative act can be said to have three distinct dimensions: *temporality, involvement,* and *control.*

Temporality is the experience of time in a given communication situation. This encompasses the idea of mediation across time and the awareness of time during a communication act. We are most aware of the temporality of communication when we use systems like postal mail or telephone answering machines; we are less conscious of it when we communicate face-to-face or on the telephone. That is, a nonsimultaneous medium like postal mail can be thought of as a channel for high temporality communication, while a face-to-face interaction is a low temporality communication act. Related constructs include simultaneity and linearity of communication.

Involvement is the degree to which cognitive, affective, and sensory capabilities are employed by the communicator in creating or perceiving messages in a given communication situation. This is the most complex of the three dimensions, encompassing both mediation across physical space and across psychological distance. Related constructs here include social presence (Short, Williams, & Christie, 1976); propinquity (Korzenny & Bauer, 1981); bandwidth, as richness or multichannel communication; proximity; distance; disinhibition (Sproull & Kiesler, 1986); system transparency, enmeshment (Pearce & Cronen, 1980); and immediacy (Mehrabian, 1966; 1971).

Control is the degree to which communicators can exert influence in a given communication situation. This can be represented as a continuum ranging from sender control, to roughly shared or equal control, to receiver control. Note that this dimension is really comprised of two distinct aspects of control: the degree of control and the balance or symmetry of control among communicators. Related constructs include certainty of contact; communicator style; anonymity; conflict resolution; turn taking; symmetry; feedback; consensus; and system reach or ubiquity.

If our readers are still unclear about how these dimensions operate, we suggest that they follow the name of each dimension with the phrase "in an interaction." Thus, the three dimensions include the experience of temporality in an interaction, involvement in an interaction, and control in an interaction. It is important to stress that these three dimensions represent *clusters* of concepts, which may pertain variously to the characteristics of communicators, the characteristics of technologies, or to any other environmental factors that would shape a particular communication situation. Each dimension, therefore, is comprised of multiple concepts or aspects. Likewise, the dimensions are not strictly proportional in a quantitative sense. They are instead intended to suggest general "ranges" of the three qualities of communication behavior.

Using the definitions offered above, we have constructed the following 3-dimensional representation of the dimensions of communication (see figure 3.1). While we believe these three dimensions to be first and foremost attributes of communication, we also find it instructive to illustrate the model using examples of communication systems (rather than

FIGURE 3.1
Dimensions of Communication Behavior

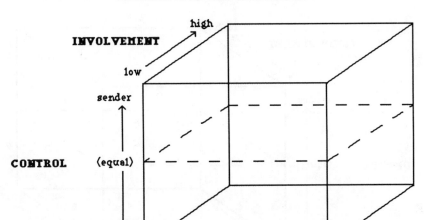

simply examples of communication behavior). While various FtF interactions can be imagined as examples of the range of involvement in an interaction, and even of the range of control in an interaction (peers vs. superior/subordinate) it is more difficult to understand the temporality dimension without examples that go beyond the FtF situation.

It is possible to array particular kinds of communication systems in the space of the 3-dimensional "cube," according to judgments that can be made about their respective degrees of temporality, involvement, and control. In figure 3.2, we have arrayed the least "technological" system: FtF interaction. This system is low in temporality (FtF communication by nature occurs in real time), and offers participants substantial opportunity to exert control over the interaction. In addition, FtF communicators are assumed to be highly involved sensorily, cognitively, and perhaps emotionally in the interaction.

Figure 3.3 indicates the relative positions of several communication systems which are ordinarily simultaneous, but which are mediated electronically: the telephone, live television, and live radio. They are all simultaneous systems, but differ in that the telephone call allows both partners of a dyad (or members of a small group in a conference call) to interact, while live radio and television transmissions typically give control of the communication to the sender (talk shows might be an exception). In

FIGURE 3.2
Face-to-Face Communication within Dimensions of Communication Behavior

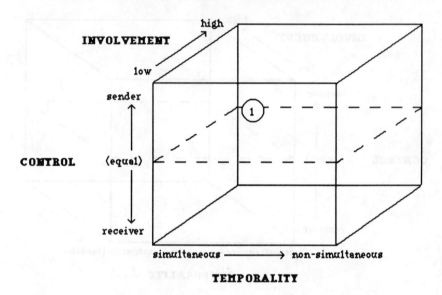

1 Face-to face interaction. small groups

addition, television is typically thought of as being more involving than radio because it supplies more stimuli or bandwidth to the viewer (visual and aural) than does radio to the listener; therefore, in this particular illustration we have depicted it as being higher on the involvement dimension.

We can proceed to even more complex systems, using the 3-dimensional array to place mediated systems that are not simultaneous, systems which have the ability to store and relay messages in a nonsimultaneous way (see figure 3.4). The main effect of the technological ability to store messages electronically is to allow relatively rapid nonsimultaneous communication, resulting in systems that are lower in temporality (such as electronic mail, voice mail, videotex, television via VCR, and telephones with answering machines) than more traditional storage media like postal mail or books. Notice that temporality interacts with the other two dimensions. For example, in television, control no longer lies solely with the producer; the widespread adoption of home VCRs has turned a certain degree of control over to viewers.

For the sake of convenience we have attempted to place selected

FIGURE 3.3
Communication Systems Arrayed within Dimensions of Communication Behavior

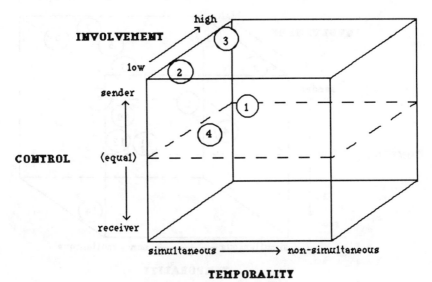

1 Face-to face interaction, small groups
2 Live radio
3 Live television
4 Telephone

communication systems at particular points in the 3-dimensional space. Yet many of these communication systems should actually be represented as bubbles in the space rather than as points. The placement of a system relative to the dimensions may vary enormously according to the social context of the communication taking place via that system and the features of the system that may be deemed most important, given the situation. Moreover, the model is not intended to imply preference for any particular type of system. Systems are seen simply as functional responses to communication behavior in particular social contexts.

In this section, the placement of systems within the involvement dimension has relied on the tradition of defining a medium by its bandwidth, or its potential for providing a rich, complex set of messages. As we have already observed, in actual usage bandwidth may have little relation to the involvement experienced by individual communicators: wide-bandwidth systems (such as FtF) may be used for very low-involvement communication, while relatively narrow bandwidth systems (such as text) may be used for very high-involvement communication.

FIGURE 3.4
Communication Systems Arrayed within Dimensions of Communication Behavior

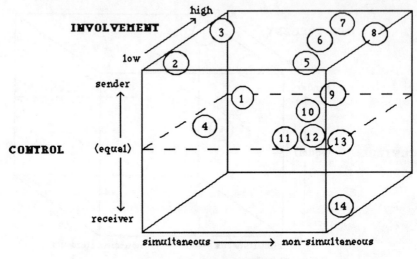

1 Face-to-face interaction, small groups
2 Live radio
3 Live television
4 Telephone
5 Books
6 Records
7 Television w/VCR
8 Movies
9 Telephone w/answering machine
10 Voice mail
11 Electronic mail
12 Overnight postal delivery
13 Postal mail
14 Database systems

Thus, to account for the rich variety of communication experiences we need a model that allows for more than just the classification of communication behavior and systems along their common dimensions. We must take account of the antecedents of a communication act as well as the content. These topics are addressed below under the rubric of "social context."

The Social Context of Communication

What is meant when we say that communication occurs in a particular social context? We have already characterized communication itself as three dimensional; but in addition, this "cube" exists in a general social context. For the purposes of this discussion, several main elements of social context are most relevant, ordered from the general to the specific: (1) the prevailing culture surrounding a given communication situation, that is, the social expectations or givens specific to a particular time, place, and people; (2) the nature of the specific interpersonal relationships among the communicators within that culture; and (3) the precise content or meaning to be shared among communicators (i.e., the messages) who interact in a specific relationship.

Communication itself, and therefore communication systems, evolve within the boundaries of these contextual elements; systems can become so context-specific that we cannot image them outside of their contextual settings. For example, videotex systems have proven to be most successful in social contexts where government or private underwriting has ensured the system's survival through the initial prototype and implementation stages (Finn & Stewart, 1985). Accordingly, consumer videotex has been introduced more successfully in Canada and France—nations that provided the start-up support—while it has encountered a lack of interest and a resistance to the high cost of videotex terminals in the U.S., where the system has had to compete with more established systems in a free market environment. Some observers have come to conclude that the success of videotex is so dependent on this level of start-up support that it cannot survive in a strictly free market context.

We can depict social context graphically, where the most general element—culture—subsumes the other two elements, relationships and content. In this scheme, culture tends to influence social relationships among individuals; and those relationships, in turn, tend to influence the actual content of the communication among individuals. We can now combine the two components of the model into a single illustration, with the 3-dimensional cube of communication nested within the three concentric spheres or shells of social context.

We depict the cube of communication as being within the shells of social context, not to indicate any particular directionality in the model, but to show that communication cannot take place unless culture, relationship, and content have been accounted for. Without these contextual elements, the attempt at communication will be nonsensical. In any given communication situation the context may influence communication and vice versa. Figure 3.6 depicts an ideal situation in terms of the directions that influence can theoretically take between communication behavior and its context.

Discussion

The communication dimensions are useful for the examination of communication behavior across a wide range of situations and social contexts.

FIGURE 3.5
The Social Context of Communication

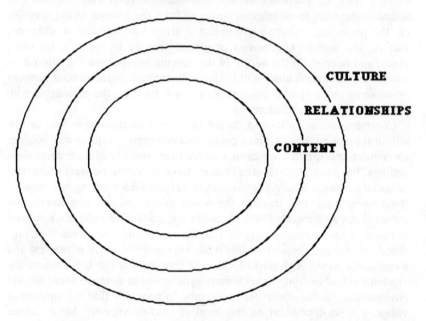

CULTURE

RELATIONSHIPS

CONTENT

In the following discussion we have attempted to apply the model to fundamental questions in each of four traditional areas of communication research: media effects, uses and gratifications, studies of group process, and communication policy. Each of these areas represents a shared effort to understand communication behavior in particular contexts; the communication systems model allows us to outline areas for further research and discussion within each of the traditions. The examples we have selected are by no means exhaustive; but they demonstrate that certain familiar concepts may change when the communication systems model is applied to them.

Media Effects

Media effects studies, whose purpose has been to clarify the actions of mediated messages on audiences and individuals, form the dominant core of American mass communication research. In this area, preeminence has been accorded to the electronic mass media, especially television. This emphasis seems to be based on the high degree of sender control exerted in television broadcasting; but sender control is equally high in radio, and almost as high in storage systems such as books and records, and these

FIGURE 3.6
The Communication Systems Model

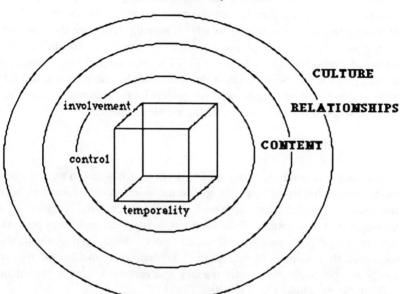

media have not been studied nearly as much as television. Ignoring the size of the audience reached for the moment, another explanation offered for the dominant impact of television is the high degree of (potential) viewer involvement, given the apparently great amount of bandwidth transmitted by television.

We reject this argument on the grounds that it only accounts for the sensory stimuli received by viewers—only sender control and purely sensory (visual, aural) involvement are accounted for. The remaining aspects of the dimensions have a role in media effects as well. We might, for example, pose the simple question: how involving can a one-way medium be for receivers? This question may place our perspective closer to a McLuhanesque view that television is inherently uninvolving ("cool"), precisely because there is so little receiver control. Television systems that afford viewers more control (e.g., VCRs) are more involving than broadcast programming. It can be argued that this quandary among media effects researchers has led, in part, to reassessments of the importance of social context (e.g., multistage theories of mass media effects and the role of opinion leaders). This emphasis on social context is essential, precisely because a system high in sender control is not necessarily high on the involvement dimension. At least one group of the most knowledgeable students of mass media effects seems to agree—advertisers. The ratings services are currently revising their long-standing approach of simply measuring whether the message is coming into the home, in favor of more precise measurements of who is actually receiving the message. Concerns over the shift of control from the sender to the receiver of televised messages—in such forms as VCR use, zapping and zipping of commercials with remote control devices, and the use of home satellite dishes—have sent advertisers and pay television programmers scrambling for new ways to regain control over the viewing audience.

Media Uses and Gratifications

One of the theoretical schools of thought that has arisen among communication scholars in response to the media-effects tradition has been the uses and gratifications approach. In this framework, receivers of a message are not seen as passive elements in the communication process, but as active participants who seek, select, shape, and evaluate the messages they want or need. At least in that tradition, the motives or needs of communicators, both senders and receivers, play a prominent role (Williams, Phillips, & Lum, 1982).

In a complex society or organization with multiple communication systems, the uses and gratifications perspective might prompt us to ask: how do communicators choose the system they use for a given communication act? We argue that, whether consciously or unconsciously, people select communication systems based on an evaluation of the intended interaction vis-à-vis the three dimensions of communication and the social context in which it will take place. We would hypothesize that individuals with a large organization, with multiple systems available to them, might choose a particular system based on:

- An assessment of the probability of reaching the intended receiver (1) at all, and then (2) within an acceptable time frame. That is, the sender takes account of the temporality dimension in choosing a communication system.
- The needs of the specific task to be accomplished. We take a broad view of "task," and see task as directly related to the involvement dimension.
- The perceived ability to exert control in the interaction. Specific aspects of the control dimension taken into account would include the desire for reciprocal control and the facility of the sender with particular systems.

While hypotheses like these are clearly empirical questions, several examples may prove instructive here. Organizational directives are typically issued as memos (rather than delivered FtF or even on electronic mail). In this case, the sender has chosen a distribution system high in temporality, low in involvement, and high in sender control (and the message is clear: no discussion, thank you). Discussion items, on the other hand, are typically communicated FtF or over the telephone, where low temporality promotes quick resolution and roughly equal control facilitates the discussion itself. Print media are frequently used for complex discussion items (reactions to written ideas and proposals) and in such situations the communicators consciously accept high temporality because they specifically want discussion only after reflection.

Furthermore, our model sheds light on the role of electronic messaging systems, which give communicators the time for reflection but reduce the temporality (turnaround time) of the interaction. It strikes us that there is an interesting difference in the use of electronic communication systems that are organized by receiver (electronic mail) and those that are organized by topic (computer conferencing): electronic mail is heavily used in organizations relative to computer conferencing systems (Sproull & Kiesler, 1986). We believe this usage pattern is consistent with our model, since the computer analog for mail moves the communication toward lower temporality, while the computer analog for conferencing moves the communication toward higher temporality (relative to FtF conferencing).

The Study of Group Processes

Two hypotheses have been advanced in research on computer-based messaging systems which have clear implications for the study of group interaction processes. The first is that computer conferencing systems are more democratic than FtF meetings (Johansen, Vallee & Spangler, 1979; Hiltz, 1978). While at first glance the notion of democracy seems roughly equivalent to equal control between sender and receiver, we might attribute the democratic atmosphere of computer conferencing to its high temporality (the ability for participants to contribute as much as they wish to the discussion whenever they wish because of reduced time constraints).

A second hypothesis which relates mediated communication systems and group processes is that the more affective cues that are permitted by a system, the less effective that system is for completing particular tasks (Hiltz & Turoff, 1986). In terms of our model, this suggests that high involvement interferes with task completion. It seems to us that this hypothesis is an oversimplification because it does not take account of social context. Studies of task effectiveness over computer-based communication systems have examined a very narrow range of tasks, typically some form of problem solving in which the criterion is consensus, the solution to a standard problem, or a combination of both. The Hiltz and Turoff hypothesis assumes that simply because a system permits affective cues (a form of high involvement) that it will necessarily be used for such cues; it underestimates the ability of communicators to focus on the task at hand even when they use a communication system which permits layers of involvement not required in that context. Our model would lead us to reject the hypothesis on theoretical grounds, and, indeed, Hiltz's & Turoff's (1986) own data show little support for the hypothesized relationship.

Communication Policy

One of the frequently discussed results of the explosive growth of new communication systems has been the breakdown of the Federal Communication Commission's (FCC) traditional model of regulating telecommunications systems. The distinctions among broadcasting, common carriers, and computers have become blurred with the introduction of systems that share attributes of two or more of these categories. These three classes of technology fit neatly along our dimension of control. Referring to figure 3.4 again, broadcasting belongs in the top place of the control dimension (high sender control), computers (conceptualized here as data base or mail systems) belong in the bottom plane (high receiver control), and common carrier systems belong in the middle plane (shared control).

Two of the most common examples of systems that have forced the reconsideration of these distinctions are cable television and the use of sophisticated computers in the common carrier (telephone and data transmission) business. The first example poses the question of whether cable television should be regulated like broadcasting or as a common carrier business. The United States has opted to treat cable as a common carrier at the local level (in the form of municipal franchise of cable operators). The control dimension of our model raises the question of who should be considered the sender in cable television—the creator of the content or the operator of the conduit who chooses the content in the local area? While this is hardly the first time the issue has come up, the control dimension of our model would lead us to conclude that, from the point of view of the receiver, cable television is more similar to traditional broadcasting than to traditional common carrier systems (such as postal mail and the telephone).

The second example, the heavy use of computers in the common carrier business, has implications for a number of policies being considered today. While the FCC acknowledged the need for the use of high-speed digital computers by AT&T as early as the 1956 Consent Decree, it has attempted to maintain the distinction between these two areas even today. Tradition may now be giving way to the logic that as long as computer storage has added the ability to mediate time to the existing ability of common carriers to mediate space, efficiency suggests that common carriers should be allowed to provide certain additional enhanced services. Services that local telephone companies are currently seeking to offer include voice messaging (storage of person-to-person messages) and electronic Yellow Pages (storage of mass communication messages).

The primary point here is that new communication systems have been reducing the usefulness of the FCC's distinctions. From the point of view of our model, these new systems—or enhancements to old systems (such as calling features on the telephone)—are simply located at different points in the 3-dimensional space of temporality, involvement, and control.

Conclusions

The discussion of the implications of the communication systems model has necessarily been rather cursory. We began this paper by stating that the model was developed as a conceptual tool for the study of specific new technologies; however, the model has turned out to be a framework for all kinds of communication, not just telecommunication technologies that have been characterized as new media. We believe that the model has a good deal of untapped explanatory power as a tool for:

- Description of any type of communication behavior in terms of three qualities of temporality, involvement, and control.
- Determination of the general attributes of particular communication systems in terms of communication behavior as well as in terms of technical system features (an approach typical of the media characteristics studies in the literature on new communication technologies).
- Comparison across systems on the basis of the three dimensions, allowing inferences about the impacts of various systems on the process of communication.
- Generation of hypotheses about similarities among systems that may appear different, and about differences among systems that may appear similar.
- The examination of how systems have actually been used in particular social contexts, considering them in terms of their relative efficiency, desirability, applicability, economy, or any other criteria investigators wish to apply.

The proof of this explanatory power must await our future efforts, and the efforts of others who employ the model.

Notes

This paper was originally presented at the annual meeting of the International Communication Association, May 1988, New Orleans, LA. The authors would like to thank Rob Kling, Brent Ruben, Jorge Schement, Stan Deetz, Guy Fielding, and anonymous reviewers for their helpful comments.

1. Early systems that provided telecommunication—communication at a distance—also used the natural media of light and air, such as smoke signals and drums. The primary difference between these systems and FtF communication is the use of some artifact or tool to create symbols rather than the use of the human body to create the symbols. Today the term telecommunication carries with it the connotation of using the electromagnetic spectrum.
2. For a somewhat representative sample see Pool (1977), in which only 3 of 21 articles are devoted to empirical studies of interpersonal communication via the telephone. See also Pool (1982).
3. Of course, the regulatory principle that has been employed to justify such restrictions is the "public interest, convenience or necessity." Underlying this principle is the idea of *scarcity,* i.e., the electromagnetic spectrum is a scarce resource and as such should be used in the public interest. Because print is *not* scarce, the reasoning goes, similar requirements are unnecessary for publishing. It has been argued that due to technological progress, the electromagnetic spectrum is no longer a scarce resource, and therefore continued restrictions on broad- or narrowcast content "in the public interest" are unjustified and possibly unconstitutional (Pool, 1983; Dordick, Bradley & Nanus, 1987; Krasnow, Longley & Terry, 1982). However, the argument over scarcity seems to us to be a red herring concealing the real concern about electronic media, that is, that they have an unnatural power over human perception in and of themselves, apart from content. Electronic media have historically been perceived, as Pool points out, to have "a uniquely pervasive presence." This perception has been the real impulse behind the restrictions placed on electronic media content (Justice J. P. Stevens, quoted in Pool [1983], p. 134).

References

Ball-Rokeach, S. J., & Reardon, K. K. (1988). Telelogic, dialogic and monologic communication: A comparison of forms. In R. P. Hawkins, J. M. Wiemann, & S. Pingree (Eds.), *Advancing Communication Science: Merging Mass and Interpersonal Processes.* Newbery Park, CA: Sage.

Barefoot, J., & Strickland, L. (1982). Conflict and dominance in television-mediated interactions. *Human Relations, 35*(7), 559–66.

Carey, J. (1981). Interaction patterns in audio teleconferencing. *Telecommunications Policy, 6,* 304–14.

DeFleur, M. L., & Ball-Rokeach, S. (1982). *Theories of mass communication* (4th ed.). NY: Longman.

Dervin, B. (1983). *An overview of sense-making research: Concepts, methods, and results to date.* Paper presented to the annual meeting of the International Communication Association, Dallas, Texas.

Dordick, H. (1987). Personal communication with the authors.

Dordick, H., Bradley, H., & Nanus, B. (1987). *The emerging network marketplace.* (2d ed.) Norwood, NJ: Ablex.

Dutton, W., & Lievrouw, L. (1982). Teleconferencing as an educational medium. In L. A. Parker, & C. Olgren (Eds.), *Proceedings of Teleconferencing and Interactive Media '82.* Madison, WI: University of Wisconsin-Extension.

Ferment in the Field. (1983). *Journal of Communication, 33*(3) (Special issue).

Finn, T. A. (1985). *A comparison of organizational uses of voice and electronic (text) messaging systems.* Working Paper #85-06, Technology and Productivity Research Center, AT&T Communications End User Computing Division, Piscataway, NJ.

Finn, T. A., & Stewart, C. M. (1985). From consumer to organizational videotex: Will videotex find a home at the office? In M. McLaughlin (Ed.), *Communication Yearbook 9.* Beverly Hills, CA: Sage.

Finn, T. A., & Strickland, D. E. (1982). The advertising and alcohol abuse issue: A cross-media comparison of the content of alcohol beverage advertising. In M. Burgoon (Ed.), *Communication Yearbook 6.* Beverly Hills, CA: Sage.

Hiltz, S. R. (1978). Impact of a computerized conferencing system upon scientific research specialties. *Journal of Research Communication Studies, 1,* 111–24.

Hiltz, S. R., & Johnson, K. (1987). *Measuring acceptance of computer-mediated communication systems.* Presented at the annual meeting of the International Communication Association, Montreal, Canada, May.

Hiltz, S. R., & Turoff, M. (1986). Experiments in group decision making: Communication process and outcome in face-to-face versus computerized conferences. *Human Communication Research, 13*(2), 225–52.

Hunter, L. (1987). Gadgets for Utopia. (Book review of *The Media Lab,* by Stewart Brand.) *New York Times Book Review,* 4 October, p. 38.

Johansen, R., Vallee, J., & Spangler, K. (1979). *Electronic meetings: Technical alternatives and social choices.* Reading, MA: Addison-Wesley.

Johansen, R., Vallee, J., Spangler, K., & Shirts, R. G. (1977). *The Camelia Report: A study of technical alternatives and social choices in teleconferencing.* A report from the Intermedia Project, Institute for the Future, Menlo Park, CA.

Johnson, B. M., & Rice, R. E. (1984). Reinvention in the innovation process: The case of word processing. In R. E. Rice, et al., *The New Media.* Beverly Hills, CA: Sage.

Kiesler, S., Siegel, J., & McGuire, T. W. (1984). Social psychological aspects of computer-mediated communication. *American Psychologist, 39* (10), 1123–34.

Kiesler, S., Zubrow, D., Moses, A. M., & Geller, V. (1985) Affect in computer-mediated communication: An experiment in synchronous terminal-to-terminal discussion. *Human-Computer Interaction, 1*(1).

Kling, R. (1980). Social analyses of computing: Theoretical perspectives in recent empirical research. *Computing Surveys, 12*(1), 61–110.

King, R., & Gerson, E. M. (1978). Patterns of segmentation and interaction in the computing world. *Symbolic Interaction, 1*(2), 24–43.

Kling, R., & Scacchi, W. (1980). Computing as social action: The social dynamics of computing in complex organizations. In M.C. Yovit (Ed.), *Advances in Computers: vol. 19.* NY: Academic Press.

Knorr-Cetina, K. D. (1981). *The manufacture of knowledge: An essay in the constructivist and contextual nature of science.* NY: Pergamon.

Korzenny, F., & Bauer, C. (1981). Testing the theory of electronic propinquity. *Communication Research, 8*(4), 479–98.

Krasnow, E. G., Longley, L. D., & Terry, H. A. (1982). *The politics of broadcast regulation*. NY: St. Martin's.

McLuhan, M. (1964). *Understanding media: The extensions of man*. NY: New American Library.

Mehrabian, A. (1966). Immediacy: An indicator of attitudes in linguistic communication. *Journal of Personality, 34*, 26–34.

Mehrabian, A. (1971). *Silent messages*. Belmont, CA: Wadsworth.

Nightingale, V., & Webster, I. (1986). Computer users as media audiences. *Prometheus, 4*(1), 128–40.

Nilles, J., Carlson, F., Gray, P., & Hanneman, G. (1976). *The telecommunication-transportation tradeoff*. NY: Wiley.

Pearce, W. B., & Cronen, V. E. (1980). *Communication, action and meaning: The creation of social realities*. NY: Praeger.

Phillips, A. (1982a). Computer conferencing: success or failure? *Systems, Objectives, Solutions, 2*, 203–18.

Phillips, A. (1982b). *Attitude correlates of selected media technologies: A pilot study*. Los Angeles: Annenberg School of Communications, University of Southern California.

Pool, I. de Sola. (Ed.) (1977). *The social impact of the telephone*. Cambridge, MA: MIT Press.

Pool, I. de Sola. (1982). *Forecasting the telephone: A restrospective technology assessment*. Norwood, NJ: Ablex.

Pool, I. de Sola. (1983). *Technologies of freedom*. Cambridge, MA: Belknap/Harvard University Press.

Restivo, S., & Loughlin, J. (1987). Critical sociology of science and scientific validity. *Knowledge: Creation, Diffusion, Utilization, 8*(3), 468–508.

Rice, R. E., & Case, D. (1983). Computer-based messaging in the university: A description of use and utility. *Journal of Communication, 33*(1), 131–52.

Rice, R. E. and associates (1984). *The new media: Communication, research and technology*. Beverly Hills, CA: Sage.

Rogers, E. M. (1986). *Communication technology*. NY: Free Press.

Rogers, E. M., & Agarwala-Rogers, R. (1976). *Communication in organizations*. NY: Free Press.

Rogers, E. M., & Kincaid, D. L. (1981). *Communication networks: A new paradigm for research*. NY: Free Press.

Ruben, B. (1988). *Communication and human behavior* (2d ed.). NY: Macmillan.

Schramm, W. (1949). The nature of news. *Journalism Quarterly, 26*(3), 259–69.

Schramm, W. (1977). *Big media, little media*. Beverly Hills, CA: Sage.

Schramm, W., & Roberts, D. (1971). *The process and effects of mass communication*. Urbana, Il: University of Illinois Press.

Short, J., Williams, E., & Christie, B. (1976). *The social psychology of telecommunications*. London: John Wiley & Sons.

Siegel, J., Dubrovsky, V., Kiesler, S., & McGuire, T. W. (1986). Group processes in computer-mediated communication. *Organizational Behavior and Human Decision Processes, 37*, 157–87.

Sproull, L. S., & Kiesler, S. (1986). Reducing social context cues: Electronic mail in organizational communication. *Management Science, 32*(11), 1492–1512.

Steinfield, C. (1983). *Communicating via electronic mail: Patterns and predictors of use in organizations*. Ph.D. diss. University of Southern California, Annenberg School of Communications.

Steinfield, C., & Fulk, J. (1987). On the role of theory in research on information technologies in organizations. *Communication Research, 14*(5), 479–90.

Stewart, C., & Finn, T. A. (1985). *Voice messaging: Organizational aspects of implementation and use.* Working Paper #85-03, Technology and Productivity Research Center, AT&T Communications, Piscataway, NJ.

Svenning, L., & Ruchinskas, J. (1984). Organizational Teleconferencing. In R. E. Rice, et al. *The new media.* Beverly Hills, CA: Sage.

Vallee, J., & Gibbs, B. (1976). Distributed management of scientific projects: An anlaysis of two computer-conferencing experiments at NASA. *Telecommunications Policy,* December, pp. 75–85.

Wilkens, H., & Plenge, G. (1981). Teleconference design: A technological approach to satisfaction. *Telecommunications Policy,* September, pp. 216–27.

Williams, F., Coulombe, J., & Lievrouw, L. A. (1983). Children's attitudes toward small computers: A preliminary study. *Educational Communication and Technology Journal, 31*(1), 3–7.

Williams, F., Phillips, A., & Lum, P. (1982). *Some extensions of uses and gratifications research.* Los Angeles: Annenberg School of Communications, University of Southern California.

Wilmot, W. W. (1979). *Dyadic communication* (2d ed.). Reading, MA: Addison-Wesley.

Woolgar, S. (1980). Discovery: Logic and sequence in a scientific text. In K. D. Knorr, R. Krohn, & R. Whitley (Eds.), *The Social Process of Scientific Investigation* (vol. 4). Holland: D. Reidel, 239–68.

4

Using Contextual Analysis to Bridge the Study of Mediated and Unmediated Behavior

Joshua Meyrowitz

This essay uses the notion of social context to examine both mediated and face-to-face interaction as part of one larger system of behavior and response. The concept of social context is extended beyond its typical definition of physical setting and location to include the types of "settings" that are fostered by the use of various media. After developing common-denominator concepts that bridge place-contexts and media-contexts, the essay demonstrates how contextual principles offer insight into the impact of media on two levels: (1) the micro, single-situation level, where choices among various communication options affect individual psychological experience, and (2) the macro, societal level, where shifts in the matrix of widely used media have an impact on social structure and on the situational geography of numerous social roles.

> *I asked a Polish peasant what was the extent of an "okolica" or neighborhood—how far it reached. "It reaches," he said, "as far as the report of a man reaches—as far as a man is talked about."*
>
> —William I. Thomas,
> *The Unadjusted Girl*

Considering how often the terms "context" and "situation" are used with respect to communication and behavior, they have been, until very recently, surprisingly underdefined terms. Their meanings are usually left implicit, embedded in traditional assumptions about the structure of communication and social life. Further, both in their implicit use and in the relatively few and recent instances of their explicit definition, such notions as "social context," "social situation," and "behavioral setting" have generally been conceived of in terms of time/space coordinates: where one is, who else is there, the date and time, and the overall definition of the event taking place in that particular time/space frame (funeral vs. wedding, for example).

Such a limited, place-bound definition, preserves the traditional distinction drawn between "real life" and "the media," between direct and indirect experience—a distinction that goes back as far as Plato's parable of the cave and continues in Goffman's (1967, p. 167) division of the universe of behavior into activities that occur either in each other's "immediate physical presence" or "solitarily."

The present essay suggests that the relationship between contexts and behavior provides a means of bridging the study of mediated and unmediated behavior, but only after the definition of context is broadened to extend beyond location-indexed settings to include the types of social situations that are fostered by the use of various media of communication.

After developing common denominator terms and concepts to study both place-contexts and media-contexts, I will show how contextual principles illuminate the influence of media on behavior, both on the micro, single-situation level such as when a spouse abandons a loving embrace to answer the telephone, and on the macro, societal level such as when changes in media environments tend to reshape the relative and absolute "life spaces" of people of different social categories.

Contextualizing Behavior

In 1964, Erving Goffman published an article titled "The Neglected Situation" in the *American Anthropologist*. Goffman argued that while attention was being focused on the behavioral implications of age, sex, class, and dozens of other social and psychological variables, researchers were not paying enough attention to the social situation itself as a key unit of analysis. In that article Goffman (1972) makes explicit a plea that he had already made implicitly in several of his earlier works (e.g., Goffman, 1959; 1963): that social situations "need and warrant analysis in their own right, much like that accorded other basic forms of social organization" (p. 63).

The following year Stanley Milgram published an article in *Human Relations,* "Some Conditions of Obedience and Disobedience to Authority." Milgram summarized there his controversial research that had found that a remarkable percentage of subjects—seemingly average citizens—followed the demands of an experimenter even when the subjects thought they were inflicting great pain to, or causing the death of, another human being through severe electric shocks. Milgram concluded that his research was not studying one of the typical provinces of psychology—personality—but rather the social context:

Many people, not knowing much about the experiment, claim that subjects who go to the end of the board are sadistic. Nothing could be more foolish than an overall characterization of these persons. It is like saying that a person thrown into a swift-flowing stream is necessarily a fast swimmer, or that he has great stamina because he moves so rapidly relative to the bank. The context of action must always be considered. The individual, upon entering the laboratory, becomes integrated into a situation that carries its own momentum. (1977, p. 118)

Milgram, like Goffman, called for a fuller study of situations:

Ultimately, social psychology would like to have a compelling *theory of situations* which will, first, present a language in terms of which situations can be defined; proceed to a typology of situations; and then point to the manner in which definable properties of situations are transformed into psychological forces in the individual. (Pp. 119–20)

The two subsequent decades have seen a dramatic increase in the examination of social contexts, situations, and settings.

Recent studies, theories, and critiques have suggested that personality measures are often poor predictors of everyday social behavior and that behaviors such as assertiveness, anxiety, hostility, leadership, and persuasibility are largely shaped by situational factors (see, for example, Argyle & Little, 1972; Mischel, 1968). Psychologists have been experimenting with teaching people to control compulsions and addictions such as overeating, drug abuse, alcoholism, and smoking, by monitoring the situational cues that stimulate the behaviors (for a review of this literature see Furnham & Argyle, 1981, pp. xli–xliii).

Researchers have also begun to examine the ways in which situational definitions affect a person's accent, vocabulary, and other linguistic variables (e.g., Giles & Powesland, 1975; Gregory & Caroll, 1978; Hymes, 1967). Even competence and skill are coming to be viewed as situation-specific rather than person-specific variables (Furnham & Argyle, 1981, pp. xix–xx).

One study of behavioral contexts found that otherwise normal students who were randomly assigned to be guards in a simulated prison began to display uncharacteristic cruelty, aggression, and sadism. Indeed, a hostile guard-prisoner relationship developed so quickly and with such intensity that the experiment had to be abandoned in less than a week (Haney, Banks, & Zimbardo, 1973). This research offered disturbing support for the earlier work of Milgram.

Ethnomethodologist Harold Garfinkel (1967) has developed a method of making situational conventions visible by breaking the rules of situations and then observing the resulting confusion and the process of reconstruction that follows. Philosopher Rom Harré and psychologist Paul Secord (1973) have argued that people's own accounts of the rules of social situations should be used as the foundation of a new scientific approach to the study of social behavior.

In *Ecological Psychology,* Roger Barker (1968) summarized more than a decade of research on behavioral settings at the Midwest Psychological Field Station by suggesting that there is less variation in behavior across individuals within a situation than there is for one individual across settings. In studying children, for example, Barker and his colleagues began their research with a "traditional person-centered approach," but concluded that they "could predict some aspects of children's behavior more adequately from knowledge of the behavior characteristics of the drugstores, arithmetic classes, and basketball games they inhabited than from knowledge of the behavior tendencies of particular children" (p. 4).

The rise of interest in situations has posed a challenge to the significance of social psychological experiments. Situation-sensitive critics of the laboratory method have argued that rather than studying raw behavior in isolation from extraneous variables, many psychologists have actually been studying the way people behave in a newly defined social situation— the psychological experiment. For example, Barker (1968), observes sardonically that "the science of psychology has had no adequate knowledge of the psychologist-free environment of behavior" (p. 4).

That critique has been supported by research that has shown that subjects in experiments try to please the experimenter, that people who volunteer to be in experiments differ in a number of significant ways from the general population, and that the expectations of the experimenter often unintentionally influence the results of an experiment or his/her perception and interpretation of the results (Rosenthal & Rosnow, 1969, 1975).

Initially, studies on the effects of experiments were conducted as means of perfecting the methodology of experimentation. But as the effects of the experimental situation have come to seem unavoidable, the more such work has evolved into a critique of the experimental method itself, especially in those areas of behavioral research where it has been applied almost to the exclusion of other methods. Psychologist Ralph Rosnow, for example, has called for a more pluralistic social psychology that embraces a variety of methods and approaches, including more contextualist studies that examine "where, when, and before whom the behavior is performed" (Rosnow, 1983, p. 333). Similarly, Adrian Furnham and Michael Argyle (1981) have suggested that as a result of "disillusionment and limited success" with old perspectives and methods, the "social situation, rather than the individual, may develop into a new unit of psychological research" (p. xxiii).

The Traditional Focus on Place

The recent interest in contextualizing human behavior has not yet led to clear agreement on exactly what a "context" or "situation" is. Different situationists have focused attention on different characteristics of contexts, including tasks, goals, rules, roles, traditions, temporal factors (season, month, day, time, and length of encounter), the number and characteristics of people present, and the subjective perceptions of participants.

Lawrence Pervin (1978) and Joseph Forgas (1979, pp. 10–12) have demonstrated how much ambiguity and disagreement surround situationist terminology. In 1972, Norman Fredericksen lamented that "we lack a satisfactory classification of situations. We need a systematic way of conceptualizing the domain of situations and situational variables before we can make rapid progress in studying the role of situations in determining behavior" (p. 115). A decade later, Furnham and Argyle (1981) were similarly declaring that in social psychology "there exist no theoretical models suggesting how situations function and what their components are" (p. xxii).

Yet underneath the ambiguity and disagreement in situational research, there has been one general commonality: an implicit or explicit concern with behavior in a physical location. For example, Goffman (1959) defines a behavioral region as "any *place* that is bounded to some degree by barriers to perception" (p. 106, emphasis added). Barker (1968) sees "behavior settings" as "bounded, *physical-temporal locales*" (p. 11, emphasis added). Albert Scheflen (1972) notes that transactions ordinarily occur in "a highly stable *physical* environment," likely a "bounded *place*" in which the "boundaries limit egress and ingress" (p. 123, emphasis added). Lawrence Pervin defines a situation as "a specific *place,* in most cases involving specific people, a specific time and specific activities" (quoted in Furnham & Argyle, 1981, p. xvi, emphasis added). Pervin (1978) also notes that despite differences in view, a person-place-action conception of a situation is consistent with all the current strains of situationism.

It is not surprising that most studies of situations and behavior have focused on immediate physical presence. Face-to-face communication is the most intense form of communication, involving one's full sensorium, including smell, touch, and taste. Every face-to-face encounter holds the possibilities of embrace or attack, however rarely those possibilities are realized. In addition, place-bound, face-to-face interaction was until relatively recently the only means of experiencing the sights and sounds of others' behaviors. Physical barriers and passageways once defined the boundaries and patterns of communication. As the saying goes, "You had to be there."

But this is no longer always the case. Through electronic media—such as the telephone, radio, television, and audio and video recordings—we have access to others in ways that defy traditional laws of time and space. When two friends speak on the telephone, for example, the situation they are "in" is only marginally related to their respective physical locations. Indeed, in some respects, the telephone brings two people closer to each other than they are to those in their immediate physical environments. Electronic communications pass through walls and leap across vast distances, thereby demoting the status of place as a determinant of social context. Such recontextualizing of behavior demands more attention than it has received so far.

Ironically, those who have taught us the most about the contextual nature of human behavior often have the least to say about media contexts. For example, when Goffman (1963, pp. 14–15) asks us to consider the importance of situations, he explicitly limits his interest to information received through the "naked senses" and not through sensory augmentors (for a fuller discussion of the general lack of attention to media in Goffman's work see Meyrowitz, in press).

Perhaps it is no coincidence that attention to the power of situational location and physical boundaries should grow intense as the integrity of location-bound situations has been challenged by an array of media of communication that have little respect for place. For the electronic reduction of the power of place-bound settings weakens the spell that place holds over us just enough for us to become aware of the spell.

As Furnham and Argyle (1981) note, video cameras and tape recorders have been among those developments that offer "new techniques and strategies to record, describe, and analyze social situations" (pp. xxv–xxvi). Yet situationists have generally seen new media only as lenses to look through in order to examine location-indexed face-to-face behaviors more closely. The study of the transformation of situations through new media, including the transformation that is inherent in a researcher's "removal" of events from their original situations by recording them on video or audio tape, has gone largely unexplored. (This new awareness on one level combined with blindness on another is analogous to the awareness we achieve through movies that reveal the making of another movie; as we gain awareness on how the effects in the original movie took us in, we often remain unaware of the techniques used in making the second movie.)

Beyond Place: Contexts as Information-Systems

While there is no question that face-to-face encounters are a very special form of interaction, there is also no doubt that, for most members of our society, direct encounters are now only one kind of social interchange. In business and pleasure, our two-way interactions on the phone and our vicarious relationships with others through radio and television (Horton & Wohl, 1956) are often more numerous, if less intense and meaningful, than encounters in immediate physical presence.

Moreover, electronic media are now present in nearly all physical settings in our country. About 96% of American homes have at least one telephone (American Telephone & Telegraph, 1981, p. 87); 98 % of American households own at least one television set (Nielsen, 1982, p. 3). There are more radios in the country than people (Hiebert, Ungurait, & Bohn, 1982, p. 10). Electronic media are considered necessities rather than luxuries even by prisoners and welfare families (see Meyrowitz, 1985, pp. 341n.3, 350n.4). Increasingly, our interpersonal encounters are interrupted by, or interwoven with, encounters with or through media.

The traditional development of media research and interpersonal research as two largely distinct fields of inquiry has benefited neither. Media research has been hampered by a narrow focus primarily on media messages and resulting concerns over distorted representation of reality, imitation, or persuasion. Interpersonal behavior theory has been limited by a general tendency to ignore the ways in which face-to-face behavior may be reshaped by media-induced changes in the boundaries of social contexts. Few studies examine both media and interpersonal interaction as part of the same system of behaving or responding to others' behavior.

Studies of media content, while important, are limited to the extent that they view media only as new links among preexisting environments. Like the commuter perusing the television listings on a train ride home from work, the content analyst is more concerned with what media bring into the house than with the possibility that media transform the home and all other interaction settings into new social contexts with new patterns of action, feeling, and belief.

One way to bridge the study of mediated and nonmediated behavior is to rethink the place-bound definitions of "context." Goffman (1959, p. 106) provides a clue when he focuses, as noted above, on "any place that is bounded to some degree by barriers to perception." For in addition to place, this definition contains another key element that tends to get lost in most of his and other situationists' discussions of behavioral settings: "barriers to perception." I suggest that place is actually a subcategory of this more inclusive notion of a perceptual field. For while situations have usually been defined in terms of who is in what location, the implicit issue is actually the types of behaviors that are available for other people's scrutiny.

One way to think of contexts, then, is as information-systems, that is, as specific patterns of access/restriction to social information, of access/restriction to the behavior of other people. The concept of information-systems suggests that physical settings and media settings are part of a continuum rather than a dichotomy. Places and media both foster set patterns of interaction among people, while set patterns of social information flow.

Parallels between Place-Contexts and Mediated-Contexts

It has long been observed that individuals project different behavior in front of different audiences (e.g., Cooley, 1922/1964; Duncan, 1962; Goffman, 1959). We behave one way in front of our parents and another way with our friends; one way in the presence of employers and another way with coworkers; and so on. When we find ourselves in a given setting, therefore, we often consciously or unconsciously ask, "Who can see me, who can hear me?" "Whom can I see, whom can I hear?" The answers to these questions help us decide how to behave. And although these questions were once fully answered by an assessment of the physical environment, they now require an evaluation of the media environment as well.

There are many rough parallels between the flow of information through media and the flow of information in physical settings. A phone conversation between two people, each of whom is also in the physical presence of another person, for example, is roughly analogous to the situation that occurs when four people go to a lecture, movie, or play together, and sit side-by-side in one row of seats. The people on the two ends often feel isolated from each other and from conversations that take place between the two people in the center. Conversely, the two people in the center may feel that they share a small conspiracy and can say things to each other that are not fully accessible to the other two people.

Similarly, when we ring a doorbell and then quickly check the neatness of our hair or clothing, we are in a situation structurally analogous to when we dial a telephone number and then clear our throats before the phone is answered. Before the door is opened and before the phone is answered, we remain "offstage." In both cases, the dividing line between private and public is informational, not necessarily physical.

Most interactions through media can be described by using an interpersonal analogue (Meyrowitz, 1974, 1979; Levinson, 1979, 1988). Watching television is structurally similar to watching people through a one-way mirror in a situation where those being watched know they are being watched and those watching know there are many other isolated and invisible viewers. Radio listening resembles overhearing people speaking in the next room with a similar awareness on the part of the participants; and so on.

This is not to say that mediated encounters are by any means identical to live interaction. The vocal intimacy and the absence of the visual image in a telephone conversation may be something like "pillow talk," that is, an intimate conversation with another person in the dark, but the two forms are certainly not identical. On the phone (or a CB radio) there is no chance for immediate physical intimacy, no risk of physical harm. But it is precisely this kind of analysis of similarities and differences that offers insight into the nature of telephone conversations. The intimate aspects of telephone interaction foster informality, even in business phone conversations. The physical isolation enhances most people's willingness to answer the phone much more freely than they would open the door to strangers. This odd mixture of intimacy and distance may explain why it is often easier to be flirtatious or aggressive on the phone than in person. The point is that while mediated and live encounters are obviously different in many ways, they can be analyzed using similar principles. The patterns of information flow, whether direct or mediated, help to define the situation and the notions of appropriate style and action.

Mediated interactions are also analogous to interpersonal encounters in the ways in which individuals modulate their behavior to signal different definitions of relationships and various degrees of involvement. The behavior of participants in a telephone call, for example, can be analyzed in the same way that Scheflen (1972, pp. 32–33) analyzes an interpersonal "with," that is, a kinesic frame that suggests togetherness in opposition to others in the same physical vicinity. The intensity of "withs" varies. Two people may convey their "coupleness" simply by walking next to each other in synchrony, or by sitting closely to each other on a bench while leaving a larger space between themselves and others. Or they may display a more intense, "excluding with" by turning their backs on others, by hugging, by gazing into each other's eyes, or by displaying any deep engrossment with each other to the exclusion of others. Similarly, a person on the phone may signal degrees of involvement in the "phone couple" by using hushed tones, by turning his/her back on others in the same room, or by tightly hugging the receiver. Viewers may signal similar involvement with noninteractive media—to the exclusion of real people in real physical space with them—by wearing headphones, by gazing at the television screen and not at the live people, or by singing along with the stereo or the radio.

The relationship between live and mediated contexts is made most apparent by electonic media, which often simulate part of the sight and sound spectrum of live interaction. But once we think of media and physical settings as being structurally parallel, relationships between non-electronic media and live settings also become apparent. For example, when two parents pass notes to each other or spell out words to avoid having to say certain things in front of their children, they are distancing their children from their communications in a manner somewhat similar to moving the children to another room.[1] And the differences between literate and nonliterate parents is functionally similar—in terms of some forms of interaction—to the differences between families with multi-room vs. single-room dwellings.

When we conceive of contexts as information-systems rather than physical settings, we realize that social situations may be modified without building or removing walls, without opening or closing doors or window shades, and without changing customs and laws concerning access to places. The use of media of communication may restructure contexts and foster new behaviors in ways that go beyond the traditional concerns over the imitative or persuasive appeal of media messages.

Contextual Characteristics of Media

The physical characteristics of a setting have behavioral implications. The size of a room, for example, tends to set a minimum and a maximum number of people who can interact within it comfortably. A basketball court is not a very romantic spot for two lovers to interact, and a telephone booth is not a suitable place for a meeting of the local PTA. The thickness of doors and walls, the size and location of windows, the availability of window shades, and the distance of the setting from other encounters in other locations, among many other factors, serve to support or undermine various potential behavior patterns.

Further, the physical characteristics of settings interact with the characteristics of individuals. The height of a window, for example, may make it accessible to adults but not to young children.

While we usually tend to think of contexts in terms of what and who is in them, contexts are also defined by what and who is excluded from them. The way male high school students speak in a locker room, for example, is influenced not only by the presence of other male students but also by the absence of female students, parents, teachers, principals, and so on.

The membranes around social situations influence behavior through full and partial inclusion and exclusion. We may be visually excluded from the next motel room but aurally included by the thinness of the walls. Or, in an office, we may be aurally insulated through thick glass but remain on visual display. Such features determine which of our behaviors are public and which are private, and therefore influence how we behave.

In a parallel manner, media may affect the boundaries of contexts by bypassing traditional physical limitations on information flow and by creating new patterns of access and restriction. Political and sports figures who are being watched through long lenses (but not microphones) may find that they have to project a visual display appropriate to their roles, but may speak profanely without social consequence. Conversely, Richard Nixon found that, although visually insulated, his tape recorder in the Oval Office led to his private and profane locker room style conversations being evaluated as public pronouncements. Most politicians have since learned to be more aware of the potential indirect media audiences.

Media, then, may be thought of as functionally similar to physically defined settings—e.g., towns, buildings, and rooms—in that their characteristics and typical patterns of use tend to include and exclude people in particular ways and to encourage different styles of behavior.

Relevant contextual characteristics of media include the following:

1. The type of sensory information the medium can and cannot convey (sight, sound, smell).
2. The form of information that the medium conveys. This differs from sensory information in that sound could be either dots and dashes or voice; visual could be either words on a page or images.
3. Speed and degree of immediacy of communication. How quickly messages can be encoded, sent, and received; how quickly feedback can be sent and received.
4. Unidirectional vs. bidirectional. Compared with the telephone, e.g., broadcast radio and television are primarily unidirectional, in that feedback by the listener is rare and, when existent, indirect and limited.
5. Simultaneous or sequential interaction. On the telephone, e.g., one can

hear the other person sigh or comment as one speaks, as opposed to a CB radio where one must take turns communicating.

6. Relative ease or difficulty of learning to use the medium to code and decode messages (it is more difficult to learn to read and write than to learn to speak and listen). Also, whether one learns to use the medium all-at-once or in stages.

7. Physical requirements for using the medium, for example, whether one has to sit still or is able to move around; whether one has to stop what one is doing to convey a message about it, as in writing, or whether the medium simply captures what one is saying or doing, as with a camcorder; the need for modifying the situation to mediate it, as with electronic flash for photography.

8. The scope and nature of dissemination of the mediated communication: How long can it last? How far can it travel? (What Innis [1951] refers to as time vs. space biases.) How many and what types of people will have access to it?

Other variables that are not immediately apparent from examining the physical media themselves also have contextual relevance. These include political and economic patterns of control over media, the cost and relative availability of media, and cultural patterns that influence whether, how, and when media are used. Such variables would include everything from explicit or implicit censorship, to rate setting (i.e., long-distance phone charges), to the custom of not telephoning people after midnight except for emergencies.

Such contextual characteristics of media affect behavior on the micro and macro level, that is both when individuals make choices among available media, and when the addition of a new medium to the existing matrix of media has an impact on a broad range of contexts, thereby affecting social structure and broad categories of roles.

Modifications of Psychological Experience

Contextual characteristics play a role in an individual's decisions concerning media use and affect communication styles and psychological experience. For example, people often choose to end an intimate relationship by letter rather than by telephone call. The letter (which is sequential rather than simultaneous and deals primarily with written symbols) allows us to "have our say" without any interruption or response from the other party as well as to objectify our message, removing it from the emotional overtones that would be conveyed by vocalizations. Further, the contextual nature of letter writing allows the sender to write and rewrite the letter until it has the desired tone and content, and then send off the completed communication.

In contrast, a similar message conveyed over the telephone (a simultaneous medium that conveys information largely indistinguishable from real-life vocalization and speech) tends to be more "give and take" in character, more emotionally charged, and less polished in form. Indeed, a "Dear John" telephone call is somewhat paradoxical; for one conveys a message of a desired end to an intimate relationship by using a medium that highlights interaction and intimacy. On the telephone, we remain *in* the relationship.

Similar contextual factors operate in our choice of other media, including noninteractive ones. A person may choose to watch television after returning home from a hard day at work (rather than reading, writing, or making telephone calls) because the television simulates some aspects of human contact but without even the slightest demand on the viewer. In everyday face-to-face behavior, we tend to maintain an "interaction tonus" (Goffman, 1963, pp. 24–25) where our facial and body muscles are tensed enough to show that we are ready to "come into play" at any moment. Writing and reading also demand effort. But television allows us to watch the interactions and gestures of others while we remain unwatched and expressionless. For similar reasons, we may turn on the radio in the car when we pick up a hitchhiker to avoid feeling the need to fill the silence with conversation.

In a different social context, however, loud music may play a very different role—that of social lubricant, easing us into and out of potentially intimate relationships. In a singles' bar, for example, the loud music requires strangers to come very close to each other in order to say even the simplest phrase. The music gives what would normally be intimate distance (Hall, 1966) an ambiguous meaning. (Are we close because we want an intimate relationship, or because we *must* come very close in order to say anything at all?) This context allows for brief trials of close interaction without a clear commitment to intimacy. While the distance is intimate, little substantive interaction can be had until leaving the establishment.

Media also differ in the degree to which they saturate an environment. Goffman (1959) discusses "saturation" as a characteristic of Anglo-American societies where one definition of a situation tends to fill an indoor space and to involve all the people in the time/space frame (p. 106). Any medium can pull a person out of the location-bound definition of the situation. But various media challenge the integrity of the time/space frame in different ways.

Print media tend to create new, engrossing definitions, but only for one person at a time. Reading is best done alone, in a quiet place, and to the exclusion of other activities. Indeed, special places are often designated for reading, which is linear and absorbing.

Electronic media often invade places, yet without occupying them the way reading and writing do. It is difficult to walk, talk, eat, exercise, make love, or drive an automobile while reading or writing. Most of these activities are possible while watching television, and all are possible while listening to the radio. Electronic media, then, tend to change the definition of the situation in places, but in an incomplete and relatively unstable manner.

For example, I recall a visit to my parents' house in New York for a Sunday dinner in the late 1970s. But as it turned out, I also attended a state funeral. Senator Hubert Humphrey was being buried that day, and my father had the television on so we could watch the funeral. Were we at a carefree Sunday dinner or at a funeral? We were at both, but not quite at either. We did not feel right about being very jubilant because the funeral was a sad event, yet we did not feel obligated to be completely dour-faced and mournful, because we were at home enjoying dinner. (There was, after all, no danger of offending Humphrey's widow or other mourners with our "improper" funeral behavior, because broadcast television is unidirectional.) Further, because the funeral was very slow and depressing, we occasionally flipped the channels, so that we left and returned to the funeral many times. The Humphrey funeral was broadcast live on ABC and NBC; Channel 9 carried a monster movie with hundreds of people being killed (which seemed to put Humphrey's death into perspective); Channel 5 broadcast a music and dancing program, "Soul Train"; Channel 11 provided another monster movie, a Japanese one dubbed into English; and the PBS station, Channel 13, broadcast "Zoom," showing at one point a boy helping his father to catch fish. Not only were we not required to travel to any specific place to see the Humphrey funeral, but the experience of the event did not saturate a time/space frame. Even the combined situation—eating dinner and attending a funeral—was itself unstable. We could easily change our place by flipping channels. Through television, my parents and I traveled to and through many different psychological spaces in a matter of minutes. The disrespect for place and occasion inherent in the use of television was even more dramatically demonstrated when one network stopped in the middle of the Humphrey funeral service to broadcast a golf match. (Similarly, a few years later, one network switched back and forth between "live" coverage of Anwar Sadat's historic peace mission to Israel and "live" coverage of the Ohio State-Michigan football game.)

Depending on one's perspective, such recontextualizing of behavior could be said to splinter psychological experience or to unify it. On the one hand, experience is now more disjointed. It is increasingly rare for people to spend an uninterrupted hour or two within a single mode of communication. The videocassette player can be stopped, run backwards, or rushed forward. The ringing of a phone can derail almost any interaction; for some people, it will even halt lovemaking. Wireless remote controls allow for convenient travel through psychological space. The newest generation of television sets even allow for the viewing of many stations simultaneously, with smaller pictures inset in the corners of the screens. Many family encounters now take place in front of the television set, which often results in fragmentary and defocused interaction. (While the amount of close family interaction in the past is probably often overstated, we should consider the possibility that nearly constant television use in some households makes it almost impossible to ever have focused family interaction.)

On the other hand, electronic media have been homogenizing experience, so that what happens in one place is now more similar to what can happen in another. The special and distinct meanings of distinct locations are blurring. Television, radio, and telephone turn once-private places into more public ones by making them more accessible to the outside world. And car stereos, wristwatch televisions, and Walkman stereos make public spaces private. The availability of similar media in different locations and to different types of people blends experience. Through the phone we can be partly at home while at the office and partly at the office while at home. Through similar television programs, the distance between different homes, different parts of a city, different cities and regions of the country—once very distinct experiential realms—is somewhat narrowed.

Electronic media, then, both break traditional ties to place and create new links. They often distance us from those in the same room with us. At the same time, they often bind us with others who are far away, both through "direct" electronic interaction (telephones, computer networks, etc.) and through the widespread—often simultaneous—indirect sharing of similar electronic experiences (through television, radio, records, etc.).

The ease and speed with which one can tune into the national television forum or connect with other people through the telephone make it more difficult for us to isolate ourselves in specific places. With electronic media, one is always in range, others are always within reach. Of course, we are not physically coerced into using the media around us. We can resist, but there are many subtle social pressures to remain connected. It is now considered strange and antisocial for a person to be isolated and out of touch. Living or working in a place without a phone may be taken by others as a sign of abnormality. To take one's phone off the hook is often interpreted as an insult. The media embrace has both broadened and tightened. Television screens now flicker even in many convents and monasteries (Meyrowitz, 1985, p. 353n.36), and some travelers take portable sets to wilderness camp sites and so-called retreats.

While we often hear about the advantages and wonders of modern communication, we can also view them as burdens. In many situations, the possibility of communicating leaves us with the responsibility of communicating. Because we are able to call home when away on a trip, we are often expected to call home. In many professions, people are required to wear beepers that make them accessible wherever they are and whatever they are doing.

The trend toward accessibility seems only to be increasing, with the spread of such technologies as computer mail networks and car phones. At present, for example, if I forget to convey an important message to my introductory course of over 100 students (such as a room change for an exam), no one would reasonably expect me to try to contact each of the students individually outside of class. Once I leave the lecture hall, I am unable to communicate with them—but I am also free of having to try. It is conceivable, however, that in a few years, each of my students will have a Bitnet or other computer mail account number and that professors will be expected to contact students through a program that automatically sends messages to each address on a list. With an especially important message, I may be expected to call my secretary even as I am driving home and have him/her send out the message immediately.

In this regard, telephone answering machines are a double-edged sword. They offer one of the few remaining shields to direct and immediate accessibility (such as when we leave them on even when we are home). But they also make us available when we would otherwise be inaccessible. The increase in use of systems for retrieving messages from remote locations now has people fielding business phone messages even while on vacation overseas. Those technologies that seem to give us greater control, therefore, also can be seen as controlling us.

The blurring of contexts through electronic media does not simply give us a sum of what we had before, but rather new, synthetic behaviors that are qualitatively different. To use an interpersonal analogy, if a child always sees his/her parents together, then the child will have a single set of behaviors that constitute "interaction with parents." If, on the other hand, the child also sees his/her mother and father individually, the child will likely have three different sets of behaviors: mother-child, father-child, parents-child. The father-child relationship may include behaviors and discussion of topics and issues that do not arise in mother-child or parents-child contexts. All separate interactions and relationships among relatives, friends, and business associates may include feelings and behaviors that would be inappropriate or impossible when others are present.

In general, the more isolated contexts are from each other, the more isolated behavior patterns and psychological orientations can be. This principle applies to all situation combinations and divisions, including those that are fostered by media. If, say, we celebrate our child's birthday at an isolated picnic spot, the joy of that event can be our sole experience for the day. But if we have a radio with us and we hear that our Navy accidentally shot down a commercial airliner, or learn of the death of a popular movie star, or of the assassination of a world leader, we not only lose our ability to rejoice fully, but also our ability to react deeply to the mediated situation.

The arrangement of physical locations is relatively stable, and there are generally established and routine forms of physical and social passage from one place to another (Van Gennep, 1960). To travel from one location to another takes time. And the temporal and spatial isolation traditionally allowed for very distinct experience within one place and for a period of adjustment and transition from one psychological space to another. But electronic media do not follow rules of social and physical passage. Even the potential of the phone ringing at any moment makes the home a less-isolated sphere of interaction. Electronic media also alter the meaning of individual rooms within the home. Sending a child to his/her room—once a form of "excommunication"—takes on a new meaning today, when the child's room is often linked to the outside world through telephone, radio, and television.

It is no coincidence, perhaps, that as electronic media have altered the meaning of "being alone," the number of single-member households in the United States has risen dramatically, nearly tripling between 1960 and 1981 (U.S. Bureau of the Census, 1982, p. 44).[2]

Electronic media blend time as well as space by extending the arena for communications into the future. The current widespread use of camcorders, for example, suggests the likelihood that many members of the next generation of young adults will have an opportunity to watch hours of early interactions between themselves and their parents. The form of information on video is quite different from verbal descriptions in letters or reminiscences (and even from the usually short, silent, and relatively staged home movies of a generation ago). Among other things, children will likely see the early awkwardness and discomfort (and even slight signs of annoyance) that new parents often feel. Will the videocassette player save some people from the need for therapy by allowing them to rediscover aspects of their repressed childhood at the push of a button? Or perhaps the VCR player will become a staple in family therapists' offices as another key source of information. (What, I wonder, will happen to primal therapy when one will be able to recreate one's own birth with the help of the videotaped record of the real thing?) One can even imagine the multilayered levels of situational frames when therapists videotape their clients' reactions while watching such videotapes. We need not wait for the children to grow up to see the effects of such temporal extensions. A colleague recently described his own shock at viewing his early videotaped play with his son, which he then realized was much too rough. I have had similar shocks of recognition in viewing early videotapes of interactions with my daughter. Through such extensions, then, the past becomes part of the present, and the present part of the future.

Whether such spatial and temporal alterations of context are ultimately good or bad is not immediately clear. The technologies that weaken our ties to the present also enrich our experience of the past and give us a small increased measure of immortality. The same process that dilutes our interactions with family members who live with us, also gives us more access to family members who live across the globe. Indeed, the telephone and other electronic media have reduced the emotional strain of travel, relocation, and living alone, since we can remain communicationally close while physically distant. Ironically, then, the same forces that allow Grandma to speak to future unborn generations also dilute the significance of her words for her contemporaries. And the same process that may help Grandma continue to live on her own rather than in an institution, may have sent her children and grandchildren hundreds of miles away, leaving her with few other options for residence.

Changes in Social Structure and Relative Roles

If we accept the arguments of such thinkers as George H. Mead (1934), Charles H. Cooley (1964), Hugh D. Duncan (1962), and Erving Goffman (1959), we learn that identity, roles, and statuses are inextricably tied to social communication. Social identity is not within people but in a network of social relations.

Further, once roles and statuses exist, they are not simply occupied; they must be constantly recreated in daily interaction. To perform various roles, the appropriate settings must be available. One cannot be a professor, boxer, or a beauty queen without the settings of universities, boxing rings, and beauty pageants. And because, as Goffman (1959) has shown, each of us plays different roles in different settings (professor, parent, spouse, friend, neighbor), we manage and balance our different subselves through the segregation of settings and the availability of passageways between them.

Media-induced changes in social contexts, then, ought to have an impact beyond individual psychological experience. Changes in social information-systems also alter basic elements of the social structure and reshape broad categories of social statuses and roles. But once again such changes are obscured by the traditional focus on place-contexts.

Distinctions in status have traditionally been associated with physical separation. People of the same social status usually have access to the same or similar social settings. People of different social statuses usually have access to different social settings. To support differences in roles and status, managers keep customers out of restaurant kitchens; in the armed services, the officers' club is off limits to enlisted personnel; and students are usually excluded from faculty meetings. Without such distinctions, differences in status would begin to blur.

Anthropologist Van Gennep (1960) refers to society as "a house divided into rooms and corridors" (p. 26), and he links changes in social category with a "change in residence" (p. 192). Similarly, Duncan (1962) suggests that our movement from social position to social position, both across our lifetimes and within a single day, involves physical movement from location to location: ·

> We move from one position to another through *dramas* of passage. As we move, we change *scenes*. Up to a certain age children live at home in intimate and daily contact with their parents, then they are separated and given their own quarters. As puberty nears, boys are separated from girls. But in these same years they have also been learning to play with other children in the neighborhood. Such play involves leaving one scene, the home, to enter another, the play place. There are also other stages outside the home. These are the school and the place of work. Thus each passage is a passage from one stage to another. These stages must be carefully prepared, and the individual must be given proper cues for his entrances and exits. (P. 261, emphasis in the original)

While the focus in traditional discussions of status and context is usually on physical location and physical passage, the underlying dynamic is the pattern of access/restriction to various experience and information—a variable that was once naturally linked with place, and therefore confused with it.

Traditionally, segregation into different places (1) gave members of different social groups and categories different sets of experiences and knowledge, (2) allowed them to be mysterious to each other, and (3) afforded time and space to rehearse for and relax from performances before the other. Situation segregation thereby encouraged the playing out of complementary rather than reciprocal roles.

In general, the more people get away from their audiences when they want to, the more time they have to polish and perfect an impressive image. The more individuals can isolate one performance arena from another, the more distinct different roles can be.

When social networks are seen as stable, we become very aware of the changing behavior of individuals as they move from setting to setting, from audience to audience. When the structure itself is seen as variable, however, we can begin to see how different patterns of contexts (including media-contexts) would foster different social roles in a society overall.

All roles associated with group identities (e.g., men vs. women), socialization (e.g., child vs. adult), and hierarchical arrangements (e.g., president and voter) are influenced by the degree of segregation of social information-systems (Meyrowitz, 1985).

Social status is not linked simply to access to a particular setting or information-system, but to a whole set of situations. The child-saving movement of the nineteenth century worked to extend the status of childhood to lower-class children by fostering children's access to certain types of situations (nurseries, playgrounds, homes, schools) while restricting them from other situations (factories, battlefields, hospitals).

The general set of situations which is associated with any given status or role might be called the status's "metasituation" or "meta-information-system." The degree of overlap of meta-information-systems for different statuses ranges between two hypothetical extremes: (1) completely distinct information-systems for every individual and (2) a common set of information-systems for everyone in society. Neither extreme is possible, but there is a great deal of possible variation in between.

It could be argued that the more we can separate people into different groups of experience and knowledge, the more we keep people in one group from closely observing others in another group, and the more we can keep people's experiences closely tied to their particular physical locations—the greater will be the number of distinct group identities, the greater the number of distinct socialization stages, and the greater the number of ranks and grades of hierarchy. Conversely, the more experiences overlap, the more we are exposed to each other's personal spheres and can watch each other closely, and the less our experiences are tied to the particular locations we are in—the more we can expect to see a blurring of group identities, a merging of socialization stages, and a raising of the lowly along with a lowering of the mighty.

Traditional distinctions between men's and women's roles (and other social groups), in Western culture, for example, were supported by separating men and women into two different experiential spheres (Degler, 1980), where they had different world views, and where they could privately rehearse for and relax from traditional gender roles (Meyrowitz,

1985). Similarly, traditional distinctions between children and adults (and other roles of socialization) were supported not only by biological and cognitive stages of development, but also by adult control over the speed and sequence of children's learning of adult "secrets" (Meyrowitz 1984, 1985). In the same way, distinctions among followers and leaders are enhanced when leaders can horde some information and isolate themselves from followers (Goffman, 1959; Duncan, 1962; Meyrowitz, 1977, 1985).

When we look at broad patterns of media use in a society, we can see that media contribute to the variation in the pattern of situation overlap and segregation. Thus, the widespread use of new forms of media in a society may have different effects on social status by changing "who knows what about whom" and "who knows what compared with whom."

The distinction between adult-adult and adult-child communication made possible by parental word-spelling, for example, is echoed on the societal level when spreading literacy fosters the separation of the roles and experiences of most adults from the roles and experiences of most children (Eisenstein, 1979; Meyrowitz, 1984, 1985). The segregating/integrating tendencies of media are parallel to the effects of physical integration and segregation. Thus, when the men of a primitive tribe restrict women from entering a male hut, they are engaging in a practice similar to that of Western man from the sixteenth through the nineteenth centuries who tried to restrict women's access to literacy and education (Meyrowitz, 1985).

Since the significant variable in fostering distinctions among social categories is *relative* access to information, new media can have a revolutionary effect even when their content is traditional or reactionary. When new media make old information available in new patterns, they restructure relative social status. Thus some social critics miss the effects of new media by focusing only on message content rather than on new patterns of disseminating information. Todd Gitlin (1987), for example, has argued that television is misnamed because rather than "seeing far" television "lets us see only close up: shows us only what the nation already presumes, focuses on what the culture already knows" (p. 3). But he misses the point that television has altered the balance of what different segments within the society know *relative* to each other.

Television, for example, has altered the boundaries of the perceptual world of those traditionally isolated in segregated physical locations. Women and children and minorities have been given outside perspectives from which to view their traditional isolation. They have also been exposed to information and experiences that were once restricted to them. Of course, the notion of "access" to social information is not absolute, but relative. There is a big difference, for example, between knowing in the abstract that the president is a human being who must have some flaws, and actually hearing a president speak nonsense, or seeing a president fall down a flight of stairs, collapse while jogging, or fall asleep during an audience with the Pope—even if the latter experiences are mediated through television.

There are at least four degrees of types of access/restriction that are relevant to an analysis of information-systems and social roles:

Type *A*: complete ignorance.
Type *B*: abstract knowledge about (such as oral or written verbal descriptions).
Type *C*: mediated sensory experience of (such as through photography, radio, or television).
Type *D*: direct experience with.

Type *A* (complete ignorance) is the only absolute. It involves lack of knowledge of the content of an information-system as well as lack of knowledge of the existence of an information-system. Types *B, C,* and *D* are each continua that range from minimal to maximal access.

In Type *B*, for example, a boy's abstract knowledge about his father's place of work could range anywhere from the fact that it exists to detailed abstract knowledge of the type of business it is, how it operates, the people who work there, and so on.

Type *C* (mediated sensory experience of) offers a major leap from Type *B* in that it mimics part of direct sensory experience. The example of two different forms of knowing about a president's flaws, above, points to the difference between abstract knowledge and mediated sensory experience. Another example is the difference between knowing in the abstract that one's parents make love and seeing a videotape of it (another increasingly likely possibility since the growth of home video). Mediated sensory experience can be further divided into two types: "fictional" and "documentary." But from the perspective discussed here, these two categories are not always consonant with the traditional labels applied to media content. For example, even in what we normally think of as a fictional television program, a viewer may get a documentary look at what another city looks like, at the closeup appearance of people of both sexes, and at what actors do when acting.

Type *D* (direct experience) involves unmediated experience with the naked senses. It is a very special sort of experience and we often remember the "firsts" of direct experience for the rest of our lives (our first day in school, our first date, the first time we made love, the birth of our first child).

The information-systems accessible to individuals, and the general scope of the meta-information-systems accessible to various categories of people are made up of a mix of all four of the above types. For example, children may be completely ignorant (Type *A*) of some things, have partial knowledge about (Type *B*) other things, have mediated sensory experience (Type *C*) of a third set of things, and have direct experience (Type *D*) with a fourth set of things. More typically, there will be many social phenomena about which children, or another social category, have partial access through various combinations of types *B, C,* and *D.*

Each medium of communication has different potential for access and restriction to information. Thus, access to information-systems will vary with individual access to media, but there will also be general social shifts in relative information-systems as new media are added to the media matrix.

In newspapers, for example, quotes from politicians (abstract knowledge about) often sound more impressive than television speeches because the flesh-and-bones body of the politician, along with his or her peculiarities of gesture and vocal expression, are absent. Mediated *sensory experience of* is also highly variable. Radio allowed citizens to hear FDR's powerful voice but not to see that he was in a wheelchair. Thus an individual's perception of politicians may vary with individual media habits. Yet at the same time, the evolution in dominant political medium from newspaper to radio to television may foster a general decline in the image and prestige of political leaders.

The spread of literacy and printing greatly enhanced the degree of Type B (abstract knowledge about) information, but it did so in an uneven manner. It not only separated literate from illiterate and preliterate, it also separated people into different information-systems based on *degrees* of literacy and on the highly segregated bodies of literature that tended to be read by different types of people. Thus literacy fostered different print contexts for people of different ages, sexes, classes, professions, and so on.

Literacy also created a new segregated forum, where adults could communicate with other adults without children overhearing. Advice books for parents, for example, allowed adults to discuss privately what to tell and not tell children. With the help of such books children were not only kept in the dark about many things, they were also kept in the dark about being kept in the dark. In this example, literacy enhanced Type B information for adults while fostering Type A ignorance for children.

In contrast to print, television tends to encourage relatively shared information-systems for people of different ages, sexes, and other social categories. While it is difficult to imagine the same set of books being best sellers among people of all ages, both sexes, and different educational backgrounds, it is quite common for the same television programs to be top-rated across many social categories. In recent years, for example, programs such as "Dallas," "The A-Team," "The Muppets," "Three's Company," "The Bill Cosby Show," "Family Ties," "Cheers," and others have been among the top 15 programs in every age and sex category (Nielsen, 1981; 1983; 1984; 1986; 1988).

Even beyond the top-rated shows and best-selling books there is much more overlap in what people will watch on television than in what they will read. While young children rarely read newspapers regularly, Atkin (1978) found that about 30% of kindergarten through fifth graders claimed they watched a national news program almost every day. A British study discovered that although many children expressed little interest in television news and appeared not to be paying much attention to it, about one-half of the children were able to mention items on the news, including crises, fires, accidents, and bombings in Northern Ireland (Howitt, 1982, pp. 43–44).

Much of the information available to children and others through television is Type C (mediated sensory experience), which not only requires less training to comprehend and less effort to attend to, but also gives one the sense of having witnessed or experienced that which is portrayed. The contextual features of television make it difficult for adults to use it as a "private" forum to view or discuss adult topics among themselves. Even when the typical content of a parental advice book becomes the subject of a television talk show, a paradox arises: Discussions about controlling what children know are overheard by thousands of children. Through such programs, children gain abstract knowledge (Type B) about many adult topics, which they may or may not immediately comprehend. But the major and more immediate impact on traditional parent-child roles may come from gaining mediated sensory experience (Type C) of anxious and unsure adults. Through news, talk shows, and other programs children are exposed both to many adult "secrets" and to the traditional "secret of secrecy."

Mediated sensory experiences are highly edited and packaged. Television sequences can approximate but never quite match direct experience (Meyrowitz, 1979). Everyday life does not come prefocused and visually framed. In a sense, a television viewer gains a perception of a perception. Access to mediated sensory experience, therefore, is not as liberating as it is sometimes taken to be. At the same time, access to media contexts and access to place contexts often evolve in the same direction. When media contexts begin to separate information-systems for various statuses, rules of segregated access to place often evolve. After literacy separated children from adults, many new separate places for children and adults developed. Conversely, as television has been reintegrating children in terms of mediated sensory experiences of adult situations, we have seen a tendency toward reintegrating children physically into many adult situations. (If Johnny has seen a thousand real and dramatized deaths on television, it now seems to make less sense not to take him to Grandpa's funeral.) Similarly, once women are exposed to countless all-male interactions on television, there is a movement to sexually integrate formerly all-male preserves.

Conclusion

While traditional research paradigms have tended to deal with mediated and unmediated communications as two completely separate realms of experience, this essay has suggested, through preliminary propositions and examples, that it is profitable to study both forms of communication as components of one large system of behaving and responding to the behavior of others. Further, this essay has suggested that while most attention in media research has focused on message content, media also influence us by altering the situational geography of everyday life.

Situational geography is significant because selves and social reality do not lie in the sum of situations and behaviors, but in the particular pattern of segregated settings. When we change the boundaries of social settings, therefore, we change who we can be. It is for such reasons that workers in an office may feel that their identities are in crisis when management decides to tear down walls and change from private offices to the open concept style. In a similar way, the introduction and use of new media may rearrange who communicates to whom and who else is "here" when the communication takes place, thereby inviting new forms of interaction and discouraging other forms. Such rearrangements are significant on at least two levels: (1) the level of individual psychological experience as we make choices among various communication options, and (2) the level of social structure and broad categories of relative social status.

Although I have focused on similarities between mediated and unmediated communications, there remain many obvious differences, and for full consideration of the media environment such differences as well as similarities need to be considered. In mass communication in particular it is important to assess the economic and political forces that drive the system and the relative lack of input and control effected by average citizens. Nevertheless, traditional approaches have tended to focus exclusively on such differences between mediated and unmediated communications, leaving us unaware of the ways in which both mass and non–mass media work to establish new interaction settings.

Interaction settings themselves are not the only source of situational definitions and behavioral norms. The shared meanings of situations and roles develop over time and through social traditions. Religious ritual, social custom, and legal codes all contribute to the stock of situational definitions, and they guide our use of available settings. A change in settings alone, therefore, will not bring about immediate or complete change. Nevertheless, while the social scripts develop through many sources, appropriate stages are necessary for the social dramas to be performed. If the settings for situations merge, divide, or disappear, it will be difficult to maintain old situational definitions and behaviors.

Notes

1. While spelling out words in front of children may help parents keep a secret, it may also expose the fact that a secret is being kept. A more secure form of secret keeping is afforded by segregated spaces and by books.
2. In their study of single-member households, Hughes and Gove (1981) are surprised to discover that, contrary to earlier findings, people who live alone today no longer seem to have many pathalogical behaviors, not even higher rates of suicide. In keeping with the often ahistorical perspective in sociology and a general lack of awareness of media as social environments, they interpret their findings as undermining previous thinking concerning the importance of social integration and the detrimental effects of social isolation. What they overlook, however, is that many people who live alone today would not have done so in the past, when there was less opportunity for mediated integration. In an electronic age, people who live alone physically are no longer necessarily socially isolated.

References

American Telephone & Telegraph (1981). *The world's telephones*. Morris Plains, NJ: AT&T Long Lines.

Argyle, M., & Little, B. R. (1972). Do personality traits apply to social behaviour? *Journal for the Theory of Social Behaviour, 2*(1), 1–35.

Atkin, C. (1978). Broadcast news programming and the child audience. *Journal of Broadcasting, 22,* 47–61.

Barker, R. G. (1968). *Ecological psychology: Concepts and methods for studying the environment of human behavior*. Stanford: Stanford University Press.

Cooley, C. H. (1964). *Human nature and the social order* (Rev. ed.). New York: Schocken. (Originally published, 1922.)

Degler, C. N. (1980). *At odds: Women and the family in America from the revolution to the present*. New York: Oxford University Press.

Duncan, H. D. (1962). *Communication and social order*. New York: Bedminster Press.

Eisenstein, E. L. (1979). *The printing press as an agent of change: Communications and cultural transformations in early modern Europe*. New York: Cambridge University Press.

Forgas, J. P. (1979). *Social episodes: The study of interaction routines*. London: Academic Press.

Fredericksen, N. (1972). Toward a taxonomy of situations. *American Psychologist, 27*, 114–23.

Furnham, A., & Argyle, M. (Eds.) (1981). *The psychology of social situations*. Oxford: Pergamon.

Garfinkel, H. (1967). *Studies in ethnomethodology*. Englewood Cliffs, NJ: Prentice-Hall.

Giles, H., & Powesland, P. F. (1975). *Speech style and social evaluation*. London: Academic Press.

Gitlin, T. (Ed.) (1987). *Watching television*. New York: Pantheon.

Goffman, E. (1959). *The presentation of self in everyday life*. New York: Anchor Doubleday.

Goffman, E. (1963). *Behavior in public places: Notes on the social organization of gatherings*. Glencoe: Free Press.

Goffman, E. (1967). *Interaction ritual: Essays on face-to-face behavior*. New York: Anchor Doubleday.

Goffman, E. (1972). The neglected situation. In P. P. Giglioli (Ed.), *Language and social context*. Harmondsworth, UK: Penguin.

Gregory, M., & Carroll, S. (1978). *Language and situation: Language varieties and their social contexts*. London: Routledge & Kegan Paul.

Hall, E. (1966). *The hidden dimension*. New York: Doubleday Anchor.

Haney, C., Banks, C., & Zimbardo, P. (1973). Interpersonal dynamics in a simulated prison. *International Journal of Criminology and Penology, 69*, 69–97.

Harré, R., & Secord, P. F. (1973). *The explanation of social behaviour*. Totowa, NJ: Littlefield, Adams.

Hiebert, R. E., Ungurait, D. F., & Bohn, T. W. (1982). *Mass media III: An introduction to modern communication*. New York: Longman.

Horton, D, & Wohl, R. R. (1956). Mass communication and para-social interaction: Observations on intimacy at a distance. *Psychiatry, 19*, 215–29.

Howitt, D. (1982). *The mass media and social problems*. Oxford: Pergamon.

Hughes, M., & Gove, W. R. (1981). Living alone, social integration, and mental health. *American Journal of Sociology, 87*(1), 48–74.

Hymes, D. (1967). Models of the interaction of language and social settings. *Journal of Social Issues, 23*(2), 8–28.

Innis, H. A. (1951). *The bias of communication*. Toronto: University of Toronto Press.

Levinson, P. (1979). Human replay: A theory of the evolution of media. Ph.D. diss., New York University. *Dissertation Abstracts International, 1979, 40*(3) (University Microfilms No. 79-18, 852).

Levinson, P. (1988). *Mind at large: Knowing in the technological age*. Greenwich, CT: JAI Press.

Mead, G. H. (1934). *Mind, self, and society: From the standpoint of a social behaviorist* (C. W. Morris, Ed.). Chicago: University of Chicago Press.

Meyrowitz, J. (1974). *The relationship of interpersonal distances to television shot selection*. M.A. thesis, Queens College (ERIC Document Reproduction Service No. ED 210 734).

Meyrowitz, J. (1977). The rise of "middle-region" politics. *Et cetera, 34*(2), 133–44.

Meyrowitz, J. (1979). Television and interpersonal behavior: Codes of perception and response. In G. Gumpert, & R. Cathcart (Eds.), *Inter/Media: Interpersonal communication in a media world.* New York: Oxford University Press.

Meyrowitz, J. (1984). The adultlike child and the childlike adult: Socialization in an electronic age. *Daedalus, 113*(3), 19–48.

Meyrowitz, J. (1985). *No sense of place: The impact of electronic media on social behavior.* New York: Oxford University Press.

Meyrowitz, J. (In press). Redefining the situation: Extending dramaturgy into a theory of social change and media effects. In S. H. Riggins (Ed.), *Beyond Goffman.* The Hague: Mouton-de Gruyter.

Milgram, S. (1977). *The individual in a social world: Essays and experiments.* Reading, MA: Addison-Wesley.

Mischel, W. (1968). *Personality and assessment.* New York: Wiley.

Nielsen, A. C. (1982–1988). *Nielsen report on television* (annual). Northbrook, IL: A. C. Nielsen.

Pervin, L. A. (1978). Definitions, measurements, and classifications of stimuli, situations, and environments. *Human Ecology, 6*(1), 71–105.

Rosenthal, R., & Rosnow, R. L. (Eds.) (1969). *Artifact in behavioral research.* New York: Academic Press.

Rosenthal, R., & Rosnow, R. L. (Eds.) (1975). *The volunteer subject.* New York: Wiley-Interscience.

Rosnow, R. L. (1983). Von Osten's horse, Hamlet's question, and the mechanistic view of causality: Implications for a post-crisis social psychology. *The Journal of Mind and Behavior, 4,* 319–37.

Scheflen, A. E. (1972). *Body language and social order.* Englewood Cliffs, NJ: Prentice-Hall.

Thomas, W. I. (1925). *The unadjusted girl.* Boston: Little, Brown, p. 44.

U.S. Bureau of the Census. (1982). *Statistical abstract of the United States: 1982–83.* 103d ed. Washington, D.C.: U.S. Government Printing Office.

Van Gennep, A. (1960). *The rites of passage* (M. B. Vizedom & G. L. Caffee, trans.). Chicago: University of Chicago Press. (Originally pub. 1908.)

5

A Sequel to the "False Dichotomy" Perspective: Applications to the Challenge of Teaching Children about AIDS

Kathleen Kelley Reardon

It is becoming apparent in the literature, that communication scholars are ceasing to ask which form of communication—interpersonal or mass media communication—is superior, but instead they ask what are the likely effects of each medium. To answer this question we need to define clearly the terms "certain circumstances" and "certain criteria" for each case. This paper focuses on the circumstances surrounding attempts to persuade children to avoid behaviors that put them at risk for AIDS; it also explores the criteria of each medium that render it more or less helpful in this regard.

For decades communication scholars have identified themselves in terms of an affinity for research focused on either interpersonal or mass media communication. Recently, this division of scholarly endeavor has come under attack by a number of communication researchers. Reardon and Rogers (1988) contend that this "false dichotomy" between interpersonal and mass media communication has been overestimated and has had detrimental effects on the progress of communication theory and research. Chaffee and Mutz (1988) argue that comparisons between interpersonal and mass media communication often exist because we are anxious to assign blame or praise for communication effects. The problem with such comparisons is that "it is exceedingly difficult to calibrate observations

95

and assign to them numbers that mean the same thing when mediated and interpersonal communication behaviors are being measured.'' Ball-Rokeach and Reardon (1988) take a similar position. They argue that comparisons among communication forms are useful only to the extent that criteria shared to a greater or lesser extent are used in the comparisons. Communication forms are not so much distinctly different as they are varied in the extent to which they share certain characteristics. For example, potential interactivity, equality of goals, and geographic range are criteria that might be used to compare communication forms.

It is obvious from the above literature that communication scholars are ceasing to ask which form of communication is superior but, rather, under certain circumstances and given certain criteria, what are the likely effects of each medium answering this question requires that the terms ''certain circumstances'' and ''certain criteria'' be clearly defined for each case. This essay focuses on the circumstances surrounding attempts to persude children to avoid behaviors that put them at risk for AIDS, and explores the criteria of each medium that render it more or less helpful in this regard.

Certainly, the fight on AIDS cannot be won by a myopic focus on either interpersonal or mass media communication. In the area of health there is no room for the false dichotomy that has separated interpersonal and mass communication scholars. There is no vaccine for AIDS. The vital ingredient in fighting this problem is prevention, and the fundamental key to prevention is effective communication, both mass media and interpersonal. In this essay we look at (1) children's perceptions of health and their responsibility for its protection, (2) the potential of interpersonal and mass media messages for conveying health-related information to young people, (3) the utility of traditional and nontraditional methods of persuasion in encouraging young people to reduce their risk for AIDS, and (4) steps required to determine which of these approaches are suited to particular target groups.

Children's Knowledge about Health

Perhaps the best place to begin is with the question—What do children know about protecting their health? The answer gives us a starting place from which to examine how communication theory and research might contribute to the development of effective mass media and interpersonal communication interventions.

The number of articles concerned with children's knowledge about health protection measures is limited. Existing research demonstrates that children often do not understand the causes of illness and have generally been deprived of learning how to take responsibility for their own health (Lewis & Lewis, 1977). Research by Nagy (1951) and Blos (1956) indicate that children's perceptions of the causes of illness change with age. Nagy found that children between the ages of 3 and 5 did not understand the origin of illness; they cited symptoms of disease. Children aged 6 and 7 were only able to indicate that infection came from the environment; they did not speak of other causes of illness. Children between the ages of 8 and 10 indicated that infections were caused by microorganisms; however, they were unable to differentiate illnesses due to different organisms. Children ages 11 and 12 were able to associate different illnesses with different germs.

Research by Blos (1956) demonstrated that the ability to identify multiple factors related to causation increases markedly among 9- and 10-year-olds. Blos points out:

> Before the age of 9–10, healthy children find it difficult to understand causal relations with regard to illness. This should not mean that one should not attempt to explain illness and its causes to the younger child. . . . It appears that children can benefit from sympathetic, intelligent discussion of illness, since they probably acquire a great deal of the feelings and attitudes toward illness before they can really understand the facts.

Gochman (1972) explored the relation of perceived vulnerability to health problems (illness and injury) and actual behavior. This study was designed to test the following hypothesis: Children who have (1) an awareness of potential health behaviors (specific ways to prevent illness) and (2) an internal locus of control, i.e., those who perceive that they have some ability to control their environment, will have relatively low perceptions of personal vulnerability, if health is important to them. Gochman suggested that anyone who considered health to be important, and yet who felt at the mercy of the environment, would feel vulnerable if he did not know how to avoid illness. One hundred and ten people aged 7 to 28 were tested. Perceived vulnerability was estimated by using the Health Ideation Pictures method developed by Gochman. Bailer's scale was used to determine the locus of control. The hypotheses of the investigator (Gochman, 1972) were confirmed.

According to Lewis and Lewis (1982:501), a key research finding regarding health perceptions of children 5 to 12 years is that "children are far more competent in a variety of dimensions, including decision making, than adults perceive (or want) them to be." Unfortunately children rarely have been encouraged to see themselves as partly responsible for their health. Physicians tell parents how to take care of their child's illness. Rare is the physician who talks to the child about his or her responsibility for prevention or recovery. It should come as no surprise then that when children who have taken little responsibility for their health mature, they are often unprepared to protect themselves from illness and even disciplined to make the effort.

How then can young people suddenly be persuaded to take responsibility for their health when their actions begin to place them at risk for AIDS? To answer this question it is important to explore the sources of influence that guide the behavior of young people. Family, peers, and mass media are three important sources of children's health information. Each has considerable potential with regard to encouraging or discouraging health protective behavior. An understanding of how each of these sources contributes to young people's views of health is an important step in attempting to develop programs to discourage risk for AIDS.

The Influence of Family and Peers

The development and maintenance of health values in children depends upon the nature of the family. Families can be viewed as information-processing units. Over time family members develop a collective view or schema of the world; they develop a set of assumptions about the world that shape their explorations and interpretations of new information.

Socioeconomic status, years of education of the mother, and ethnicity, to the extent that symptom sensitivity is learned from social groups or family members, are the important demographic factors. The family constitutes an important social unit for the production of children's health-related beliefs and behaviors. Parenting style has been demonstrated to be significantly associated with acquisition of preventive health-care behaviors.

Parents who ignore their children, or who deal with them in an authoritarian fashion, and who are excessively concerned about "doctoring their child" rather than encouraging positive self-care habits, tend to produce children with poor health-care-related beliefs and behaviors. Health-care behaviors are communicated best by individuals who model the desired behaviors and simultaneously explain the reasons they are taking certain actions.

In a study of children's health attitudes and behaviors, Mechanic (1979) explored family characteristics, mother's attitudes toward the child's health, their generalized values about health, attitudes toward doctors, use of medical care, family illness, and the use of medical facilities. Data obtained from children included their willingness to report symptoms and their attitudes toward health and medical facilities. The major part of the study was aimed at investigating some assumptions about how health-related behavior patterns develop. It was hypothesized that children's patterns of illness behavior are influenced by child-rearing practices, family stress, and family definition of health resources.

The data supported Mechanic's contention that age and sex are significant determinants of children's responses. Males at both age levels were less afraid of getting hurt and reported less attention to pain than females, and these trends increased with age. The mother's educational achievement was the best predictor of social status, and her attitudes toward health and illness depended upon her educational status. Although the data from mothers did not predict the child's use of services, there were striking associations between mother and child's illness behaviors. Mothers with high inclinations to use care, when compared with mothers with lower inclinations to do so, were much more likely to take their children to the doctor frequently and to allow their children to assume the "sick role."

Research clearly indicates that supportive messages from parents lead to higher self-esteem, more conformity to the wishes of the parents, inhibition of aggression or antisocial behavior in a variety of settings (Fitzpatrick & Badzinski, 1985). Moreover, maternal responsiveness, the discussion and acceptance of feelings, and the reinforcement and modeling of prosocial behavior encourages prosocial behaviors in children. The research also suggests that the potential contribution of family to the ability of children to protect their health cannot be overestimated. To the extent that parents are attentive to their own health, their children are likely to be attentive to their health as well.

Families also develop styles of communication and problem solving that influence the way children respond to persuasion. This is important to the establishment of health-protective behaviors, especially among children who are frequently confronted by peer pressure to take risks.

Styles of responding to persuasion are likely to influence the extent to which children are willing and able to resist pressure from others to engage in health risks. For example, Wood (1981) explains that strict guidelines based on status relationships within the family can lead to closed-communication patterns with little room for discussion or dispute; here are a few examples of strict status-dependent rules:

1. In matters of money, your father always decides.
2. Never speak angrily with your mother.
3. Male children deserve more (money or possessions) than female children.
4. The female children must take care of the younger ones.
5. Never argue with your father.

6. You must always do as your mother says (p. 67).

There are always rules of family behavior. However, when there are too many rules or if the rules are too rigid, the child's reasoning ability and communication development may be threatened.

In a closed-communication family, rules for appropriate and effective behavior are strictly enforced. There is little self-autonomy—freedom to behave as you prefer—unless it does not conflict with the established rules. This type of environment stifles creativity of thought and action. It teaches children that there are only two categories of action: proper and improper. There is little room for imagination or discussion. Right and wrong are not subject to interpretation, and problems are not presented for consideration by family members.

Open communication helps the child learn to reason. It also teaches the child that there is usually more than one way to solve a problem. Communication competence requires the ability to deal constructively with people who do not share the same rules. Closed-communication environments foster communication myopia—the belief that there is one way to solve a problem, and if it fails to work, nothing will. Such closed-communication family environments foster inflexibility in solving health problems as well.

A second problem associated with closed-communication families is severe limitations on the expression of feelings. Children need to experiment with emotions. This does not mean that they should be encouraged to throw tantrums. It means that emotions are a fundamental aspect of human existence. We must learn to use them to facilitate communication. In many families, boys are expected to thwart emotional expression. In families where communication is closed, discussions of emotional reactions are discouraged. For example, junior is told: "Act your age," or "Don't be a wimp." The reasons behind his emotions are ignored, and he is deprived of the chance to express what may be legitimate feelings. Since saying No to health risks often involves risking relationships with peers, adolescents need emotional support. A recent study on adolescent pregnancy, for example, indicates that a significant number of girls who become pregnant do so not as a result of insufficient knowledge about birth control but rather because they wanted to become pregnant. One explanation given for this finding is that, especially among youth who have not received adequate parental nurturing themselves, a baby may be seen as a means of meetings one's own emotional needs.

In an open communication environment, decisions are derived through discussion rather than handed down. Feelings are not suppressed without regard for their reasons. It may be impossible for any family to be completely open in their communication. Sometimes authority rule must abide. The key is to avoid excessively stringent rules so children can learn that there are a variety of ways to accomplish the same goal. They must also learn that they have the ability to make such decisions even in the face of peer pressure.

An alternative and more complex model of family communication patterns was developed by McLeod and Chaffee (1971). They proposed a model consisting of four family communication patterns: Laissez-faire, protective, pluralistic, and consensual families.

The family communication patterns in that model differ according to their social vs. concept orientation. Socio-oriented families place considerable emphasis on harmony and pleasant social relationships within the family. Concept-oriented families encourage children to develop their own views on issues and to consider more than one side of those issues. Laissez-faire families are characterized by a lack of either socio- or concept-oriented relations; there is simply little parent-child communication. In protective families, obedience and harmony are very important; there is little concern with conceptual matters. Children from such homes are typically easy to persuade since they have not learned to defend their own opinions. In pluralistic families, open communication and discussion of ideas are encouraged; family members have respect for each other's interests. The consensual family is characterized by pressure toward agreement. Children in consensual families are encouraged to take an interest in issues but to do so without disturbing the family power structure.

McLeod's and Chaffe's (1971) model suggests that children from different types of families are likely to approach communication situations within and outside the home in very different ways. For example, while the child raised in a pluralistic family is likely to feel comfortable exploring and discussing many sides of the AIDS issue, a child raised in a consensual home may shy away from expressing such views since they might contradict those of authority figures. Health educators could certainly benefit from understanding how family communication patterns influence children's willingness to protect their own health and the health of those with whom they associate.

Research on family communication patterns and problem-solving capacities suggests that the families play an important role in the success of any community- or school-based AIDS intervention for children. To the extent that their support can be elicited, and to the extent that the predominant family communication style is or can become one of open discussion, the likelihood of long-term AIDS program success is increased.

Peers

It is one thing to value health and quite another to believe that you can actually protect it. Aside from family attempts to encourage a value for health among children, it is imperative that children come to believe that they have what it takes to resist pressure from peers to risk their health. Furstenberg, Moore, & Peterson (1985), in their study of 500 cases of 15- and 16-year-olds, found that sex education programs, while effective, were not as influencial as peers on level of sexual activity.

Reardon, Sussman, and Flay (1988) found that adolescents who were at risk for becoming smokers were less likely than other adolescents to resist aggressively peer pressure to smoke, even when they did not wish to smoke. That research suggests that adolescents who are willing to take health risks either are ill-equipped to resist peer pressure or are unwilling to do so with any significant level of forcefulness.

Other research suggests that adolescents who belong to especially cohesive groups with little access to extragroup information, experience considerable pressure toward informational conformity (Gottlieb, 1985; Hall & Wellman, 1985). According to Sussman (1988), such groups develop inflexible roles, which discourage intrapersonal changes. Loose-knit groups with more weak ties can provide access to new social contacts and alternative information (Granovetter, 1973). According to Sussman, two variables inhibit making such ties: first, membership in a high-density network may result in the existence of strong informational control over the individual on a day-to-day basis; and second, the individual may not have learned those skills needed to make bridging ties with other groups. This perspective implies that some adolescents may be literally stuck in an information trap with regard to health information. To the extent that their families are not open about such matters and their peer network is dense and closed, adolescents are unlikely to receive extragroup health opinions.

Research also indicates that peer groups often transform or reinterpret information derived from the mass media, parents, and other informational sources (Flay, et al., 1983; Hansen, et al., 1985). For example, to the extent that a group values the appearance of independence, risk taking may be encouraged. Such groups may also encourage overestimation of the amount of risk that is typically engaged in by adolescents. Smoking research indicates that inflated prevalence estimates are a predictor of smoking onset (Chassin, et al., 1984; Collins, et al., 1987). Adolescents who are led by peers to believe that health risks are common are more likely to engage in such behaviors.

The implications for AIDS risk reduction are clear. Children who are members of groups characterized by informational conformity and by either an appreciation for health risks or inflated perceptions of the extent to which their peers take such risks are at risk themselves. For these children behaviors that place them at risk for AIDS may even be admired. The youngster who proudly insists, "I never use condoms," may believe that most other young, sexually active people feel as he does. Without access to extragroup contacts which dispute that perception, this child is struck with information that is dangerous to his health and the health of those with whom he has intimate contact.

It is not enough to gain access to groups that encourage behaviors that place children at risk for AIDS. Educators must establish credibility with the members before they can encourage them to consider outside views. Utilizing teenage idioms is one approach. Peer models is another. Former or current group members who have changed their behaviors in order to protect their health, or ones who have watched a family member suffer from AIDS may have a better chance of penetrating the sturdy boundaries of tight-knit groups than educators who have nothing in common with the group members.

The Influence of Mass Media

Much social learning occurs on the basis of casual or directed observations of others. The third source of social learning for children is the mass media. Children and adults acquire attitudes, emotional responses, and new styles of conduct through film and television viewing (Bandura, 1973).

Evaluations of mass media health compaigns indicate that it is difficult, at best, to develop methods of influencing the public, especially the young, to adopt health-enhancing behaviors. Flay (1981a; 1981b) found that most of the mass media programs that have been effectively evaluated were unsuccessful in terms of influencing attitudes and behavior for any length of time. Those few that were successful did more than focus on information alone. It appears that successful mass media health campaigns require attention to a number of steps in the persuasion process. Flay explains, for example, that it is of little use to reach people's living rooms if they do not attend to the program. He suggests appeals to multiple motives (e.g., improve health, social and/or self-image, decrease cost of living, improve quality of life) in novel ways, with repetition across sources, channels, and times. He adds that involvement, active participation, and social support increase the likelihood of changes in attitudes and behaviors being maintained over time as was the case in at least two smoking campaigns (Warner, 1977; Cook & Flay, 1978).

Recent research suggests that getting children to attend to media messages may also be a matter of learning how they perceive the media and the qualities they attribute to it (Solomon, 1984). Researchers have argued that people receive messages in more or less mindful or mindless ways. According to studies by Langer (1984) and Langer, Blank, and Chanowitz (1978), mindlessness in information processing means ignoring information perceived to be already known. In contrast, mindful processing takes full account of information. These terms are similar in meaning to shallow and deep processing (Craik & Lockhart, 1972; Craik & Tulving, 1975).

In a study of children's processing of television and print material Solomon (1984) found that, when no clear instructions are imposed on learners, perceptions of the media (e.g., how realistic it is) and perceptions of self-efficacy (ability to obtain information and learn from a particular source) influence investment of processing effort that is in turn related to inferential learning. Solomon argues that perceptions of information sources and of one's self "come from somewhere and reflect past experience, abilities, and social norms." Over time it is possible for them to become "self-sustaining prophecies" and continue to influence the way various media messages are processed (p. 656).

We may surmise from this research that the way children receive, interpret, and store information about AIDS from media sources likely depends upon their expectations concerning those sources. It may be insufficient merely to present children with media messages about AIDS without considering their styles of interaction with the media sources and the qualities they attribute to them.

Works by Ball-Rokeach, Rokeach & Grube (1984) and Ball-Rokeach (1988) on media dependency suggest that people develop ways of using the media in terms of acquiring information. They become more or less dependent upon media for the information they need in their daily lives. Ball-Rokeach (1988) argues that dependency differences account for much of the confusion about whether, and to what extent, media messages have effects: "The media system's power lies in its control over scarce information resources that others—individuals, groups, organizations, social systems, societies—depend upon to attain their goals." She proposes that survival and growth are fundamental human motivations. These motivations lead us to achieve understanding, orientation, and play goals. The level of one's dependency on mass media sources for the achievement of these goals is what Ball-Rokeach describes as media dependency.

To the extent that children depend on media sources to attain goals, they are said to have established a dependency relationship with those sources. Of course, like adults, children do not always consciously approach the media with goals in mind. Sometimes they are what Ball-Rokeach (1988) calls "active selectors"; at other times "casual observers." Active selectors expose themselves to media content which they expect will help them achieve one or more of their goals. Casual observers encounter the media without expectations regarding the attainment of goals. It is possible, however, for casual observers to find that one or more dependency is activated during their casual observation of a media message, thus motivating them to continue exposure. Further according to Ball-Rokeach, the active selectors and the casual observers who become motivated to continue exposure are more likely to be affected by the media. This view is consistent with Solomon's (1984) assertion that the amount of energy expended to interpret media messages influences their effects.

One aspect of media dependency theory renders it especially relevant to the issue of AIDS education. According to Ball-Rokeach (1988): "Media dependency relations become more intense when the social environment is rapidly changing, ambiguous, and/or threatening." To the extent that children do not perceive AIDS as a personal threat to them, it is unlikely that they will turn to the media, or for that matter, to interpersonal sources, to learn about protective measures. If we assume that there are hundreds of thousands of children who consider AIDS a remote threat, then we may expect low levels of attention to media messages about AIDS. To the extent that children are convinced that they should be concerned about AIDS but are confused about how it is acquired, they are more likely to attend to media messages about AIDS. Add to this Solomon's (1984) perspective, and we may also conclude that the more seriously children take the media sources, the more likely it is that they will attend to and retain AIDS-related information from those sources.

It appears that merely throwing large sums of money at media campaigns against AIDS may not be effective if funds are not also provided for research that assesses (1) the degree to which children feel threatened by AIDS, (2) the extent of their confusion about how to protect themselves, and (3) the degree to which they consider various media as serious, reliable sources of information (both in general and in terms of health information). Moreover, it is imperative that the media themselves be assessed for the likelihood that they take seriously the role they might play in halting the spread of AIDS. In a study of the perceptions of doctors (both heterosexual and homosexual), healthy gay men, and ARC patients Reardon and Richardson (1989) found that on the topic of AIDS, homosexual males often distrust the objectivity of the media and even perceive a tendency in the media to be biased against homosexuals. They conclude that such perceptions limit the potential effectiveness of the mass media to stay the tide of AIDS transmission.

While similar research pertaining to the perceptions of children about media coverage on AIDS does not exist, research on other health issues suggests that the media may actually encourage rather than discourage some forms of health promotion behaviors.

Research by Dearing, Rogers, and Fei (1988) indicates that the mass media dragged their feet, so to speak, in taking the AIDS epidemic seriously. Now AIDS receives a considerable amount of coverage by the media, but the quality of that coverage has not yet been assessed. If indeed the media are the watchdogs of the nation, then the AIDS epidemic is a reasonable field upon which to judge the media's effectiveness. It remains to be seen whether they can make up for lost time with accurate, unbiased information about AIDS.

These findings suggest that creating AIDS media messages that will be attended to, believed, and retained by children requires preliminary investigations into children's perceptions of the various media and investigations into the potential of each medium to take seriously their role in the fight on AIDS. If we assume that AIDS may also become a means of amusing listeners or viewers, then serious media messages about AIDS protection may be compromised.

Persuasion Strategies for Interpersonal and Mass Media AIDS Campaigns

Having established that there are a variety of ways by which interpersonal and mass media communication can encourage or discourage behaviors that place young people at risk for AIDS, the next step is the selection of persuasion strategies suited to each medium. Reardon (1989) explored how prior research in persuasion might be used in the development of interpersonal and mass media AIDS interventions for adolescents. Within the realm of traditional persuasion methods Reardon describes the development of health values and four persuasion approaches as offering some promise with regard to their inclusion in interpersonal and mass media AIDS campaigns. These four approaches include instilling confidence and motivation to protect one's health, involving adolescents in finding ways to respond to health threats, teaching them to reason about health risks, and utilizing some degree of fear.

Each of these persuasion models is based on the premise that people are basically rational beings, torn, for example, by inconsistencies between what they do and what they know to be the better thing to do or to have done. According to such models, the key is to identify which strategies are likely to increase discomfort with the current behavior and thus facilitate the adoption of a persuader-preferred behavior.

Rational models suggest that attempts to persuade children to adopt behaviors that protect them from AIDS should involve getting children in touch with reality—letting them see that they are vulnerable to AIDS and that their current risk-taking behaviors are in conflict with rationality. Once this is accomplished, children can be guided toward the adoption of protective behaviors. Reardon (1989) argues that in a world where normal people are those in touch with, or at least willing to be in touch with, reality, such an approach may indeed work. Reardon does not rule out traditional models of persuasion as useful in the fight against AIDS among adolescents. Yet she points out that recent work in psychology suggests that most people are not in touch with reality but rather function from day to day on the basis of fundamental illusions that guide their actions and interpretations of information and events.

Taylor and Brown (1988) argue that the widely held view of the healthy person as one who maintains close contact with reality may actually be erroneous. According to the traditional model, people gather data in an unbiased manner, combine it in some logical, identifiable fashion, and reach generally good, accurate inferences and decisions. Recent work indicates that the social perceiver's actual inferential activity and decisions making is fraught with incomplete data gathering, shortcuts, errors, and biases (for reviews see Fiske & Taylor, 1984; Nisbett & Ross, 1980). Fiske and Taylor (1984) note: "Instead of a naive scientist entering the environment in search of truth, we find the rather unflattering picture of a charlatan trying to make the data come out in a manner most advantageous to his or her already-held theories" (p. 88).

Taylor and Brown (1988) propose that most individuals, rather than having a firm grasp on reality, operate on the basis of at least three illusions: unrealistically positive view of the self, exaggerated perceptions of personal control, and unrealistic optimism. They argue that there is a pervasive tendency for individuals to see themselves as better than others. Moreover, with the exception of depressed individuals and those with low self-esteem, most individuals are convinced that they have more control over events than they really do. Finally, most people are future oriented and hold unrealistically positive views of the future. The fact is that most of us are actually unprepared to accept reality. As Taylor and Brown explain: "A variety of social norms and strategies of social interaction conspire to protect the individual from the harsher side of reality."

Research indicates that people are generally reluctant to give feedback to others. When feedback is given, it is generally positive (Blumberg, 1972; Parducci, 1968; Tesser & Rosen, 1975). Moreover, people tend to seek feedback when it is likely to be positive (Brown, 1987) and select friends who are relatively similar to themselves (Eckland, 1968; Hill, Rubin, & Peplay, 1976). Research also indicates that negative feedback is seen as less credible, especially by people with high self-esteem (Snyder, Shenkel, & Lowery, 1977; Shrauger & Rosenberg, 1970).

Given people's tendencies to avoid giving others negative feedback as well as to surround themselves with positive messages and to deny the credibility of negative messages that do sneak through, it seems reasonable to ask why anyone should listen to, let alone be influenced by, negative information. In all likelihood, people vary in the extent to which they can cope with negative feedback. If, however, we accept that most people prefer to be told good things about themselves, it follows that persuasion strategies that focus on the positive may prove more effective.

Even if one does not accept the premise that people are more out of touch than in touch with reality, Taylor's and Brown's (1988) perspective suggests that presenting children with the vivid reality of AIDS may fall on deaf ears. If children, especially those at risk, have a vested interest in maintaining a positive self-image, a strong sense of control, and a positive view of the future, perhaps the last thing we want to do is try to convince them that they are not different from anyone else, highly vulnerable to AIDS, and thus perilously on the brink of a short, unpleasant future.

Further, since the children most at risk for AIDS are minority children and those deprived in terms of socioeconomic status—reality training may be the last thing they need or want. How then can such children be reached? The answer may lie in our ability to identify interpersonal and mass media messages that build on, rather than tear down, the "illusions" held dear by children at risk for AIDS. For example, rather than bombarding them with images of their vulnerability, we could focus attention on how protective behaviors increase their control. Rather than tear down the self-images of those who have placed themselves at risk, or terrorize them with the fear that they are already the carriers of death, why not use positive models of young people who changed their behaviors and are free of AIDS. And rather than present them with bleak depictions of their futures, we might employ positive images of the healthful and happy times ahead, for those who protect their health.

This approach is not altogether new. Marketers appeal to such illusions. They know that more hamburgers are sold based on fun than on fact and more toothpaste is sold on the basis of its positive effects on future relationships than on the basis of taste. AIDS is certainly a more serious issue than hamburgers and toothpaste, but the idea of selling by association with the buyer's positive self-image, sense of control, and optimism may prove useful.

Persuasion research has been guided by the commonly held belief that normal people are either in touch with reality or capable of being directed toward it. Traditional persuasion theory asserts that people can be wrestled into change by inconsistent cognitions or reasoned into change by rational arguments. In many cases such approaches are indeed effective. However, when one considers that over 95% of the U.S. population has heard of AIDS and yet a significant portion continue to place themselves daily at risk of AIDS, the answer simply may not lie in traditional persuasion strategies.

Implications for Interpersonal and Mass Media Messages about AIDS

Knowing that interpersonal and mass media communication channels have considerable potential to determine whether children behave in ways that place them at risk for AIDS or not, but not knowing whether traditional or nontraditional persuasion approaches are best suited to the task at hand, is a bit like having a boat without oars. Rather than blindly relying on either traditional persuasion approaches or appeals to illusions, some preliminary research is in order. Based on this chapter's review of theory and research on children's sense of responsibility for health, the potential of interpersonal and mass media sources to influence their sense of responsibility, and promising persuasion approaches, the following steps should be taken prior to the development of AIDS campaigns for young people:

1. Designate the group to which the campaign will be directed.
2. Identify language barriers and relevant idiosyncracies of that group, including illusions about health and AIDS.
3. Determine their level of media and interpersonal dependency as well as the level of credibility they assign to each source with respect to health information.
4. Select messages types and persuasion appeals that are relevant to the group and to their stage of education and progress in AIDS prevention.

Designation of Group

Since Aristotle's *Rhetoric,* knowing one's audience has been touted as a major ingredient for persuasion success. It is tempting to think that all children are alike, but they are no more alike than all adults. Young people differ in the extent of their knowledge about AIDS, familiarity with protective measures, family openness with regard to discussion of AIDS, availability of positive role models, skill in resisting peer pressure to take risks, and sense of self-efficacy regarding their ability to protect themselves from AIDS (see Reardon, 1989).

These differences are the primary reason why mass media alone or interpersonal communication alone are unlikely to be as effective as a conjoint effort. Research indicates that Blacks and Hispanics use television as an information source more than other groups (Atkin, 1981; Department of Health & Human Services, 1985; McGuire, 1985) and radio is effective for reaching teenagers (Atkin, 1981; Worthington, 1988). Whether these media outlets are a sufficient means for persuading youngsters to avoid behaviors than put them at risk for AIDS is a question that remains unanswered. Longshore (1988) argues that some combination of mass media and interpersonal messages is likely to be more effective than either medium alone. He proposes the use of invitation-only meetings in private homes, during which health educators will offer AIDS information. Former drug users or people with AIDS might add credibility to such meetings. Another option is an AIDS hotline that allows teenagers to ask questions about AIDS without having to divulge their identities.

Each of these options is useful only to the extent that the target audience is willing to attend to or participate in them. More research is needed to determine how adolescents with different ethnic backgrounds and different levels of experience with AIDS-risk behaviors might be reached.

Identify Idiosyncracies of Target Group

Recent research by Reardon, Sussman, and Flay (1988) indicates that adolescents differ in their ability to resist pressure to smoke. The key differentiating factor was risk-taking behavior. It appears that adolescents most at risk for smoking are also least capable of assertive rejections of pressure to smoke, even when they do not want to smoke. This research underscores the importance of determining those idiosyncracies that prohibit certain groups of adolescents from adopting health-protective behaviors.

Here is where Taylor's and Brown's (1988) view of illusions may prove useful. As mentioned above, if young people harbor illusions of invulnerability to AIDS, an overly optimistic perception of their ability to identify and avoid people who put them at risk, or a self-image that predisposes them to reject advice from people who would be considered by adults as credible sources, then persuasive campaigns designed with reality-based messages in mind may fall on deaf ears.

A necessary precursor of any AIDS campaign for children is assessment studies of the attitudes, actions, and illusions of the target group with regard to AIDS.

Determine Level of Media and Interpersonal Dependency

As discussed earlier in this paper, the effectiveness of AIDS messages is dependent on the extent to which they are delivered via channels that the target group attends and assigns a reasonable degree of credibility. Scant research exists on the extent to which adolescents depend on interpersonal vs. mass media channels for health information. Television and magazines are the primary sources of AIDS information among a sample of Seattle high school students.

Williams (1986) argues that effective media messages depend upon the availability of credible role models. She points out that local media messages about AIDS are typically delivered by news reporters of nonminority status. The result may be the unwillingness of minority adolescents to assign credibility to health messages conveyed via such news reports. She further argues that barriers to effective mass media campaigns are often rooted in the value systems and social structures of minorities. If these are not identified and dealt with constructively, then mass media effectiveness is likely to be limited.

The extent to which family and peer communication might serve effectively to convey AIDS information depends on their willingness to discuss AIDS, the degree to which families and peers regard AIDS as a threat, and how willing they are to provide supportive environments that discourage risks for AIDS.

There is a desperate need for research that provides answers to these questions. The National Institutes of Health recently released a call for research identifying factors that encourage adolescents to engage in risks for pregnancy and health risks related to adolescent sexuality. Equally important is research that assesses how mass media and interpersonal channels of communication might be used to discourage such behaviors.

Identify Language Barriers and Relevant Cultural Idiosyncracies

One of the most obvious and yet often overlooked barriers to effective communication is language. The answer to this problem is simply to provide interventions in the primary language of the recipient. Overcoming cultural barriers is more difficult. Research indicates that Blacks and Hispanics are at considerable risk for AIDS. Cancer research indicates that these minorities are least likely to have access to cancer information (American Cancer Society, 1981; 1985; 1986). Moreover, excess mortality among Black males under age 70 is 16%, and 10% for Hispanics. Excess mortality is the difference between the observed number of deaths and the number expected if there were similarities in age and socioeconomic status-specific rates in the nonminority populations.

Research that provides guidelines for conveying health information to minorities is imperative. Williams (1986) argues that the role that mass media play in creating awareness and conveying knowledge may be less significant in minority communities. She explains: "Strategies to induce attitudinal and behavior changes among members of the black community relative to AIDS prevention and risk-reduction activities would undoubtedly encounter a powerful traditional medical belief system that exists among blacks. Some illnesses may be judged to be God's punishment and a form of social control" (p. 414).

To the extent that people perceive AIDS to be divine intervention, they are unlikely to take a proactive response. To the extent that adolescents perceive this, they are unlikely to believe that their future with regard to AIDS is in their own hands. Combine with this the illusions of self-regard, control, and optimism described by Taylor and Brown (1988), and the likelihood of risk reduction is further decreased.

Conclusions

The fight against AIDS cannot be won on one front, nor can it be won with one strategy. Unlike many other diseases that threaten society as a whole, AIDS is transmitted primarily through sexual relations with an infected person. For this reason it is a sensitive topic. Alcoholism and drug abuse, for example, are not contagious. Preventive measures for them do not require discussions of sexual activity. As offensive as they may be, mass media and interpersonal communications about these health problems rarely meet with protests from people whose sensibilities have been offended.

This paper proposes that the influences of family, peers, and the media are important in convincing children that they are responsible for their own health. It also proposes that traditional persuasion methods may not prove as useful as appeals to the illusions that guide risk-taking behvior. A few lessons from marketing may thus be in order. Effective selling of a product requires identification of the customer's needs, illusions, and emotions with regard to the product. It involves associating the product with needs, illusions, and positive emotions. AIDS prevention is a product to be sold to young people and adults alike. To do so effectively requires study of their needs, illusions, and emotions with regard to AIDS. It also requires a thorough understanding of the extent to which they depend on various communication channels for health information and the degree of credibility they assign to each.

This approach to AIDS prevention among children debunks the false dichotomy that has devided communication researchers. A channel for AIDS prevention messages is only as good as the target's degree of dependency on it for health information, and credibility that person assigns to it. To the extent that family, peers, magazines, newspapers, film, and other communication channels are valued sources of health information for children, they are the most promising avenues of intervention. Determining these preferences and identifying promising persuasion approaches for both interpersonal and mass media are two important goals of future health communication research.

References

American Cancer Society. (1981). A study of Black Americans' attitudes toward cancer and cancer tests. New York: ACS.

American Cancer Society. (1985). A study of Hispanics' attitudes toward cancer and cancer prevention. Prepared by Clark, Matire & Bartolomeo, Inc. New York: ACS.

American Cancer Society. (1986). Cancer in the economically disadvantaged. New York: ACS.

Atkin, C. K. (1981). Mass media information campaign effectiveness. In R. E. Rice, & W. J. Paisley (Eds.), *Communication campaigns*. Beverly Hills, CA: Sage.

Ball-Rokeach, S. J. (1988). Media system dependency theory. In M. L. DeFleur & S. J. Ball-Rokeach, (Eds.), *Monologue, dialogue and telelog: Comparing an emergent form of communication with traditional forms*.

Ball-Rokeach, S. J., & Reardon, K. K. (1988). Telelogic, dialogic, and monologic communication: A comparison of forms: In R. P. Hawkins, J. M. Wiemann, & S. Pingree (Eds.), *Advances in communication science: Merging mass and interpersonal processes*. Newbury Park: Sage.

Ball-Rokeach, S. J., Rokeach, M., & Grube, J. W. (1984). *The great American values test: Influencing behavior and belief through television*. New York: Free Press.

Bandura, A. (1973). *Aggression: A social learning analysis*. Englewood Cliffs, NJ: Prentice-Hall.

Blos, P. (1956). An investigation of the healthy child's understanding of the causes of disease. Unpublished M.D. thesis. Yale University.

Blumberg, H. H. (1972). Communication of interpersonal evaluations. *Journal of Personality and Social Psychology, 23,* 157–62.

Brown, J. D. (1987). Evaluating one's abilities: The self-assessment versus self-enhancement debate revisited.

Chaffee, S. H., & Mutz, D. C. (1988). Comparing mediated and interpersonal communication data. In R. P. Hawkins, J. M. Wiemann, & S. Pingree (Eds.), *Advances in communication science: Merging mass and interpersonal processes*. Newbury Park: Sage.

Chassin, L. A., et al. (1984). Predicting the onset of adolescent cigarette smoking: A longitudinal study. *Journal of Applied Social Psychology, 14,* 224–43.

Collins, L. M., et al. (1987). Psychosocial predictors of young adolescent cigarette smoking: A sixteen-month, three-wave longitudinal study. *Journal of Applied Social Psychology, 17,* 554–73.

Cook, T. D., & Flay, B. R. (1978). The temporal persistence of experimentally enduced attitude change: An evaluative review. In L. Berkowitz (Ed.), *Advances in experimental psychology*, Vol. 11. New York: Academic Press.

Craik, F. I. M., & Lockhart, P. (1972). Levels of processing: A framework for medical research. *Journal of Verbal Learning and Verbal Behavior, 11,* 671–84.

Craik, F. I. M., & Tulving, E. (1975). Depth of processing and the retention of words in episodic memory. *Journal of Experimental Psychology: General, 104,* 208–294.

Dearing, J., Rogers, E. M., & Fei, X. (1988). *The agenda-setting process for the issue of AIDS.* Unpublished ms., University of Southern California.

Department of Health and Human Services. (1985). *Report of the Secretary's Task Force on Minority Health, volume II: Cross-cutting issues in minority health.* Washington, D.C.: U.S. Department of Health and Human Services.

Eckland, B. K. (1968). Theories of mate selection. *Eugenics Quarterly, 15,* 71–84.

Fiske, S. T., & Taylor, S. E. (1984). *Social cognition.* Reading, MA: Addison-Wesley.

Fitzpatrick, M. A., & Badzinski, D. M. (1985). All in the family: Communication in kin relationships. In M. L. Knapp, & G. R. Miller (Eds.), *Handbook of interpersonal communication.* Beverly Hills: Sage.

Flay, B. R. (1981a). On increasing the chances of mass media health promotion programs causing meaningful changes in behavior. In M. Meyer (Ed.), *Health education by television and radio.* Munich: Saur.

Flay, B. R. (1981b). The evaluation of mass media prevention campaigns. In R. R. Rice, & W. Paisley (Eds.), *Public communication campaigns.* Beverly Hills: Sage.

Flay, B. R., et al. (1983). Cigarette smoking: Why young people do it and ways of preventing it: The Waterloo study. In P. Firestone, & P. McGrath (Eds.), *Pediatrics and adolescent behavioral medicine.* New York: Springer-Verlag.

Furstenberg, F. F., Moore, K. A., & Peterson, J. L. (1985). Sex education and sexual experience among adolescents. *American Journal of Public Health, 75,* 1331–32.

Gochman, D. S. (1972). The organizing role of motivation in health beliefs and intentions. *Journal of Health & Social Behavior, 13,* 285–93.

Gottlieb, B. H. (1985). Social networks and social support: An overview of research, practice, and policy implication. *Health Education Quarterly, 12,* 5–22.

Granovetter, M. (1973). The strength of weak ties. *American Journal of Sociology, 78,* 1360–80.

Hall, A., & Wellman, B. (1985). Social networks and social support. In S. Cohen, & S. L. Syme (Eds.), *Social support and health.* et al. New York: Academic Press.

Hansen, W. B., et al. (1985). Self-initiated smoking cessation among high school students. *Addictive Behaviors, 10,* 265–71.

Hill, C. T., Rubin, Z., & Peplay, L. A. (1976). Breakups before marriage: The end of 103 affairs. *Journal of Social Issues, 32,* 147–68.

Langer, E. J. (1984). Playing the middle against both ends: The influence of adult cognitive activity as a model for cognitive activity in childhood and old age. In S. R. Yussen (Ed.), *The development of reflection.* New York: Academic Press.

Langer, E. J., Blank, A., & Chanowitz, B. (1978). The mindlessness of ostensibly thoughtful action: The role of "placebic" information in interpersonal interaction. *Journal of Personality and Social Psychology, 36,* 635–42.

Lewis, C. E., & Lewis, M. A. (1977). Child-initiated care: The utilization of school nursing services by children in an adult-free system. *Pediatrics, 60,* 499–507.

Lewis, C. E., & Lewis, M. A. (1982). Children's health-related decision making. *Health Education Quarterly, 9,* 129–41.

Longshore, D. L. (1988). AIDS education for higher-risk populations. Unpublished ms., General Accounting Office, Washington, D.C.

McGuire, W. J. (1985). Attitudes and attitude change. In L. Gardner, & E. Aronson (Eds.), *Handbook of social psychology*, vol. 2 (3d ed.). New York: Random House.

McLeod, J. M., & Chaffee, S. R. (1971). The construction of social reality. In J. Tedeschi (Ed.), *The social influence process*. Chicago: Aldine.

Mechanic, D. (1979). The stability of health and illness behavior: Results from a 16-year follow-up. *American Journal of Public Health, 69,* 1142–45.

Nagy, M. H. (1951). Children's ideas of the origin of illness. *Health Education Journal, 9,* 6–13.

Nisbett, R. E., & Ross, L. (1980). *Human inference: Strategies and shortcomings of social judgment.* Englewood Cliffs, NJ: Prentice-Hall.

Parducci, A. (1968). The relativism of absolute judgments. *Scientific American, 219,* 518–28.

Reardon, K. K., & Rogers, E. M. (1988). Interpersonal and mass media communication: A false dichotomy. *Human Communication Research, 12.*

Reardon, K. K., & Richardson, J. L. (1989). The important role of mass media in the diffusion of accuratae information about AIDS. *Journal of homosexuality.*

Reardon, K. K., Sussman, S., & Flay, B. (1988). Can adolescents "just say 'No' " to smoking. Paper presented at the International Communication Association Conference, New Orleans.

Reardon, K. K. (1989). The potential role of persuasion in the fight on AIDS. In: R. E. Rice, & C. Atkin (Eds.), *Public campaigns.* Newbury Park, CA: Sage.

Shrauger, J. S., & Rosenberg, J. E. (1970). Self-esteem and the effects of success and failure feedback on performance. *Journal of Personality, 38,* 404–17.

Snyder, C. R., Shenkel, R. J., & Lowery, C. R. (1977). Acceptance of personality interpretations: The "Barnum effect" and beyond. *Journal of Consulting and Clinical Psychology, 44,* 564–72.

Solomon, G. (1984). Television is "easy" and print is "tough": The differential investment of mental effort in learning as a function of perceptions and attributions. *Journal of Educational Psychology, 76,* 647–58.

Sussman, S. (1988). Two social influence perspectives of tobacco use development and prevention. Unpublished ms. University of Southern California.

Taylor, S. E., & Brown, J. D. (1988). Illusion and well-being: A social psychological perspective on mental health. *Psychological Bulletin, 103,* 193–210.

Tesser, A., & Rosen, S. (1975). The reluctance to transmit bad news. In L. Berkowitz (Ed.), *Advances in experimental psychology*, vol. 8. New York: Academic Press.

Warner, E. (1977). The effects of anti-smoking campaign on cigarette consumption. *American Journal of Public Health, 67,* 645–50.

Williams, L. S. (1986). AIDS risk reduction: A community health education intervention for minority high risk group members. *Health Education Quarterly,* Winter, 407–21.

Wood, B. (1981). *Children and communication.* Englewood Cliffs, NJ: Prentice-Hall.

Worthington, G. M. (1988). Adolescence and youth: Some educational and epidemiological aspects of the AIDS crisis. Unpublished paper.

6

The Death of Intellectual History and the Birth of the Transient Past

Sari Thomas and Michael Knippendorf

The issues related to technology and media have long been serious matters to the discipline of communication. Some might argue that these issues circumscribe, if not define, a good portion of the discipline. In this context, "technology" typically refers to those mechanical processes pertinent to information production such as television. "Mediation" is used to refer to different channels of information recording and transmission such as film or video. While this typical employment of terms certainly fits most extant definitions, there remain many systems and subsystems of information production and dissemination that are commonly overlooked but, nonetheless, might be shown to play important roles in aspects of the communication process. These alternative systems may interact with interpersonal communication to create specialized environments for communication that are often not obvious. This essay attempts to examine some of these technologies and media and their attendant social circumstances that have not been explored much. Intellectual history is used here as a particular example of an area where we may find such nonobvious communicative environments or circumstances. Manuscripts, personal correspondence, and other historical sources are analyzed to determine the differences in the historical record left by certain literary circles, according to the media the writers themselves employed during their lives. We find that, at least for the examples presented here, our historical understanding of the intellectual and creative processes might be deeply influenced by the records left behind by the media commonly in use at the time.

The chronicling of intellectual movements varies considerably as a function of the era in which these movements themselves occurred. Intellectual historians have traditionally relied on various kinds of material (such as letters, journals, public artifacts, and hearsay) to create their subject matter. However, the availability of these sources may vary as a result of changes in technology and social practice, and that which constitutes the formal intellectual history of our civilization may demonstrate important methodological change. This study attempts to examine the course of intellectual history in the context of literary circles. It compares the scholarly treatment of literary circles from several different centuries in terms of the sources of documentation used in creating history.

Literary circles are the subject of analysis because professional writers, more than most other types of professionals, might be likely to create and keep written records of their lives through letters, journals, and so forth. Six literary circles are studied: (1) Elizabethan writers of the sixteenth century (Shakespeare and Bacon), (2) Johnson/Boswell of the eighteenth century, (3) the Romantic poets (Shelley, Byron, and Keats) of the early nineteenth century, (4) the Wharton circle (Wharton, James, and Berenson) of the turn of the twentieth century, (5) the Bloomsbury circle (Virginia Woolf, Roger Fry, E. M. Forster) of the early twentieth century, and (6) the post–World War II Beat Generation (Kerouac, Ferlenghetti, and Ginsburg). For each of these groups, all available volumes in two major library collections (the libraries of Temple University and the University of Pennsylvania) were considered. Specifically, all biographies of leading figures in each circle as well as all books about these circles (excluding readings of texts) were systematically analyzed to determine the number and nature of citations that biographers, historians, critics, and other scholars have made to illustrate and substantiate their findings and interpretations. Thus, our analysis provides a description of how documentation patterns in the intellectual histories of literary circles vary with respect to the time period studied.

As indicated, the six circles named represent different historical periods. The Wharton and Bloomsbury groups were chosen because they were, at one point, contemporaries, and thus, their comparison would help to eliminate a possible bias of style in a particular literary circle. That is, two groups of close temporal proximity were chosen so that it might not be claimed that the particular styles of individual writers accounted for their record keeping.

The reference citation constituted the unit of analysis. Considering all volumes analyzed, this study examined patterns among over 14,000 citations. Each citation was coded as one of eleven mutually exclusive types, that is, either as (1) personal correspondence—letters between friends, family, lovers; (2) professional correspondence, i.e., business letters; (3) journals and diaries; (4) magazine or newspaper articles about the circle or particular individuals in it; (5) government documents; (6) hearsay/rumor (which sometimes is formally cited); (7) interviews; (8) published fictional work of members of the circle; (9) published nonfictional work of circle members; (10) fictional works of others not in the circle; and (11) nonfictional work of others not in the circle (including all cited scholarly work on the subject.)

Of major concern is the use of what might be called "personal and direct" sources of documentation such as personal correspondence, journals, and diaries. Specifically, we shall compare the percentage of citations relying on personal documents vs. that relying on secondary reports (articles, scholarly or otherwise, hearsay, interviews with nonmembers) and public artifacts (documents as well as fictional and nonfictional work by circle members.) While personal sources are not necessarily the fundamental arbiters of truth, we suggest that there is an important methodological distinction between history as built from the direct observations of those having intimately experienced it, and history as inferred and interpreted from secondary information and/or fictional artifacts.

With regard to the use of personal documents, there is an absence-> growth-> decline documentation pattern. The history and biography of the Elizabethan writers show little reference to such artifacts (less than 5% of the near 1,900 citations from Elizabethan histories.) For the Johnson/Boswell era, 21% of slightly over 2,000 citations came from letters, journals, and diaries. About 30% of approximately 3,000 citations from the Romantic poets' histories and biographies rely on personal sources. The peak is reached with the Wharton circle, where over 50% of documentation (approximately 3,100 total citations) derives from personal letters and journals; the contemporary, but nonetheless younger and more modern Bloomsbury circle (with about 3,800 citations) is chronicled nearly 40% of the time through personal artifacts. The most recent, Beat Generation history and biography—which is, perhaps, the most recent literary movement to be historicized—relies on personal documents for only 11% of its nearly 1,200 citations.

For documentation, histories of the Beat Generation rely mostly on interviews (typically with people on the very periphery of the circle) and also on newspaper articles—that is, mainly on secondary material. Secondary reports also figure heavily in the histories of the earlier circles—

Shakespeare and Boswell. However, unlike the histories of the Beat Generation, the major source of secondary documents for these sixteenth- and eighteenth-century groups is earlier scholarly writing. Many of these earlier scholarly works (also included in the sample) were written with relatively little documentation beyond actual fictional and nonfictional publications authored by members of the circle.

Overall, there are more references cited in the intellectual histories and biographies of the late nineteenth- and early twentieth-century literary circles—the Wharton and Bloomsbury groups. The least amount of citations of any kind occur in the chronicling of the Beat Generation. Moreover, the histories of the Wharton and Bloomsbury groups are those most heavily substantiated by direct, personal artifacts from members of the groups themselves. Very early and very recent histories seem to rely largely on secondary, indirect sources of information, when citation occurs at all. The histories of all the groups rely on published work by circle members for between 15% and 25% of citations. The question, then, is what these patterns might mean in terms of the course of intellectual history. Two major issues must be considered.

The first issue might be called the sociology-of-fame (cf. Braudy, 1986; Margolis, 1977; Schickel, 1985), and it encompasses two factors: (1) self-consciousness as celebrity, and (2) public treatment of public figures. Self-conscious celebrity pertains to how writers seemed to understand their roles as (potentially) important historical figures. On the one hand, Edith Wharton, for example, prepared a large package of personal documents that she labeled "for my biographer" (Lewis, 1975, p. xi). This suggests a definite awareness or, at least, presumption of her status in intellectual history. On the other hand, the assembling of such materials in the days of Shakespeare would have been less probable; the notion of such self-importance in the course of history did not befit the popular Elizabethan poet (Braudy, 1986, pp. 315–26). While this may partially explain why available documents from Shakespeare differ from those emerging from Wharton or Woolf, it does not explain why the distribution of Kerouac's records are more similar to those of Shakespeare than to those of Wharton or Woolf. In this context, then, we must turn to the issue of public treatment of public figures and consider the effect of the style and substance of mid-twentieth-century biography.

From the point where writers could easily recognize the possibility of worldwide fame and immortality, there was also a long-standing tradition that biographies were undertaken by the subjects' admirers (Boorstin, 1961, p. 51; Nadel, 1984, p. 176). Shakespeare probably did not fear what historians would say, but also probably doubted that they would say much at all. By the 1940s and 1950s, conditions were radically different. Critical biography and the commercialization of public scandal became increasingly commonplace (Boorstin, 1961, pp. 51–52). Thus, even if voluminous personal records were kept by relatively recent writers, there is much reason to question whether or not such records would be assiduously maintained for subsequent public scrutiny. One might even consider the course of future history in light of the progress of contemporary critical biography and events such as Watergate. It would seem that public or potentially public figures might well be developing a media fear, knowing the use to which private records of their lives might be put (Margolis, 1977, pp. 208–210). In addition to the commercial benefits, many public figures may be prematurely rushing to their (possibly sanitized) autobiographies to provide the "definitive" account of their lives, to compete with those accounts, written by others, that may follow. It is not unreasonable to assume that life review by authors writing in the vein of Bob Woodward or Albert Goldman is undesirable.

The second issue to consider—communications technology—is equally important. Here, communications technology broadly refers to three things: postal systems, transportation, and the telephone.[1] Among our literary circles, vast personal travel does not become commonplace until at least the period of the Romantic poets, who travelled more than most members of their social class. At that time, among those separated by distance, letter writing was the only means of interpersonal communication, using an already-developed postal system (Robinson, 1953). In earlier eras, although letters and messages were regularly delivered, the world tended to consist more of one's immediate community. Until the twentieth century, travel was typically a lengthy process involving long separations; thus, letter writing increases with the Romantic poets. Edith Wharton's generation traveled extensively by ship and motorcar in Europe, England, and the United States. Air travel and long-distance phoning were not particularly accessible to her group; however, letter writing among members of that circle was common and extensive. Ultimately, with the advent of commercial air travel and, obviously, extended uses of the telephone (both innovations occurring during the life of the Bloomsbury group), the post, while readily available, probably became less used for close, interpersonal interaction and even for business dealings. From a psychological perspective, the immediacy of the telephone, in particular, was extremely influential in limiting the kinds of artifacts which writers were to leave to posterity. While calculating the fate of intellectual history, one must also consider the present and future uses to which the telephone can be put.

In all, there seem to be a number of interlocking variables which may serve to explain the changes found in documentation patterns and, thus, the evolution of intellectual history. We should stress that this study involved individuals committed to writing, hence one might expect to find even stronger trends in the directions noted when examining the history of other professional movements. Before concluding, two important methodological considerations must be introduced. First, in our comparison of literary-circle histories, we have included a movement, the Beat Generation, whose major figures are not yet all deceased. With the passage of time, it is highly probable that personal documents, thus far unavailable to scholars, will emerge. Nonetheless, on the basis of our aforementioned arguments concerning the sociology-of-fame and communications technology, we would predict that the future totality of personal documentation in histories of the Beat Generation will never significantly approach the proportions reached in the histories of the Wharton or Bloomsbury groups.

The second matter pertains to an assumption of parity between documentation sources cited and sources available, i.e., we have attributed the evolution of intellectual history to changes in social organization rather than to changes in history writing. Could it be that the various types of documentation are proportionately constant throughout time, but that the patterns of their scholarly employment differ? The answer clearly seems that the changes we detect in our research are overwhelmingly the result of actual changes in the sources of documentation. Although it is certain that the techniques of scholarship in all disciplines evolve and transmute through time, the materials of biography have certain generic properties all of which demand confrontation, if not reliance on documentation from the chronicled life (Nadel, 1984). One must assume that the availability of documentary evidence will necessarily affect the biography. While the literary circles sampled represent different time periods, their written histories are not correspondingly varied; it is a fact that a present-day historian of Francis Bacon, for example, would necessarily have a distinctly different set of archival possibilities from the scholar chronicling Henry James. To assume that these different sets of possibilities would be irrelevant in history construction would be intellectually naive.[2]

To the extent that scholars are able to rely on personal, direct artifacts (as well as indirect sources) on which to construct their histories of intellectual movements, we should obtain a more enlightened and substantiated history. Conversely, to the extent that these personal, direct sources are scarce, a more interpretive and present-bound mode of recounting our intellectual foundations should prevail.[3] As we approach the twenty-first century, it would seem that it is this second model of intellectual history that may dominate.

Notes

1. For the history and social effects of these technological innovations see the following works—Fuller (1972), Robinson (1953), and Staff (1956) for histories

and social effects of postal systems; Aronson (1979), Brooks (1976), Pierce (1977) on the development and role of the telephone; Gwilliam (1978), Ogburn (1937, 1938, 1942, 1946, 1951, 1964), Ogburn & Gilfillan (1933), Partridge (1968), and Willey & Rice (1933) with regard to the social impact of transportation and technology.

2. La Capra (1980) does argue that interpretive history results not because of a scarcity of information but in response to what some current philosophical and hermeneutic readings consider the fallacy of reconstructing "true" history. Our claim is that documentary-source availability must not be dismissed as a variable in the overall equation.

3. Several articles take up this issue of reconstructing vs. interpreting history. Shore (1981) offers an argument for more psychohistorical and prosopographical methods of history in response to both excessive idealization in the Victorian biography and to the mere accumulation of facts. Approaches with interpretive bents are found in Tamke's (1977) examination of the use of oral history as a method for exploring popular culture, Loesberg's (1980) reading of Victorian autobiography as epistemological view, and Nadel's (1984) efforts toward the construction of a poetics of biography.

References

Aronson, S. H. (1979). The sociology of the telephone. In G. Gumpert, & R. Cathcart (Eds.), *Inter/Media*. New York: Oxford University Press.

Boorstin, D. J. (1961). *The image: A guide to pseudo-events in America*. New York: Harper Colophon.

Braudy, L. (1986). *The frenzy of renown: Fame and its history*. New York: Oxford University Press.

Brooks, J. (1976). *Telephone, the first hundred years*. New York: Harper & Row.

Fuller, W. E. (1972). *The American mail: Enlarger of the common life*. London: Heinemann.

Gwilliam, K. M. (1978). The development of the world transport market. In T. I. Williams (Ed.), *A history of technology, 1900–1950: Vol. 7*. Oxford, UK: Clarendon Press.

La Capra, D. (1980). Rethinking intellectual history and reading texts. *History and Theory, 19*(3), 245–76.

Lewis, R. W. B. (1975). *Edith Wharton: A biography*. New York: Harper & Row.

Loesberg, J. (1980). Self-consciousness and mediation in Victorian autobiography. *University of Toronto Quarterly, 50*, 199–220.

Margolis, S. (1977). *Fame*. San Francisco, CA: San Francisco Book Company.

Nadel, I. B. (1984). *Biography: Fiction, fact, and form*. New York: St. Martin's.

Ogburn, W. F. (1937). The influence of inventions on the social institutions of the future. *American Journal of Sociology, 43*(3), 365–77.

Ogburn, W. F. (1938). Technology and sociology. *Social Forces, 17*(1), 1–8.

Ogburn, W. F. (1942). *Man and his machines*. National Association of Secondary School Principals, National Council for the Social Studies, NEA.

Ogburn, W. F. (1946). *The social effects of aviation*. New York: Houghton Mifflin.

Ogburn, W. F. (1951). How technology changes society. *Sociology and Social Research*, November–December, 75–83.

Ogburn, W. F. (1964). Technology, populations, history. In *Culture and social change: Selected papers of William Fielding Osgood.* Chicago: University of Chicago Press (original work pub. 1942).

Ogburn, W. F., & Gilfillan, D. (1933). The influence of invention and discovery. In *Recent Social Trends in the United States: Report of the President's Research Committee on Social Trends: Vol. 1.* New York: McGraw-Hill.

Partridge, D. (1968). The revolutionary impact of the automobile. In N. F. Cantor & M. S. Werthman (Eds.), *The history of popular culture.* New York: Macmillan.

Pierce, J. R. (1977). The telephone and society in the past hundred years. In I. De Sola Pool (Ed.), *The social impact of the telephone.* Beverly Hills, CA: Sage.

Robinson, H. (1953). *Britain's post office: A history of development from the beginnings to the present day.* New York: Oxford University Press.

Schickle, R. (1985). *Intimate strangers: The culture of celebrities.* New York: Doubleday.

Shore, M. F. (1981). Biography of the 1980s: A psychoanalytic perspective. *The Journal of Interdisciplinary History, 12*(1), 89–113.

Staff, F. (1956). *The transatlantic mail.* New York: J. De Graff.

Tamke, S. (1977). Oral history and popular culture. A method for the study of the experience of culture. *Journal of Popular Culture, 13*, 267–79.

Willey, M. M., & Rice, S. A. (1933). The agencies of communication. In *Recent Trends in the United States: Report of the President's Research Committee on Social Trends: Vol. 1.* New York: McGraw-Hill.

Winslow, D. J. (1978). Current bibliography on life-writing. *Biography, 4*, 76–81.

7

Interacting with Media: Para-Social Interaction and Real Interaction

Sheizaf Rafaeli

This study is about interactive use of mass media. "Interactivity" is a construct related to the use of computers and other new communication media. As part of a broader interest in interactivity as a variable quality of communication settings, we focus here on the apparent growth in interactive use of the traditional, historically one-way media. Real interaction is contrasted with para-social interaction in the context of the relationship between sociability and mass media use. This study demonstrates one potentially positive outcome of the incorporation of interactive arrangements in mass communication settings.

Introduction

Use of communication media in an interactive manner is growing. The use of media in an overtly interactive rather than a completely passive or just reactive fashion is termed here "interactivity." Interactivity has been studied in the context of new communication technologies, especially computers as media. The present study begins with the assumption that interactivity is a characteristic of communication settings, and is therefore of some interest in the study of traditional mass media.

It is possible to conceive of a continuum of interactivity along which all communication settings can be located (Rogers, 1986). Media use, the individuals making this use, and perhaps even the messages transmitted, should be studied in relation to this dimension. In addition, the degree of interactivity of a given medium is not chiseled in stone. Since interactivity is a characteristic of the setting and not the medium (Rafaeli, 1984a; 1984b), we might find media evolving historically toward the higher end of the interactivity continuum.

Media once considered one-way now seem to be taking on a different nature. Beniger (1987) refers to the outcome as the formation of a pseudo-community; the process is one of a "rapid blurring of the distinction between interpersonal and mass communication" (p. 354). Mass mediation can now simulate interpersonal communication, transmit personalized messages. One may (and several scholars do) treat this phenomenon as newly exploited avenues for manipulating sincerity, or dismiss the "blurring" as an artifact of deception in appearances.

An alternative path, taken here, is to focus on the real portions of the process. Some of the apparently disappearing distinctions between mass and interpersonal processes are really disappearing, not just seemingly so. The nostalgic request-shows on radio have been replaced. In several mediated contexts, once-passive audiences are now more active. The "letters to the editor" page in a newspaper is one example; talk-radio shows are another. Community, legal, and political action groups attempting to affect mass-mediated content are a case in point. The growth in marketing studies employed by most mass media organizations is yet a fourth way in which mass media are becoming (or at least giving the impression of becoming) both bidirectional and potentially more responsive to their users. This phenomenon is, therefore, of interest in the domain of mass media research.

Realization of the role of interactivity entails a focus on the audience/ receivers. As the present review shows, one question of interest with regard to interactive use of media involves the social dimensions of the user's media-use behavior: Is interaction indeed just a delusion? Both supplementation and substitutional models have been proposed to explain the relationship of sociability to mass media use. This issue is now raised with regard to the new technologies and computers. The present essay begins by introducing the relevance of studying interactive use to the study of mass media use. Next, the literature on writing letters to the editor and participation in radio call-in talk shows is being reviewed. The communication research tradition on the question of sociability and mass media use is reviewed, to examine the evidence provided for both the substitutional and supplementary dynamics. Finally, I focus on the concept of para-social interaction, and the way in which it is used to explain the notion of escape and substitution of media use for sociability.

Interaction, of both real and para-social nature, is a social phenomenon. The research reported here is a juxtaposition of the way in which para-social interaction mediates the relationship of sociability to media use, with the role of real interaction in the same relationship.

Interactive Behaviors

Interactivity should be viewed as a variable quality of communication settings. Think of interactivity as the degree to which, in a given series of communication exchanges, any third (or later) transmission (or message) is related to the degree to which previous exchanges referred to transmissions that transpired even earlier.

This complex definition clarifies several points regarding interactivity. First, that interactivity as a variable represents at least a continuum, not just a dichotomous quality. Second, that interactivity is much more than just the presence of channels allowing communication to flow in two or more directions. Third, the definition highlights a subjective condition for the presence of interactivity. Because of the subjective and continuous nature of interactivity, it is best viewed as a special subset of feedback: not all systems which have feedback are interactive, but all interactive systems have incorporated feedback loops. And last, while interactivity can be enhanced by changes in or of a medium, the level of interactivity is a quality of the communication setting, not the medium. Thus levels of interactivity may vary widely within a given medium.

In the terminology of computer technology, interactivity is a software-driven characteristic. Interactivity is of interest in the study of computer-based communication settings. But the metaphor of software and the algorithms that compose software can be extended to other realms of organized human behavior. Similarly, there can be interest in interactivity as it is implemented in noncomputerized, traditional communication systems.

What are interactive behaviors in the context of mass media? First, they are instances of communicative behavior with and through a medium of communication shared by others she or he does not know (qualifying the behavior to be of interest in the mass media literature). Second, most of these behaviors have an interpersonal angle. So much so that these behaviors become unclassifiable in the traditional and now-deceased non-paradigm scheme of who says what to whom through which channel, and with what effects. (These behaviors qualify to be of interest to the literature of interpersonal communication, too.) Third, the behaviors of interacting with media, as distinct from behaviors that are either integral parts of attending to media or intended effects of doing so, are true instances of mass communication. Interacting-with-media behaviors are neither inputs to nor outputs of a linear process connecting senders to receivers. Thus, a theoretical focus on interacting behaviors is less likely to fall into the trap of categorizing communication behaviors according to the number of receivers (Ball-Rokeach & Reardon, 1988). Finally, these behaviors seem to obviate an all-too-common distinction—the juxtaposition of interpersonal and channel-mediated communication according to degree of impersonality. Instead, the prominence of these behaviors in the real world, and the possibility that they are becoming popular behaviors raise some questions: Does mass-mediated communication have to be impersonal? Is it true that media of communication come between people, or do they (just as often) link people who would not have been joined otherwise?

Overt interactions with media (writing letters to the editor, calling-in to talk-radio open microphone shows, using citizen band [CB] radio, using electronic bulletin boards, even libel suits against mass media organizations) have been the subject of generous treatment in the literature of communication reserach. An unofficial count of articles in five journals reaches well over seventy items of empirical research. However, all these treatments focus singularly on one specific behavior. There is no analysis of these as a coherent set.

Writing letters to the editor is the most frequently studied interacting-with-media behavior. An initial reflection on this entire body of literature is that very little of it is theoretically based or derived. The behavior is only rarely studied in the context of other media-use behaviors, or treated as anything other than an instance of itself, rather than a part of a broader theoretical construct. Further, the statements made, and (less frequently) the theories tested with regard to these behaviors, are somewhat contradictory. None of the hypotheses forwarded at different times achieve the role of an accepted theory or a working paradigm. Thus, for example, some articles proceed on the assumption that people who write letters to the editor are representative of the larger audience; others presume that this is not true, looking instead for differentiation; yet a third group use that assertion as their null hypothesis, one they proceed to disprove. Similarly, several debates rage in the literature over the demographic character of those who write letters. Results are presented regarding educational level, gender, SES, political affiliation, etc., unaccompanied by a theoretical organizing theme.

One characteristic does cut across a large portion of this eclectic section of the literature—a pervasive condescending attitude toward those who make use of interactive channels and means. In the worst cases, those who write letters to the editor or participate in talk-radio shows are being ridiculed as "eccentrics and gladiators," "extremists," "cranks," or "occupants of the loafers' bench on the courthouse square." At best, their strategy is being questioned. Several researchers are quick to point out that there is a wide difference between what interactants hope to achieve and what they actually do get. What is achieved, say some, is a mere letting out of steam on the part of the writer. Almost none of the research on letters to the editor accepts audience behavior on the audience's terms.

Compassion for the interacting audience is not the only thing lacking. Closure on some of the main points researched is absent too. Some good examples could be drawn from the literature on writing letters to the editor. The published literature on that matter varies in methodology, scope, rigor, and approach. It could be summarized as dealing with three interrelated research questions:

1. Who writes letters to the editor? How many people write? Are those who write (or their letters) representative of members of the general public and their opinions?
2. How can one explain the phenomenon of writing letters to the editor? Why do people write? What function(s) does the institution of the letters page in the newspaper fulfill?
3. Is the subject of letters to the editor important at all?

Much attention has been given to the question of the demographics of those who write letters (Abel & Thornton, 1975; Chu & Chu, 1981; Klempner, 1966; Lewis, 1970; Singletary, 1976; Singletary & Cowling, 1979; Tarrant, 1957; Vacin, 1965). The findings are contradictory, and consequently there is no final answer to the question of whether the letters that get published (or even the larger population of those that are sent) are representative of anything (Hill, 1981; Roberts, Sikorski, & Paisley, 1969). Often, the writer is envisioned as an older, more educated, better off economically male conservative (Buell, 1975; Volgy et al., 1977). Buell locates the only statistically significant differences in education, income, and political stance.

Estimates of the number of people who ever engage in this form of interaction with the media also vary much. The range of estimates is anywhere from an inconsequential 3% to a substantial 20% of the adult population (Converse, Clausen, & Miller, 1965; Grey & Brown, 1970; Rosenau, 1974; Singer, 1972; Sussman, 1959, 1963; Verba & Brody, 1970). Interestingly, the estimates seem to vary linearly with time, growing in recent years.

Several hypotheses are forwarded in the literature regarding the reasons for writing letters, and the functions fulfilled by their publication. The most frequently offered hypotheses or null hypotheses are:

1. Letters are not from individuals: Letters are mainly outcomes of concerted campaigns—initiated, organized, and written mostly by organizations, political interest groups, or individuals in their employ. Letters to the editors are, therefore, not an individual-level phenomenon (Brown, 1976; Inkeles & Geiger, 1952, 1953; Kefauver & Levin, 1960; Renfro, 1979).
2. The safety-valve hypothesis: Letters serve a cathartic function for the individual, providing a safety valve for society; "A letter column gives the irate, the antagonist, the displeased, a chance to speak out and be heard" (Davis & Rarick, 1964). (See also Forsythe, 1950; Lander, 1972.)
3. The extremist hypothesis: Letters to the editor are written mostly by extremists and/or political activists, specifically people located on the political right (Buell, 1975; Converse, Clausen, & Miller, 1965; Forsythe, 1950; Verba & Brody, 1970; Volgy et al., 1977).
4. A functional hypothesis: Letters to the editor function to stimulate public debate and discussion of important issues. (Grey & Brown, 1970; Lemert & Larkin, 1979)

The single consensual dimension in the literature is that this behavior is important, a matter of great interest, and deserving of more research. One author even quips: "I have always threatened to end an article or book with the line: 'However, *less* research is needed in this area.' Without question, I cannot do that with this topic" (Singer, 1972). Writing letters to the editor is important, because the readers of newspapers pay attention (Singletary, 1976). Its importance is validated by the testimony of those who write; they think their writing is important and has an effect (Eyal, 1985; Vacin, 1965). This criterion for choice of research area is refreshing, in its being set by the audiences as well as the media outlets' interests.

More important, many believe that the right to write is a primary manifestation of a constitutional privilege of access to media (Barron, 1967; Pasternack, 1983; Wilcox, 1969). The importance of the behavior is also linked very often to the establishment of "feedback loops" in society and government (Bauer, 1967), and, more generally, to the working of democracy. Although these two underlying ideologies (the constitutional role of letter writing in preserving freedoms, and the functionality of feedback for society) are widely cited, their execution remains untested, and invoking them is in conflict with the disdain in which most of the literature holds the letter writers.

With regard to other behaviors on the list of behaviors of interaction with mass media, the literature is more sparse. Nevertheless, there is some similarity to the literature on letters to the editor, in both the questions asked about these behaviors and the findings reported. Further, that literature tends to be more theoretical.

Here, too, much attention is devoted to the question of whether or not the content of receiver-initiated interactions with media is a reliable expression of sentiments held by the general population. Are the participants in this genre of interaction significantly different from the general population? The discriminant function of interaction is raised with regard to audience participating in talk radio (Avery, Ellis, & Glover, 1978; Crittenden, 1971; Turow, 1977; Zweibelman & Rayfield, 1982). Even CB radio and fan mail to broadcast celebrities face the same research question (Bierig & Dimmick, 1979; Dannefer & Poushinsky, 1977; McGuire & Leroy, 1977; Marvin & Schultze, 1977; Winick, 1964).

Despite the relative abundance of published research, the important questions remain largely unanswered. We have collected along the way some pieces of the puzzle. We know, for example, that people who are mentally troubled or lonely are more likely than others to call-in to talk-radio shows. People who write fan mail are not very good spellers. We also know that CB radio is more likely to carry male voices, and that these voices are more than likely to be owned by dedicated amateurs or truck drivers, rather than just random users. These findings are not terribly surprising; they illuminate the differences between the demographic groups used in each particular analysis more than the communicative behavior or the media used for it.

Interestingly, and in contrast with the literature on letters to the editors, the theoretical issues of interaction with media are given more attention. For example, there are some empirical assessments of the degree to which talk radio "stretches the envelope" of democracy and freedom of speech (Carlin, 1976; Crittenden, 1971; McEachern, 1970; Touchiest topic, 1973). Further, in some cases there is even an articulated call to recognize these behaviors as a "unique media phenomenon," deserving of research in its own right. Nevertheless, the highlighted distinction is the degree to which the interacting behaviors *differ* from regular interpersonal or mass-mediated communication (Avery & McCain, 1982; Bierig & Dimmick, 1979; Turow, 1974).

One major interest is the degree and manner in which interacting behaviors *integrate* with other communication behaviors. Setting them apart from other communication instances is the easier of the tasks. Identifying the continua along which they reside is the more interesting challenge. This study focuses on sociability and mass media use as elements in the same model with interactive behaviors. We turn, therefore, to a review of the relation of traditional mass media to sociability.

Sociability and Mass Media Use

Rather than compete with each other, the communication of individuals through interpersonal channels and their use of mass media are simultaneous, feed into each other, interact, and could (each) be understood only in reference to the other. Katz (1959), Noelle-Neumann (1977), and Chaffee (1972; 1979; 1982) are among the more eloquent in making this point.

The nature of the mutual influence process between sociability and mass media use is rather complex. There is certainly more than one direction of causal flow. The very discrimination upon which this relationship is based, of mass-mediated vs. interpersonal sources, is problematic from the outset. People communicating with others are not altogether concerned with a classification of sources. The "mass" and "interpersonal" labels might be, in part, an artifact generated by the self-perception of the sources themselves.

It is likely that a combination of supplementation, complementation, and substitution plays a role in the interplay between mass communication and face-to-face communication. An elaboration of discussions of the uses and gratifications of mass media with respect to personal relations (McQuail, Blumler, & Brown, 1972) deals with this prospect. The authors show that there is at least the logical possibility of individuals using either mode (interpersonal or mass) for either purpose—supplementing, complementing, or substituting for functions otherwise performed by or via the other mode. From an empirical/statistical point of view, both positive and negative bivariate covariations are likely, subject to different contingencies. Researchers have, indeed, documented both types. The challenge is in identifying the contingencies.

The Positive Correspondence-Supplementation Dynamics

An interest in the way the use of mass media augments interpersonal communication dates from the earliest years of empirical research on mass communication. In the process of showing that face-to-face contacts are the most important influences in stimulating opinion change, Lazarsfeld, Berelson, and Gaudet (1944) show a high covariation between mass media exposure and interpersonal communication. Opinion leaders (who are, almost by definition, sociable and high on sociometric evaluations and amount of face-to-face contact) were shown to use more campaign-related mass media content. The amount of mass media use by opinion leaders was reported to exceed the levels which could be predicted by their interest in the campaign. In the second seminal campaign study, Katz and Lazarsfeld (1955) advance this point by showing that opinion leaders, who have more or stronger communication links to others, also choose to have a greater exposure to media sources of information relevant to their areas of special interest.

Rogers (1983) draws the following syllogism regarding social connectedness and media consumption; innovation and early adoption are related to social participation, interconnectedness, cosmopoliteness, and information seeking through interpersonal channels. At the same time, innovators and opinion leaders are likely to have more change-agent contact and greater exposure to mass media communication channels. Having high levels of both interpersonal and mass communication reflect the quality of belonging to highly interconnected social systems. At least in this sense sociability and media use are positively related.

In the same vein, Riley and Riley (1951), Schramm, Lyle, and Parker (1961), Bostian and Ross (1965), Kuroda (1966), Donohew (1967), and Klein (1971) all report positive correlations for a variety of sociability measures with amount of media use, and especially the use of print and newspapers. The measures of sociability used in these projects include number, duration, and frequency of interpersonal communication with friends, relatives, neighbors and fellow workers, social participation in meetings, organizational membership, the propensity to give political advice, as well as measures of sociometric and psychological integration and adjustment to peer group.

Media-disseminated content serves as fuel for interpersonal discussion. Here, the claim is for a causal flow from media use to interpersonal communication. Some media content is consciously designed to encourage recirculation, consumers comply; mass media gatekeepers may select content by its gossip value. This is so in the case of curiosity content such as cartoons (Bogart, 1955), but it is also true for news of both major and minor import (Chaffee, 1982; Greenberg, 1975).

The most powerful explanation for the complementation dynamics and positive correlations between sociability measures and mass media usage is that offered by Atkin (1972; 1973). In both survey and experimental settings Atkin demonstrates the instrumental-social-utility explanation of information seeking and attendant media exposure. People who are better connected with relevant others have a greater anticipated communication utility for what they can get from the media. They use more of it, because their connections motivate them to do so. In Atkin's experiment (1972) it becomes evident that the effect is even stronger on *selective use* than on *amount* of use. The motivation to select or use more could be for persuasion purposes (most common, and reminiscent of Lazarsfeld, Berelson, & Gaudet [1944]). But it is also a matter of gaining prestige, or just collecting fodder as a basis for one kind of interaction—"small talk" (Chaffee, 1979; 1982).

Yet a third explanation for the positive covariation between media use and sociability is rooted in the nature of the use of mass media. At least some of the use of media is, in itself, a social act. The most obvious example is the act of going to the movies, clearly an interpersonal, as well as mass-communicated experience. Evidence shows that television is often watched in groups and the presence of close others (Chaffee, 1982; McQuail, Blumler, & Brown, 1972).

The Negative Correspondence-Substitutional Dynamics

A large portion of the research that reports substitution effects (i.e., negative correlations between mass media use and sociability) concerns children; almost all of these involve television. Riley and Riley (1951) report increased exposure to adventure stories among children who were relatively distant from those in their age group. Schramm's, Lyle's, and Parker's (1961) seminal study of television use by children located higher use of television among children who were in conflict with their parents, and those whose educational aspirations were at odds with (and usually lower than) those of their peers.

In two separate studies, Johnstone (1961; 1974) illustrates the same reverse covariation. Johnstone employs measures of sociometric status, feelings of attraction to the peer group, extent of friendship networks, and the extent the child felt "out in the cold." All measures correlated negatively with mass media use (especially television). In a creative interpretation of his and other's cross-sectional data longitudinally, Johnstone explains the sharp drop in television use among adolescents ages 15- to 18-year-old, as part of this same phenomenon. His argument is that maturation and introduction to significant others render obsolete the previous reliance on television.

All of the substitutional findings above are among children. Yet, the reversed relationship has been detected among adults as well. Using social organization participation, church membership, and frequency of visits to town among the rural poor of Appalachia as the gauges for sociability, Donohew (1967) found that the same sociability variables that had a positive covariation with newspaper and magazine use had a negative relationship to television and radio use. In at least one sense, Donohew's study is a replication of the diffusion of innovation studies reported earlier. Use of print mass media loaded highly on the same factor which included tolerance and openness to change; this factor included social isolation (coded inversely). A separate factor emerged in which "isolation from change" characteristics were found to go together with use of radio and television. Tellingly, Donohew labeled this the "housewife factor."

Also among adults, several empirical attempts within the literature on para-social interaction have attempted to replicate this finding of negative covariance. The para-social interaction research is reviewed separately

below. In that literature several different measures are used for gregariousness and social interaction. These measures vary from having leisure time
and owning a car, through having a partner and being married, to number
of friends, coworkers, etc., with whom one had a personal contact.
Rosengren and Windahl (1972), Nordlund (1978), and Levy (1979) report
negative associations between these measures and television use.

The temptation at this point could be to associate the negative relationship between sociability and media use with the differences between
television and print. This approach would attribute the seeming discrep-
ancy to channel differences. Chaffee (1979; 1982) suggests that, alternatively, the focus should be on the source, not the channel. From the
receiver's perspective the difference between print and television is in
accessibility to important sources and the likelihood of finding the needed
content with them. To the extent that interpersonal contexts create a need
for information, one is more likely to find any specific kind of desired
content in print. Most mass media users know this. From the receiver's
perspective, print is really a different set (and arrangement) of *sources,*
not so much a different channel. This source-rather-than-channel distinction is important is generalizing this model to the treatment of new
technologies, the computer in particular.

Katz and Foulkes (1962) provide the theoretical underpinnings for a
motivational explanation of the reverse, substitutional findings. Their
explanation is based on the concept of escape. Some media use, they say,
is a result of tensions or drives that stem from alienation or deprivation.
At least one dimension of this escapist function extracted from the mass
media by some people is to compensate for inadequacies in social interaction. Thus the lonely, socially deprived person can turn to mass-communicated images and messages to compensate for deficiencies in the social
environment.

In the same explication of escape, Katz and Foulkes join the rejection
of the simplistic channel-related explanation. From their perspective,
escapist use of media can be a form of use applied to any of the mass
channels, as well as to any content transmitted through them. The distinction between news and entertainment is also not very fruitful because both
can serve the escapist function. It just so happens that television fare (both
news and entertainment) contains more potentially escapist content. Chaffee (1979; 1982) enumerates the accessibility and availability reasons for
this difference. He emphasizes that they are not irreversible or fixed.

Summary

Both the communicatory utility explanation and the escape explanation
are instrumental approaches to understanding people's behavior in the

sociability-media context. Thus, while the predictions derived from each are in contradiction to the other, the overall approach to audience members and the behavior of media use is similar. Both approaches treat the receiver as rational, choice making, and acting on a perceived set of needs and defined motives. The escape-seeking viewer of television or reader of romantic stories in a magazine is just as motivated and rational an audience member as the stock-quotes reader of the *Wall Street Journal,* or recipe-hunter fan of (televised) Julia Child.

The two approaches seem to differ on the priorities of these uses and gratifications. Given the availability of some simultaneous evidence for both motivation-sets in simultaneous operation (Riley & Riley, 1951; Schramm, Lyle, & Parker, 1961; Donohew, 1967) we must accept the validity of both arguments. Further research requires the identification of one or more sociability scales that will allow—but could disprove—the discrimination between supplementary or substitutionary use of media as well as a more detailed examination of the kinds of sociability—Are there different dimensions?—in predicting media use.

Para-Social Interaction

Para-social interaction (PSI) is an illusion of face-to-face interaction. It is termed "para-social" because it is a figment of the imagination, a form of self-delusion. Para-social interaction is a subjective activity carried out by members of the audience, but it is a suggested (and alluring) intimacy that can be cultivated and maintained by designers of mass media content, especially radio and television, for their own commercial benefit.

The concept was introduced and defined by Horton and Wohl (1956), in an early treatment of the way mass media encroach on the interpersonal domain. Horton and Wohl contrast para-social interaction with ortho-social interaction. Para-social, or make-believe, interaction is a form of manipulation used by some mass media, especially by television and television celebrities. The manipulation of perceived interaction is intended to form a "bond of intimacy" between television and the personalities starring on it on one hand, and the audience television needs for survival on the other. PSI is invoked by several strategies of the television personae. The intended result is a larger, more loyal audience.

For the audience, the result is compliance and engagement in an unhealthy, one-sided, nonreciprocated, and controlled relationship. Audience members who find the experience unsatisfying have only one alternative to the self-delusion—to withdraw. Horton's and Wohl's (1956) observation has negative undertones for both the medium and its faithful audience. As Katz and Foulkes (1962) point out, the escapist outcome is not necessarily dysfunctional. Nevertheless, the connotation in use is commonly disapproving of the phenomenon, its victims, and those who exploit it.

Horton and Wohl conclude their seminal article by outlining two research questions. They state that the para-social interaction concept is a challenge to the then-pervasive assumption of a passive audience. Acknowledging the dynamics of para-social interaction required, for Horton and Wohl, a reexamination of the accredited hypothesis of the relatively passive audience. Para-social interaction, negative as it might be, is a form of audience activity, sense making, overt manipulation by the supposedly passive receivers. It also discriminates between members of the audience, identifying some who indulge in this process, and others who do not.

The second research challenge Horton and Wohl (1956) make is to "approach the phenomena from the viewpoint of interactional social psychology, [to] learn in detail how these para-social interactions are integrated into the matrix of usual social activity" (p. 207).

Several scholars in the communication field have responded to this challenge. All of the work done on the concept since the original publication in a psychiatry journal has been within the field of communication research. Further, all references to PSI since Horton and Wohl treated the concept from the receivers' perspective—as an individual difference, not a source strategy.

In a theoretically innovative departure from Horton's and Wohl's formulation, Rosengren and Windahl (1972) and Rosengren, Windahl, Hakansson, and Johnsson-Smaragdi (1976) define PSI as a condition that occus only in the absence of identification: when an audience member reaches the point of identifying with one or more personae, she or he is captured (presumably a state even worse than the self-delusion involved in PSI). Katz and Foulkes (1962), too, distinguish between identification and PSI. They point out that the former overwhelms the ego, while PSI has at least the potential positive effect of bolstering the ego of the person engaging in it. Other scholars conducting research on PSI such as Nordlund (1978), Levy (1979), and Houlberg (1984), steer away from this distinction.

The Measures

The operationalizations used in PSI research have evolved considerably. Rosengren and Windahl (1972) relied on a content analysis of responses to questions about media content preferences. Responses in personal terms classified their owners into the high PSI category. Those who responded to the question in programmatic or content terms were taken to be detached, or not engaged in PSI. Nordlund (1978) used a very similar measure based on the specific language used in answering an open-ended question about content preferences in each of the cases of television, radio, newspapers, and magazines.

The two most recent empirical studies of PSI employed closed-option questionnaire items as indices of PSI. Both Levy (1979) and Houlberg (1984) developed their own set of questions, each based on extensive focus group discussions and pretests. The items generated were in the form of propositions about the way the respondent perceives, thinks, or feels about media content or personae. Levy (1979) cites one participant in a focus group to illustrate sentiments captured by the PSI phenomenon: "I grew up watching Walter Cronkite. I guess I expect him to be there when I turn on the news. We've been through a lot together. Men on the moon and things like that" (p. 180).

The measures employed for sociability in the investigations of this model do not differ from those used in studies of sociability and mass media exposure (reviewed earler). Both Levy (1979) and Rosengren and Windahl (1972) used variations on an index of gregariousness consisting of the items introduced originally by Katz and Lazarsfeld (1955), in which the respondent was asked for the frequency of interpersonal discussions with friends, coworkers, and family. In addition, respondents were asked whether they usually watched television alone or with others. Secondary measures used as surrogates for sociability included age, education, sex (assuming men are more sociable), access to car and leisure time, and marital status. Nordlund (1978) employed a similar gregariousness item, as well as the Eysenck and Eysenck (1969) neuroticism scale.

The Model

The focus below is on the theoretical model shared by most of these studies, in which PSI is integrated into a larger scheme. The studies have in common a basic model of media use. The model relates psychological and social needs and drives to the needs and motivations for media use, as well as mass media exposure patterns, resulting in intended and unintended consequences. Para-social interaction is a link imposed between the social and psychological needs and the media exposure elements.

The empirical tests for the model are fairly similar and render comparable results. The association between PSI and media use is, as expected, positive and relatively strong (usually on the order of $r = .15$ to $.28$). This relationship fails to replicate for print use (Rosengren & Windahl, 1972; Nordlund, 1978); Levy (1979) focused solely on television.

The more complicated links in the model are those between sociability and media use on the one hand, and between sociability and PSI scores on the other. Measures for both associations (which are expected to be negative) were of questionable magnitude and borderline statistical significance. Regarding the relationship between social interaction and media use, Levy (1979) reports a positive, nonsignificant correlation. Nordlund (1978) found that the hypothesized negative covariation was neither particularly strong nor did it reach customary levels of statistical significance. Rosengren and Windahl (1972) report C coefficients of .09 and .16 for this relationship (in two different samples). This covariation is low and barely significant, and the C coefficient does not even provide information about the direction of covariation.

The direct link between social interaction and the propensity to engage in para-social interaction is even weaker than that between sociability and media consumption. Rosengren and Windahl (1972) find no significant covariation. Nordlund (1978) explains that the expected negative associations "were not manifested to any extent worthy of mention, [they were] neither strong nor significant." Levy (1979) reports an expected negative correlation ($r = -0.12$, $p < .05$), which is reduced to zero when educational level is controlled statistically.

In the face of such weak support for the theory, the choice is between abandoning the construct and a search for other ways to substantiate it. Two observations are offered here in line with the option of persisting with theory until measurement improves and data conforms. One probable reason for the weakness of the sociability-media use relationship is reviewed earlier. Sociability can and does operate both ways. It can affect the motivation and the actual use of mass media in both positive and negative ways. Following this logic, the low correlations reported may be interpreted as a reflection of the aggregate result, which explains the failure to confirm any part of the model for the use of print, but it also illuminates the difficulty in achieving statistical significance for the model with television use.

The second observation relates to the disappointing lack of association between para-social interaction and sociability. The authors mentioned above resort to secondary measures of sociability (i.e., education, age, having a car) whose covariation is more conforming to the predictions of the theory. The assumption is that education and physical mobility are powerful positive covariates of sociability, and age represents negative constraints on it. These secondary measures covary with television use in a more predictable manner. Relying in part on the support provided by these secondary measures, the authors refuse to give up on the concept. A reexamination of the theory that underlies the analysis may offer one more way out, and a circumspect validation for their stance.

Logically, the model is iterative, as any process implied by a use-and-gratification approach should be. Members of the audience go through a cycle of sensing needs and mechanisms for their fulfillment, constantly reassessing both the needs and the means and extent of satisfying them. Thus para-social interaction is hypothesized to be a vehicle through which some needs are fulfilled (the substitutional, escapist motivations discussed earlier). But PSI is also a moderating construct for the readjustment of the process. Since the model is iterative, better tests for its validity might be found in examining the role of PSI in a different way, perhaps better suited to test this nature of the model. One technique could be to view PSI as a moderating construct, which interacts with sociability to affect media exposure. Alternatively, PSI may be viewed as a step on an indirect path that leads from sociability to amount of media use. Both these options require information on more than just the bivariate associations of elements in the model, but neither are as sensitive to the weakness in measuring the bivariate covariation alone.

Both models have attendant statistical techniques designed to represent the theoretical argument in quantitative terms, and offer measures of goodness of fit. The former approach (PSI as a condition) can be represented as a general linear model in which mass media use (as the dependent variable) is regressed on sociability, PSI, and the interaction term (product of sociability and PSI). The contribution of the interaction term in explaining the variance in media use—over and above the additive contribution of the main effects—constitutes the test for the specific prediction that sociability covaries negatively with media use, especially in the presence of high levels of PSI. A schematic model of this approach is given in figure 7.1. The top figure depicts the basic sociability-media use relationship, conditioned by varying levels of PSI. The middle figure expresses the interaction in causal terms, highlighting the independent—and crucial for this model—role of the statistical interaction term. The bottom scheme shows the predicted interaction: only those who engage in much parasocial interaction should have their sociability affect the amount of their television watching.

The alternative approach (PSI as one indirect path of the effect of sociability on mass media use) is tested via the decomposition of the effects on mass media of the two independent variables in the model. Such a decomposition is possible via the statistics of causal models. The application of this technique requires only one additional assumption beyond that of the general linear model. The assumption of temporal asymmetry (i.e., sociability precedes PSI in time) is a fairly risk-free assumption. The schematic depiction of the path analysis appears in figure 7.2. The required assumption that para-social interaction is predetermined by sociability levels is not hard to accept. Such an assumption is implicit

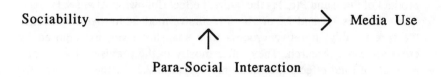

FIGURE 7.1
PSI as a Condition

PSI as a Condition in Causal Terms

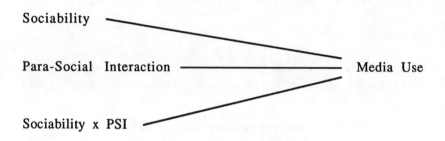

The Predicted Interaction

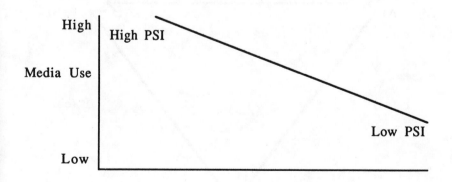

in the definition of para-social interaction. This model allows a decomposition of the total effect of sociability on media use into a direct and an indirect component (see figure 7.2): P(ab) is the direct effect, and the product of P(ac) and P(cb) is the indirect effect (following Alwin & Hauser, 1975). Figures 7.1 and 7.2 are both recursive models, in that they reduce the (presumably) iterative process to a snapshot level, as required by cross-sectional research. They differ mostly in the provision for decomposition of total effects afforded only by figure 7.2 vs. the provision for testing of an interactive effect afforded only by figure 7.1. While the causal model of figure 7.2 allows a quantitative gauge for the role of PSI in the indirect effect of sociability on media use, it requires an assumption of linear, and additive effects. Figure 7.1, on the other hand, assumes a conditioned interaction, which is ruled out by the assumptions of figure 7.2.

Summary

In summary, research on the concept of PSI has concentrated on the psychological aspects of the phenomenon. Measures of sociability and

FIGURE 7.2
Temporal Assymetry: PSI as a Path

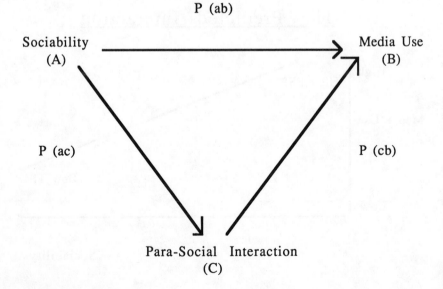

P (ab)

Sociability
(A)

Media Use
(B)

P (ac)

P (cb)

Para-Social   Interaction
(C)

media use employed in this literature were similar to those used in other literature about these concepts. The theory of PSI views it as a link in the uses and gratifications chain of reasoning, which connects social and interpersonal psychological needs to media-use behavior.

However, empirical work on the topic has failed to demonstrate the bivariate relationship between PSI and sociability. Although PSI has been shown to covary positively with media use, most projects that attempted to show the expected negative link between sociability and media use have been disappointed in their efforts. Two multivariate alternative approaches are suggested, in an attempt to demonstrate better the theory and to adhere to its logic better.

Research Questions

The following research questions serve as an outline for investigating the relationship of sociability to media use as modified by para-social interaction and real interaction.

Extent of Interactive Use

The degree to which people make use of any opportunities to interact with mass media is examined first. A substantial amount of active engagement in real, ortho-social interactions is a precondition for any of the ensuing discussion. As was stated earlier, interactivity should be viewed as a continuum. Various communication settings, interpersonal as well as mass, can be located along that continuum, but for this research project to shed any light on "interactivity" and its meaning, proof must be offered that the settings studied here (television and newspapers) are not at the very extreme low end of the interactivity continuum. Of interest are both the absolute extent of interactive behaviors and the degree of change over time. The hypotheses are that the degree of participation in interactive behaviors is both substantial and at a higher level in recent years than in the past. Has there been a spill-over of the interactivity trend to traditional media?

Demographics for Writers and Callers

As was shown, a dominant theme in the available literature on letters to the editor focuses on the demographic uniqueness of the letter writer and the talk show participant. Because of technological, social, and value-system changes, as well as the growth in opportunities afforded by the media themselves, some of the demographic "strangeness" of persons more apt to interact is likely to have eroded. Cross-sectional comparative analyses as well as (where possible) an across-time analysis of the demographic correlates of those engaging in these behaviors will be carried out to see which, if any, of the demographic predictors of ortho-social interactive use of the mass media have lost predictive power.

The hypothesis is that beyond the raw growth in the percentage of people interacting with the media there is also a change in the nature and demographic composition of those people. The design of earlier literature on writers of letters to the editor will be replicated to see whether the growth in numbers alters the demographic character of writers and callers.

Para-social Interaction as an Explaining/Intervening Construct in the Sociability-Media Use Correlation

The distribution across the para-social interaction (PSI) scale used in previous literature will be replicated, and the bivariate relationship of para-social interaction with sociability and television use will be tested.

The explanatory validity of the construct will be tested by examining two statistical models. On the one hand, the relative magnitude of the indirect path from sociability to television use via PSI, compared with the direct path connecting the two concepts, should provide a quantitative estimation of the relative role of PSI in the theoretical model of escapist use of media. The second approach will test the significance of the contribution of the interaction term representing the conditioning by PSI in a regression model for television use by sociability, over and above the main effects of sociability and the PSI construct alone. In addition to providing a statistical test for the contribution of the interaction beyond the main effects, this approach allows a graphic illustration of the way in which sociability and PSI interact in producing the variance they are hypothesized to produce in television use.

Both approaches are undertaken based on the hypothesis of a significant, negative effect of sociability on television use. At least part of this negative effect should be traced over a significant indirect path from sociability via PSI, to television use, or expressed as a significant statistical interaction of the two terms.

Real Interaction as an Explaining/Intervening Construct for the Relationship of Sociability and Media Use

Borrowing from the logic behind the analysis above, the examination of the role of ortho-social, or real, interactive behaviors will be conducted by substituting these behaviors for PSI in the models described above. Here, too, the interest is in the statistical significance of the interaction term over and above the contribution of the main effects of sociability and the act of using media interactively itself. In addition, in this section of the analysis sociability will be gauged in two different ways. The traditional, situational measures of sociability used by most authors (as well as in the former portion of this analysis) will be augmented by a measure of sociability disposition. The likelihood of people to desire friends, conversations with others, and opportunities to link into ortho-social interactions is separated from the actual behaviors or situations they are in. The entire model is, then, analyzed for both measures of sociability.

Analyses for real interaction are conducted only for the sociability-newspaper relationship and not for television. The relationships predicted here should hold across the different media (i.e., no independent channel main effect is implied). However, the literature's prediction of positive relationship between situational sociability and newspaper use is more robust than the predicted negative association of sociability and television use. Further, newspapers are likely to be placed much higher on what was termed here the interactive continuum. Appropriately, the indicator for interactive use of newspapers (writing a letter to the editor) represents a more clear-cut interaction than, for example, the act of calling a radio station, for a possible wide variety of reasons. This interactive behavior is also more frequent.

The assumption is that those who write letters to the editor are heavier users of newspapers than those who do not. Those who are (situationally) sociable read newspapers more often than the less sociable; they would also be expected to be more interactive in their use of newspapers. Similarly, people who are not disposed to be social are expected to be lower consumers of newspapers. Those who do not place a positive value on social interaction are also hypothesized to be less likely to interact with the mass media.

The last hypothesis holds for both measures of sociability, having social interactions in everyday life, and favoring the theoretical proposition of social interaction. The prediction is that a high score on sociability, together with interactive use of media (writing letters) are precursors of even higher consumption of newspapers than would be predicted from the additive effects of sociability and letter writing alone.

In the terminology of the path analytic model, the hypothesis is that the indirect component of the total effect of sociability on newspaper use which winds through ortho-social interaction with media is statistically significant.

Summary

The research questions begin with a descriptive question. Are mass media such as newspapers and television sufficiently interactive (at least in potential) so that a discussion of interactive use made of them can make sense?

The relationship of sociability to media use is the central concern. The hypotheses are predictions of the different manners in which this association is manifested, and more important, the different ways in which para-social interaction and real interaction intervene to explain this relationship. While para-social interaction ought to moderate (by strengthening) a substitutional dynamics between sociability and media use, the theoretical analysis predicts an interaction of ortho-social interaction on the supplementation effect. Or, in path analytic terms, a significant, positive, indirect effect via letter writing of sociability on newspaper use.

Method

Procedure and Sampling

The following analyses make use of data collected in two surveys. One was a random-digit-dialing telephone survey of adults in the San Francisco Bay Area. The survey was conducted in two phases, during January and February of 1985, and then during April and May of that year. Telephone numbers were selected on the basis of a table of random numbers, in conjunction with the telephone book. This method was used to ensure equitable inclusion in the sample of owners of unlisted and recently installed telephones, while minimizing the costs of dialing inoperative prefixes. Interviewers were instructed to make up to three calls to the same number, until response was achieved, or the number found to be disconnected or in a nonresidential location.

Interviewers were trained students. The interview schedules included 90 questions, all but one of them closed-ended, multiple-choice type. Interviewers introduced themselves as students and the survey as a study of mass communication use. The questionnaire was computerized. Interviewers, each seated in front of one microcomputer, read each question in turn and punched in the responses, causing the answer to be recorded and the next question to be projected. This procedure was employed to cut down on measurement error and processing time and costs. It also ensured that the only missing values were those introduced intentionally, by overt refusal to answer.

The instrument was an omnibus questionnaire, designed to explore several topics related to mass media use. Only the items relating to interactive use of media, para-social interaction, and general media use were used here. In all, 522 interviews were completed.

The population reached by the Bay Area survey is urban and suburban, therefore slightly higher in educational background and income and slightly younger than the general population. Very little difference from the general population is found on any other demographic distributions. Demographic comparisons between this sample and a national cross-section sample are available by examining the marginals of table 7.3.

Also reported here are secondary analyses of the Center for Political Studies' 1976 American National Election Study, Michigan University (Miller & Miller, 1977). The data were made available through the Inter-University Consortium for Political and Social Research. The study was designed to explore political attitudes and behavior in the context of the 1976 presidential campaign and elections in the United States. Items used included mass media behavior measures, measures of interpersonal interaction, social participation, social attitudes, and personal and political demographic information.

The CPS 1976 survey was conducted in two waves, in a pre- and postelection design. Items used there were drawn from both schedules. The total number of interviews completed was 2,248 in the preelection phase, and 1,909 in the postelection phase. A weighting variable, designed to form a representative cross-section and compensate for inadequacies resulting from the construction of the sample from subpanel groups, was applied to all responses according to specifications of the principal investigators.

Measurement and Scales

The scales used in the following analyses include indices of television and newspaper use, para-social interaction, sociability, and writing letters to the editor. The scale measuring para-social interaction was constructed following the items used by Levy (1979). Cronbach's alpha for interitem reliability on this scale as measured in the Bay Area survey was alpha = 0.70 (N = 522). The six items constituting this scale are detailed in table 7.4.

Two distinct scales were employed to measure situational sociability in the two samples. The items included in each of the scales are similar in nature to those used in previous research on sociability and media use. The purpose of the scales was to capture the amount of social, face-to-face interaction the respondent experienced in day-to-day life. The sociability scale constructed for the Bay Area survey consisted of eight items.

Respondents were asked whether they thought they had more or less friends than other people they knew. They were asked whether they usually watched television alone or in the presence of others. Respondents were asked about membership in social and fund-raising organizations. Marital status and number of persons in the respondents' household were also included in that scale. Respondents were asked for their self-assessment of how talkative they thought they were. Finally, the scale included the gregariousness item from Katz's and Lazarsfeld's (1955) seminal study: "How many friends (not coworkers or relatives) have you spoken to in the last week?" The sociability index formed by these eight items generated a Cronbach's alpha of 0.64.

The CPS 1976 National Election Survey data allowed the construction of scales for both situational sociability and dispositional sociability. Situational sociability was measured by fourteen items that closely approximated those used in the Bay Area setting. The items included five gregariousness questions about whether the respondent discussed important problems with close family, friends, coworkers, neighbors, and others. Two items asked about the degree to which other people tried to influence the respondent, and the degree to which the respondent tried to influence others' political opinions. Five items (addressed only to the posttest sample) inquired whether the respondents have discussed election results with close family, friends, etc. An organizational membership and activity item was also included. The overall Cronbach alpha reliability coefficient for this 14-item index was measured as 0.60. Dispositional sociability was measured by averaging the responses on two items taken from Rokeach's (1979) instrumental values scale: "How important is it to be well liked and friendly," and a reversed score on the question of how important it is to the respondent to be independent and self-reliant. The dispositional and situational sociability indices are slightly negatively correlated ($r = -0.10$).

Newspaper and television use were measured for the Bay Area survey using questions about weekly consumption of each medium, averaged respondent's self-assessment on the amount of use. The resulting newspaper-use scale varied between one and four, with a mean of 2.87. Television use was measured by the mean of the reported average number of hours of television watched each day, with the self-report on the overall use of television. This scale varies from zero to nine, with a mean of 4.03. Newspaper use was measured in the CPS National Election Survey by using an arithmetic mean index of eight items, each asking about how often the respondent reads daily newspaper reports about eight topics of interest—national politics, state and local politics, community events, sports, the election, international affairs, home gardening and hobbies, crime and accidents. Cronbach's alpha for the interitem reliability of this 8-item scale was measured at 0.66. Means and standard deviations for all the scales are provided in tables 7.5 and 7.10 for the Bay Area survey and the CPS 1976 secondary analysis, respectively. Breakdowns in tables 7.7, 7.10, 7.14, and 7.17 are around the median.

Results

The presentation of results begins with findings regarding the extent of interactive use of mass media. The tests for the role of para-social interaction follow. The results chapter concludes in an examination of ortho-social interaction in the context of the same model.

Some dimensions of the extent of interactive use of mass media are described in tables 7.1 and 7.2. In contrast to earlier literature on the topic, Bay Area survey estimates the level of letter writing (measured as the self-report of having written at least one letter to either a local or national newspaper) at almost one-third of the population. Not surprisingly, more people (27.3%) have written to daily newspapers than to magazines (20.8%). These figures are essentially a replication of the levels of letter writing found by the secondary analysis of the CPS 1976 National Elections survey, but much higher than previously reported levels of 3%–15%.

Writing to a newspaper is the most common mode of interacting with the print media. More people have written a letter than either canceled a subscription in protest (a surprisingly high 13.1%) or called a newspaper newsroom (24.6%). With the sole exception of canceling subscriptions, people who reported engaging in each of the interactive situations are likely to have done so more than once; that is, writing letters to the editor as a way of communicating with print mass media for most people who have done so was not a one-time experience. The evidence in table 7.1 stops short of proving or even indicating an addictive effect. However, this tendency to write more than once, if one writes at all, does seem to rule out aversion by experience. The items in table 7.1 are not mutually exclusive, hence the percentages do not add up to 100%. Summing across all interactive options, we find that over 40% of the population surveyed have found one or more ways to send a message back to the print mass media.

The findings for real interaction with broadcast mass media do not differ in essence from those for the interactive use of the print media. As seen in table 7.2, the preferred mode of interacting with the medium is closely tied to the syntax of the medium. People would more likely call a radio station than write to it, just as they are more likely to write to a newspaper than call it. Slightly more than one in five persons in the population surveyed

TABLE 7.1
Interacting with Print Mass Media, Percentages of Interactants and Noninteractants
(N = 522)

	% Yes Many times	% Yes 2 or 3	% Yes once	% No (total)	% Yes
Interacting Behavior:					
Written letter to editor of daily newspaper?	7.2	13.0	7.2	72.7	27.3
Written letter to editor of any other periodical publication?	4.0	10.8	6.2	79.2	20.8
Have written ANY letter?				68.6	31.4
Cancelled a subscription to a newspaper in protest of something published	1.7	3.8	7.6	86.9	13.1
Called a newspaper newsroom for information about news	5.5	14.0	5.1	75.4	24.6
Had ANY interaction with print mass media?				59.8	40.2

Source: Bay Area Sample.
Note: The items are not mutually exclusive. Some respondents engaged in more than one of these behaviors.

TABLE 7.2
**Interacting with Electronic Mass Media, Percentages of Interactants and
Noninteractants**
(N = 522)

Interacting Behavior:	% Yes Many times	% Yes 2 or 3	% Yes once	% No (total)	% Yes (total)
Called-in to radio or television talkshow?	3.2	7.8	7.2	81.8	18.2
Called radio or television station to give information	3.5	7.3	5.8	83.5	16.5
ANY participative use of radio or television? (summing across both items)				79.5	20.5
Called radio or television station to get information	8.1	21.3	13.2	57.4	42.6
Written to radio or television station	4.2	9.3	7.6	78.8	21.2
ANY interaction with broadcast media? (summing across all four items)				52.9	47.1

Source: Bay Area Sample.

Note: The items are not mutually exclusive. Some respondents engaged in more than one of these behaviors.

have taken part in the participative contexts of radio and television talk shows or other opportunities for getting on the air. An even larger portion of the population surveyed (42.6%) have called radio or television stations in order to get information. Unfortunately, the data at hand do not disclose the proportion of people who did so with the provision that they not be "put on the air." Here, too, the items are not exclusive. Nearly one-half of the respondents (47.1%) have chosen to interact with radio or television in ways more active and more individualized than just being an anonymous part of what might be a supposed mass, passive audience.

National data show that the number of radio stations in the United States that were licensed to broadcast in the talk show and all-news formats has grown by almost 60% in the decade between the mid-1970s and the mid-1980s. This figure reflects only the number of stations whose *primary* format (as licensed by the FCC) is the talk show format. In addition, many stations with other formats have, in the past ten to fifteen years, instituted call-in and participation forums as part of their daily schedule, or as segments of programs under another primary format.

The growth of talk-show radio does not seem to be at the expense of a number of other interactive electronic mediated forms. In fact, this growth parallels (in time) the first implementations of interactive cable television (Becker, Dunwoody, & Rafaeli, 1983), and the emergence of videotex and teletext (Rogers, 1986). It is not even at the expense of the closely related radio format of all-news, which has exhibited accelerated growth (of over 150%) itself.

Who Are the Writers?

Table 7.3 presents a replication of the demographic analysis of letter writers reviewed earlier. The 1972 column (table 7.3) repeats the findings reported by Buell (1975). It should be recalled that, of those who studied the question, Buell reported the *least* demographic differences between writers and nonwriters. His data are based on the CPS 1972 National Election Study (NES). His findings were that writers were wealthier, more educated, and significantly more likely to be Republicans in their political orientation. Buell found no statistically significant differences for sex, race, or age of nonwriters and writers. The 1976 and 1985 columns in table 7.3 repeat the analysis of the 1972 sample. The overall trend is toward decreased differences between letter writers and others. The difference in education levels is the only demographic discriminator that retains discriminating power across all three samples and over the time span studied here. Age, sex, and race are unrelated to the choice of writing or not. Furthermore, whatever (nonsignificant) differences initially existed on these crite-

TABLE 7.3
Demographic Characteristics of Writers and Nonwriters, by Group, in Percentages
(1972, 1976, 1985)

Category	1972 (1)		1976 (2)		1985 (3)	
========	========		========		========	
	Wr	N.Wr	Wr	N.Wr	Wr	N.Wr
Sex:	n.s.		n.s.		n.s.	
Male	49	42	43	42	44	42
Female	52	58	58	57	56	58
Race:	n.s.		n.s.			
White	93	89	88	86	N.A	
Non-white	7	11	11	14		
Age:	n.s.		n.s.		n.s.	
17-25	16	18	15	17	15	27
26-35	20	20	29	22	22	20
36-45	22	17	18	13	29	19
46-55	20	16	13	15	12	13
56 or older	22	29	24	34	23	21
Income:	**		*		n.s.	
Less than $9,999	25	55	29	46	36	37
$10,000-14,999	26	23	22	23	9	19
$15,000 or more	39	19	49	31	55	44
Education:	**		**		**	
Less than h. shc.	4	21	5	21	4	9
High school	38	51	42	54	38	54
College or more	58	28	53	26	58	38
Party Identification:	**		*		n.s.	
Republican	26	25	25	22	21	20
Independent	41	27	34	27	35	36
Democrat	32	40	35	41	40	34
Other, no pref.	1	8	6	10	4	10
Sample Size (N =):						
Writers	163		766		164	
Non-Writers	2027		2104		358	
Overall	2190		2870		522	

Sources: Buell (1975).

1 Based on 1972 CPS NES.

2 Based on 1976 CPS National Election Study.

3 Based on 1985 Bay Area Survey.

*   = Significant at p < .05 for this demographic category.

**   = Significant at p < .01 for this demographic category.

n.s. = No significant difference for this demographic category.

ria, they have eroded over time. Regrettably, data for racial distributions are not available for the 1985 data. Both financial status and political stance have diminished as predictors of letter writing: the statistical significance of the demographics predictors of letter writing has shrunk by 1976, and vanished altogether by 1985.

Para-Social Interaction

Table 7.4 replicates the distribution of Bay Area responses to Levy's (1979) para-social interaction items. A comparison of the distribution of responses in table 7.4 to Levy's findings (p. 180) shows no meaningful differences. The items were all phrased in such a way that agreement with them is indicative of para-social interaction. At least one-third of the respondents agreed with each of the six items, and only two of the items were rejected by more than one-half of the sample. All but one of the items received endorsements from nearly one-half of the sample. Such level of support for most items indicates that para-social interaction occurs on

TABLE 7.4
Distribution of Responses to Para-Social Interaction Items
(N = 522)

Question:	Strongly Agree	Agree	Not Sure	Disagree	Strongly Disagree
"Television newscasters are almost like friends you see every day"	2.3	38.6	4.4	46.1	8.5
"I like hearing the voices from television in my house"	2.0	47.6	13.9	32.7	3.7
"When newscasters show how they feel it helps me make up my mind"	0.2	33.5	6.7	51.4	8.1
"I like comparing my own ideas with what newscasters say"	7.9	65.6	4.3	21.1	1.0
"The joking around on television makes the news easier to take"	1.6	42.8	7.2	39.8	8.6
"I feel sorry for television personalities when they make mistakes"	2.4	43.3	7.4	43.9	3.0

Source: Bay Area Survey, 1985.
Note: Response scale as displayed.

both the emotional and the cognitive levels. The sentiments that refer to friendship, joking, and empathy received about the same level of support as the items about "comparing ideas" and "making up my mind." As indicated in the literature on para-social interaction, the even distribution of agreement with these statements points to the validity and applicability of the concept.

PSI and the Sociability-Media Use Model

The bivariate correlations associated with the hypothesized model involving sociability, para-social interaction, and television use are reported in table 7.5. Television use is positively associated with PSI ($r = 0.25$). As expected, there is only a weak (but significant) negative correlation between television use and sociability ($r = -.06$).

The hierarchical regression reported in table 7.6 serves as the test for the hypothesized model. Only a very modest 6% of the variance in television use is explained by the complete model which contains all three terms: the effect of sociability, the effect of PSI, and the interaction term of sociability and PSI. But the increments in R square for each step of the model are significant, as are the standardized beta coefficients of the newly added term at each step. In the transition from the second to the third

TABLE 7.5
Univariate and Bivariate Statistics for Scales Used in Tables 7.6 and 7.8
(N = 522)

	Y1	Y2	X1	X2	Mean	S.D.
Y1 Television Use	-				4.03	1.78
Y2 Print Use	.10	-			2.87	0.87
X1 Sociability	-.06	.13	-		1.64	0.25
X2 PSI	.25	-	.25	-	1.93	0.75
X3 Writing letters	-.11	.12	.10	-.12	0.32	0.47

Source: Based on Bay Area Survey, 1985.
All reported correlations are significant at the p < .05 level.

TABLE 7.6
Hierarchical Regression of Television Use, by Sociability and PSI

Step Number	Variable Entered	Multiple R	Increment in Adjusted R squared	F for increment	D.F.
1	Sociability	.10	.01	4.2 (*)	1,482
2	PSI	.21	.03	11.9 (*)	2,481
3	PSI X Sociability	.24	.02	9.4 (*)	3,480

Standardized Coefficients

Equation	Variable	Value
1	Sociability	-.10 (*)
2	Sociability	-.10 (*)
	PSI	.19 (*)
3	Sociability	-.14 (*)
	PSI	.06
	PSI X Sociability	.15 (*)

Source: Based on 1985 Bay Area Survey
* p < .05

hierarchical step, when the interaction term is added to the model, the significance of the contribution of PSI's main effect is eliminated. That could be due to high correlation between PSI and the interaction term. Thus, the hypothesis is provided limited support, pending an examination of the elimination of one of the main effects.

Such an examination is provided in table 7.7. Two graphic depictions of the statistical interaction are displayed at the bottom of the table. Subjects were grouped into low- and high-sociability and PSI groups, around the respective medians. Graphing the cell means separately for the two sociability groups (on the right-hand side) shows how the positive association between PSI and television use is stronger for those in the low-sociability group. This is consistent with the hypothesis, since PSI is supposed to serve as the vehicle for negative sociability effects on television use.

On the other hand, the graph on the left of table 7.7 explains why the main effect for PSI "washes out" once the interaction term is introduced into the regression model. One way of reading this graph is to observe a form of ceiling effect in operation here. People who are high on para-social interaction watch so much television that sociability cannot account for any more variance. This interaction is in line with the underlying logic behind the original hypothesis but takes a different form than predicted. The current form strengthens the statement about the importance of PSI. An alternative explanation for the graph on the left (which partitions for PSI levels) is that PSI is an effect of television watching, and should be viewed as following television temporally. This explanation is still in line with the escapist theory of sociability and media use, but is untested by these cross-sectional data. However, acceptance of this alternative explanation renders the analysis in table 7.8 invalid.

The path model displayed in table 7.8 conducts a decomposition of the studied effect into direct and indirect paths. Given the rather modest total effect of sociability on television use reported in table 7.6—($r = -.06$)— it is not surprising that the decomposed paths (which sum to it) are so small. However, the direct contribution of sociability to television use is, as expected, in an opposite direction to that of the direct effect of PSI.

The indirect contribution from sociability via PSI to television use is at the center of the escapist model studied here. The total indirect effect is small, but it consists of paths that are in the hypothesized direction, and each is larger than sociability's direct effect on television use. We may, therefore, conclude that although the model is consistent with the statistical test, there are still other ways through which sociability takes away from television watching. The indirect path leading from sociability through PSI to television use is only one course this influence can take, and by no means the largest.

TABLE 7.7
Interaction Pattern and Cross-Tabulation for Television Use, by Para-Social
Interaction, and Sociability
(N = 522)

Average Television Use

Para-Social Interaction

		Low	High
Sociability	Low	3.81 (N=122)	4.83 (N=139)
	High	3.47 (N=105)	4.36 (N=126)

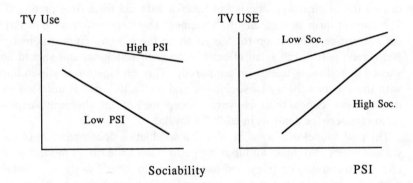

Source: Based on Bay Area Survey, 1985.

TABLE 7.8
A Path Model of Sociability Effects on PSI and Television Use

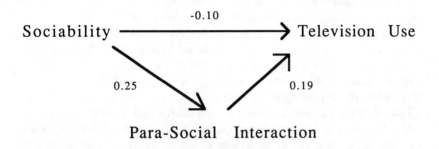

The Decomposition of the Total Effect of Sociability on Television Use

Total Effect	Indirect Effect via PSI	Direct Effect
-0.06	0.05	-0.10

Source: Bay Area Survey.

Sociability and Print-Media Use

Turning now to evidence on the role of real, ortho-social interaction in the context of sociability and print media, we first examine the findings on the basic sociability-media use relationship. Returning to table 7.5, we find that the bivariate association between sociability and print-media use (as measured in the 1985 Bay Area sample) was a low positive correlation ($r = .13$, $p < .05$). This is in accordance with the hypothesis and the theory of communicatory utility from which it was derived. The interpretation is that sociable people—those who consider themselves more talkative, have more interpersonal interactions, think of themselves as surrounded by friends, watch television with others, and are not living alone—are more likely to read more newspapers. Other people, who score lower on this sociability index, have less of an instrumental reason to seek information in print.

However, as table 7.9 reveals, when sociability is separated into the two components of situation and disposition, as became possible by using the CPS 1976 data, a more complex pattern emerges. The two sociability measures are not associated in the same way with print use. The situational measure for sociability yielded findings comparable to those from the Bay Area survey. The correlation here is rather strong in relation to customary findings in this field ($r = 0.38$, $p < .01$). Since the two indices are similar, the interpretation is identical: situational sociability is positively associated with print use, because the two supplement each other. This is in accordance with the hypotheses.

TABLE 7.9
Univariate Statistics and Intercorrelations for Scales Used in Tables 7.10–7.12, 7.16–7.18
(N = 2340)

	Y	X1	X2	Mean	S.D.
Y Newspaper Use	—			3.38	0.98
X1 Sociability #1 (Situational)	.38	-		1.69	0.93
X2 Sociability #2 (Dispositional)	-.14	-.10	-	2.92	1.15
X3 Letter Writing	.30	.33	-.08	0.29	0.45

Source: Based on CPS National Election Survey, 1976.
All reported correlation coefficients significant at $p < .01$.

But the correlation for print use with the disposition toward sociability is negative and statistically significant ($r = -0.14$, $p < 0.01$). This negative association between disposition toward sociability and media use could be interpreted in one of two ways. We may view dispositions as either a precursor of situations, an outcome, or an attitude that exists in relative independence of the reality of the person's life. The data at hand do not allow a test of this fundamental social science issue.

If we assume reasoned action in the social arena—that the actual sociability of a person is partly a product of one's motivation to be sociable—then the negative correlation between situational sociability and the dispositional measure of sociability ($r = -.10$; table 7.9) can only be interpreted as reflecting an even-stronger negative association between the attitude about being friendly and yet a third theoretical component of sociability. This third component is, logically, some measure of objective opportunities for, and barriers to, interaction. Under these conditions, the objective opportunities for social interaction that one has must vary inversely with attitudes about sociability. This circumstance is not likely.

Alternatively, we might assume that dispositions about interacting with others are relatively independent of situations, or codetermined by preceding factors (inter alia, the objective opportunities to interact). In this case, the interpretation of the observed negative association between preference for interaction and the use of print media is similar to the substitutional dynamics, previously elaborated only for broadcast media. The instrumental utility-driven supplementation-process is not in force here. Instead, a substitution process is indicated.

People with a highly favorable disposition toward being sociable are likely to spend more of their resources (primarily time and psychological energy) seeking face-to-face interactions. They might not actually find more of these opportunities—witness the slight negative association between disposition and situational sociability ($r = -.10$, $p < .01$; table 7.9). But they are less likely to be spending time with other, "irrelevant" activities (such as reading the newspaper). Their counterparts, those who do not value social interactions, will do other, presumably more valuable, things with their time. One of these subjectively more valuable activities can be reading newspapers. The study of Schramm, Lyle, and Parker (1961) on reading and the work ethic comes to mind. In their Denver Study they found that use of reality-oriented media is related positively to adherence to some social norms about future orientation. Those who believed in working harder today so that tomorrow could be enjoyed better were much higher consumers of print.

The role of the objective opportunities for face-to-face interactions is also central to sketching the picture here. Unfortunately, reliable measures of social opportunities (as distinct from measures of making use of such opportunities) are not available. However, the focus of the present study is on the opportunities for real interaction provided by mass media arrangements, so we now return to examining the role of these in the sociability-print-use context.

Real Interaction and the Sociability-Media Use Model

The hypothesized positive effect of the interaction between writing letters to the editor and situational sociability was found to be statistically significant. Table 7.10 displays the hierarchical regression (for the CPS 1976 data), in which both the terms for the main effect for writing letters

TABLE 7.10
Hierarchical Regression of Newspaper Use, by Situational Sociability and Letter Writing

Step Number	Variable Entered	Multiple R	Increment in Adjusted R squared	F for increment	D.F.
1	Situational Sociability	.37	.14	387.9 (*)	1,2359
2	Letter Writing	.42	.03	249.2 (*)	2,2358
3	Writing X Sociability	.44	.01	173.2 (*)	3,2357

Standardized Coefficients

Equation:	Variable	Value
1	Situational Sociability	.37 (*)
2	Sociability	.31 (*)
	Writing	.19 (*)
3	Sociability	.36 (*)
	Writing	.37 (*)
	Writing X Sociability	.12 (*)

Source: Based on CPS National Election Survey, 1976.
* p < .05

and for sociability, and the interaction with situational sociability, produce a significant and positive coefficient. A graphic display of this effect is provided in the two graphs at the bottom of table 7.11. The path model (table 7.12) reveals that the indirect effect of sociability on print use via letter writing is not a very large portion of the total effect (only one-sixth of the total effect, $r = 0.38$), but it is statistically significant, and in the expected direction.

Situational sociability is associated with higher use of newspapers. Letter writing is related positively to the consumption of print media, as hypothesized. The presence of both conditions (many situations of interacting with others plus writing letters to editors) is associated with even

TABLE 7.11
Interaction Pattern, Cross-tabulation for Newspaper Use, by Letter Writing and Situational Sociability
(N = 2340)

Average Newspaper Use

Letter Writing

		No	Yes
	Low	2.93	3.42
		(N=999)	(N=192)
Sociability			
	High	3.29	3.98
		(N=718)	(N=493)

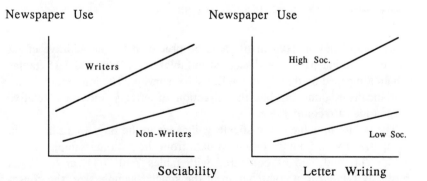

Source: Based on CPS National Election Survey, 1976.

TABLE 7.12
**A Path Model of Situational Sociability Effects on Real Interaction and
Newspaper Use**

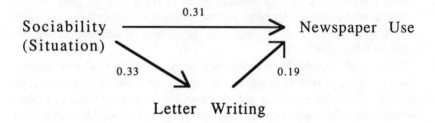

Decomposition of the Effect of Situational Sociability on Newspaper Use

Total Effect	Indirect Effect via Real Interaction	Direct Effect
0.38	0.06	0.31

Source: Based on CPS National Election Survey, 1976.

more use of newspapers than would be predicted by the additive effect alone. A similar pattern is discerned in tables 7.13, 7.14, and 7.15 (tables which are based on data from the Bay Area survey). The interaction is not statistically significant, but the direction of effects and their relative magnitudes are comparable.

The failure to achieve statistical significance in the Bay Area sample, in comparison with findings based on data from the national sample (tables 7.13, 7.14, and 7.15 as compared with tables 7.10, 7.11, and 7.12) is probably related to a combination of the smaller sample-size, the consequently relatively small size of the letter-writers low-sociability group, and

TABLE 7.13
Hierarchical Regression of Newspaper Use, by Sociability and Letter Writing

Step Number	Variable Entered	Multiple R	Increment in Adjusted R squared	F for increment	D.F.
1	Sociability	.13	.01	8.0 (*)	1,482
2	Writing Letters	.16	.01	6.7 (*)	2,481
3	Writing X Sociability	.17	.01	4.5 (*)	3,480

Standardized Coefficients

Equation:	Variable	Value
	========	======
1	Sociability	.13 (*)
2	Sociability	.12 (*)
	Writing	.10 (*)
3	Sociability	.07 n.s.
	Writing	.002 n.s.
	Writing X Sociability	.12 n.s.

Source: Based on Bay Area Survey, 1985.
* p < .05

the weak total effect that serves as the backdrop for this analysis (r = 0.10, table 7.6). The sociability scale used for the Bay Area survey is, perhaps, not as good a gauge for communication utility.

The interpretation of the relatively small portion of the indirect effect (as displayed in the path models, tables 7.12 and 7.14) is of special interest. It is important to realize that the supplementation hypothesis with regard to real interaction does not necessarily predict a large share for the indirect path. Unlike the analysis for para-social interaction, only the presence of such a path is predicted, and (the observed) positive sign. The direct path from sociability to print use (explained by the instrumental utility hypothesis) is still the major effect. The process of supplementing one's social ties by seeking more information and using (print) media more is revalidated (the direct effect). The added information provided here is that when the opportunity for real interaction with mass media is used, the result for sociable people is even more supplementation between sociability and media use.

TABLE 7.14
Interaction Pattern and Cross-tabulation for Newspaper Use, by Letter Writing
and Sociability
(N = 522)

<u>Average Newspaper Use</u>

Letter Writing

		No	Yes
Sociability	Low	2.75 (N=191)	2.83 (N=73)
	High	2.86 (N=144)	3.16 (N=86)

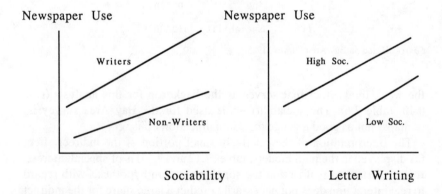

Newspaper Use   Newspaper Use

Writers   High Soc.

Non-Writers   Low Soc.

Sociability   Letter Writing

Source: Based on Bay Area Survey, 1985.

Finally, we turn to the problematic model of disposition toward sociability and print use (tables 7.16, 7.17, and 7.18). As was stated earlier, a full interpretation of these findings is complicated by the absence of a counterpart measure of objective opportunities for social interaction. The weak evidence here speaks to a possible substitutional relationship, in which dispositions about the importance of social relations have a slight negative

TABLE 7.15
A Path Model of Sociability Effects on Real Interaction and Newspaper Use

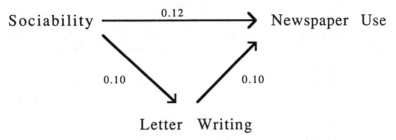

The Decomposition of the Total Effect of Sociability on Newspaper Use

Total Effect	Indirect Effect via Letter Writing	Direct Effect
0.14	0.01	0.12

Source: Based on Bay Area Survey, 1985.

relationship to print use. As is shown in table 7.16, the act of writing letters to the editor interacts significantly with dispositions about sociability in explaining newspaper use. The beta for the interaction term is positive and significant, as is the increment in percent of variance explained (change in adjusted R square). However, both are rather small.

The meaning of the curious interaction between disposition toward sociability and letter writing is better elaborated by examining the left-hand graph in table 7.17. Writing letters to the editor contributes to decreasing the negative relationship between dispositions and newspaper use. In other words, the act of writing letters to the editor detracts from the substitution process. Looking at the same interaction plotted on the right-hand side of the table we find the same relationship. The positive association of letter writing and newspaper use is even stronger for those who say they value interpersonal relations. The respondents for whom interpersonal relations are of high priority are likely to have a weaker relationship between letter writing and newspaper consumption. As can be viewed by examining the path model displayed in table 7.17, this phenomenon is not a very powerful one and accounts for only a small portion of the modest total negative effect of dispositions on newspaper use.

TABLE 7.16
**Hierarchical Regression of Newspaper Use, by Sociability Disposition and
Letter Writing**

Step Number	Variable Entered	Multiple R	Increment in Adjusted R squared	F for increment	D.F.
1	Sociability Disposition	.14	.02	49.2 (*)	1,2359
2	Letter Writing	.32	.10	134.1 (*)	2,2358
3	Writing X Sociability (Disposition)	.33	.11	91.3 (*)	3,2357

Standardized Coefficients

Step:	Variable ========	Value ======
1	Sociability (Disposition)	-.14 (*)
2	Sociability (D)	-.12 (*)
	Writing	.28 (*)
3	Sociability (D)	-.15 (*)
	Writing	.17 (*)
	Writing X Sociability	.12 (*)

Source: Based on Bay Area Survey, 1985.
* p < .05

Summary

    Interactive use of mass media, in the form of writing letters to the editor and calling broadcast talk shows are shown to be large scale and growing behaviors. The two central hypotheses in our study received some support. The psychological exercise of engaging in para-social interaction was shown to play a significant role in the *substitutional* dynamics predicted by the literature: the use of television for escape purposes, which results in more television use when there is less social interaction. In contrast, the role of one overt manifestation of ortho-social interaction, the behavior of writing letters to the editor, is significant in the reverse, *supplementation* process. The choice people make to carry out real interactions with the mass media is a significant (though small) part of supplementing their sociability with media consumption.

TABLE 7.17
Interaction Pattern, Cross-tabulation for Newspaper Use, by Letter Writing and Disposition toward Sociability
(N = 2340)

Average Newspaper Use

Letter Writing

		No	Yes
	Low	3.32	3.88
		(N=821)	(N=388)
Sociability (Disposition)			
	High	3.08	3.79
		(N=860)	(N=293)

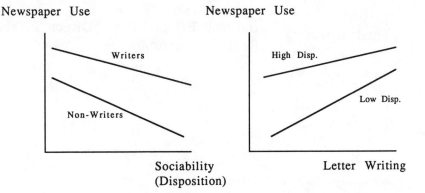

Newspaper Use   Newspaper Use

Writers   High Disp.

Low Disp.

Non-Writers

Sociability   Letter Writing
(Disposition)

Source: Based on CPS National Election Survey, 1976.

The exceptions to these findings (or unconfirmed hypotheses) are illustrative, too. Contrary to expectations, the favorable dispositions regarding sociability were found to relate inversely to newspaper consumption. This curious failure to confirm the hypothesis is, again, reminiscent of Schramm's, Lyle's, and Parker's (1961) Denver Study. The role of letter writing in this relation is to mitigate the negative, or substitutional effect.

At least in the case of the use of newspapers and the situational measures of sociability, our study provides support for a supplementation process, explained as information seeking driven by communication-utility motivations. The findings proceed to offer support for the argument that the

TABLE 7.18
A Path Model of Sociability Disposition Effects on Real Interaction and Newspaper Use

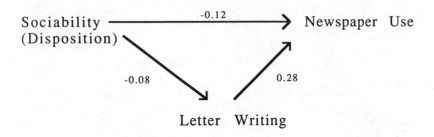

The Decomposition of the Effect
of Sociability Disposition on Newspaper Use

Total Effect	Indirect Effect via Real Interaction	Direct Effect
-0.14	0.02	-0.12

Source: Based on CPS National Election Survey, 1976.

interactive element of using newspapers, represented here as writing letters to the editor, contributes to this supplementation process in a manner similar to the way para-social interaction contributes to the reciprocal substitution between sociability and television use.

Discussion

The approach taken in this study differs from previous work on interactivity in at least three ways: (1) in its survey approach to a problem currently being studied mostly in the laboratory; (2) the act of interactivity is studied here with relation to traditional mass media rather than new media of communication; and (3) the focus is on a mediating or intervening role of media-generated interaction rather than on interactivity either as an effect or as an independent variable.

Nevertheless, some motivation for the interest in the relationship of interactivity to sociability and mass media use is of mainstream communication research nature. There is a growing interest in the sociability of the users of new communication technologies (and especially computer-mediated communication systems). The question is addressed on several levels by researchers. In a seminal statement on the social psychology of telecommunication, Short, Williams, and Christie (1976) devote an entire discussion to the "social presence" of a medium. In their footsteps, Hiltz and Turoff (1978), Kiesler, Siegel, and McGuire (1984), and Rice (1984) study the connectivity, consensus, and emotional arousal associated with communication via computer-mediated systems. Dependent measures vary from content analyses of the nature of responses to the number of malt balls eaten by participants in group discussions. Findings vary as well, but the overall approach is to test notions about computer users that have become folk wisdom. Beniger (1987) broadens this psychological variable to sociological dimensions. He argues that a major societal change is forming, pushing "upward the curve of trade-off between population size and societal control."

In this "folk" wisdom, computer users are no longer depicted as just maladjusted "nerds" (or low in sociability, using the present terminology). Armed with modems, and equipped with esoteric secrets, the ominous "hackers" are cracking bank safes as well as hastening World War III in the popular media image. As long as these images are ascribed to the sociability (or lack thereof) of computer users, they are of little interest. But once the connection is made between attributes of computers and these awful outcomes, the leap from folk wisdom to generalization might be made. Kiesler, Siegel, and McGuire (1984) are among the first to analyze this concern. They say that because of the qualities that typify the computer-mediated communication setting (most of which can be related to interactivity), there is at least a potential of depersonalization and social anonymity. According to them, this can invite "stronger or more uninhibited text and more assertiveness in return. It might be especially hard to communicate liking or intimacy without writing unusually positive text. . . . [Users may] lose sight of the fact that they are addressing other people, not the computer" (pp. 1125–26).

The modest findings of the present research project should be examined within this framework. At least in the context of interactive use of newspapers, and with regard to writing letters to the editor as the form of interactive use under study, the role of interactivity was shown to be more complex. In fact, our findings do not address the effect of a medium at all.

The findings reported here do not contest untested antisocial effects such as alienation or anomie, but they do show that interactive use of media can make a positive contribution to a functional supplementation process associated with interpersonal communication.

Let us contrast the findings regarding real interaction and print mass media with the link between para-social interaction and broadcast media. Both print and television are forms of mass communication. Both PSI and writing letters to the editor are forms of interaction. The difference between them is that PSI is a psychological illusion held by those engaging in it. Writing letters to the editor is a reality made possible by adding interactivity potentials to a communication setting that, otherwise, is a one-way (not even reactive) system. But the difference in their roles is that PSI acts to enhance a use of the medium by people for purposes of escape. Letters to the editor, on the other hand, are part of the process of using print media to bolster social contacts.

If one accepts a view of the press as generally reflecting reality, and if situational sociability is taken to be a positive attribute, the effect of introducing a facilitating mechanism for mutual supplementation of both can be viewed as favorable. Interactivity allowed by letters to the editor is, under these conditions, functional to both individual and society. In the same vein, the present findings can be contrasted with the tone of research on letter writing reviewed earlier. Beyond showing that the behavior is more widespread than had been reported, the model tested here relates to the safety valve hypothesis of letters to the editor (Davis & Rarick, 1964) and the observation that call-in talk radio houses a disproportionate amount of mentally-ill participants. Beyond diffusing negative energy, interactive use of media makes a modest but significant contribution toward a proactive end. Interactivity, as represented here by letters to the editor, is not only associated with more use of mass media but with more use by the more situationally sociable, to a degree that exceeds that predicted by the misleading bivariate covariations.

Treating situational sociability and more use of print media as exclusively positive notions is, of course, presumptuous. No claim is made here that interactivity is an unblemished, completely functional characteristic, and that every medium should always have two of it. One can think of some of the dysfunctions interactivity can account for in the context of mass media. As in other communication contexts, a more responsive system is both slower and expensive, and can be less accurate. Comprehensibility may be hindered, so making the press more responsive to its writing-readers could hinder other functions it needs to provide. Under some conditions, the effect might even be the paradoxical detraction from the democratic values of a medium.

The functionality of interactivity in mass media for either the individual or society is not a linear, positive one. To some extent, letters to the editor do not get published and/or do not get read or heeded. It is even possible that the supposed interaction provided by letters to the editor is a form of self-deluding, para-social interaction rather than the relatively constructive ortho-social variety of interaction. The point here is different. Interactivity may have both functions and dysfunctions for those engaging in it and for the society. Similar to the sociability-media use model in which this analysis is rooted, the relationship may flow either way. Real interaction may provide the backdrop for either real participation or escape and vicarious participation. Either of these paths can be either functional or dysfunctional. The preceding analysis has shown the operation of one of these four possibilities, but it does not test or disconfirm any of the others.

As in many empirical studies, our research has limitations of method, scope, and potential generalization. It begins with an interest in behaviors of interaction with mass media. The psychological dimension of para-social interaction is measured using a scale validated elsewhere, and is based on work of several researchers in different places. However, both the sociability scales and the measure of letter writing can be improved. This is evident empirically by the modest levels of interitem reliability achieved for each of the scales. It is even more evident at the conceptual level. Sociability should be measured at the very least on three levels—the objective opportunities, the disposition, and the actual situational sociability. The survey materials at hand allowed only a partial, therefore deficient, gauge of this concept. Also on the conceptual level there is the problem of substituting letter writing for real interaction. The justification here is in the study's exploratory nature. But as indicated above, a better test for the notion forwarded here should distinguish between people whose letter writing resulted in real gratification and those for whom it did not. The more general notion of interacting with media should be represented by more than just one behavior.

The regression models and resultant path analyses at the heart of this study are based on several assumptions that deserve elaboration. Regression models require the assumptions of no specification error, no measurement error, and an expected error-term with a mean of zero, constant variance for all levels of the independent variables, and no correlation of the error terms with other error terms or the independent variable (Kerlinger & Pedhazur, 1973). Given the simplicity of the model used here, and especially the expectation that both the media use measures and the interaction measures are likely related to dimensions other than sociability, some of these assumptions may not be met to an optimal degree. In addition, the models studied here are misleading if they are seen as explanations of variance in the dependent variables. The amount of explained variance in either television or newspaper use is significant in these analyses only in the narrow, statistical sense.

Because our purpose is not predicting levels of a dependent variable but a comparative examination of relations in a model, the regression technique and the path-analysis model are judged robust enough to withstand these violations of assumptions (Asher, 1976; Kerlinger & Pedhazur, 1973; Lewis-Beck, 1980). There is a lesson here for future research on this question. Data about expected covariates of both media use and letter writing need to be collected and included in the model to validate the pattern of relations presented here.

Finally, the greatest limitation of the study is its scope. The theoretical question involves all mass media, various forms of real interaction, and various forms of psychological illusion of interaction and mechanisms for escape. The empirical operationalizations for these included only a rather limited subset of operationalizations. Employed here were a scale of para-social interaction, mostly with newscasters on television vis-à-vis television use, and a crude measure of writing letters to the editor vis-à-vis the use of newspapers. One of the two samples used was selected randomly, but from a nongeneral population. The other sample was collected almost a decade ago, using a questionnaire designed for purposes other than the current one. For all these reasons, pending validation of the findings reported here in studies designed in such a manner that the uncovered portions of the research question are tested, the conclusions should be considered tentative.

The goal of this study was to examine corollaries of a historical growth in the interactivity in the use of mass media. Real interaction with mass media was defined as the likelihood and opportunity for audience members to interact with mass media and their audience. Para-social interaction was defined as an imagined relationship between an audience member and personae of a mass medium. The theory about relationship between sociability and mass media use leads to a set of hypotheses of a contrasting role of para-social interaction and real interaction in explaining that relationship.

The findings of the study offer some support for the hypotheses. Ortho-social (or real) interaction with mass media in the form of writing letters to the editor and participation in call-in talk-radio shows was found to be rather high and, at least by some indices, followed a pattern of growth over the last few years. This finding qualifies the previous assumptions that letter writing can be completely understood on the organizational and political level. It also questions the assertion that letter writing is the act of extremists. The erosion over time of the predictive power of structural variables for letter writing underscores the importance of the social and socio-psychological elements in understanding this behavior.

Two hypothesized patterns of relationship between sociability and media use have been confirmed. The escapist pattern suggests a substitutional dynamics: sociability is related to inverse levels of television use. The communication-utility pattern suggests a supplementation dynamics: sociability is related positively to print use. Both patterns were replicated simultaneously in this study.

In accordance with the escape-substitution hypothesis, the covariance of para-social interaction with television use was found to be negative, and the interaction of PSI with a measure of the audience member's sociability was found to have a weak but significant effect on television use in the hypothesized direction. Similarly, real interaction was found to covary positively with print use. Furthermore, and as expected, it has been found to interact positively with a situational measure of the audience member's sociability. Real interaction is also associated with even higher levels of print mass media use.

One implication for future research involves the sociability-media use model. The simultaneous replication of these findings, previously reported only separately, helps refine the question of the association between media use and sociability. It is tempting to accept the distinction between the two reversed effects as based on media differences. The implication would be that the reason communication utility-originated process of supplementation has never been documented for the use of media other than print, is that it only operates for print. Chaffee's (1979) reasoning of availability and access notwithstanding, people exercise more use of print alone when confronted with the prospect of need for information for social transactions.

Similarly, escape and the consequential substitution are mainly a television phenomenon. Katz's and Foulkes's (1962) caveats that this process holds for all media of communication, and even Riley's and Riley's (1951) findings about adventure reading to the contrary, notwithstanding. Alternatively, the discrimination may be in the sociability pole of this axis. Two prehypotheses can compete for future research attention: if we accept the belief that such processes cannot be attributed to channel differences alone, we can expect the reverse relation to be attributable to different dimensions of sociability. On the other hand, we might find that both dynamics operate in both cases, with different results for each medium because of other reasons. This is the content-related hypothesis suggested by Chaffee (1972).

The support offered here for the para-social interaction hypothesis is in line with previous research. A slightly more stringent test was posited here for the theory. Although the results were not statistically strong, they were without exception in the expected direction, which indicated a need for a better scale for measuring para-social interaction. One likely area for the development of such a scale and the continuation of efforts utilizing that concept is in the domain of entertainment content, both for television and other media of communication.

One study to fantasize about in this context is a comparison of readers of a Dear Abby–like column. In this design, people who use such a column can be divided in two ways: (1) those who use the interactive format to have their own problems commented on or solved, vs. those who do not; and (2) those who think the advice is directed at them personally, or identify with Abby's recent divorce, etc., vs. those who do not. A future study in this line of research would allow simultaneous measures of real interaction and para-social interaction, and would do so in the context of a single medium, even a single type of content.

Finally, we turn to the implications for the study of interactivity. That interactivity is a central concept in the study of computer-based media—from teletext to videodisc and from the microcomputer itself to interactive cable—is becoming an accepted view. But the bridge between research on these new media and the traditional (and much more widespread) mass media has yet to be built. Interactivity is one building block. An implication of the findings is that mass media do not just come between people, they may also link people in an active fashion, when interactive arrangements are in place and used. The stereotype of modern life and new technologies is that they cause people to write less, visit with friends and neighbors less, interact less. The findings question parts of this simplification.

Is it fruitful to think of para-social interaction in the context of computer-based communication? Some studies of computerized videogames, and the interaction of users with those games come to mind. How closely does the imagined relationship taken on by a Dungeons and Dragons player with the Dragons or the Wizard resemble the relationship some people had with Walter Cronkite? And conversely, what is the effect that the player's actions do affect the Dungeon Master's action (while for Cronkite it was still "the way it is," no matter what)? The relationship of sociability and the amount of use for computer-based media is already under heavy scrutiny. Much of current research is driven by the reverse model, concerned with the isolation computers might impose on their users. Once computers become a relatively old hat and the novelty effect erodes, it might be interesting to study the model with this temporal ordering: the flow from sociability to computer-based media, as moderated by levels of interactivity.

References

Abel, J.D., & Thornton, L.R. (1975). Responders and nonresponders to television editorials: A comparison. *Journalism Quarterly, 52,* 477–84.

Alwin, D.F., & Hauser, R.M. (1975). The decomposition of effects in path analysis. *American Sociological Review, 40,* 37–47.

Asher, H.B. (1976). *Causal modeling.* Beverly Hills, CA: Sage.

Atkin, C.K. (1972). Anticipated communication and mass media information seeking. *Public Opinion Quarterly, 35,* 188–89.

Atkin, C. K. (1973). Instrumental utilities and information seeking. In P. Clarke (Ed.), *New models for communication research.* Beverly Hills, CA: Sage.

Avery, R.K., Ellis, D.G., & Glover, T.W. (1978). Patterns of communication and talk radio. *Journal of Broadcasting, 22,* 5–17.

Avery, R.K., & McCain, T.A. (1982). Interpersonal and mediated encounters: A reorientation to the mass communication process. In G. Gumpert, & R. Cathcart (Eds.), *Inter/Media: Interpersonal communication in a media world.* (2d ed.). New York: Oxford University Press.

Ball-Rokeach, S.J., & Reardon, K.K. (1988). Monologue, dialogue, and telelog: Comparing an emergent form of communication with traditional forms. In R.P. Hawkins, J.M. Wiemann, & S. Pingree (Eds.), *Advancing Communication Science: Merging Mass and Interpersonal Processes. Annual Reviews of Communication Research: Vol. 16.* Newbury Park, CA: Sage.

Barron, J.A. (1967, June). Access to the press: A new First Amendment right. *Harvard Law Review, 80,* 1641–78.

Bauer, R.A. (1967). Societal feedback. *Annals of the American Academy on Political and Social Sciences, 373* (September), 182–92.

Becker, L., Dunwoody, S., & Rafaeli, S. (1983). Cable's impact on the use of other news media. *Journal of Broadcasting, 27*(2), 127–40.

Beeping toms (1964). *Newsweek,* March 30, p. 74.

Beniger, J.R. (1987). Personalization of mass media and the growth of pseudo-community. *Communication Research, 14*(3), 352–72.

Bierig, J., & Dimmick, J. (1979). The late night radio talk show as interpersonal communication. *Journalism Quarterly, 56,* 92–96.

Bogart, L. (1955). Adults talk about the comic strips. *American Journal of Sociology, 61,* 26–31.

Bostian, L.R., & Ross, J.E. (1965). Functions and meanings of mass media for Wisconsin farm women. *Journalism Quarterly, 42,* 69–76.

Brown, R.V. (1976). Letters to the editor. *Editor and Publisher, 109,* 68.

Buell, E.H. Jr. (1975). Eccentrics or gladiators? People who write about politics in Letters to the Editor. *Social Science Quarterly, 56,* 440–49.

Carlin, J.C. (1976). The rise and fall of topless radio. *Journal of Communication, 26,* 31–37.

Chaffee, S.H. (1972). The interpersonal context of mass communication. In F.G. Kline, & P.J. Tichenor (Eds.), *Current perspectives in mass communication research.* Beverly Hills, CA: Sage.

Chaffee, S.H. (1979). *Mass media vs. interpersonal channels: The synthetic competition.* Paper presented at the annual meeting of the Speech Communication Association, San Antonio, Texas.

Chaffee, S.H. (1982). Mass media and interpersonal channels: Competitive, convergent, or complementary? In G. Gumpert & R. Cathcart (Eds.), *Inter/Media: Interpersonal communication in a media world* (2d ed.). New York: Oxford University Press.

Chu, G. C., & Chu, L.L. (1981). Parties in conflict: Letters to the editor of the People's Daily. *Journal of Communication, 31,* 74–91.

Converse, P.E., Clausen, A.R., & Miller, W. (1965). Electoral myth and reality: The 1964 election. *American Political Science Review, 59,* 321–36.

Crittenden, J. (1971). Democratic functions of the open mike forum. *Public Opinion Quarterly, 35,* 200–210.

Dannefer, W.D., & Poushinsky, N. (1977). Language and community: CB in perspective. *Journal of Communication, 27,* 122–26.

Davis, H., & Rarick, G. (1964). Functions of editorials and letters to the editor. *Journalism Quarterly, 41,* 109.

Donohew, L. (1967). Communication and readiness for change in Appalachia. *Journalism Quarterly, 44,* 679–87.

Eyal, C. (1985). *Letters to the editor and their writers.* Unpublished ms., Ohio State University.

Eysenck, H.J., & Eysenck, S.G.B. (1969). *Personality structure and measurement.* London.

Forsythe, S.A. (1950). An exploratory study of letters to the editor and their contributors. *Public Opinion Quarterly, 14*(1), 143–44.

Greenberg, S.R. (1975). Conversations as units of analysis in the study of personal influence. *Journalism Quarterly, 52,* 128–31.

Grey, D.L., & Brown, T.R. (1970). Letters to the editor: Hazy reflections of public opinion. *Journalism Quarterly, 47,* 450–56.

Hill, D.B. (1981). Letter opinion on ERA: A test of the newspaper bias hypothesis. *Public Opinion Quarterly, 45*(3), 384–92.

Hiltz, S.R., & Turoff, M. (1978). *The network nation: Human communication via computer.* Reading, MA: Addison Wesley.

Horton, D., & Wohl, R.R. (1956). Mass communication and para-social interaction: Observation on intimacy at a distance. *Psychiatry, 19*(3).

Houlberg, R. (1984). Local television news audience and the para-social interaction. *Journal of Broadcasting, 28*(4), 423–29.

Inkeles, A., & Geiger, K. (1952). Critical letters to the editors of the Soviet press: Areas and modes of complaint. *American Sociological Review, 17* (December).

Inkeles, A., & Geiger, K. (1953). Critical letters to the editors of the Soviet press: Social characteristics and inter-relations of critics and the criticized. *American Sociological Review, 18,* 2–22.

Johnstone, J.W.C. (1961). *Social structure and patterns of mass media consumption.* Unpublished Ph.D. diss., University of Chicago.

Johnstone, J.W.C. (1974). Social integration and mass media use among adolescents: A case study. In J.G. Blumler & E. Katz (Eds.), *The uses of mass communication.* Beverly Hills, CA: Sage.

Katz, E. (1959). Communication research and the image of society: Convergence of two traditions. *American Journal of Sociology, 65,* 435–40.

Katz, E., & Foulkes, D. (1962). On the use of the mass media as "Escape": Clarification of a concept. *Public Opinion Quarterly, 26,* 377–88.

Katz, E., & Lazarsfeld, P.F. (1955). *Personal influence.* New York: Free Press.

Kefauver, E., & Levin, J. (1960). Letters that really count. In D. Katz, D.

Cartwright, S. Eldersveld, & A. McLung-Lee (Eds.), *Public opinion and prop- aganda*. New York: H. Holt.

Kerlinger, F.N., & Pedhazur, K. (1973). *Multiple regression in behavioral research*. New York: Holt, Rinehart & Winston.

Kiesler, S., Siegel, J., & McGuire, T.W. (1984). Social-psychological aspects of computer-mediated communication. *American Psychologist, 39*(10), 1123–34.

Klein, F.G. (1971). Media time budgeting as a function of demographics and life- style. *Journalism Quarterly, 48*, 211–21.

Klempner, A. (1966). *People who write in: Communication aspects of opinion letter writing*. Unpublished Ph.D. diss., Michigan State University.

Kuroda, Y. (1966). Political role attributions and dynamics in a Japanese commu- nity. *Public Opinion Quarterly, 29*, 602–613.

Lander, B.G. (1972). Functions of letters to the editor: A reexamination. *Journal- ism Quarterly, 49*, 142–43.

Lazarsfeld, P.F., Berelson, B., & Gaudet, H. (1944). *The people's choice*. New York: Columbia University Press.

Lemert, J.B., & Larkin, J.P. (1979). Some reasons why mobilizing information fails to be in letters to the editor. *Journalism Quarterly, 56*, 504–512

Levy, M.R. (1979). Watching TV news as para-social interaction. *Journal of Broadcasting, 23*(1).

Lewis, A. (1970). The jungle drum of the British establishment. *Esquire, 70*, 52–64.

Lewis-Beck, M.S. (1980). *Applied regression: An introduction*. Beverly Hills, CA: Sage.

McEachern, M. (1970). The town meeting is not dead–It's alive and well on radio. *Today's Health*, June, pp. 32–71.

McGuire, B., & Leroy, D.J. (1977). Audience mail: Letters to the broadcaster. *Journal of Communication, 27*, 79–85.

McQuail, D., Blumler, J.G., & Brown, J.R. (1972). The television audience: A revised perspective. In D. McQuail (Ed.), *Sociology of mass communications*. Middlesex, UK: Penguin.

Marvin, C., & Schultze, Q.J. (1977). The first thirty years: CB in perspective. *Journal of Communication, 27*, 104–117.

Miller, W.E., & Miller, A.H. (1977). *The CPS 1976 American National Election Study*. Ann Arbor, MI: Inter-University Consortium for Political and Social Research.

Nordlund, J.E. (1978). Media interaction. *Communication Research, 5*, 150–75.

Noelle-Neumann, E. (1977). Turbulences in the climate of opinion: Methodological applications of the spiral of silence theory. *Public Opinion Quarterly, 41*, 143– 58.

Pasternack, S. (1983). Editors and the risk of libel in letters. *Journalism Quarterly, 60*(2), 311–15.

Rafaeli, S. (1984a). If the computer is the medium, what is the message? (I) Explicating interactivity. Paper presented to the annual conference of the International Communication Association.

Rafaeli, S. (1984b). If the computer is the medium, what is the message? (II) Interactivity and its correlates. Paper presented to the annual conference of the International Communication Association.

Renfro, P.C. (1979). Bias in selection of letters to the editor. *Journalism Quarterly, 56*, 822–26.

Rice, R.E. (1984). Mediated groups. In R.E. Rice (Ed.), *The new media*. Beverly Hills, CA: Sage.

Riley, M.W., & Riley, J.W. (1951). A sociological approach to mass communication research. *Public Opinion Quarterly, 15,* 444–50.

Roberts, D.F., Sikorski, L.A., & Paisley, W.J. (1969). Letters in mass magazines as outcroppings of public opinion. *Journalism Quarterly, 46*(4), 743–52.

Rogers, E.M. (1983). *The diffusion of innovations* (3rd ed.). New York: Free Press.

Rogers, E.M. (1986). *Communication technology: The new media in society.* New York: Free Press.

Rokeach, M. (1979). Value theory and communication research: Review and commentary. In D. Nimmo (Ed.), *Communication Yearbook 3.* New Brunswick, NJ: Transaction.

Rosenau, J.N. (1974). *Citizenship between elections.* New York: Free Press.

Rosengren, K.E., & Windahl, S. (1972). Mass media consumption as a functional alternative. In D. McQuail (Ed.), *Sociology of mass communications.* Middlesex, UK: Penguin.

Rosengren, K.E., Windahl, S., Hakansson, P-A., & Johnsson-Smaragdi, U. (1976). Adolescents' TV relations: Three scales. *Communication Research, 3*(4), 347–66.

Schramm, W., Lyle, J., & Parker, E.B. (1961). *Television in the lives of our children.* Stanford, CA: Stanford University Press.

Short, J., Williams, E., & Christie, B. (1976). *The social psychology of telecommunications.* London: Wiley.

Singletary, M.W. (1976). How the public perceives letters to the editor. *Journalism Quarterly, 53,* 535–37.

Singletary, M.W., & Cowling, M. (1979). Letters to the editor of the non-daily press. *Journalism Quarterly, 56*(1), 165–68.

Singer, B.D. (1972). *Feedback and society.* Lexington, MA: D.C. Heath.

Sussman, L. (1959). Mass political letter writing in America. *Public Opinion Quarterly, 23,,* 203–212.

Sussman, L. (1963). *Dear FDR: A study of political letter writing.* Totowa, NJ: Bedminster Press.

Tarrant, W.D. (1957). Who writes letters to the editor. *Journalism Quarterly, 34,* 501–2.

Touchiest topic on radio now: Talk about sex (1973). *Broadcasting, 77* (March 19), 118–19.

Turow, J. (1974). Talk show radio as interpersonal communication. *Journal of Broadcasting, 18,* 171–79.

Turow, J. (1977). Another view of citizen feedback to the mass media. *Public Opinion Quarterly, 41*(4), 534–43.

Vacin, G. (1965). A study of letter writers. *Journalism Quarterly, 42,* 464–65.

Verba, S., & Brody, R. (1970). Participation, policy preferences, and the war in Vietnam. *Public Opinion Quarterly, 34,* 325–32.

Volgy, T.J., et al. (1977). Some of my best friends are letter writers: Eccentrics and gladiators revisited. *Social Science Quarterly, 58,* 321–27.

Winick, C. (1964). Children's television fan mail. *Television Quarterly, 42,* 464–65, 510.

Wilcox, W. (1969). Public favors right of reply whether question refers to newspaper or individual. *American Newspaper Publishers Association: Bulletin No. 10,* May 29, pp. 31–40.

Zwibelman, B.B., & Rayfield, G.E. (1982). An innovation in counseling research: Using the campus radio station. *Journal of College Student Personnel, 23*(4), 353–54.

PART II
INFORMATION SOCIETIES: DEVELOPMENTS
IN RESEARCH AND POLICY

**Selected papers from a research forum
sponsored by the Annenberg Washington
Program in Communication Policy Studies,
Washington, D.C., December 1984.**

8

Introduction: The Emergence of Information Societies

Everett M. Rogers

In this article, current research on the information society is reviewed and some policy implications of the information society are explored. The question of what is an information society is discussed along with such related issues of information overload, social problems, the role of information technology, and the nature of public policy in such a society.

The purpose of this article is (1) to review current research on the information society, and (2) to explore certain policy implications of the information society.

Perhaps the promising stream of research begun by Machlup (1962), Bell (1973), and Porat (1978), and carried forward by several other social scientists, needs to stand still for a moment and take stock of where it is going. Much has been learned that is useful, but I think that we do not just need more of the same. Further, the scholarly research accomplished to date on the information society implies policy alternatives for government officials in the United States, and in other nations. If indeed the United States, Japan, and several Western European nations are going through a historical transformation to become information societies, their public and private leaders need to consider the implications of this watershed social change.

Several important recent events focus attention on the topic of information societies:

- The Microelectronics and Computer Technology Corporation (MCC) announced in 1983 its decision to locate in Austin, Texas. In two years after that announcement, Austin became a boom town, with new housing values shooting up about 50% (and then collapsing in 1986–1987). Here is a case of instant high-technology industry, with the boom-and-bust that such rapid change often implies.
- The promise of high technology is very much in the air, with a U.S. president having given it considerable attention, with each of the two national political parties organizing a high-tech group (Rogers & Larsen, 1984), and with some spokespersons suggesting that high-tech industry might offer solutions to such social problems in America as unemployment and failing smokestack industries.
- U.S.-Japanese competition in such high-technology industries as computers and semiconductors is much discussed in both nations, with one best-selling book in America explaining why Japanese management is superior and another best seller telling Americans that certain of their own firms are being managed with excellence compared to Japanese companies.
- The New York/New Jersey teleport is a kind of information harbor with facilities for satellite transmission of messages. Similar facilities are now operating in several other U.S. cities.
- Microcomputers, invented in Silicon Valley in 1971, are having important social impacts on homes, businesses, and schools, leading to the realization that the new information technologies are playing a key role in the transformation of the United States to an information society.
- Silicon Valley–like centers are springing up in a dozen or so locations around the United States, mainly in the Sunbelt, usually with a research university in the center of each high-technology complex.

Each of these events carries implications for students, investigators, policy makers, and the public. In general, they help illustrate the trend for the United States to become an information society.

What Is an Information Society?

For the past decade or so, various authors have been proclaiming that the information society has arrived. The new society differs in important ways from the past industrial society. Empirical indicators (mainly based on occupational or other economic data) support the observation that a transition may presently be underway in American society. The new system has been labeled an "information society." What is it?

In his pioneering work on this concept, Bell (1973) stated: "A post-industrial society is based on services. Hence, it is a game between persons. What counts is not raw muscle power, or energy, but information." Later scholars referred to the postindustrial society as the "information society." There are detractors from the prevailing view that we now live in an information society (for example, Dupuy, 1980, pp. 3–17). Nevertheless, most scholars feel that a basic change in society has occurred.

Porat (1978) argued that "the essential difference between an industrial and an information society is that the locus of economic activity and technological change has shifted away from manufacturing 'objects' towards handling information and symbols." Porat dates 1954 as an important transition point because, according to his calculations, in that year information workers comprised larger numbers than industrial workers, service workers, or agricultural workers in the United States. Today, information workers constitute about one-half of the U.S. workforce and earn a slightly higher share of the gross national product (GNP). "Information workers" were defined by Porat (1978) as individuals "holding a job where the production, processing, or distribution of symbols is the main activity."

In studying information societies, researchers need to go beyond strictly economic interpretations of their data to show how the information society implies changes in human communication behavior. From the start, scholarly work on the information society has profited from the attention of several disciplines—economics and sociology at first, now joined by communication scholars and political scientists, among several others.

In Japan, the term *johoka shakai* (information society) was coined in 1966 (Ito, 1981), and the issues raised by the concept have probably received at least as much research attention as in the United States or Western Europe. *Jokoka shakai* is defined by Ito as "a society characterized by abundant information in terms of both the stock and flow, quick and efficient distribution and transformation of information, and easy and inexpensive access of information for all members of society." Notice that in Japan, the information society is defined (and measured) in terms of information, rather than in terms of occupational classifications or economic contributions to the GNP.[1]

Information Overload

The research approach of Japanese communication scholars investigating the information society tends to focus on social problems (somewhat as the Chicago School of Sociology concentrated on studying the urban social problems accompanying the industrial society early in this century). The chief social problem investigated in Japan is information overload.[2] In the decade from 1960 to 1970, the information supply in Japan increased by 400%, while consumption increased only 140% (Bowes, 1981). The Japanese public consumed 40% of the information available in 1960, but only 10% in 1975. What caused the rapid growth in information in Japan? Not surprisingly, more than 70% of the information growth was traced to such information technologies as computers, television receivers, and telephones (Bowes, 1981). As these technologies are more widely accepted, individuals are more likely to experience information overload.

Certain social scientists are not much interested in study of the information society concept because it has been defined in such aggregate terms that it cannot be studied with our favorite methodological tools like the survey and the experiment. In Japan, various research problems concerning the information society have been pursued at an individual or household level, as well as at the societal level. For example, an information ratio has been computed as the amount of financial expenditures for information-related activities in proportion to total household expenditures. Engel's ratio (the share of household expenditures for food) decreases with higher income, but the information ratio behaves in the opposite way. Families with higher incomes spend a higher proportion of their expenditures on information (Ito, 1981).

The information ratio can be aggregated to the national level, of course. Japanese scholars of the information society find that Japan's national information ratio is very high for its level of personal income (Ito, 1981). But the United States has the highest average information ratio among the nations that have been studied.

Following somewhat comparable procedures in the United States to those of the *johoka shakai* scholars in Japan, Pool (1983) found a similar problem of information overload: "There have been extraordinary rates of growth in the transmission of electronic communications, but much lower rates of growth in the material that people actually consume." From 1960 to 1977, the number of words made available to Americans (over the age of 10) through 17 public media of communication grew at the rate of 8.9% per year, more than double the growth rate in the gross domestic product. Words actually attended to from these media grew at just 2.9%, and per capita consumption of words grew only 1.2% per year.

One might suppose that the relatively slower rate of consumption of information than of information availability could be due mainly or partially to individuals' feelings of information overload. Perhaps the growing overabundance of information in society is really not a social problem;

maybe citizens simply take what they need or want and leave the rest. We do not yet know much about how individuals cope with the increasing amount of information available to them in society.

Social Problems

Comparative analyses of two or more information societies are surprisingly rare in the scholarly literature. One such investigation has been completed by Salvaggio (1983), who argues that all information societies must have some means of coping with such social problems as unemployment, the invasion of privacy, information inequality, etc. In Japan, government agencies like the Ministry of International Trade and Industry (MITI) and the Ministry of Posts and Telecommunications (MPT) are the main policy-making organizations, with a small number of large private firms producing information technologies under the guidance of government officials. In contrast, free market forces and the dynamics of competition are more likely to be the arbitrator in U.S. decisions about what information technologies to produce and what social impact they will have (Salvaggio, 1983).

In Japan, the government takes a main responsibility for dealing with the social problems that accompany the advances in information technologies (that make the information society possible); this is a public policy model. The United States depends more on market forces to help cope with these social problems; this is a competitive model for society.

One of the most serious social problems is unemployment. When the U.S. industrial society occurred, the millions of off-farm migrants were absorbed by urban/industrial jobs which were then expanding fast. Can we today make up for the drop in employment in industrial jobs through the creation of new jobs in services and information?

The Role of Information Technology

The new information technologies of computers, satellites, and cable help move nations toward becoming information societies. But how much of this societal transformation can be traced directly to the new information technologies, and how much is due to other, more contextual factors? The answer is not yet clear, but most scholars agree that technological determinism is very important. Thus we need to understand more fully the new technologies and their social impacts.

In what ways are the new communication technologies different from the communication technologies that we have known in the past?

First, the new media are unlike either the electronic communication technologies of radio, television, and film, or the print media such as newspapers and magazines in that the new technologies are more highly *interactive*. This interactivity usually is provided when a computer is one component in a communication system. Such interactivity usually fosters a high degree of decentralization in the new communication systems, with widespread sharing of authority and decision making. Linear models of communication, based on source-message-channel-receiver components (Shannon & Weaver, 1949), may have been an appropriate theoretical approach for investigating the effects of mass media communication. Such effects-oriented research has been the main preoccupation of mass communication scholars for the past forty years or so. But the interactivity of the new communication technologies forces us to follow a model of communication as convergence, the mutual process of information exchange between two or more participants in a communication system (Rogers & Kincaid, 1981). Such convergence communication behavior implies that it is impossible to think of a "source" and a "receiver" in a communication system with a high degree of interactivity. Instead, each individual is a "participant in the communication process."

Second, the new media are quite *demassified* in that a message can be highly individualized to a particular member of the audience, even though a large number of people may be included as participants in one of the new media systems. For example, an interactive cable television system like QUBE in Columbus, Ohio, or Hi-OVIS in Japan, allows for almost complete individualization of messages. This is audience segmentation to an extreme.

Third, because users of the new communication systems (such as computer bulletin boards and electronic messaging systems) can retain and access messages after an extended period of time, these new media are *asynchronous*. For instance, a participant in an electronic messaging system can receive a message from another participant whenever he/she logs onto a computer in the local area network. Unlike a telephone call, both participants do not need to be in communication at the same time.

These distinctive aspects of the new information technologies are forcing basic changes in communication models and in research methodologies (Rice & associates, 1984). But even more broadly, the new technologies, through their social impacts in creating information societies, are leading to a whole new set of communication research issues that are now beginning to be addressed by scholars. The information revolution is causing a scientific revolution in communication research.

Public Policies in Information Societies

The information society is worldwide in its orientation. For example, high-technology firms in computers or semiconductors engage in global competition. Thus the policies of national governments must increasingly take into account this wide scope of the emerging information society.

In the United States, federal government policies have played a less important role in the information society of North America, where market forces (rather than public policies) are more significant in making important decisions about new information technologies. One of the key issues here is how the economies of industrialized countries might be revitalized by certain public policies that encourage the development of high-technology industry.

Within the United States, many state and local governments today have policies to promote high-technology industry, often through the role of a research university. That academic institution is considered key to the rise of high-technology private industry in an area, just as the scientist and engineer are the key occupations in the information society (Bell, 1973). We see the crucial role of the research university in the rise of Silicon Valley, Boston's Route 128, and in North Carolina's Research Triangle.

Information as a Unifying Concept

There is yet another way in which "information" has been used for scholarly purposes to understand the information society. Here the concept of information is utilized to explain a series of important historical events, leading up to fairly recent times when the cumulation of these events seems to cause the point of transition to an information society. In this sense, information offers a means to better understand history.

One example of this approach to information as a unifying concept is Campbell's (1983) book, *Grammatical Man*. He feels that the development of information theory by Claude Shannon in about 1949 was the crucial turning point in recent times: "He had been able to make the concept of information so logical and precise that it could be placed in a formal framework of ideas" (Campbell, 1983, p. 17). The concept of information is then shown to be fundamental to understanding such important scientific discoveries and inventions as DNA, how the brain functions, and Einsteinian physics. To Campbell, information is the unifying, fundamental concept that explains a very broad range of phenomena.

Jim Beniger (1986) raises four questions in his book that also serve to guide our discussions and thinking about information societies:

1. Is there an information society?
2. Why "information"?
3. When did information society begin?
4. What can we do about it?

Answers to these questions are being pursued by communication scholars in various nations, but the answers are not yet fully developed.

Notes

1. Obviously the concept of ''information'' (defined as the patterned matter-energy that affects the probabilities of alternatives available to an individual making a decision) underlies these definitions of the information society.
2. ''Information overload'' is the state of an individual or a system in which excessive communication inputs cannot be processed.

References

Bell, D. (1973). *The coming of post-industrial society*. New York: Basic Books.

Beniger, J. (1986). *The control revolution: Technological and economic origins of the information society*. Cambridge, MA: Harvard University Press.

Bowes, J.E. (1981). Japan's approach to an information society: A critical perspective. *Keio Communication Review, 2,* 39–49.

Campbell, J. (1983). *Grammatical man: Information, entropy, language, and life.* New York: Simon & Schuster.

Dupuy, J.P. (1980). Myths of the information society. In K. Woodward (Ed.), *The myths of information*. Madison, WI: Coda Press.

Ito, Y. (1981). The ''Johoka Shakai'' approach to the study of communication in Japan. In G.C. Wilhoit, & H. de Bock (Eds.), *Mass Communication Review Yearbook 2*. Beverly Hills, CA: Sage.

Machlup, F. (1962). *The production and distribution of knowledge in the United States*. Princeton, NJ: Princeton University Press.

Pool, I. (1983). Tracking the flow of information. *Science, 221,* 609–613.

Porat, M.U. (1978). Global implications of the information society. *Journal of Communication, 28,* 70–79.

Rice, R.E., & associates (1984). *The new media*. Beverly Hills, CA: Sage.

Rogers, E.M. (1986). *Communication technology: The new media in society*. New York: Free Press.

Rogers, E.M., & Kincaid, D.L. (1981). *Communication networks: Toward a new paradigm for research*. New York: Free Press.

Rogers, E.M., & Larsen, J.K. (1984). *Silicon Valley fever: Growth of high technology culture*. New York: Basic Books.

Salvaggio, J.L. (1983). Social problems of information societies: The U.S. and Japanese experiences. *Telecommunications Policy*, 228–42.

Shannon, C.E., & Weaver, W. (1949). *The mathematical theory of communication*. Urbana, IL: University of Illinois Press.

9

Silicon Valley: A Scenario for the Information Society of Tomorrow

Judith K. Larsen

The transition from an industrial society to an information society is inevitably accompanied by widespread societal and individual change. A consequence of this change is the rapid breakdown of traditional patterns and supports of the old society, a change often causing problems for social systems and for people as they try to define new models and superimpose them on existing patterns. The life-style changes occurring in the information society may be as critical and as difficult as the earlier transition from an agricultural to an industrial society. It is clear that we are moving into a different way of life, but without an adequate understanding of its character- istics or consequences. In this article, the social patterns evolving and emerging in Silicon Valley, where these changes are highly developed, are examined as possible precursors of the future of other, high-tech communities.

Technology is creating a new information society in which knowledge, or information, forms the basic resource. The postindustrial or information society is a society in which information technology supports manufactur- ing and administration. While tool technology is an extension of the individual's physical powers, information technology is an extension of perception and knowledge, and thus enlarges our consciousness. In this sense, information technology is basic to all other technologies.

The transition from an industrial society to an information society is accompanied by widespread societal and individual change. Nowhere is this change more developed than in Silicon Valley, America's high-tech heartland. Like the technological innovations developed in Silicon Valley then flowing to the rest of the world, social patterns now evolving in Silicon Valley may be precursors of the future for other communities.

As the information society spreads and replaces the industrial society, social and cultural characteristics of the new society also emerge. A consequence of this change is the rapid breakdown of traditional patterns and supports of the old society; a change often causes problems for social systems and for people as they try to define new models and then superimpose them on existing patterns. The life-style changes occurring in the information society may be as critical and as difficult as the earlier transition from an agricultural to an industrial society. What is clear is that we are moving into a different way of life, but without an adequate understanding of its characteristics or consequences.

Silicon Valley Today

Just as Manchester, the Saar Valley and Pittsburgh were once the centers of an industrial society, today's information society has a heartland— Silicon Valley. Silicon Valley is located in a 30- by 10-mile strip between San Jose and San Francisco. Almost all of Silicon Valley lies in Santa Clara County, which in 1950 was the prune capitol of America. The county had only 800 manufacturing employees then, and one-half of them worked in canneries and food-processing plants. The fruit trees have all but disappeared, and in their place have come semiconductors.

Today Silicon Valley is the nation's ninth largest manufacturing center, with sales of over $40 billion annually. The electronics industry on which the information society is based presently accounts for $100 billion in annual sales. By the end of this decade, electronics will reach annual sales of $400 billion, and be the world's fourth largest industry, after steel, autos, and chemicals. Electronics, the source of information technology, is the largest employer in Silicon Valley, providing 162,000 jobs in 1983 (Bank of America, 1983). About 40,000 new jobs are created in the Valley each year. Its economy is the fastest growing and wealthiest in the United States, with a median family income of over $26,000 according to the U.S. Census.

Specifically, it is the semiconductor industry, centered in Silicon Valley, that earns Silicon Valley the title of America's high-tech heartland. Semiconductors, popularly called "chips," are the basic component in virtually all microelectronics products; therefore, the semiconductor industry can be considered the basic technology-producing industry. Of the approximately 150 semiconductor companies in the United States, all but a handful are centered in Silicon Valley.

Naturally, semiconductor users are attracted to locate close to semiconductor suppliers, and as a result, other microelectronic industries have congregated in Silicon Valley. Computers, one of the largest users of semiconductors, is a major Silicon Valley industry, along with computer peripherals, instrumentation, and software.

Like some other areas of the United States, Silicon Valley includes a large production of information workers, people whose work mainly involves processing information. Scholars studying the information society (Machlup, 1962; Porat, 1978) assign the majority of people in the information society to this category. By contrast, the information society contains a relatively smaller number of information-technology producers.

Unlike most other communities, a large proportion of the Silicon Valley work force consists of people who produce information technology. People employed in Silicon Valley's microelectronics industries produce tools that enable knowledge workers to perform their jobs. Almost all Silicon Valley high-tech employees can be considered information workers, and nearly all would also be classified as information-technology producers. Information-technology producers are in some sense particularly basic to the information society. The technology they produce affects knowledge workers and the information society at large. Likewise, changes in societal patterns and interpersonal relationships experienced by information-technology producers, and even more so by people who are both knowledge producers and information users, may be harbingers of the future for the rest of the world.

Entrepreneurism

Entrepreneurial Silicon Valley represents the work ethic of the information society in the extreme: fast pace, long hours, and a high commitment to work. The workaholics who want job success and money are bright, and they devote their disciplined minds to work. Virtually everyone, from line operators to executives, complains about the fast pace, intensity, and stress of the electronics industry. Yet they all acknowledge that the long hours are dictated by the need to be first to market with a new product, to be competitive. New information technologies on the cutting edge of development may be truly unique, but usually only for a few months, until a competitor brings out a newer and better version of the technology. The pace suggests that one's job depends on speed, and often it does.

Many social observers state or imply that the transformation of the

United States and other industrialized nations into information societies is caused, at least in part, by new information technologies, especially by the semiconductor and the computer. While the technology is crucial, an equally important component in the current social transition is an entrepreneurial spirit. Entrepreneurism and information technology, the two critical factors in today's social change, are complexly interrelated. Silicon Valley is the world center for microelectronic innovation; it also extols the entrepreneurial spirit and its associated work ethic, life-style, and social values. Technological innovation and entrepreneurship support today's emerging information society.

Entrepreneurial Spirit Today

Silicon Valley's information society represents a trend from organization man to entrepreneur. A spurt of entrepreneurial activity has occurred in recent years. In 1950, 93,000 new companies opened their doors in the United States; in the 1980s, there are nearly 600,000 start-ups annually.

Silicon Valley has produced an amazing number of new electronics firms. Companies are constantly starting up, growing, merging, being acquired, or fading away, making it difficult to know how many firms exist at any one time. A recent count (Schmieder, 1983) identified 2,736 electronics-manufacturing firms in Silicon Valley. In addition to manufacturing companies, Silicon Valley includes companies supporting the electronics manufacturers, companies engaged in marketing, advertising, R&D, consulting, training, venture capital, legal, and other support services. There are at least as many of these companies as manufacturers, so the total number of firms in the electronics industry in Silicon Valley is probably about 6,000.

In addition to the surprising number of firms, another startling fact is their small size. Over two-thirds have from one to ten employees and 85% have fewer than fifty staff. Media attention is concentrated upon the 54 electronics firms with more than 1,000 employees, firms such as Hewlett-Packard, Intel, and Apple Computer. These giants constitute only 2% of the electronics companies in Silicon Valley, although they represent one-half or more of the total work force.

Key Factors in Entrepreneurism

Several factors are characteristic of entrepreneurism in Silicon Valley, and these are probably necessary for the successful development of other high-technology heartlands (Rogers & Larsen, 1984).

Availability of skilled technical people. More than any other single factor, Silicon Valley's high-tech companies depend on the people who can design the clean rooms, tool delicate features, and design innovative operating systems. This priceless human resource is placated and wooed; few other places in the world can offer the pool of experienced, specialized high-tech brainpower. Companies that want access to that expertise have little choice but to locate where those intellectual resources are concentrated.

Infrastructure. Sunnyvale, a city in the middle of Silicon Valley, is the only city in the world with eight miles of hydrogen mains under its city streets, along with water and sewer lines. Clean rooms, daily deliveries of liquid gas, and local machine shops with tolerances measured in microns, are part of the infrastructure of the industry. Hundreds of specialized services support this industry: transportation vans for computers and delicate equipment; venture capitalists who understand high technology; advertising and public relations firms that can tell Winchesters from floppies; and lawyers specializing in bringing companies public.

Venture capital. Silicon Valley is a prime center of venture capital activity. Over one-third of the nation's largest venture capital companies have an office located in or near Silicon Valley. Many of the remaining venture capital firms, though based elsewhere, are heavily invested in Silicon Valley. In 1983, over $5.8 billion were at work in venture capital investments.

Job mobility. The annual rate of job turnover in Silicon Valley is about 30% among professionals (Murray, 1981). This means that the average professional will have three different jobs in ten years. Such turnover is encouraged by the shortage of qualified, experienced personnel. Thus, companies often are oriented toward the near-term, offering benefits and incentives attractive now such as stock options, recreational facilities, and extensive training programs. High job-mobility is a boon or a disaster, depending on one's perspective. For employees, the assurance of being able to leave one company and move to another with an increase in salary provides an ultimate security. Companies have quite a different view of job-hopping. For them, the loss of experienced employees is a major problem. The constant turnover among staff creates difficulties in establishing internal operating networks. If an engineer who is key on a design project leaves, much of the thinking behind the project also goes—information which is not written down.

The most common incentive for job-hopping is money; a move to a new job usually represents a raise of 15%. For the company, problems caused by the shortage of technical people means that paying more is sometimes the only way to attract needed personnel. Job-hopping is also a way of advancing a career through a series of moves up the corporate ladder.

Paradoxically, in Silicon Valley job-hopping provides greater opportunity for advancement than staying with one company. By job-hopping the employee can move to a more respectable position with more pay; in contrast, there is less chance of being promoted by staying with one company.

Information-exchange networks. Everyone knows everyone in Silicon Valley, due to the high rate of job mobility and the concentrated geographical location of the industry. The extensive network of personal contacts facilitates information exchange. A Federal Trade Commission report states that the unique strength of the U.S. semiconductor industry derives from its firms' rapid copying of each others' innovations.

Information exchange is the predominant purpose of networks, and there are widely held norms for what constitutes ethical information exchanges. According to the Semiconductor Industry Association (Davis, 1981): "Information exchange is fine under ethical conditions but not under non-ethical." The definitions of these terms are unwritten but well known to those in the information society: "It is ethical if you leave a company and take your ideas and plans with you. In this way, spin-offs occur and are considered ethical. However, it is unethical if another company identifies someone who might have the information they want, and they come in and steal that person away. That creates hard feelings all the way around" (Davis, 1981).

A primary norm of information exchange in the information society is that of reciprocity. It is acceptable for an individual to give technical information to another as long as the first person expects to receive information in return. It is not considered acceptable to provide information when there is no expectation of reciprocity; then the individual is considered an informer and untrustworthy.

Another norm is that of personal relationships. Personal networks thrive in Silicon Valley's information society, and even in a cut-throat industry, warm personal relationships exist. It is generally acceptable for information-technology producers to exchange certain technical information with a colleague working for another firm, if such information exchange is based on close personal ties. However, it is not considered ethical to share critical corporate proprietary information, regardless of the strength of personal ties.

There is a point at which information exchange must stop, both for the firm and for the individual. Most professionals have a good idea of where this thin line is, and most observe it. Generally, people are wary of information requests coming from competitors, and will provide information to competitors only if it is "behind the times." They will not exchange information on current processes or activities that might hurt their present employer.

Local role models. Spin-off companies from established firms is an example of a modification in industrial structure that is occurring with the change to an information society. In Silicon Valley, the technology is expanding so rapidly that no one company could possibly develop all potential innovations. This climate encourages spin-offs, and many are successful. Soon the belief is accepted that almost anybody can try to form a new company: "If he can start a new company, why can't I?" As the entrepreneurial spirit spreads and gains support, the technological innovation and social change that accompany it also begin to gain acceptance.

The Toll Exacted by Silicon Valley

In the extremely competitive work environment of Silicon Valley's information society, the fast pace and long hours take their toll on personal life and families. Human relationships can be strained, with the results affecting not only employees but spouse and family as well. In 1980, Santa Clara County reported 10,900 divorces, more than the number of marriages (*San Jose Mercury,* 1981). This divorce rate is higher than the rate for California as a whole, and California's rate is 20% above the U.S. average.

Silicon Valley family life also is in the midst of change. According to the 1980 census, one of five families with children under 18 was headed by a single parent. Women headed slightly more than one in every ten households (Watson, 1981). As a result of the high divorce rate, there are a large number of single-parent households, most headed by women.

The Silicon Valley work ethic may be the wave of the future. Perhaps it is functional in an information society where technology prevails and individual competence is rewarded. Nevertheless, if this ethic is the model for the emerging information society, certain serious social problems with far-reaching implications are raised.

Families and Households

Although Silicon Valley may be the "permanent" location for most information technology producers, their immediate living arrangements are often transient. According to a recent study of Silicon Valley employees (Larsen & Gill, 1984), nearly one-half of the respondents had lived in their present location less than five years. The rate of housing turnover was reported by people at all age levels; therefore, it appears that living arrangements for many people in Silicon Valley do not stabilize with age but continue to change and evolve over a lifetime.

The range of household configurations is also broad. The traditional American household—mother, father, and two children—is characteristic of less than one-half of Silicon Valley's technology producers (Larsen, 1984). Other household arrangements commonly reported include self and children; self and spouse with no children; and self living with related and nonrelated persons. About one-half of the Silicon Valley people report that their household has experienced change within the last two years. To underscore the rate of household change, about one-third report that they expected their present household to remain as it was no more than six months.

Time pressures of working in entrepreneurial Silicon Valley directly affect families and children. About one-half of the mothers in our study and three-fourths of the fathers spent less than two hours a day with their children, yet nearly one-half of the respondents were satisfied with that time arrangement. Those who were not satisfied regretted that there was not more time to spend with their children.

Like their parents, children's lives are very full; one-third of the mothers reported that their children had little free time available outside of school, so the children's flexibility for participating in family activities also was limited. About one-fourth of the families were able to get together as a group only on holidays or other such occasions; however, about one-half of the families did things together as a group once a week.

This high rate of change in personal living-arrangements and the lack of time for families to spend together contributes to the sense of instability frequently described as characterizing the emerging information society. For many members of the emerging society, their personal living-situation fails to provide a dependable base.

Working in the Information Society

Work is a central component in the lives of many information users and information-technology producers in Silicon Valley. One-third of our respondents reported that for them, work was a basic requirement for their overall well-being: "Work is completely central to me. It is the most important thing I do." For another one-third, work was important but not predominant. These people described themselves as career oriented but thought there was more to life than work. The remaining one-third said they thought about work from eight to five, but not otherwise. They perceived work as an economic necessity, not as a primary aspect of life.

If dedication to work can be measured by hours worked per week, those participating in the information society constitute a very dedicated group. Over 63% of the respondents reported working more than forty hours per week. Indeed, many people at higher job levels observed that there was a peer culture of working extra hours, and that they felt guilty if they went home on time rather than staying late. The dedication required by Silicon Valley's information society demands that people work long hours and relinquish personal concerns for the sake of professional success. Respondents also were asked for their observations of the place of work in the information society. Nearly two-thirds thought that people in Silicon Valley's information society were more work oriented than elsewhere, a statement consistent with their assertion that for them, work is very central in their lives.

Quality of Life

People comprising Silicon Valley's information society have given considerable thought to the emerging society and related issues regarding the quality of life; discussion of such topics was not unusual. In general, those in the information society in our sample thought that the positive elements of the information society outweighed the negative aspects. "There is excitement in being part of a revolution. You watch it grow and change, and you realize you're at the vanguard of what everyone is going to experience." Most people thought the opportunity for jobs provided by the information society was its greatest asset. This was followed closely by the exciting nature of the work, educational programs, recreational and cultural activities, and by the belief that they were making a substantial contribution to the industry and to an emerging society.

What is the impact of the emerging information society on the attitudes and values of its people? Most people believe that interpersonal values in Silicon Valley are different from the society in which they grew up. Specifically, they state that life in Silicon Valley is more competitive, more career oriented, faster, and places greater emphasis on the individual than on family and community. Further, they feel sexual mores are more permissive, and that there is a more tolerant attitude toward different kinds of people. Indeed, most people feel that traditional values of home, family, and community do not apply in this information society.

Traditionally, the institutions of church, school, and public government have been viewed as the foundations of society by most Americans. Virtually every individual and family has come in contact with these institutions and has been affected by them. However, these traditional institutions are not central to life in Silicon Valley. Most people noted little or no interest in church-related activities or in community or civic activities. One area in which people reported a good deal of interest was in school-related activities of their children. Yet while most parents expressed interest in their children's school activities, they had little involvement in school-related activities. One explanation for this apparent paradox is time constraints faced by working parents. These parents experienced long and concentrated work days and by night they were too tired to go out and participate in school activities.

The negative aspects of Silicon Valley's information society are also part of the reality. The disregard for established institutions and the lack of traditional values is a problem faced by many. As one person expressed it: "Traditional values place the center of life in the home, family, and community. That's not the way it is here. People focus on themselves, or on one significant person—that's all. There's a withdrawal of concern for others. I don't know where I fit into this. I still think it's good to have those old values, but they aren't part of the way I'm living now."

Many Silicon Valley observers note that the information society overwhelms all other societal forms. "Everyone here works in electronics. So when you meet people who work in other industries, you don't know what to talk about." The industry producing new information technologies is both a benevolent supplier of jobs and a temptor. "It is easy to get so caught up that you lose perspective." Most people want to rid themselves of work-related concerns when they deal with their family and friends, but many have trouble backing off. The fast pace of life, stress, and dilemma of having to choose between work and personal life pervade the society.

Summary

Silicon Valley represents a special kind of information society based on technology, continuous innovation, vigorous economic competition, and entrepreneurship. Understandably, the entrepreneurs of Silicon Valley take extreme pride in the system they have created. Technology has rewarded them personally, spawning millionaires at a remarkable rate. It also has been good to the local area, contributing new jobs and tax dollars. As the cornerstone of the information society, high-tech industry has been good for the nation, providing one of the economic bright spots in a rather dreary picture of smokestack industries and displaced workers. Given these achievements, it is understandable that high-tech entrepreneurs survey their efforts with pride.

But what about the future? Can and should such a record continue? Presently there is a paradox of troublesome changes in social and personal life, along with the challenges and rewards of work life. The information society emerging in Silicon Valley presents an inconsistent reality for its people. The challenges and opportunities are there as well as the stresses and traps. Many of the people who are part of this society are aware of the changes occurring around them and to them, and wonder about the impact of this emerging social environment on themselves and their families.

Work is a central component in the lives of most people in Silicon Valley's information society, with many stating that work is essential to their overall well-being. Meritocracy is the positive side of the Silicon Valley work ethic: the single most important criterion in determining success is work performance. But there is also a sinister side to the work ethic: one is left with few resources and little self-esteem when one's job is pulled away.

A troubling characteristic of the emerging information society is the absence of stability. Information-technology producers experience a high rate of job mobility, most having been at their present job two to three years or less. To exacerbate the situation, there is a high rate of change in personal living-situations as well. Traditionally, people have depended on jobs and on families or households to provide support, but many of the Silicon Valley technology producers were able to depend on neither. For many, change was pervasive, continual, and unsettling.

Families in Silicon Valley's information society also are changing. The traditional nuclear family is less common than it once was. New family forms are emerging, often without intention or planning. The large number of families headed by single parents face special problems. Single parents are usually also working parents, and as such have special problems with time. High-tech industry demands commitment and long hours from its employees, and does not stop to ask whether those employees also face responsibilities at home, or whether there is anyone else to share those responsibilities. Time becomes the enemy for those families.

For the industry, the rate of job growth and facilities expansion must level off as the geographical and resource limitations of Silicon Valley are reached. Already most electronics manufacturing jobs are located elsewhere. But as yet there are no signs that Silicon Valley's entrepreneurial spirit is slackening. Technical expertise and entrepreneurial spirit are firmly established there, and to a far more pervasive degree than elsewhere in the country. Silicon Valley is still the heartland of the information society. The network, the human chain of vital information, is still working.

In the information society, information and innovation combine to produce economic value. Information is the society's resource and it is inexhaustible. Entrepreneurship is the society's driving force, and it is moving with deep strength and conviction. The entrepreneurial spirit and sense of innovation that characterized the growth of the industry is very much alive in its people today. If the workaholic single-mindedness of purpose can be melded with the desire for a fuller quality of life, the emerging information society may be as significant as the technology that spawned it.

References

Bank of America (1983). *Regional perspectives: Santa Clara County. 1983 outlook.* San Francisco, CA: Bank of America.

Davis, W. (1981). Personal interview.

Larsen, J.K. (1984). Workaholism in the valley. *Business Woman, 3*(6).

Larsen, J.K., & Gill, C. (1984). *Changing lifestyles in Silicon Valley.* Los Altos, CA: Cognos Associates.

Machlup, F. (1962). *The production and distribution of knowledge in the United States.* Princeton, NJ: Princeton University Press.

Murray, T.J. (1981). Silicon Valley faces up to the people crunch. *Dun's Review, 16,* 60–62.

Porat, M.U. (1978). Global implications of the information society. *Journal of Communication, 28,* 70–79.

Rogers, E.M., & Larsen, J.K. (1984). *Silicon Valley fever: Growth of high technology culture.* New York: Basic Books.

San Jose Mercury (1981) June 28.

Schmieder, R. (1983). *Rich's complete guide to Silicon Valley.* Palo Alto, CA: Rich's Enterprises.

Watson, A. (1981). Census data portrait of a typical San Josean. *San Jose News* (October 1).

10

The Research Triangle of North Carolina: Its History and Influence as an Information Society Component

Quentin W. Lindsey

The early history of the Research Triangle Park is described. Information society aspects became more pronounced in 1980 with the establishment of the Microelectronics Center of North Carolina in the Park. This has led to much more development of sophisticated computer hardware and software by institutions and firms operating within the park and within the state. Libraries of universities and industry have expanded and utilized more sophisticated systems of information management. However, the point is made that information, regardless of its form and content, can be used for creative or destructive purposes. Concepts of the humanities—e.g., wisdom, justice, beauty, and truth—are more likely to guide the use of information toward constructive purposes than will the strict objectivity of science.

Establishing the Research Triangle Park

Six years after taking the initial steps in 1955 to establish the Research Triangle in North Carolina, former governor Luther Hodges is quoted as describing it as "an idea that has produced a reality—the idea that the scientific brains and research talents of . . . three institutions, and their life of research in many fields, could provide the background and stimulation of research for the benefit of the state and nation. In a way, the Research Triangle is the marriage of North Carolina's ideals for higher education and its hope for material progress'' (Wilson, 1967, p. 1).

For several years prior to 1955, Howard W. Odum, a sociologist at the University of North Carolina at Chapel Hill, had made repeated attempts to foster a research complex involving the University of North Carolina at Chapel Hill in association with Duke University in Durham and North Carolina State University at Raleigh. All three institutions are within a 15-mile radius of the center of the triangle formed by these institutions. Over the period 1952–1955, Romeo Guest, a North Carolina developer, sought to promote the establishment of industrial laboratories and other forms of research and development with this triangle. But not until Hodges, as governor, combined the support of state government with academic and industrial interests did concrete action begin to take place.

In 1984, the triangle consists of the three universities plus the 5,000 acre Research Triangle Park located in its center. Within this park, some 50 public and private research organizations now function, plus another 50 organizations providing hotel, travel, banking, and other services. More than 20,000 people work in the park each day, and the total payroll amounts to approximately half a billion dollars per year. Private satellite parks are now springing up outside the Research Triangle Park itself.

The Research Triangle is a great asset to the State of North Carolina. It has become known as a state committed to scientific research and the development of advanced technology industries. The Triangle has averaged nearly $2 billion in new investment in industrial plant and equipment each year of the past eight years. Throughout most of the recent recession, the unemployment level was running about 2 percentage points below the national average.

In 1980, an additional step was taken that qualified North Carolina as a distinct component of the so-called information society: the creation of the Microelectronics Center of North Carolina. The center is designed to unify electronics research and education efforts of the three triangle universities, plus that of the Research Triangle Institute in the Park, the University of North Carolina at Charlotte, and the North Carolina Agricultural and Technical State University at Greensboro. The Microelectronics Center enables these six institutions to share in the use of extremely expensive, state-of-the-art equipment. It has a core staff that relates closely to the faculties and staff of the universities and to the professional staff of industrial affiliates of the center. Microwave links with the six associated institutions are being developed to enable two-way telecommunications between them. State appropriations for the center total about $47 million. Additional investment in land and equipment, and in operating costs thus far, now bring the total expenditures to around $80 million since 1980.

Justification for this investment in the center rests on its influence in creating and maintaining jobs by attracting additional industrial firms to the state, particularly those that utilize microelectronics directly or indirectly in their operations. In the long run, justification will be through the creation of more and better jobs by virtue of spin-off industrial growth in the state, stemming from research by the center and associated research institutions. This growth will consist of new microelectronics-related firms; the modernization of traditional industries in the state, such as textiles and furniture; the expansion of existing small-business firms; and the associated growth of many other aspects of society such as financial institutions, advertising agencies, transportation systems, and so on. It will also include increased use and support of the library system.

Since the establishment of the Microelectronics Center, the North Carolina Biotechnology Center has also been created and the State Legislature is considering a plan to invest $70 million in this field. There are also plans for a major expansion of microsphere capabilities, i.e., research into the microphenomena of molecular biology, microelectronics, and related fields.

The Establishment Struggle

The establishment of the Research Triangle Park and the Microelectronics Center has not been simple. In creating the park, the differing views and interests of the universities, state government, and private industrial and financial institutions had to be dealt with. In creating the Microelectronics Center, competition for resources by the Triangle Universities, two public and one private, had to be resolved. The research orientation and physical characteristics of the center, the equipment requirements, and other potential bases for disagreement were significant causes of debate. National cycles of recession and prosperity constituted another disturbing factor.

Throughout all aspects of the Research Triangle development, including the development of the Microelectronics Center and subsequent development of biotechnology and other fields, the informal partnership of state government, universities, and the private sector has been essential. Governor Hodges provided the external leadership and support required to draw the interested parties together behind a common, sustained purpose. Later, Governor Hunt helped negotiate the compromises, persuade the legislature to provide financial support, recruit industrial firms, and otherwise bring the Microelectronics Center and associated university programs into being.

However, state government alone is not enough. Without the universities, state government could not have created the park, nor the Microelectronics Center and other facilities as they exist today. And without initial industrial support, and subsequent further growth of industry, neither the universities nor state and local governments could have developed the park and the center to the world-class scale and standards that now prevail there.

One main conclusion can be drawn from the Research Triangle experience. It is similar to the experiences in Silicon Valley, and to the emerging information-oriented developments in and around Austin, Texas. A combination of academia, industry, and government (federal, state, and local) is required to bring about major developments pertaining to accelerated economic growth through technological innovation. The industrial factory to which Everett Rogers refers in this volume has been replaced not just by the university but by a growing university-industry-government complex.

Information and the Structural Design of Society

Analysis of the Research Triangle development highlights two main issues. First, the transformation of basic research in microelectronics, or in any other field of science and engineering, into manifestations of the information society requires consideration of the process of technological innovation. Technological innovation consists of two interrelated parts, *technical* and *organizational* innovation. Computer chips, robots, telecommunications systems, and other tangible products and processes that emanate from the use of information drawn from basic microelectronics research are examples of *technical* innovation. The changes in the organization of industry, of methods of communication, of industry-university-government relations, and other institutional structures, constitute examples of *organizational* innovation. Economic, sociological, political, and other forms of information are utilized in organizational innovation.

Second, analysis emphasizes, in a more controversial way, fundamental questions related to the design of the emerging information society. These questions deal with the nature and purpose of universities, of industrial firms, of government, and of other components of society. More important, they deal with people's relations with each other and with these institutional structures and their functions. They are the questions that are answered, one way or another, as we make use of information in the design of society. Use of information does change society, whether it is intended to do so or not.

Science and engineering information does not provide the wisdom nor the appreciation of aesthetic considerations needed to guide the design of society. Instead, we must turn to concepts such as justice, integrity, beauty, and truth. These eternal verities of the humanities, and their integration with concepts of science, are also required in creating the information society.

Information, whatever its form and content, can be used for good or evil, for creative or destructive purposes. It can be used intensively and extensively, or it can remain underutilized, even dormant. Information can be transmitted rapidly to entire populations through modern communications and education systems, or it may be used selectively to preserve power for the few at the expense of many. Information can range from knowledge of the fundamental principles of relativity and quantum physics to unorganized accumulation of trivia. Information can consist of inspiring expressions of truth and integrity, or deliberate misrepresentation of facts through malicious spread of propaganda.

It is my impression that information aspects of the information society are viewed from the perspective of scientific objectivity. If we are tilting in any direction, it is to assume that information is mostly good and relevant. Although we do not rule out the possibility that some information may be bad, irrelevant, or malicious, we apparently assume that all such deficiencies will be exposed or construed somehow as not being "information." However, on the cutting edge of change, i.e., in making decisions that determine the form and character of the information society, the mode of scientific objectivity does not prevail. Science knows no moral choice, as exemplified by the use of scientific information in building destructive weapons of war. It is true that scientific and engineering evidence is essential in developing a new product or process. Economic considerations are required in determining market feasibility and hence in deciding whether to start a new firm or expand an existing one. Information pertaining to political, sociological, and economic issues must be used in determining government support for university research, in deciding tariff or quota questions, and in dealing with many other policy issues that relate to the structures of society. But in every case, none of the information available will serve, in whole or in part, as the basis for decisions in a completely deterministic sense. There are no absolute answers, although valid and relevant information helps.

Moreover, technical and organizational innovation constitutes a process of creative destruction. As new products are introduced, existing products and processes become obsolete. Textile mills and automobile and steel plants need to be modernized or replaced. Inner cities need to be rebuilt and new jobs created. New ecological balances with the environment need to be struck. New relations among nation-states must be devised, and even the concept of the nation-state may be superseded over time—in the manner in which ancient feudal structures have given way—through several transformations, by the modern industrial state.

It is for these and similar reasons that we cannot deal with the design of the information society without explicitly referring to subjective concepts such as "justice," "integrity," "beauty," and "truth." The decisions we must make in the design of society must translate such criteria into the vision, values, and the creative purposes in accordance with which information may be used.

Reference

Wilson, L.R. (1967). *The research triangle of North Carolina*. Chapel Hill, NC: Colonial Press.

11

High Technology Development in Brazil

Luiz Fonseca

The times in which we live are characterized by one of the worst economic crises of contemporary society. But at the same time, our age is also characterized by wonderful conquests in every field of the sciences and knowledge, creating new opportunities for the generation of wealth and new patterns of organization in the production of goods and services. Historically, crisis and technology tend to be intimately associated. This article addresses the question to what extent the way out of deep economic crisis will be directly influenced by the expansion of information technologies through an examination of the development of high technology in Brazil.

Technological advancement, the fruit of the exercise of labor, is the conquest of all men in directing the forces of nature at their service. Nothing more just than that the fruits of technical progress be made available to those that participate in production, aiming at eliminating poverty and bringing together all people. The dominion shown by technology in the use of the forces of nature must also indicate the road to the preparation of a new society where material resources are at the disposition of the people. The dominion shown by technology in the use of the forces of nature must also indicate the road to the preparation of a new society where material resources are at the disposition of the people. This principle indicates that it is necessary to prepare a society in which the beneficial effects of technical progress will reach all men and at the same time eliminating its negative effects.

—From the report of the Manufacturing
Automation Commission of the Special
Secretariat of Informatics of Brazil

211

Technology in the Central Countries

The present time is characterized by one of the worst economic crises of contemporary society. But our age is also witnessing wonderful conquests in every field of the sciences and knowledge, creating new opportunities for the generation of wealth and new patterns of organization in the production of goods and services. These conquests, which appeared in the form of sophisticated technologies, bring with them the expectation of large increases in labor productivity and the hope for substantial improvements in the quality of human life.

Historically, crisis and technology tend to be intimately associated. In the last decades the economic crisis, caused mainly by the increase in the import price of oil in the beginning of the 1970s, forced the appearance of new technology in the central countries. Among them, and in a intensely dramatic form, there emerged the application of informatics and microelectronics that put in march a veritable revolution in world production, by turning the dream of automation into a reality.

To what extent the way out of the deep economic crisis in which the world is immersed will be directly influenced or even conditioned by this technological expansion and to what extent these innovations will benefit equally the central and the peripheral countries is still obscure. Castro et al. (1984, pp. 1–2) suggest that "by contributing decisively towards the production of certain types of goods which demand greater precision and quality, microelectronic technology has asserted its position of economic importance and technical prominence among other types of production techniques. Additionally, it confirms the value of its technical progress insofar as it permits levels of productivity and economic competitiveness which surpass those of the traditional technologies."

One of the outstanding features of information technology is that it is something entirely different from whatever existed before, and that it cannot be considered as an expansion of the previous technological processes. Because it requires for its utilization a complete reorganizing of production patterns, that technology alters profoundly the conventional forms of work—be it work of a qualified, semiqualified, or nonqualified nature.

According to Coriat (1984), what makes this technology so fascinating and spectacular are the multiple possibilities of associations and combinations of production patterns that it permits, such as (1) *automated integration,* through which the machine not only substitutes man but also allows the operation of a set of productive tasks in an integrated way, optimizing the whole system of production; and (2) *flexible integration,* through which a given set of machines is able to produce families of parts, starting from

a common matrix. This eliminates the need for the mechanical reorganization of the production line to attend to specifications of a certain
product, since the modifications are done through programming.

What that means for human beings has not been sufficiently analyzed.
However, there is no doubt that we are living in a new transition period,
with profound effects on the intensity, quality, and the quantity of labor
used in industrial production and services.

Day by day, informatics is confirming itself as an effective factor of
wealth generation. As a result, new industries and new products are
successively appearing, especially in the developed countries, which are
the first beneficiaries of its development and application. According to
Rattner (1983), "in spite of the high risks inherent to the market of new
technologies, these offer also large profits for the firms that succeed in
taking hold early of the emerging technologies and are able to successfully
protect them against the attack by potential competitors."

However, in the capitalist and highly competitive society in which we
live, the distribution of the benefits derived from technological innovation
do not tend to produce an equitable pattern. What seems to be happening
is a new reinforcement in the direction of the income concentration in the
central, in relation to the peripheral, countries and, within each country,
in the big companies, in relation to the medium-size and the small ones.
For Rattner (1982), this is largely due to microelectronics having the ability
to potentialize the centralized integration and management of immense
and powerful conglomerate groups. The expansion of these conglomerates
forcefully introduces profound changes in the international division of
labor, restructuring the whole process of production and market, both at
the national and international levels, giving birth to the global markets.

The global market is the answer to the need created mainly by the
necessity of huge investments in research and development (R&D) of new
technologies. Since the gains and benefits flow more abundantly to the
countries and companies that innovate earlier, we are involved in a real
race in the direction of accelerating scientific findings through R&D, with
the consequent increase of the rate of investment in the sector. Most of
the investment is done by the big companies of the industrialized nations.
The poorer countries and the small firms, not having the conditions to
meet these costs, are kept outside of the process.

Technology itself can become a direct source of income. The common
pattern is that, after applying the results of R&D in its own production,
the transnationals transfer part of it to the intermediate countries, mostly
through providing know-how for the production of parts and components
or through technical assistance, for which they receive payment of royal-

ties. This scheme necessarily intensifies the technological dependence that characterizes the industrial relations in the West.

The Dependency of the Peripheral Countries

The transnationalization of the world economy is a fact that is accepted as occurring to a high degree as a function of the new technology. The economic strength of the central nations, acting through their multinationals, are clearly affecting the newly industrialized countries. These countries, caught in the net of the global markets, are realizing that the absorption of the new technology is causing deep social, political, and economic changes of great implications for the whole community. In view of this, the intermediate countries are awaking to the need of facing this stage from a broader perspective, by considering technology as a problem of the whole society and not just of businessmen, workers, university professors, scientists, technicians, or the government.

Surely, the item that brings more drama to this changing context is the fear that the new technologies, especially those related to microelectronics, will lessen the requirements of labor, which is the most abundant production factor in the newly industrialized nations. In reality, the competitive capacity of these countries is centered in the export of the low cost of its labor. To the extent that the developed nations find the means to produce with less manpower requirements, the present point of equilibrium will tend to be altered, with yet more unfavorable consequences for the Third World.

In the words of Castro et al. (1984):

> Countries like Brazil will be affected in a significant way and there is already a discussion about the changes caused by microelectronic technology, which will have considerable influence on the international division of labor. Such effects could lead to the erosion of the comparative advantages of developing countries in international trade and cause a reduction of the importance of the wage differential, which has been responsible for the competitiveness of these countries in some industrial sectors. Through the decrease in the proportion of direct labor costs within the total costs of production, the introduction of microelectronics, via automation of the production process, may minimize the advantages of low labor costs and lead to a profitable relocation of production from the developing countries to the developed countries themselves.

One of the biggest problems of the intermediate nations today is unemployment. The millions of jobless people that live in these countries are not fully participating in society, either from the social or the economic point of view. Hence, anything that tends to aggravate the problem of unemployment will necessarily have a great impact on the community, which could be the case of the microelectronic innovations. By promoting the change of the technical basis from the theory of the value of labor to that of the theory of the value of information, microelectronic technology might jeopardize the only comparative advantage that favors the intermediate countries, that is, their abundant and cheap manpower. On the other hand, the workers and their labor unions in the less-developed countries tend not to be able to cope with this change on a technical basis. In many instances, because they are not politically prepared, they do not actively participate in the process, thereby becoming much more vulnerable to the perverse effect of technological innovation.

Castro et al. (1984) further state that

> the impact of microelectronic automation on the workers' control of the labor process and on the unions' bargaining power seems evident. This will be immediately reflected in the situation of the work and life of employees, to the extent that it will profoundly affect the conditions of employment, qualification and wages. The consequences tend to be more serious in countries like Brazil, where we have to consider the precariousness of social security mechanisms relating to unemployment as well as to the difficulties faced by the unions in concluding comprehensive agreements, which would contain items such as stability of employment, control over introduction of technical information, etc.

This is perhaps the main justification of government interference that tries to solve the dilemma between the utilization of a more efficient technology and the maintenance of the national level of employment.

It should also be considered that in the peripheral countries, the inevitable reorganization and adaptation of internal structures to receive the new technology gives birth to a series of crises that are not always easily solved. In the first place, there is occurring in the countries of the Third World a form of technological dualism, through which conventional and traditional production processes coexist with enclaves of high-technology industry. The competition between old and new processes can go on for a greater or lesser period of time. But sooner or later the criteria of quality, uniformity, and cost will displace the less-advanced technology (usually practiced by the local, medium- and small-size companies) to the benefit of the more advanced one (usually practiced by large foreign companies).

Second, the countries that want to modernize by using domestic technology face the problem of R&D. In the words of Rattner (1982), "the countries of Latin America, even the more advanced ones like Argentina, Brazil and Mexico, present economies of late capitalism, in which the market structures and the presence of transnational conglomerates greatly inhibit the emergence and the development of an autonomous science and technology system.'' This problem is manifold. It requires well-qualified scientists and researchers, and the support of strong institutions and sophisticated equipment. These conditions are not exactly abundant in the intermediate countries. They have to confront the problem of how to meet the costs of domestic R&D; since their economies are depleted, and considering the enormous investments that R&D requires, they face enormous difficulty in allocating funds for that purpose, at least at the necessary level.

The natural reaction to these drawbacks is the emergence of technological nationalism—prevailing in the intermediate countries today—which does its best to create barriers against the invasion of foreign technology. Analyzing the consequences that might be felt on a global scale, even in the 1980s, Rattner (1982) foresees that for economic and political reasons, the wave of technological nationalism will expand, making local governments provide support and incentives of all sorts, particularly in the newly developed countries, where there can already be found several attempts to implant explicit technological policies.

According to Rattner, the governments of the Third World are directly sponsoring the companies that enter into the global markets and are giving explicit incentives to those companies in their country, which contribute to the expansion of exports and the level of employment. The forms of patronage vary from legal protection and incentives for exports to declared support of projects of joint ventures for marketing and R&D. Market reserve or import restrictions, besides fiscal incentives and tax exemption, are among the array of mechanisms adopted by the governments to stimulate job generation and the conquest of external markets, while trying to protect the national industries against foreign competitors. Conversely, when technological nationalism becomes too critical, the transnational companies unleash their powerful methods to counterbalance its effects. The measures taken go from the offering, at very competitive prices, of their high-quality products, use of specifications that impair the compatibility of their machines with national peripherals, and the use of extremely aggressive lobbying, to the purchase of national firms at highly advantageous prices.

In this true technological warfare, it becomes very difficult for the national companies of the peripheral countries to compete in the global markets or even in their own national markets. After the partition is made and the lion's share is taken by the transnationals, only the smaller areas, of little commercial interest, will remain.

The Specific Case of Brazil

Due to the amazing technological performance of the central nations and the pressure they exert in the global markets, the options are apparently few for the developing countries. In the case of the intermediate nations, Brazil among them, the situation is not altogether clear.

It is generally accepted in Brazil that the microelectronic technology is here to stay and to expand. At this moment any discussion about the good or bad qualities of informatics and automation becomes meaningless. For many Brazilians the right questions are how to prepare the country to receive the impact of the new technology, and how to monitor that process, to the extent that it is possible.

Historically, the struggle for Brazil's industrial emancipation started back in the last century. The difficulties of internal provisioning during the Depression years and World War II forced Brazil to move toward a policy of import substitution for manufactured products. This policy was severely criticized on the grounds of its high social cost and because it diverted from the priority of agriculture, recognized as the major economic vocation of the country. Notwithstanding, due to that policy, Brazil is today self-sufficient in almost every line of manufacturing, except for certain highly sophisticated products, and its present imports are raw materials such as oil, coal, and wheat, besides a few chemicals that are scarce in the country. It was that policy that made it possible for Brazilian manufacturing to contribute 58.5% of total exports in 1982. Parallel to that, Brazil developed its educational system, which, in spite of being far from the ideal level, has expanded considerably. The present university system in the country enrolls around 1,407,655 students in 889 educational units. Some of the Brazilian universities have achieved high standards in many different fields.

In order to provide vocational education for the workers from the industrial and services sectors, the National Industrial Training Service (SENAI) was created in 1942, and in 1946 the National Commercial Training Service (SENAC). These institutions are directly linked to the Federations of Industry and Commerce, respectively. During the last four decades, SENAI and SENAC have established nationwide networks for professional training, which today constitute the main mechanism for manpower training as well as an important gateway for the entry of technology into the country. The effort in vocational education is being supplemented by a large number of federal technical schools and hundreds of other institutions, both private and public, dedicated to professional training and scattered throughout different states of the country. In 1983 alone, 24 institutions offered 1,797 courses for the qualification of workers in many areas of the economy.

Having acquired valuable experience in manufacturing, and with a well-established university and professional-training system besides a few recognized research institutions, Brazil appears today as a nation able to start consolidating its position vis-à-vis other, more developed countries. An important factor that gives support to this claim is the existence of a national market of 130 million people, not to mention the growing possibilities of favorable commercial exchange with Latin American and African countries.

Although there is an impetus in Brazil in the direction of growth and modernization, it must be remembered that it is an extremely complex land that shows enormous variations in the productive capacity of different regions and economic sectors. Thus there coexist in the country the sparsely inhabited Amazon Region, the agricultural central-west, the pre-industrial northeast, and the relatively industrialized south with an enclave of high industrialization—the State of São Paulo. It is hoped that the advancement of technology, at least in the long run, might contribute to rescue economically the more backward regions with more problems of education and poverty.

In the case of open economies such as that of Brazil, the rate of adoption of new technology is closely related to its participation in the international market. To compete in the foreign market means to produce efficiently and cheaply. To attain this it is necessary to innovate, which usually implies high costs. The present conjunctural situation in Brazil is by no means attractive in terms of investment. Internally it is depleted, and externally it is struggling with the biggest external debt in the world. Of course this has a disrupting effect on production and employment. One recent study, conducted by Cunha (s.d.), indicates that the sector of capital goods has been severely affected and the worst consequence has been the degeneration of Brazilian industry and the labor market. With reference to the State of São Paulo, the major industrial center of the country, the study indicates that industrial production decreased 11% in 1981 and, accumulatively, 17% in the period from 1981 to 1983. This effect is mainly in the capital goods subsector that presents a decrease of 93% between 1980 and 1983, and the sector of durable goods that decreased 22% in the same period.

There has also been a drop in the level of employment, especially in the mechanical sector (-35%), transport (-25%), metallurgy (-26%) and nonmetallic minerals (-23%). This drop has been partially attenuated by the expansion of the salaried employment in the commercial and service sectors. The decrease in employment has been larger than the decrease in production, which indicates increase in productivity, especially after 1982. During the same period, the population occupied in the informal labor market, that is, wageless work without formal employment ties, expanded from 35% to 41%. However, for the workers who kept their jobs there was no negative interference in the process of salary formation. On the contrary, the average salary has increased for the lower salary group in the period from 1980 to 1982, in real terms. This was not the case for the homogeneous groups at the top of the salary pyramid that show a decrease in their net salaries over that period.

Use of High Technology in Brazil

In its report on the social, economic, and employment effects of automation, the Special Commission on Manufacturing Automation (Impactos, 1984) presents two hypotheses related to the introduction of automated processes in Brazil. The first one states that microelectronic equipment (such as NCMT, robots, CAD/CAM systems) should be imported, with just its utilization begin reserved to the Brazilian firms. In the case of the NCMT, at least, this hypothesis cannot be sustained, because about 20% of the existing machines already have been produced in the country. Besides that, a series of negative aspects associated with this hypothesis calls for its rejection.

The second hypothesis considers a policy that not only incorporates the use of microelectronic machines but also aims at their local production and technological development. The commission recognizes that even in this last model there might occur industrial concentration, but in this case it will be done in the context of the Brazilian industrial complex, creating the basis for the development of domestic technology. It considers that the mobilization of resources to implement this sector will generate beneficial multiplying effects on the economy, especially during the maturation of the first investments in the sector.

In both hypotheses it will be necessary to wait a long time until the economy is settled—time being measured in years for the first hypothesis and in decades for the second.

According to the same report:

> We do not have in the country and we cannot build rapidly the technical competence to construct a basis for the production of every new equipment. This, however, should not impede us from developing production competence for at least some of the necessary equipment.

> The implications of that is that we will continue to be technologically dependent on other countries, participating in an international division of labor which is already harmful to the country.

> Today we are dependent on this technology and on the global strategy of the transnationals. They interfere decisively in the restructuring and redirecting of our economy. They are already changing production processes in the country, aiming at global markets.

> The government will also act in a decisive way if it takes action promptly in a planned manner and not only by incorporating the new technologies in its

government companies. If it acts only in function of international competition it will just be following the direction dictated by the transnationals.

The present official position of Brazil is much closer to the second hypothesis in that it is interested in accelerating the rhythm of informatization of the country, using domestic capital and technology.

One very interesting analysis conducted by Castro (1983) comments on four cases that illustrate different approaches to technological development in Brazil. In the first case, related to the pharmaceutical industry, there occurred a significant decrease in the participation of the Brazilian companies while the transnationals sharply increase their share not only in R&D but also in the ownership of the firms.

The second case refers to the automobile industry. In this sector technological innovation has been highly successful. As an indicator, car production in Brazil grew from 130,000 vehicles in 1960 to 1.16 million in 1980. Besides attending the local market, this sector exported $1.5 billion in 1981. The Brazilian automobile industry today is quite competitive in many countries. In this sector, however, very little has been added in terms of Brazilian technology, with one notable exception—the development of the alcohol engine. In spite of some minor drawbacks, that program has been a success. The important fact here is that it uses vegetable fuel, a renewable resource. The conditions of being a tropical country with the immense territory of Brazil favors the viability of this project.

The third case is that of the Brazilian computer industry. Castro (1983) notes that "the development of the Brazilian computer industry has been outstanding in terms of growth and import substitution. In particular, the domestic R&D patterns set this sector apart from most others in which local efforts are nil or marginal. Mean value for R&D is 8.7% of revenues, which is above international averages."

The fourth case relates to military weapons. Although Brazil has one of the smaller armed forces (on per capita basis) plus a modest military participation in the nation's budget (only 12%), it has become the sixth major world exporter of weapons, with income in this sector estimated at $5.5 billion a year. The key to this performance seems to be the concentration of the production on intermediate types of weapons in which were incorporated simple practical solutions.

Summing up his analysis of these four cases, Moura Castro (1983) concludes that:

Brazil has reached a stage in which domestic technology generation has become possible. Yet, if the necessary conditions are there, they are certainly not sufficient. Being an internationally open economy, much exposed to technology transfers from abroad and quite inexperienced in generating its own, Brazil has to meet additional conditions before significant achievements can be obtained.

The main difficulty has to do with the immediate availability of foreign technology which in most cases is adequate, inexpensive and low risk. In addition, it is marketed aggressively by experienced firms interested in utilizing their know-how to retain control of the markets. This usually means closed packages that prevent any meaningful role for domestic R&D. . . . Hence, under the conditions of relatively free competition, technology will not be generated in the country. The inevitable consequence is a permanent technological dependence, with all the correlated lack of economic independence.

The Brazilian Informatics Law

Traditionally Brazil has shown a very receptive attitude toward foreign technology. In recent decades it has benefited from investments done in R&D by the central countries. Lately, however, the Brazilians began to feel the need for an explicit policy to promote the development of domestic technology, at least in selected areas of the economy. They considered that if adequate controls and strong stimuli are not offered to the national companies, these will easily opt for foreign technology. The appearance of informatics on the Brazilian technological scene coincided with this awakening.

Perhaps more than in any other case in Latin America, the action of the Brazilian government has intervened to protect or stimulate local activities of production, use, and R&D in relation to microelectronics, through public policies. This has been done through legislation and by offering incentives for the growing of the informatics sector. At the same time it is fostering, over the medium and long term, the building of a more independent industry, with the progressive nationalization of parts and components.

Within this model, the National Congress has recently approved the Brazilian law of informatics (Dispõe sobre, 1984), which becomes the legal instrument for monitoring the computerization of Brazilian society from now on. The main items of this law are:

1. The creation of the National Council of Informatics and Automation (CONIN), directly responsible to the president of Brazil and under which is the National Secretariat for Informatics. CONIN has the responsibility to elaborate the National Plan for Informatics, to be submitted every third year to the National Congress.
2. Adoption of restrictions on production, operation, marketing, and importing of technical goods and services in informatics. These restrictions are of a temporary character and will remain in force until the

national companies are consolidated and able to compete on the international market. This item assures the market reserve for the national firms in terms of mini- and microcomputers.

3. For the purposes of this law there are considered as national companies all juridical personalities constituted and with headquarters in Brazil whose control is permanently, exclusive by, and unconditionally in, the hands of Brazilian persons or entities of public rights. Control in this context is in terms of decision, technology, and capital.

4. For the accomplishment of R&D projects, and for the production of goods and services of informatics, national companies can receive exemptions up to 100% in taxes on imports and industrial products.

5. Foreign companies that are interested may produce their equipment in the informatics export districts, located in the north and northeast regions of Brazil, provided that their production is destined exclusively for the foreign market.

6. Creation of a line of fiscal incentives for purchase of shares of national companies linked to informatics.

7. Creation of the National Informatics Center Foundation with the objective of promoting scientific and technological research in informatics activities. Among the financing sources of the foundation is the Special Informatics Fund, also created by the same law.

The term "market reserve" is not explicitly used in the wording of the Brazilian Informatics Law. However, this issue has elicited wide interest to the point of becoming the most controversial item of the whole process. The market reserve seems to be so polemic not only because of the supplying of the Brazilian market with computers produced locally, but also because of the precedent it creates on the international level.

For many Brazilians, government support, in terms of the market reserve for mini- and microcomputers is important also from the political and social point of view. For them, the market reserve should not only protect some 150 firms that produce computers but should also be used to establish a position in terms of the technological possibilities of the country. According to Castro (1983), "the market reserve was a wise decision in the long run. To judge by the present development, technology and costs are rapidly reducing the gap between the local initiatives and the well-established foreign competition. In addition, the sector is past the stage of sheltered public firms surrounded by unprofessional university professors' risk ventures."

Castro also comments on the fierce controversy between those who advocate the market reserve for mini- and microcomputers and those who are against it. In this last group, the argument is that the transnational companies could produce in the country with less cost—and offer a product of better quality and within international standards—and with the advantage of using their facilities to export. Besides that, the consumer would get the benefit in terms of market prices. On the other hand, the group that defends the market reserve contends that that is an area of vital importance for the technological future of the country and that the efforts and the hardships of today will be fully compensated for later on. With the approval of the market reserve in the context of a law passed by the National Congress, this matter now seems to be settled, at least until the national companies are in a position to compete with their products on the international markets.

Technological Impact on Employment

The problem of unemployment arises like a ghost in the context of the technological modernization of Brazil. In the present conjuncture there is already a deficit of 2.5 million unemployed workers in the country. This deficit is increased annually by the addition of around 1.5 million young people to the labor force. In a situation like that it becomes quite natural to fear that microelectronics might worsen this already critical outlook.

There are some difficulties connected with an effective evaluation of the impact of microelectronics on employment in Brazil. In the first place, the studies that have been done so far are always of a partial or microanalysis nature, hence demanding caution as regards generalization. Second, that economic is relatively little diffused in Brazilian society, and therefore it is impossible to appraise in depth its impact on the economy and on the professional structure. Third, the entry of microelectronics coincides with the strong recession the country is facing, which tends to confound the effect of the one phenomenon with the other's. And finally, considering that the economically active population of Brazil amounts to 50 million people, from which 18 million comprise the formal market, it becomes of little relevance to inquire about the impact of microelectronics in global terms. For any meaningful evaluation it is necessary to decompose the work force in order to verify the modernizing effects on specific subsectors and occupations.

The most recent report of the Special Commissions of Evaluation of Automation (Impactos, 1984) presents some interesting information. In what concerns the Manufacturing Subcommission, two studies are mentioned. The first, conducted by Peliano (1983) is of a prospective nature. It suggests that if microelectronic automation in Brazil is to follow the pattern, rhythm, and the tendencies observed and projected for the United States until 1990, some 800,000 to 2.4 million workers will be excluded from the manufacturing sector. The second, conducted by Tauile (1982), is a field study on the effect of adoption of some 700 NCMT in the country, up to the year 1980. The findings indicate that there had been substitution or displacement of three to five workers for each NCMT introduced. This analysis, however, did not consider the compensatory indirect effect that might have occurred as a result of that innovation.

In terms of the manufacturing sector as a whole, there is no major evidence that automation is contributing to unemployment. On the contrary, there is even suspicion that those companies that resist modernizing will eventually meet more difficulties in keeping their employees.

The sector that has presented the highest growth rates during the last few years in Brazil is banking and financing. This is also a sector that has rapidly modernized its processes and services. Notwithstanding this, automation has not influenced negatively the sector's employment level. On the contrary, according to figures from the National Federation of Banks (NFB), the number of employees in the sector increased from 372,000 in 1979 to 463,000 in 1982 (this statistic does not include the Bank of Brazil, the largest banking system in the country). Using a series of indicators, the NFB demonstrated that although the sector as a whole is growing more than the employment, the increase in jobs is also quite significant.

According to the Subcommission of Automation on Commercial Operations, the financial sector is still in the beginning of its computerization process. The great majority of computerized systems in the sector have not been integrated—its processing being done in batch. The systems refer mainly to stocks updating, credit control, and printing of price lists. It is therefore premature to evaluate the impact of microelectronics in this sector, whether with regards to the amount or the nature of the effect on jobs.

A recent case study by Buarque (1984) on two Brazilian industries with a relative degree of automation presents interesting findings. One of the industries belongs to the automobile sector (Ford of Brazil) and the other to the metal-mechanics sector (Metal-Leve). Both are located in the State of São Paulo. The study, which covers the period from 1978 to 1984, indicates that:

1. In both companies the level of employment was maintained between 1980 and 1982.
2. There was a decided increase in productivity during those years.
3. There was an increase in the technological content of the products.
4. There was some flexibility in the production process, which appeared differently in the several phases of production.
5. There was also some flexibility of the organizational structure, with the more automated areas reaching a higher status than the others.

6. From the point of view of the occupational structure, there were minor alterations in certain functions, with substantial reduction in the administrative area.
7. The resources dedicated to R&D increased by about 30% in the two companies, during the period considered.

These results—maintenance of the level of employment, increase in productivity, increase in the technological content, flexibility of the production process and the occupational structure, and increase in R&D—are encouraging. But we should remember that since they are the outcome of case studies, these results require caution in their generalization.

Finally, it can be said that there is today in Brazil a favorable attitude of confidence and expectation with regard to the coming of computerization. In spite of many conjunctural problems, the structural conditions of the country as a whole are favorable, and practically all the anticipatory and preventive actions that should have been taken have indeed been taken. Brazil seems to be prepared to fight this battle and with fairly good chances of winning it.

References

Buarque, S. (1984). *Impactos da microeletrônica sobre emprego e estrutura ocupacional no Brasil;* diagnóstico e prospectiva para a próxima década. Recife, UFPe, Relatório de pesquisa.

Castro, C. de M. (1983). *High technology in intermediate countries? The case of Brazil.* Brasília: IPEA/IPLAN.

Castro, C. de M., et al. (1984). *Economic and social impacts of microelectronic technology in brazilian industry.* Brasília: IPEA/IPLAN.

Coriat, B. (1984). Novos padrões de organização da produção. In: Sim pósio sobre impactos sócio-economicos da informática. 1, Brasília, SEI/MTb/CNPq.

Cunha, P. (s.d.). *Evolução recente do mercado de trabalho assalaria do no Brasil— uma análise usando os dados da RAIS; relatório preliminar.* São Paulo, USP, Faculdade de Economia e Administração, 1v.

Dispõe sobre a Política Nacional de Informática e dá outras providências. (1984) Lei No. 7.232 de 29 de outubro de 1984. D.O. de 30/10/84, Seção I. p. 15.841.

Impactos sócio-econômicos da automação. (1984). Brasília, SEI.

Peliano, J.C.P. (1983). *Automação, emprego e qualificação de mão-de-obra na indústria brasileira;* notas preliminares. Brasília, IPEA/IPLAN/CNRH.

Rattner, H. (1982). O impacto da tecnologia do comando numérico na sociedade brasileira. *Boletim de Indicadores Conjunturais, 7* (May–June), 54–80.

Rattner, H. (1983). Inovação tecnológica e planejamento estratégico na década de 80. *Rev. Adm. Emp.* (Rio de Janeiro), *23*(1), 5–12.

Tauile, J.R. (1982). *Máquinas ferramentas de controle numérico no Brasil.* Rio de Janeiro, UFRJ.

12

Government Policies and High Technology in Japan

Ryuzo Ogasawara

Japan is presently engaged in the development of a variety of microelectronic and other high technologies. Among others, there is the Information Network System (INS), otherwise internationally known as the Integrated Services Digital Network (ISDN), which is being constructed by Nippon Telegraph and Telephone Corporation (NTT). The INS or ISDN is regarded as a large-scale nationwide project that will have a great impact on information and communications services. NTT, once a government telecommunications monopoly, was privatized in 1985, and the publication of its shares has received a tremendous response. The Japanese government has been surprised and overjoyed to receive such a large unexpected windfall that can be directed toward public spending and tax reductions. In addition, the abolition of the monopoly has brought much sought-after competition. This is, however, still restricted in many ways by administrative guidance and control. Government interference is putting increasing constraints on the private sector's activities, and is regarded as representing a "closed market" or "trade barrier" by foreign governments and businesses. There have been many successful research and development projects jointly conducted by the government and the private sector, but too much existing bureaucratic guidance and control is doing more harm than good. The bureaucracy is opposed at heart to the open market system. It is highly unlikely that bureaucracy will ever disappear. Administrative reforms initiated by the Nakasone government have not produced the expected fruits due to bureaucratic intransigence. This is the

227

problem that is preventing Japan's healthy growth in the high-technology industries and services.

National research and development (R&D) projects centering on microelectronics are progressing very well in Japan. These R&D studies are focusing on so-called Fifth Generation Computers,[1] ISDN,[2] direct broadcasting satellites,[3] Hi-Vision,[4] a national videotex network (CAPTAIN),[5] and room temperature superconductors.[6]

These studies are producing mixed results. Although some are resulting in success, other results are far below expectations. Noteworthy is that most of these projects are characterized by joint R&D efforts between the government and private sector. Take the case of ISDN or INS, for example. NTT began its experimental operations on a large scale in the Mitaka-Musashino area (outskirts of Tokyo) in 1984. Based on the results of the model ISDN system, NTT plans to extend this new communications system throughout the country over the next 10 or 15 years. It is estimated that the aggregate investment will amount to more than $150 billion. The ISDN is an integrated digital communications network that makes use of such state-of-the-art technologies as optical fiber cables, large-capacity communication satellites, and electronic digital-switching systems. It enables the provision of highly advanced information communications services through a single nationwide system, including basic services such as voice transmission and advanced communications services such as computer communications, facsimile and video transmission, and various kinds of information processing. All information will be transformed into digital signals. The charge rate system will be based on the number of information bits and not on time or distance.

Hundreds of private companies participated in the Mitaka-Musashino ISDN experiment, including many financial institutions that expect to enhance cost-efficiency of financial transactions through the ISDN electronic-banking service. Moreover, when videotex terminals or modem-attached personal computers are introduced into enough households, there will be a vast market for home-banking and home-shopping services. General trading firms, supermarkets, and department stores foresee increases in consumer demand as a result of implementing the ISDN. Specialists, however, are divided over the future share of electronic home shopping in the retail market. Some claim that home shopping would deprive people of the pleasure of window shopping. However, it is also believed that those who wish to, could always make time to enjoy this pastime even in the "ISDN age."

Transportation and leisure industries such as airlines, railroads, trucking, and travel agencies are also expecting increases in demand as a result of the ISDN. Newspapers and broadcasting stations also participated in the ISDN experiments as information providers. Needless to say, computer manufacturers and telecommunication equipment manufacturers, both domestic and foreign, have been deeply involved in developing the ISDN. These companies thought that the ISDN would undoubtedly provide them with huge new markets. It is not rare for Japanese companies, which normally compete with each other, to work together on the same nationwide project. There is a Japanese proverb that says: "In a lifeboat, even enemies must cooperate to survive."

The primary promoter of the ISDN experimental project has been NTT. For a long time it was a government-owned public corporation, which had a legally authorized monopoly over Japan's domestic telecommunications. After NTT became privatized in 1985, to introduce competition, several hundreds of competitors have emerged, but NTT is still the giant. It is comparable to AT&T of the United States before its divestiture.

The Japanese Ministry of Posts and Telecommunications (MPT) has been strongly supporting NTT's project administratively. MPT and NTT evolved together—they belonged to the same administrative organization until their separation in 1949, and even now there are many former high-ranking MPT officials holding executive NTT posts.

Despite expenditures of more than $100 million by NTT alone, the 2-year Mitaka-Musashino ISDN experiment was not the success initially expected. One of the reasons was that the quality of information to be processed and transmitted through the ISDN system has not differed from that which is transmitted through conventional telecommunications means. Another reason was that restrictions on electronic financial transaction services which come under regulations and control of the Ministry of Finance have yet to be eased. A third reason was that much ISDN-related equipment has not always been user-friendly, and many users could not take advantage of its highly sophisticated capabilities.

Although there are many existing drawbacks against full-fledged implementation of the ISDN, both NTT and MPT are determined to develop a nationwide ISDN system over the next 10 or 15 years. It is their belief that information and telecommunications businesses will grow into a key industry in the foreseeable future, replacing the steel and automobile industries in terms of strategic importance.

Another example of the cooperation between the administration and the private sector is the joint development of Hi-Vision or High Definition Television (HDTV) broadcasting. Hi-Vision R&D has been conducted by NHK (Nihon Hoso Kyokai—Japan's nationwide public broadcasting system, a counterpart to the BBC in the United Kingdom) and several television equipment manufacturers such as Sony and Matsushita. Japan's Hi-Vision (1,125 scanning lines), although not compatible with today's standard NTSC (525 scanning lines), has the potential to transmit very high-resolution, wide-screen signals across the country by means of direct-to-home broadcasting satellites (DBS).

The Japanese DBS's, which were launched by the National Aero-Space Development Agency (NASDA) in 1985 and 1986, are now transmitting two kinds of NHK television programs (NTSC signals) to about 150,000 receivers. The DBS audience is expected to exceed one million households within a couple of years. NHK is experimenting with Hi-Vision transmissions through DBS-2, and the commercial implementation of Hi-Vision by NHK and Japan Satellite Broadcasting Incorporated (JSB), which will utilize DBS-3, is planned for 1991.

Many television stations, movie makers, television equipment manufacturers, and even printing firms are participating in the development of Hi-Vision-related equipment and the experimental production of Hi-Vision programs. According to estimations by some experts, if 10 million Hi-Vision television sets are sold in the 1990s, there will be a new market worth $33 billion, because the retail price will drop to about $3,300 per set. In addition, it is thought that Hi-Vision will be very useful for movies and high-resolution printing as well.

Although both MPT and the Ministry of International Trade and Industries (MITI) are boosting the development of the Hi-Vision system, they are not cooperating. The notorious rivalry between MPT officials and those at MITI has been always frowned on by the private sector. Despite this, under the leadership of the government, the activities of each private industry are coordinated and directed toward industrial expansion through government assistance in finance, taxation, and a steady transfer of technology from public R&D institutions to private companies. This form of assistance has been adopted often by countries that have recently entered the capitalist world market. This method has been particularly prominent in Japan. Other Asian countries such as Korea, Taiwan, and Singapore are emulating Japan in pursuing economic development in line with this government-led model.

A set of telecommunications laws was enacted in 1985, which changed the government-owned NTT into a special company, privately capitalized at 780 billion yen (about $5.2 billion).[7] A portion of the shares was made public in 1986 and in 1987, and the response from investors has been so strong and the potential for NTT growth so great that securities businesses are now trading them at 40 to 60 times their par value. Profits from the sale of stocks went into the national treasury and have been used to boost the domestic economy as well as to alleviate national debt.

With the privatization of NTT, the telecommunications business became open to participation by the private sector and a number of companies entered the market. In particular, the Tokyo-Nagoya-Osaka intercity trunk lines have been considered to have the biggest demand potential in Japan. Three new entrants constructed large-capacity microwave communication circuits and optical fiber cables along these lines, providing telecommunications services in 1986, which compete with NTT. These three firms are Daini-Denden, Inc., incorporated by a group made up of Kyocera and other companies; Japan Telecommunications Co. Ltd., which is a joint corporation consisting of Japan Railways and other leading companies; and Teleway Japan Corporation, whose biggest shareholder is the Expressway Public Corporation, a quasi-governmental organization. It is strange that there are almost no differences in the tariff and other conditions of services provided by these newcomers. That is the result of MPT guidance. Regardless of the number of carriers, there will be no free market or competition in the true sense of the word, if their services and prices do not differ. This is one example of excessive bureaucratic interference.

According to newly enacted telecommunications business laws, telecommunications businesses are divided into two types. One is the type 1 carrier business, where operators provide telecommunications services through their own circuits and facilities, and the other is the type 2. Type 2 telecommunications carriers do not possess circuits of their own, but borrow such lines from type 1 carriers and use them to provide a variety of advanced telecommunications services such as value-added networks (VAN). Whereas there are presently only 16 type 1 carriers, the number of independent type 2 carriers in operation is as many as 364. This is because legal and administrative regulations for type 2 are relatively mild, compared with those for type 1; and it is also easier to enter into type 2 businesses.

Several trading companies are preparing to operate large-scale satellite communications systems in collaboration with U.S. companies such as Hughes Communications and Ford. In Japan, two satellite systems developed by the National Aero-Space Development Agency (NASDA) are presently in operation. These satellites are, however, clearly inferior to those of its U.S. counterparts in performance and are much more expensive. Space development in Japan is limited to civilian use, as military implementation is strictly prohibited under the Japanese Constitution. Government budget allocations are therefore limited. Rocket-launching technology in Japan particularly lags far behind that in such countries as the United States, the Soviet Union, and France. Demands are increasing among leading companies and other major would-be users for U.S.-made satellites that have greater capacity and are more cost effective. And U.S. manufacturers are very eager to sell satellites to Japan. Nevertheless, the development of powerful launching vehicles, which will be able to send 2-ton satellites into a geostationary orbit is under way by NASDA, and the project is scheduled to be completed by the mid-1990s.

The Reagan administration has put pressure on the Japanese government to approve purchases by Japanese companies of U.S.-made communications satellites. The U.S. government is aiming to maintain its lead in satellite aerospace technology as well as to improve the trade imbalance between the United States and Japan. Prodded by such pressure, the Japanese government has decided to allow overseas procurement of satellite systems in addition to maintaining its own plans to continue developing domestic satellites.

Japan Communications Satellite Company, Inc. (JC-SAT)—a joint venture between C. Ito, Mitsui, and Hughes Communications—intends to provide leased transponder services on a nationwide basis by utilizing two large-scale ku-band communications satellites purchased from Hughes Aircraft in the United States. These two satellites were originally scheduled to be launched by the NASA space shuttle. However, due to the 1986 Challenger disaster, launching of the first JC-SAT will be undertaken by the French Ariane, and that of the second, by a Martin Marietta's Titan rocket. Both satellites are scheduled to be launched in 1989.

Mitsubishi, a leader of the former Zaibatsu group, has set up the Space Communications Corporation (SCC) and plans to utilize two Ford-made communications of both ku- and ka-band for providing similar services to those by the JC-SAT. SCC's satellites are to be launched by the Ariane rockets in 1989. A third would-be entrant into the satellite business is the Sony-led Satellite Japan, Inc. (SJI), which intends to introduce RCA-made high-power satellites. However, MPT has suspended the approval of the SJI project on the grounds that supply will outweigh demand if a third system is introduced to the fledgling Japanese satellite market.

Many foreign companies, including such powerful multinational corporations as AT&T and IBM, are making penetrating entrances into the Japanese market for enhanced communications services. As mentioned earlier, participation by private companies, both domestic and foreign, in telecommunications businesses was forbidden by law for a long time, and it is only two years since this legislative ban was lifted in 1985. The open-door policy adopted by the Japanese government has been regarded as a big opportunity by many foreigners, for Japan has the potential to be the world's second largest market, behind that of the United States. Severe competition is expected in the near future between large U.S. companies and Japan's leading counterparts.

As far as the existing Japanese communications situation is concerned, it is said that demand and supply are well balanced. The quality of nationwide telecommunications services is deemed as being the highest in the world. Furthermore, Japan is an archepelago consisting of numerous islands with a total area equivalent to that of the State of California. The question is what would the outcome be if so many new communication companies enter this small market? Probably only the largest and strongest would survive, because of market forces.

At present, it is difficult to foresee the size and scope of long-term demand for information and communications services by both companies and individuals. However, there is a question of whether or not it is appropriate to open up completely the market. One disadvantage is that too much competition may lead to a worsening of communications services. Such worries are particularly strong among the bureaucratic institutions.

The Japanese bureaucracy has an almost instinctive dislike for U.S.-type deregulations, because these deregulations would deprive the bureaucrats of many of their administrative functions. The bureaucratic system plays a unique and significant role in present-day Japanese society, both politically and economically. The incomes of individual bureaucrats are less than those of the average Japanese businessmen working for large firms, but these bureaucrats are considered to have a certain degree of ability and integrity. Although Japan has adopted a parliamentary system similar to that of the United Kingdom, the political parties depend a great deal upon the bureaucracy for law making and policy formation.

They have a tendency to intervene in the activities of private companies in the name of administrative guidance. Japan's economic development achieved in the postwar period can be largely attributed to the presence of certain types of cartels among private companies under the guidance of these bureaucrats. With regard to Japan's economic advancement, which has been jointly promoted by the public and private sectors, Americans and Europeans are critical of the Japanese economic juggernaut and refer to it as "Japan Inc.," which is not a wholly groundless description. However, it was simply the most effective possible method to drive the once-completely-war-damaged Japan toward economic recovery.

Now that the Japanese economy has expanded to a level of more than 10% of the world economy in terms of production and income, administrative guidance by the bureaucracy has become an obstacle for private companies. Cries for deregulation are being heard more and more among private entrepreneurs. Many of them have built such a strong competitive edge in capital accumulation that they no longer require assistance from the government. Competition between private companies is fierce in every industry, and bureaucrats often gain third-party profits through "mediation" between private companies.

For example, in the case of the adjustment of steel production or agreement between companies on the extent of self-restrictions in car and integrated circuit (IC) exports to the United States, industries cannot help being subjected to bureaucratic arbitration. Therefore, companies try to recruit senior government officials by offering high-paying positions in order to exploit their influence on political and administrative decision making. This practice is called *amakudari* (literally "descending from heaven"). Private companies accept retiring bureaucrats not for their managerial skills, but to take advantage of their influence on the bureaucratic organizations they are leaving.

This is apparent in the telecommunications business. As noted before, Japan's open policy on telecommunications was introduced in 1985 to allow private companies to participate in the market. But because entrance into Japan's telecommunications market is limited by natural and other conditions, it would be difficult to make the market completely free. If competition is completely free, no single company would ever be able to compete on an equal basis with the giant NTT. NTT's capital, technology, and know-how in the telecommunications business is so tremendous that newcomers would be completely overwhelmed.

Japanese private companies have to concentrate on securing certain sections of the market through cooperation as well as competition with NTT. On the other hand, it is in the interest of NTT to help its competitors grow. This is because NTT would probably be divested (as was the case with AT&T in the United States), if it tried to preserve its monopoly.

The infrastructure of telecommunications includes intercity cables, microwave communications networks, satellites, etc. Large-scale investment as well as the approval of the Ministry of Posts and Telecommunications will be required to establish and operate such communications facilities. Since information and communications-related industries are considered to have the highest growth potential, a variety of industrial groups has been fervently competing to obtain approval from MPT for market entry. Japan's bureaucracy is attempting to control information and communications-related industries by sending retired officials to private companies, thus capitalizing on its administrative influence.

An MPT official confided recently that the administration prefers "orderly competition," not fair competition. It is suspected that orderly competition means bureaucratically controlled competition designed to balance demand and supply, thus preserving the bureaucracy's vested interests.

Local development projects using various new communications media including the INS or ISDN are proliferating. More local governments than expected have been eager to participate in projects planned by MPT and MITI for the construction of model "intelligent cities" based on the idea of advanced information-oriented society.

Information networks for office work, transportation, medical treatment, disaster relief, as well as for our daily lives and cultural advancement, are considered to be part of the infrastructure necessary for social life in the same way as electricity, gas, water, and sewers. Many local governments have been engaged in such construction projects. To gain the lead in the coming information society, each governmental ministry is working out measures aimed at local governments. Projects quite similar in content such as MPT's Teletopia and MITI's New Media Community Plan are in direct competition. Other competitors include the Construction Ministry, Transport Ministry, National Land Agency, and Home Affairs Ministry, all of which are involved in separate projects and programs for the information society.

Japanese governmental offices often compete for jurisdiction in various fields due to a lack of horizontal contact and interdepartmental coordination. Japanese local governments are often dismayed because measures differ from ministry to ministry. This is due to the vertical administration system in Japan.

Another problem in Japan is that the power of local governments is relatively weak, whereas the power of central governmental offices is too strong because of their tremendous authority over the allocation of financial assistance to individual local governments. It is not a groundless concern that, owing to the development of microelectronic technology, continued centralization, uniformity and standardization of ministerial measures might reach the point where local autonomous systems will be destroyed. It has also been pointed out that as the central government utilizes more advanced information media, citizens will be driven into an ever-weaker position. If people are uniformly controlled by the administration, it will be a threat to Japanese democracy, still considered by many not yet sufficiently mature.

In order to realize sustained improvement in the Japanese economy, there is no alternative but to focus on high technology, particularly the information and communications industries. However, these particular fields will hereafter experience even keener competition from the United States, Europe, and Asian countries. To close the door to the outside world, as Japan did a couple of hundreds years ago in the Edo era, under similar control of the imperial bureaucracy, would inhibit the survival of Japanese society and should not be permitted. In high technology as well as in many other fields, Japan has no choice but to open the door to foreign countries and practice fair competition in the true sense of the phrase.

Here is an example of international friction on account of the lingering "shut-out policy" by officials at MPT. Overseas telecommunications services in Japan have been under the monopoly of Kokusai Denshin Denwa Corporation (KDD), which is both legally and administratively protected and is under strict regulation by MPT, notwithstanding its outward status as a private company. Since the open-door policy on telecommunications was established in 1985, there have emerged potent would-be competitors in overseas services. One is International Telecom Japan, Inc. (ITJ), which is a joint venture of more than 50 private companies, including leading trading companies such as Mitsui, Mitsubishi, and Sumitomo and giant electronic consumers products manufacturers such as Matsushita. The other is International Digital Communications Planning, Inc. (IDC), which is a joint international organization consisting of 35 companies, C. Ito, and Cable & Wireless in the United Kingdom—each holding 20% of shares, Toyota Motors and Pacific Telesis International in the United States—each holding 10%, and Merrill Lynch 3%. Initially, MPT showed disapproval of participation by foreign companies in the so-called type 1 overseas telecommunications business on the grounds that it would infringe on Japanese sovereign interests in telecommunications. This angered British Prime Minister Margaret Thatcher, and she threatened to retaliate by shutting the Japanese out of financial activities in London. MPT then exhorted ITJ and IDC to merge into one company, maintaining that if two new entrants into overseas services were permitted, in addition to KDD, there would be too much competition, bringing more harm than good to subscribers. MPT's intention seemed to be that the merger would lower the shares of foreign companies.

Negotiations between ITJ and IDC for the merger came to a deadlock, for both of them are against any concessions. This illustrates that there is a limit to bureaucratic guidance and control, once considered almighty. How much skill MPT will show in dealing with this matter is presently an object of great concern among the interested parties as well as among diplomatic circles, for MPT has put itself in an awkward position in terms of international relations.

However, it would be wrong to underestimate the capabilities of the Japanese bureaucracy. Prime Minister Nakasone has spoken of "taking advantage of the vitality of the private sector" as the basis for policy implementation in proceeding with various large-scale national projects. The actual implementation of these projects, nonetheless, remains subject to the bureaucrats who steer them, as well as to investments by the private sector. Apparently Nakasone's hopes have been set on getting the private sector to participate financially. This kind of one-sided maneuvering will not necessarily bring about good results. Nakasone holds administrative reform as one of his primary policy goals. His efforts are, however, not producing sufficient results as he faces subtle and ingrained resistance from bureaucratic organizations.

Whether Japan likes it or not, it is rapidly changing itself into an advanced information society. The critical problem is not excessive competition from the United States and other foreign companies, but rather bureaucratic intransigence and intervention in the private sector. The private sector's hitherto meek stance toward the bureaucracy is also to blame.

Many adverse effects have resulted from the advent of the information society, and it is thought that they will grow into major social problems such as effects on employment, infringement on privacy, occupational health hazards, etc. It appears that Japan to date has not exerted enough effort to counter these numerous problems. Measures are of course imminently necessary, but even more problematic would be the control of information systems by bureaucrats, a condition that not only would be harmful to Japanese society but would be also a continued cause of international friction. It is strongly desired that the administration make the utmost effort to implement a fair and open policy in the field of high technology.

Notes

1. A research and development project of Fifth Generation Computers was started in 1982 by a combined team of major Japanese computer manufacturers and researchers from universities sponsored by MITI. This research organization—named Institute for New Generation Computer Technology: ICOT,''—is scheduled to complete the development of the super personal computer with artificial intelligence (AI) within ten years.
2. The Japanese version of ISDN is called Information Network System (INS). Dr. Yasusada Kitahara, senior vice president of NTT, is the most prominent person, who originally planned and is now promoting this system. He wrote a number of books on this particular system, including *Information Network System—The Telecommunications in the Twenty First Century*.
3. Broadcasting satellites which enable direct reception of television signals at each house via large-capacity high-power (more than 100 watts) satellite transponders. Japan launched DBS-e (a broadcasting satellite for experimental use) in 1978, DBS-2a in 1984, and DBS-2b in 1985. NHK, national broadcasting corporation, started 2-channel television services by means of DBS-2b in 1986. DBS-3a and -3b are also scheduled to be launched in 1990 and 1991, each of which sends out 3-channel television programs, including high-definition television as well as

high-fidelity pulse code modulation (PCM) radio broadcasting, teletext, and facsimile broadcasting.

4. Hi-Vision is the name of Japanese high-definition television, which has 1,125 scanning lines, compared with 525 of today's standard NTSC. It can transmit very high-resolution, wide-screen signals. NHK and a newly incorporated satellite broadcasting station (JSB) intend to implement Hi-Vision television on a commercial basis through DBS-3.

5. There are various videotex systems which have different names: NAPLPS in Canada and the United States, Presstel in the United Kingdom, Teletel in France, and so on. The Japanese version of videotex system developed by NTT is named as CAPTAIN (Character and Pattern Telephone Access Information Network). The commercial operation of the system began in Tokyo and other main cities in 1984. However, it could not win so much popularity, as expected, at homes as well as at offices, because its existing subscribers number only a little more than 100,000.

6. An overheated international competition among the United States, Japan, and other countries is going on for the R&D of superconducting ceramics, which are expected to have a vast extent of applications such as superconductor cables that can convey electric currents with no loss of energy, high-speed trains that float on magnetic cushions, immensely powerful computers, etc. It seems to be an almost common characteristic of those countries wherein exist government-sponsored tightly-knit cooperations between industry and university.

7. The annual revenues of NTT amount to approximately ¥ 5.5 trillion ($37 billion). There are more than 46 million telephone subscribers. The number of employees is about 300,000. It has four laboratories, which are next to the Bell Laboratories in the United States in scale.

Fifty percent of its total stocks are to be made public within five years, and finally two-thirds will be held by the private sector with one-third by the government.

13

Telecommunications and International Financial Centers

Mitchell L. Moss

Communications technologies are often regarded as space-extending phenomena; specifically, they allow individuals and firms to function within a geographically larger set of boundaries (Kellerman, 1984). For most observers, the ability to overcome traditional spatial limits implies a weakening of the city (Abler, 1975). New technologies, it is argued, allow people to exchange information and ideas without interpersonal contact; thus, the comparative advantage of cities, whose existence has been traditionally based on their role as centers for face-to-face contact, is no longer necessary (Gottman, 1977). This article argues that advances in communications technologies are not leading to the demise of cities; rather, they are strengthening a handful of principal world cities (Hall, 1984). Three critical issues are examined, to demonstrate the way in which technological change is influencing the pattern of urban development and the emergence of global finance and legal centers: (1) How has the emergence of a global economy led to the creation of major financial centers, and what role do these centers play? (2) How will the emerging telecommunications infrastructure influence future patterns of urban development? (3) What types of cities will benefit from telecommunications deregulation, and why?

Cities in a Global Economy

Telecommunication systems, by allowing firms to overcome the traditional limits of distance, permit what were once separate economic activi-

239

ties to become highly integrated functions. Multinational firms, for example, although headquartered in one location, produce and sell a diversity of goods and services in numerous countries. More precisely, information and computer systems enable a relatively small number of people to control and coordinate production, marketing, and financing from geographically remote points. Because of the widespread decentralization of manufacturing and assembly operations, there has actually been an increased need for a central headquarters responsible for the policies and financial decision making that allow such dispersion to occur. Noyelle and Stanbach (1984) have shown that such corporate headquarters rely extensively on "advanced producer services," (e.g., finance, law, accounting, management consulting, and advertising) which are predominantly situated in the central business districts of large cities; the city provides the sophisticated financial and information services that allow a firm to operate globally. As a result, according to Cohen (1981), cities that specialize in international finance and producer services have witnessed considerable growth in their economic activity.

This emergence of the internationally oriented financial capital represents a considerable departure from the traditional role of certain large cities as centers for a nation's international trade and commerce. In a report by *The Economist Publications* analyzing changes in London's financial markets, the authors highlight London's transformation into a global financial capital:

> The City of London has always been an international financial centre, or at least since the late Middle Ages. However, until recently its cosmopolitanism merely reflected the international scope of *British* trade and financial interests. British merchant banks . . . traditionally engaged in the finance of British trade, while the 'colonial and foreign banks' . . . provided a banking network throughout the Empire and British trading enclaves elsewhere. The international horizons of these institutions were essentially the global horizons of the British political and economic interests which they served. However, the recent globalization of the City's interests, occurring at a time of economic recession and stagnation in the UK, is a different phenomenon from the internationalization that occurred in the 19th century, when the City financed British trade and economic influence. The central feature of many recent changes has been the development of the City as a centre for an emerging world capital market, as opposed to its more traditional role as a financial base for cosmopolitan interests. (Hewlett & Toporowski, 1985, p. 43)

The rise of the multinational firm has been intimately connected to the globalization of banking and finance activities. Facilitated by the advent of communications technology, these activities grew for reasons that extend beyond responding to the finance demands created by the rise of the multinational firm. Specifically, the rapid rise and fluctuation of inflation and interest rates, which began in the early 1970s, created conditions of far greater uncertainty and risk. This, in conjunction with an influx of petro dollars, increased nation-state budget deficits, and the lowering of capital barriers between countries has led to the internationalization of finance activities and the proliferation of new finance-related services and products. Most important, "Technological change, particularly the advance in computer technology, has altered the environment of financial markets. . . . The increased speed and lower cost of communication have been important to the development and expansion of international markets" (Germany & Morton, 1985).

As a recent report by the *Group of Thirty* stated, "Improved telecommunications and the presence of the larger banks in several time zones have created a continuous, round-the-clock market which responds instantaneously to new developments" (Group of Thirty, 1985). This is one of the reasons given for London's continued prominence as an international financial capital. "London's position in between the U.S. and Far Eastern Time Zones make[s] it a useful centre for arbitrage between financial markets in those zones (chiefly the markets of the USA, Japan and Hong Kong); dealings on all those markets can be orchestrated from London in the course of one deal day" (Hewlett and Toporowski, 1985.) In addition, telecommunications systems are now being used to link geographically separate stock and commodity exchanges, leading to considerably longer trading days. For example, the Chicago Mercantile Exchange is linked to a futures exchange in Singapore, the Sydney Stock Exchange has agreed to do joint trading with the New York Commodity Exchange, and the London Stock Exchange and the National Association of Securities Dealers share price information on actively traded British, American, and international stocks (Lohr, 1985a; 1985b).

As Charles Kindleberger (1978) has wisely noted: "The continuous reduction in the costs and difficulties of transport and communication over the last two hundred years has favored the formation of a single world financial market" (p. 130). The emergence of international finance centers has facilitated the emergence of this global market; however, it has also weakened the role of the small- and medium-size city. The headquarters of the independent firms that once thrived in smaller cities are now subsidiaries of large, multinational companies. As a result, their headquarters have been consolidated within larger financial centers. Thus, communications and information technologies are strengthening a small number of world cities while weakening the traditional autonomy of many smaller cities.

In the Pacific Rim, Tokyo, Hong Kong, Singapore, and (to a lesser extent) Sydney have emerged as major financial centers. Tokyo's emergence as a particularly powerful financial center is closely linked to Japan's large capital base and its preeminence in the Pacific Rim economy. In 1981, Japan generated 69% of the Pacific Rim's gross domestic product. Japan's economic presence also extends beyond the Pacific Rim. In a recent report by the *American Banker,* Japan was shown to account for 35.5% of the total foreign-bank lending to business in the United States—the largest single source of such activity (Foreign Banking, 1986).

Tokyo has long been Japan's preeminent financial center. Despite stringent financial regulations that limit its role in offshore activities, Tokyo is the headquarters of 11 of the world's 50 largest banks. Moreover, the Tokyo Stock Exchange is the fastest growing major market in the world (McMurray & Browning, 1986). With the gradual loosening of Japan's finance regulations, and the admission of three major American securities firms as Tokyo Stock Exchange members, Tokyo is becoming an increasingly powerful world financial center. In Hong Kong and Singapore, their emergence as financial centers has been closely linked to their ability to facilitate offshore capital market activity. Hong Kong has a liberal regulatory environment, and both cities have strong historical ties to international trade and commerce. Most important, an infrastructure exists that adequately facilitates increasing demands for international communication and transport (Kirby, 1983).

In order to determine the location of international financial centers in the Pacific Rim, the ten largest U.S. banks were surveyed. Seven of these banks indicated that they had established a regional headquarter office in the Pacific Rim. Citicorp designated regional headquarters in three cities: Tokyo, Hong Kong, and Singapore. Of the remaining six, three banks established regional headquarters in Hong Kong and three in Tokyo. In addition, all banks had their largest operations in Tokyo, Hong Kong, and Singapore, while three had equivalently large operations in Sydney. The importance of these financial centers is underscored by a 1983 comparison of world rental levels, in which New York led, followed by Tokyo, London, San Francisco, Los Angeles, Hong Kong, and Singapore tied with Sydney for seventh place (Rowley, 1984).

As financial centers are drawn to areas with complementary services, the strength of these centers can also be measured by analyzing the location of branch offices of leading American law firms. Moreover, the location of these law firms underscores the concept that these areas serve as neutral settings that facilitate face-to-face contact and transactions. While many law firms rely on travel, telephone-based contact, and/or correspondent relationships with local counsel, a growing number of firms recognize the need for maintaining a physical presence in the Pacific Rim.

Such firms place a premium on being able to readily serve clients without encountering time differences whenever a meeting is necessary. As table 13.1 shows, Hong Kong houses the largest concentration of American law firms—followed by Singapore and Tokyo. Although one might expect Tokyo (due to Japan's economic predominance) to have a larger concentration of law firms, Japan's Practicing Attorneys Act of 1955 severely restricts the presence of foreign lawyers. Thus a regulatory impediment rather than a market impediment is constraining the growth of an international legal community in that country (Weber, 1983.)

Telecommunications Infrastructure and Cities

While the initial development of financial centers has been spurred by cultural, economic, and regulatory factors, a new optical fiber telecommunications infrastructure is being built that will further enhance the communications capabilities of national and international financial centers. As stated in *The Economist:* "The world's telecommunications are going on a high-fibre diet. Within two years, optical fibres will carry telephone calls beneath the Atlantic and Pacific" (Optical Fibers, 1986, p. 84). Although optical fiber systems have inherent technological advantages

TABLE 13.1
Location of Largest 15 U.S. Law Firms in the Pacific Rim

LOCATION	LOCATION OF ALL LAW FIRM OFFICES IN PACIFIC RIM	LOCATION OF FIRMS WITH ONLY ONE OFFICE IN PACIFIC RIM
HONG KONG	11	6
SINGAPORE	6	1
TOKYO	5	1
MELBOURNE	2	1
SHANGHAI	1	1
TAIPEI	1	0
SYDNEY	1	0
BANGKOK	1	0
PEKING	1	0

Source: Legal Times, "500 Largest Law Firms," vol. 8, pp. 15–17 (Washington, DC: September 15, 1985).

over copper wire, satellite, and microwave communication systems, the current state of the technology and economics of fiber favor high-volume point-to-point communications—from one hub to another. As a result, the new optical fiber systems are initially being built to serve the heavily used communication routes, typically those linking major cities (Moss, 1986). This pattern of development is in sharp contrast to communication satellites, where the economics favor traffic from one point to multiple points or vice versa.

In the United States and other nations, optical fiber systems are being installed along transportation right-of-ways, often following the railroad routes established in the nineteenth century. MCI has built its Northeast fiber system along the AMTRAK right-of-way; Cable and Wireless is using the right-of-way of the Missouri-Kansas-Texas Railroad to connect the Texas cities of Austin, San Antonio, Dallas, and Ft. Worth; and in England Mercury Communications is building a fiber system on British Rail's right-of-way. It is ironic that the choice of cities to be first served by advanced fiber systems is in part due to the decisions concerning transportation right-of-ways in the nineteenth century.

The initial comparative advantage fiber optics confers on financial centers is seen by examining New York City and Los Angeles, the United States' preeminent East and West Coast financial centers. These cities account for approximately 30% of all overseas telephony emanating from the United States. In addition, New York, with 43%, has the largest concentration of foreign bank offices in the United States, followed by Los Angeles with 11.8%, and Chicago with 8.4% (Foreign Banking, 1986). Further, advanced telecommunications systems have reinforced the comparative advantage that New York and Los Angeles have. Within each city, extensive fiber optic systems are being used to facilitate intraurban communication flows. New York Telephone has built three fiber optic networks around Manhattan and an interborough fiber network that links the counties adjacent to Manhattan. In the Los Angeles region, the fiber network built for the 1984 Olympics provides an advanced regional telecommunications infrastructure that can support the information-intensive firms in southern California. Clearly, telecommunications has not resulted in the economic decline of the largest central cities in the United States, but is being used to move information in, through, and out of such cities with greater speed and efficiency.

Telecommunications and the Pacific Rim

Just as the emergence of fiber optic networks in the United States demonstrates the way in which new technology can strengthen large cities, the fiber and analog networks being built in the Pacific Rim show similar trends. Due to the dramatic increase in trade between Pacific Rim nations and the United States, the current telecommunications infrastructure is being seriously challenged. Because the existing Hawaii-3/Transpac-2 (HAW-3/TPC-2) cable is saturated, satellite transmission is being increasingly used to meet communication needs. By the end of 1984, 70% of the transmission in the Pacific Rim was via satellite and 30% via cable. The estimate in 1986 was that by 1987 76% of transmission would be via satellite and 24% via cable (Logue, 1986).

The Federal Communications Commission considers this dependence on one medium of transmission to present risks, and has therefore supported the new Hawaii-4/Transpac-3 (HAW-4/TPC-3) fiber optic system. By 1991, this system is projected to shift the balance between satellite and cable traffic to 56% satellite and 44% cable (Federal Communications Commission, 1986). Further, the configuration of this cable provides valuable insights concerning the emerging pattern and location of economic activity. While the initial Hawaii/Transpac cables were oriented toward national security interests with direct links from Hawaii to Guam, the new HAW-4/TPC-3 cable is designed to accommodate both economic and military linkages. After stopping in Hawaii, the cable extends far into the Pacific and then branches in two directions—the national security link runs to Guam and then on to the Philippines via a branch called GP-2; the economic and trade connection extends directly from Hawaii to Japan. By 1990, other key Pacific Rim centers will be linked via a ring that will connect Guam, the Philippines, Hong Kong, Korea, and Japan. By 1994, Taiwan will also be connected.

Although the design of this network appears to favor the northern countries in the Pacific Rim, it is important to note that the ANZCAN cable connects Vancouver, Hawaii, the Fiji Islands, Sydney, and New Zealand. With both the Canadian and U.S. cables stopping in Hawaii, this will become an important point for information transfer. Further, it serves to mitigate the strong comparative advantage that the northern countries would otherwise have received.

As figure 13.1 shows, there is also an extensive amount of intraregional telecommunications systems being built. The systems shown on the map have been constructed since the early 1980s. As can be seen, these systems link areas that have both cultural and/or economic ties. For example, the Japan-Korean cable shows the important economic relationship between these countries. In the early 1980s, 28% of South Korea's trade was with Japan; and in 1980, 41% of South Korea's overseas telecommunications messages were with Japan (Kirby, 1983). In addition, the ASEAN cable shows how a new communications infrastructure can further the develop-

FIGURE 13.1
Pacific Rim Cables

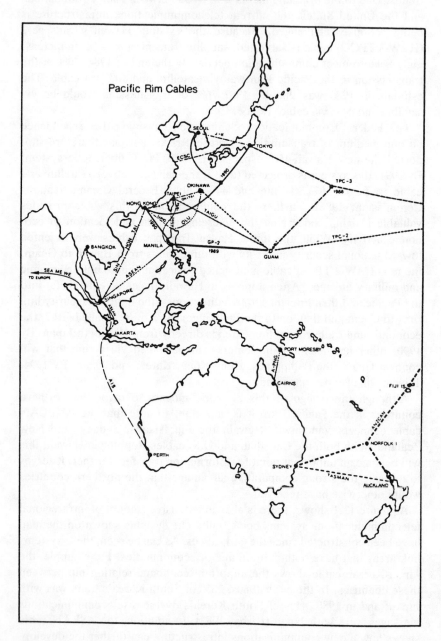

ment of a coalition whose goal is to develop stronger economic and cultural ties.

Urbanization, Trade, and Telecommunications

While the emerging web of cable systems shows that the strength of key centers with an existing comparative economic advantage will be reinforced, figure 13.2 shows that trade relationships do not completely account for international communication linkages. Although the NIC's— South Korea, Taiwan, and Hong Kong—show a strong association between trade and communication, Japan's pattern is different. Japan accounts for

FIGURE 13.2
U.S. Pacific Rim: Trade and Communication

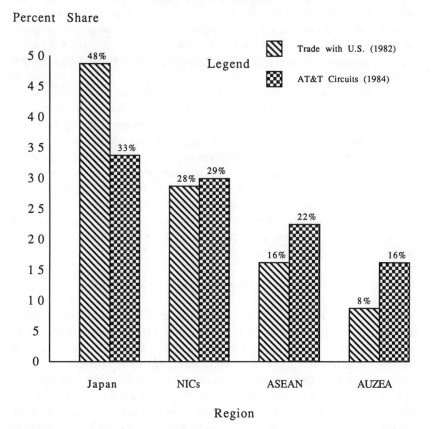

Percent Share

Legend

Trade with U.S. (1982)

AT&T Circuits (1984)

Region

Sources: "The Pacific Arrives," *The Banker, 135* (713), pp. 16–23 (July 1985); FCC, 1985.

almost half of all Pacific Rim trade with the United States, yet it has only one-third of the AT&T circuits between the Pacific Rim and the United States. Given the strong cultural ties which also exist between the two countries, one might argue that this is an area where demand for international communications should be far higher. Conversely, while ASEAN accounts for 16% of Pacific Rim trade with the United States, 22% of AT&T's circuits link ASEAN and the United States. Such disparities demonstrate that telecommunications is a permissive factor that can contribute to locational decisions, but it is not a deterministic factor that, by itself, can generate economic activity (Mandeville, 1983). The Maitland Commission has recently highlighted this complex relationship between telecommunications and economic development when it stated, "while a strong correlation has been established between the number of telephones per capita and economic development measured by gross domestic product, it has not been clear whether investment in telecommunications contributes to economic growth or economic growth leads to investment in telecommunications. That there is a link between the two is however beyond question" (Independent Commission for Worldwide Telecommunications Development, 1984).

As figure 13.3 shows, gross domestic product statistics for countries within the Pacific Rim do show a strong association with number of telephones. As a result, Japan's economic dominance and strong economy does translate into a dominance in percent of telephones as well. For ASEAN, where the greatest variation occurs, this can be largely explained by the lack of urbanization within these countries. With the exception of Singapore, countries within ASEAN are 25–35% urbanized; this compares with over 80% urbanization in other Pacific Rim countries. Thus, while ASEAN's population is dominant within the Pacific Rim, the degree of urbanization and economic development is a far better indicator of telephone dispersion and demand.

Telecommunications Deregulation and Cities

The design, development, and management of the telecommunications infrastructure in all nations (with the exception of the United States) has, until recently, been totally under public control. In the United States, the telecommunications infrastructure has been largely built by AT&T, several independent telephone firms, and numerous rural telephone companies. Although privately owned, all function under close governmental regulation. In the United States, a policy of telecommunications deregulation and the divestiture of AT&T is leading to a profound transformation in the nation's telecommunications infrastructure. Public policy at the federal

FIGURE 13.3
Pacific Rim: Concentration of GDP, Telephones, and Population

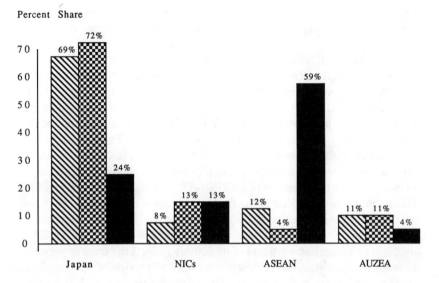

Percent Share

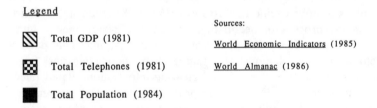

Legend

◨ Total GDP (1981)

▨ Total Telephones (1981)

■ Total Population (1984)

Sources:

World Economic Indicators (1985)

World Almanac (1986)

Sources: World Economic Indicators, 1985; World Almanac, 1986.

level is now geared toward letting market forces increasingly determine the pattern of telecommunications investment. This supplements the policy of "universal service," the goal of providing everyone (regardless of location) low-cost and reliable telephone service. As a result, new telecommunications systems are being built to serve large communications users, most of whom are located in the nation's largest metropolitan areas (Moss, 1986).

A growing movement to rely on private firms to develop telecommunications systems is occurring in other nations as well. Nowhere, however, is this competitive telecommunications environment as pronounced as in the United States. In Britain, privatization has occurred with the creation of British Telecom; presently, limited competition in telecommunications infrastructure is taking place between British Telecom and Mercury Communications. In Japan, the state-owned Nippon Telegraph and Telephone (NTT) has become a private firm; new private firms, such as the Hughes-Mitsui-C.I.T.O.H. partnership, are now developing systems to compete with NTT.

The movement toward competition in telecommunications is clearly bound to strengthen the telecommunications infrastructure in those cities that have become centers for information-intensive industries. In the United States, COMSAT and TRT (a major international common carrier) have formed a partnership and are now building urban gateway satellite stations in San Francisco, Houston, and Chicago. Further, they have already established a satellite facility at the Teleport in New York. At the international level, competition and technological innovation are largely responsible for the decision of INTELSAT to deregulate its International Business Services (IBS). For the first time, private carriers will be allowed to build earth stations and lease a portion of INTELSAT's satellite capacity for the purpose of sending data communications. INTELSAT's decision to deregulate a portion of its activity reflects the intense pressures brought by large information users who want to maximize the use of new technologies, such as Ku-band satellite transmission, that INTELSAT has not incorporated into its network. In a survey of four common carriers with plans to offer Pacific Rim IBS in 1986 or 1987, each stated that they were in the process of negotiating or concluding agreements with the PTT's of Japan, Hong Kong, Singapore, and Australia. This pattern of development again demonstrates that each of these countries' financial centers is the source of rapid and growing information-related telecommunications demand. Further, the probability that new telecommunications systems will initially serve these areas and reinforce their preeminent position is underscored. As a result of these developments, planners and policymakers concerned with regional development will need to give heightened attention to the availability of telecommunications systems in cities.

Conclusion

This essay has examined the relationship between advanced communication and information technologies and the future pattern of urban development. It has sought to demonstrate that (1) telecommunications technologies are facilitating the globalization of world financial markets and increasing linkages among principal world cities; (2) the emergence of fiber optic systems for international and interurban communications is strengthening the telecommunications capacities of large metropolitan centers; and

(3) increased competition in telecommunications will require policymakers to give greater attention to the private sector's role in providing advanced telecommunications services in cities.

Note

The author would like to acknowledge the research assistance of Mr. Andrew Dunau in the preparation of this article.

References

Abler, R. (1975). Effects of space adjusting technologies on the human geography of the future. In R. Abler, D. Janelle, & A. Philbrick (Eds.), *Human geography in a shrinking world*. Scituate, MA: Duxbury Press.

Cohen, R. B. (1981). The new international division of labor, multinational corporations, and urban hierarchy. In M. Dear, & A. J. Scott (Eds.), *Urbanization and urban planning in capitalist society*. London, UK: Methuen.

Federal Communications Commission. (1986). *Memorandum opinion, order, and automation*. File No. I-T-C-85-219, (June 7), p. 9.

Foreign banking in the United States. (1986). *American Banker* (February 14), p. 1A.

Germany, J. D., & Morton, J. E. (1985). Financial innovation and deregulation in foreign industrial countries. *Federal Reserve Bulletin* (October), p. 743.

Gottman, J. (1977). Megalopolis and Antipolis: The telephone and the structure of the city. In I. de Sola Pool (Ed.), *The social impact of the telephone*. Cambridge, MA: MIT Press.

Group of Thirty. (1985). *The foreign exchange market in the 1890s*. New York.

Hall, P. (1984). *The world cities*. London, UK: Weidenfeld & Nicolson.

Hewlett, N., & Toporowski, J. (1985). *All change in the City*. London, UK: Economist Publications. Special Report, No. 222.

Independent Commission for Worldwide Telecommunications Development. (1984). *The missing link* (December). Geneva, Switzerland.

Kellerman, A. (1984). Telecommunications and the geography of metropolitan areas. *Progress in Human Geography, 8*(2), 232.

Kindleberger, C. P. (1978). *Economic response: Comparative studies in trade, finance, and growth*. Cambridge, MA: Harvard University Press.

Kirby, S. (1983). *Toward the Pacific century: Economic development in the Pacific Rim*. London, UK: Economist Publications. Special Report, No. 137.

Logue, T. (1986). Recent major U.S. facilities-related policy decisions: Letting a million circuits bloom. In. D. Wedemeyer, & A. Pennings (Eds.), *PTC '86 proceedings*. Hawaii: University of Hawaii Press.

Lohr, S. (1985a). Global stock trading near. *New York Times,* November 27, p. D1.

Lohr, S. (1985b). The global exchange. *Fortune,* February 4, p. 9.

Mandeville, T. (1983). The spatial effects of information technology. *Futures, 15*(1), 67.

McMurray, S., & Browning, E. (1986). Merrill Lynch, other U.S. firms, expect big things from Tokyo exchange seats. *Wall Street Journal,* January 31, p. 24.

Moss, M. L. (1986). Telecommunications and the future of cities. *Land Development Studies, 3*(1), 3.

Noyelle, T. J., & Stanbach, T. M. Jr. (1984). *The economic transformation of American cities*. Totowa, NJ: Towman & Allenheld.

Optical fibres straddle the globe (1986). *Economist, 289,* March 22, p. 84.

Rowley, A. (1984). Where does the market go from here? *Far East Asian Review,* March 8, p. 45.

Weber, D. (1983). The Asian connection: Lawyers in the financial centers of the Far East. *California Lawyer, 3*(11), 29.

14

Marketplace vs. Public Utility Models for Developing Telecommunications and Information Industries

Jerry L. Salvaggio and Richard A. Nelson

The economics of information technology is emerging as an increasingly important area of study. As yet, adequate tools to make solid projections or even draw useful historical parallels do not exist. In this essay, a broad theoretical framework is outlined which attempts to address this problem by establishing a baseline from which to view national patterns for developing information technology. The models are designed to allow for the generation of hypotheses. Rather than simply concentrating on a traditional comparison of telecommunication policies in various countries, this article seeks to identify and discuss the underlying processes by which information technologies (such as cable, computers, semiconductors and telephony) are developed, adopted, and used within a society. The strength of using a cultural and social as well as a political approach—focusing on how a society develops new forms of technology as opposed to only how new laws and policies are created—is that it places greater importance on understanding national "behavior" in matters of information technology rather than the shifting vagaries of policy changes.

There is little doubt that information technologies directly impact on a nation's economy. It is thus not surprising that a growing number of

European communities and Asian countries have targeted information technologies as an answer to economic problems. The process by which societies develop information technologies is complex and subject to a number of variables. In periods of erratic monetary policy, or where inadequate investment and tax incentives exist to develop information technology, adaptation to a fully matured services economy is disrupted. Particularly in market economies (such as the United States) succeptible to inflation and the disequilibrium of the continuing international debt crises, an unstable value of the monetary unit can distort market prices and profits—altering their informational content—and misdirect resources away from higher-valued uses. Without understanding the immediately felt implications of an emerging information economy and its potential for economic dislocation, the long-term structural benefits for an information economy may be traded away for short-term political solutions. The money-supply process can easily become politicized, as it has in America, into cries for "new" protectionist policies designed to slow movement toward a cooperative postindustrial international information economy, especially in the face of mounting federal deficits, historically high trade imbalances, and large pockets of unemployment in declining industries.

In light of the above, it becomes clear that the economics of information technology is emerging as an important area of study. As yet, adequate tools to make solid projections or even draw useful historical parallels do not exist. The broad theoretical framework outlined below addresses this problem by establishing a baseline from which to view national patterns for developing information technology. The models are designed to allow for the generation of specific hypotheses. Rather than concentrating on a traditional comparison of telecommunication policies in various countries, this essay seeks to identify and discuss the underlying processes by which information technologies (such as cable, computers, semiconductors and telephony) are developed, adopted, and used within a society. The strength of using a cultural and social as well as a political approach—focusing on how a society develops new forms of technology as opposed to only how new laws and policies are created—is that it places greater importance on understanding national behavior in matters of information technology than on the shifting vagaries of policy changes.

Why concentrate on theory and modeling? While reluctant to suggest that all the various dimensions and complexities involved can be adequately represented in a model, the value of a theoretical approach makes oversimplification an acceptable risk. Irrespective of political systems, there are certain variables that influence the development and adoption of information technology in all societies. If such theoretical generalizations are rejected, the ability to recognize broad patterns and associated patterns is lost.

The factors that affect the way in which a society develops and adopts information technology are too numerous to list. Public attitudes, educational objectives, discretionary income, social mores, and even fads may influence the development of technology. Most of these can be placed within six major categories common to all societies. Ideology, political forces, economic forces, policy-making organizations (PMOs), external forces, and information infrastructure are the major variables which transcend political and cultural situations (Salvaggio, 1983; 1985a).

Of the variables listed above, national ideology generally has the greatest influence over the way technology is developed and adopted. Ideology involves the foundational doctrines (values, beliefs, and governmental policies) which prevail in a society at a given time. Lodge and Vogel (1987) in their recent study of ideology and competitiveness suggest that every nation has at least one dominant ideology, with several other alternative or congruent ideologies of importance also possible. Components of an ideology include a society's cultural traits, religious values, political institutions, and laws as they are historically formed.

The weight given to the other variables influences technological innovation and further determines the model a particular society will fall under. One variable, however, in each society tends to drive it more than the others. Referred to as "variable X" and differing from model to model, it represents the factor—other than ideology—that exerts the most influence over the development and use of information technology. For example, variable X in the Marketplace Model is the emphasis on capitalist free trade decision making as compared with industrial policy; in the Public Utility Model it is the importance of coordinated policy-making decisions. The weighted importance of X also accounts for a number of differences within societies operating under the same basic model.

Another major variable, "information infrastructure," includes the structure and physical composition of technology (satellites, computer networks, telecommunications, telex, broadcast stations), the characteristics of ownership (private vs. government, national local, concentrated vs. diversified), and the types and levels of services offered (DBS, videotex). (For a recent survey of the Japanese information environment see Tamura, 1987.) Space does not permit us to discuss the remaining variables.

Internationally, at least four basic models for the development of technology can be identified: The Communist-Totalitarian, Newly Industrialized Country (NIC), Marketplace, and Public Utility. The Communist-Totalitarian Model is represented by Marxist and other states where information technology—broadcast, telephone, computer, satellite, print, image reproduction—is owned by the government on behalf of the people and managed by a central, one-party bureaucracy.

The Newly Industrialized Country (NIC) Model is actually a catchall phrase designating those nations characterized by continued dependence on international and bilateral aid from more advanced economies for the development of information technologies. Truly developing states typified by South Korea, Taiwan, Singapore, Malaysia, Indonesia, India, and Brazil while still often referred to as Third World countries are, in fact, forging their own unique telecommunication infrastructures by adopting—or not adopting—existing information technologies to suit their particular needs (e.g., Crawford, 1984). Rather than forming their own distinct category, such national systems remain dependent on external aid and overlap in many respects with the three other major models.

Neither the Communist-Totalitarian nor NIC models are particularly appropriate for democratic industrial states seeking to advance into a prosperous postindustrial economy. This essay concentrates on the two major models used by democratic-capitalist societies. Each model, proponents argue, is most suitable for maximizing the benefits of an information society while minimizing social disruption. Obviously such arguments are contradictory; an attempt to maneuver through the minefield of competing claims will be made here.

In the Marketplace Model (also referred to as the Competitive Model), information technology is privately owned and operated, either unregulated or loosely regulated by numerous organizations, and is primarily developed by market forces (see figure 14.1). The United States is the only major country that clearly falls into this category, although several smaller nations are possible candidates. The philosophy that lies at the heart of the Marketplace Model is that society is best served by not interfering with the development and adoption of information technology. In the free enterprise system, information technology develops its full potential only if the consumer, business, and public sector marketplace accepts it. Full employment, according to that theory, is most likely to be realized if industry is producing products truly sought by members of society. In essence, society thrives when the marketplace thrives.

In the Marketplace Model, where consumer demand drives the development of information technology, policy-making organizations are relatively weak and advisory in nature. In the United States, policy-making organizations are decentralized because the idea of a powerful agency in charge of communications and information is antithetical to traditional American ideology. Power is shared by the Federal Communications Commission (FCC), the National Telecommunications and Information Administration (NTIA), Congress, and the courts. Power, however, is

FIGURE 14.1
Marketplace Model

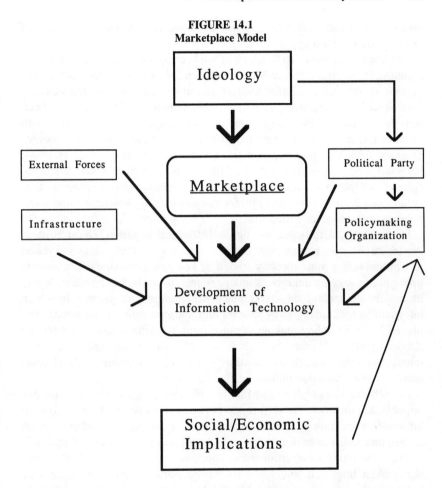

most often exercised in the form of ad hoc regulation rather than concerted policy. The FCC and NTIA would no doubt argue that they have enacted considerable policy in recent years—it just so happens that deregulation is their current policy and one they seek to export to other countries (Edgar & Rahim, 1983; Bolter, et al., 1984; Sterling, 1984; Eward, 1985; U.S. Department of Commerce, 1985).

In this atmosphere, the marketplace is actually in control of the development and adoption of information technology with only minimum service, content, or price regulatory controls. One major disadvantage of the approach is the inability to implement consistent national commitments because of the vagaries of decision making and the lack of control held by the PMOs. This places government in a reactive rather than proactive position, with little influence over the development and implementation of information technology.

There are exceptions to this lack of long-range policy agenda setting and planning in the Marketplace Model. Certain forms of information technology are developed solely for military purposes regardless of the possible commercial applications. The U.S. Department of Defense has been heavily involved in information technology design and deployment, with satellite communication a spin-off from military space research. Another example of long-range policy-making—this one by the White House—involved support for the creation of the Communications Satellite Corporation (COMSAT). The National Science Foundation has also been influential in an indirect way, recently focusing efforts on American supercomputer development and adoption.

In the Public Utility Model (figure 14.2) used in Japan, Great Britain, Australia, West Germany, and Canada, information technology is viewed as a public utility more directly guided by key policy-making organizations operating at varying degrees of independence from the government. While ultimately dependent on marketplace acceptance, the manner in which information technology is developed and adopted reflects the strong role played by such policy-making organizations working in concert with the national political leadership. This is not only true in the area of telecommunications but extends to consumer electronics, computer technologies, and the cable/television industries.

In both the Marketplace and Public Utility models the economy is very important. However, the difference between the two systems relative to information technology involves questions of initiation and guidance. What we are interested in here is large-scale development and public adoption.

The solid curved line from socioeconomic problems to the PMOs, and the broken line from the PMO to the economic system in figure 14.1 indicates that the PMO in the Marketplace is not in a major position to influence variable X. Conversely, PMOs in the Public Utility Model operate differently, depending on national ideology, but tend to be very influential and effective because these societies have a greater trust in governmental institutions (Homet, 1979). Unlike the United States, for example, information technology in Japan is usually initiated by PMOs that are in a good position to create policy relative to the development of technology—often before the technology is adopted on a mass scale. The solid lines between the PMOs and the political leadership in figure 14.2 point to the close working relationship between these two variables in the Public Utility Model, to the point that PMOs are central in such systems.

In the Marketplace Model, PMOs are only able to regulate information technology, while PMOs of the Public Utility Model tend to be more

FIGURE 14.2
Public Utility Model

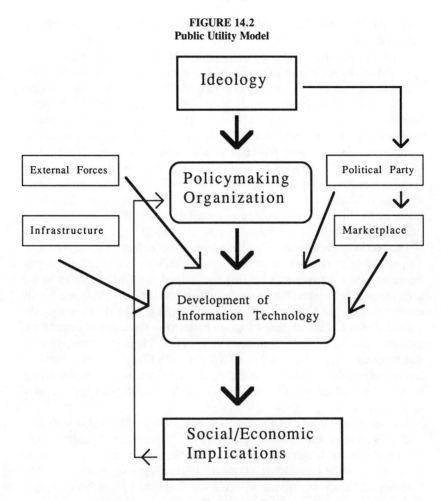

involved with long-term development and adoption. A comparison of U.S. and Japanese approaches to space technology is instructive. Japan, like the United States, supports a space program spending over $450 million per year in the early 1980s. Though the United States invested twelve times as much, most of it went into the shuttle program and explorations mapping the surface of Venus and probing the outer planets. Japan's budget went more directly into state-assisted commercial applications of satellite technology, while commercialization in the United States relative to satellites has been left to market forces. Japan's emphasis on commercialization has helped to lessen the technological gap between the two countries. Japan is now in the position to build and launch its own communication satellites, with the net effect being loss of U.S. sales to Japanese firms.

A second advantage of the Public Utility Model is the ability to target market sectors for future dominance. Japan now is the recognized world leader in the semiconductor industry—a direct result of long-range support by the Ministry of International Trade and Industry (MITI) (Okimoto, Sugano, & Weinstein, 1984). Until recently, only the United States manufactured supercomputers. Now at least three firms in Japan have supercomputers equal or more powerful than American systems. The benefits of MITI's Fifth Generation Project cannot be determined yet, but should they succeed at building computers with parallel computer architecture capable of communication through natural languages, then the consequences for the Japanese computer industry in the 1990s will be significantly enhanced.

The Marketplace Model offers the advantage of entrepreneural boldness. Those willing to take a chance on a new technology are not often encumbered by PMO bureaucracies. This has helped the United States in the area of cable television, for example, where levels of penetration are only outstripped by the Netherlands. Statistics would also likely show that the United States has the highest adoption patterns in the areas of computers, facsimile and satellite communication systems. There are exceptions to this rule. Since the divestiture of AT&T, the Fifth Circuit Court of Appeals has prevented the regional operating companies from manufacturing equipment. As a result, Japan and the Asian NICs have captured large shares of this market.

A clear disadvantage of the Marketplace Model is inequal distribution and utilization of information technologies. Information inequity results from a number of factors, ranging from existing social class differences to service availability and cost (Bolling, 1983; Siegel & Markoff, 1985). Growing illiteracy is proving a factor for formerly homogenous nations undergoing socially painful transition to multiracial, multilinguistic, and multicultural postindustrial status. The more important consideration involves what considerations are made about public adoption when a new technology is first implemented. In the Marketplace Model, technologies are often introduced with little concern about the long-term implications of such inequity. Consumer demand in and of itself may not be enough to ensure public service since the capital intensive nature of information technology limits the degree to which any society can offer inexpensive information services. The profit motive in advanced Marketplace Model countries such as the United States means that for the foreseeable future virtually all information services will continue to be marketed to businesses and professionals living in upscale residential areas. Studies of information services such as CompuServe indicate that 95% of its users are White males, more than one-half of whom are earning over $30,000 a year. Private videotex systems are far more expensive than CompuServe, limiting their target market only to the most affluent.

This contrasts with the nationalization of information systems in Public Utility Model countries committed to widespread public distribution and utilization of new technologies. While development of information technology on a national scale will not automatically ensure public use, teletext is rapidly becoming a mass medium in Europe (unlike the United States), at a cost affordable to broad population segments (see *Financial Times, Media Intelligence Unit*, 1985). This would not have been possible without strong government intervention.

An additional advantage of Public Utility Model countries involves their ability to exercise control over imports and exports. As the U.S. International Trade Commission recently pointed out to manufacturers, nations in the European Community traditionally restrict sales of American telecommunications equipment while giving preferential procurement treatment to their own manufacturers. This has led to a U.S. trade deficit with Japan that is at an all time high. The result is a significant import-export imbalance between the Marketplace and Public Utility Model nations. By 1984, U.S. imports in telecommunications exceeded exports by 3:1 (Telecommunications Imports, 1984), a trend increasing every month. As table 14.1 shows, the United States still leads in certain categories and Japan in others. The table refers to success in sales rather than technological superiority; it is important to note that Japan has targeted several of the areas listed in the left column. Thus, how long the United States will remain the leader in these important technologies is unknown.

Some scholars have argued that Japan and European countries such as Great Britain are abandoning public utility controls to mimic the American marketplace example. This view, we believe, is overstated. There contin-

TABLE 14.1
High Technology Sales

U.S. Leadership	Japanese Leadership
Microprocessors	Semiconductors
Computer technology	Computer peripherals
Satellite technology	Satellite dishes
Cable technology	Megatronics
Computer software	Telecommunication components
Value-added networks	Videocassette recorders
Optoelectronics	
Artificial intelligence	

ues to be marked differences between the process by which information technology is developed in the United States and in other countries.

Even though both Japan and Great Britain have privatized their telephone monopolies and adopted more competitive approaches to the future direction of their national communications policies, it is doubtful whether either country has actually changed the way in which it develops information technology. Competition is important to advanced applications of telecommunications, but there still exists significant differences between policy directives in such countries and in a true marketplace environment such as the United States, where there is virtually no up-front government involvement. In Great Britain, for example, the *Telecommunications Act* (1984) and the *Cable and Broadcasting Act* (1984) taken together, end the government monopoly long held by British Telecom and authorize private industry to compete in cable. But how this wiring is accomplished, what kinds of cable are used, and the switching systems selected—has been dictated by PMOs from the beginning. So the level of British governmental planning and responsibility still far exceeds interventionary powers available to U.S. regulators (Evans et al., 1984; Salvaggio & Steinfield, 1985).

Similarly, in recent years Japan has made auspicious moves toward a more competitive atmosphere (Shimizu, 1985). This is particularly true of Japanese telecommunications following the 1985 privatization of Nippon Telephone and Telegraph (NTT, analogous to the American AT&T; see Salvaggio, 1985b, for a comprehensive report on these developments). However, these changes should not be seen as a transformation to the Marketplace Model (Salvaggio, 1987). The litmus test of the question as to which model Japan most closely resembles lies in the answer to another question—Who is responsible for setting the technological agenda? Innovative projects such as Tama New Town, Hi-OVIS, the Fifth Generation Computer Program, and the Information Network System (INS) have traditionally been planned by PMOs. The same PMOs are now directing national planning for the late 1980s and 1990s (Yokoi, 1982; Tachikawa, 1983; Ikeda, 1985). In Europe, PMOs have created wired city prototypes such as Viarritz in France and Milton Keyes in Great Britain. All of these research projects were or are technological systems conceived by PMOs that envisage them as parts of an overall plan to position Japan and the European Community countries at the cutting edge in information technology.

Numerous government white papers and literature from the private sector attest to a single coherent objective—to make a quick transition from an industrial to an information society. Virtually all of the above Japanese projects, for instance, were initiated by MITI or based on the Ministry of Post and Telecommunication's (MPT) information flow census (*johoka shakai*) studies demonstrating that information distribution is more efficient via new telecommunications channels than traditional media (Ito, 1981; Zeman, 1983; Musashi, 1985). MITI was also instrumental in the development of Japan's mainframe computer, semiconductor, and artificial intelligence industries.

Such integration is in marked contrast to similar projects in the United States. PMOs in the Marketplace Model are less proactive than reactive— often mobilizing only in response to conflicts among players and then usually in forms acceptable to industry. The U.S. Cable Communications Policy Act of 1984 (U.S. Congress, 1984) was less guided by social consciousness-"public interest" considerations than marketplace exigencies leading to compromises acceptable to cable, broadcast, federal officials, and city councils responsible for regulation at the local level.

Tetsuro Tomita (1984) of MPT recently considered the merits of the American vs. the Japanese approach. His conclusion, that the ideal is a policy mix rather than leaning toward strict government controls or total reliance on market forces, reflects Japan's new balanced approach. There are other reasons why the development and adoption of information technology in Japan will continue to be a partnership influenced by government policy-making organizations such as MITI and MPT working very closely with the *zaikai* (trade associations) and the five major *keiretsu* (clusters of large firms and banks) to develop a consensus (Tsurumi, 1982; Bloom, 1984; Varan, 1987). First, a key segment of Japan's marketplace is outside of Japan, requiring orchestrated research, development, and export planning. Second, Japanese ideology sets the pattern for the kind of policy hierarchy that is seen in the area of information technology. Competition exists within the system but allows for a finality of decision to ensure consensus of voice once policy is determined. Industry leaders may not always agree with the guidance of MITI and the MPT, but they accept a vertical hierarchy that places government bureaucracy above private interests.

Unfortunately, it is still too early to definitively correlate information technology and services with a country's economic success (Babe, 1985; a useful starting point is found in Pool et al., 1984; Courville et al., 1984; and Leff, 1984). Japan's phenomenal development does not necessarily demonstrate the automatic superiority of the Public Utility Model, since a number of societies have used it with less concrete results.

Several conclusions, however, can be drawn. First, relative to economic development, we would suggest that in the area of high technology, the Public Utility Model, when effectively applied, does seem to promote orderly development and social testing of information technology. National videotex systems and wired-cities projects are only two examples. On the down side, it follows that if policy makers are in a position to positively influence national productivity and growth, they are also in a position to influence growth negatively. Various studies have shown that for all MITI's success, its planners too often concentrated in the past on aiding the wrong industries.

The Marketplace Model, on the other hand, encourages innovation and diversity of information technology. The personal computer industry is an example of the former, and the variety of database options in the United States are examples of the latter. The promised cornucopia of high-tech applications is misleading in that many forms of information technology are developed but not adopted, because the market fails to accept the technology. Bell's Picture Telephone is one example. Other forms of technology may be slow to develop nationally, because the private sector is unsure of market forces. Videotex is perhaps the most obvious example of a national interconnection developing in the Public Utility countries but not in the United States. Experiments such as those conducted by Knight-Ridder, MCC, ISDN, etc. were initiated in local markets by individual companies to test perceived consumer demand, but never incorporated in any rational federal policy. In the long run, innovation per se is unlikely to prove a crucial factor. Fiber optics, the transistor, and integrated circuits are all American innovations, but Japanese technologists are proving far more effective at realizing profits and high employment from their development. Because of these and other such differences, construction of a new social order based upon a mutually beneficial international information economy remains a difficult task.

References

Babe, R. E. (1985). Information industries and economic analysis: Policy makers beware. In M. Gurevitch, and M. Levy (Eds.), *Mass Communication Review Yearbook 5*. Beverly Hills, CA: Sage.

Bloom, J. L. (1984). *Japan's Ministry of International Trade and Industry (MITI) as a policy instrument in the development of information technology*. (October). Cambridge, MA: Harvard Program on Information Resources Policy.

Bolling, G. H. (1983). *AT&T: Aftermath of antitrust*. Washington D.C.: National Defense University.

Bolter, W. G., et al. (Eds.). (1984). *The transition to competition: Telecommunications policy for the 1980s*. Englewood Cliffs, NJ: Prentice-Hall.

Cable and Broadcasting Act 1984, Chapter 46. London, UK: Her Majesty's Stationary Office.

Courville, L., et al. (Eds.). (1984). *Economic analysis of telecommunications: Theory and applications*. New York: Elsevier Science.

Crawford, M. H. (1984). *Information technology and industrialization policy in the Third World: A case study of Singapore, Malaysia, and Indonesia* (August). Cambridge, MA: Harvard Program on Information Resources Policy.

Edgar, P., & Rahim, S. (Eds.). (1983). *Communication policy in developed countries*. London, UK: Kegan and Kegan Paul International.

Evans, J., et al. (1984). *The development of cable networks in the U.K.: Issues in the formulation of a technology policy*. Manchester, UK: Program of Policy Research in Engineering Science and Technology, Manchester University.

Eward, R. (1985). *The deregulation of international telecommunications*. Dedham, MA: Artech House.

Financial Times, Media Intelligence Unit (1985). *Videotext and teletext in the U.S. and U.K.* London, UK: *Financial Times* Business Information Service.

Homet, R. (1979). *Politics, culture, and communication*. New York: Praeger.

Ikeda, K. (1985). Hi-OVIS seen by users: Use and evaluation of Japanese Interactive CATV. *Studies of Broadcasting, 21,* (March), 95–119.

Ito, Y. (1981). The *Johoka Shakai* approach to the study of communication in Japan. In G. C. Wilhoit, and H. de Bock (Eds.), *Mass Communication Review Yearbook 2*. Beverly Hills, CA: Sage.

Leff, N. H. (1984). Externalities, information costs, and social benefit-cost analysis for economic development: An example from telecommunications. *Economic Development and Cultural Change, 32*(2), 255–76.

Lodge, G. C., & Vogel, E. F. (1987). *Ideology and national competitiveness: An analysis of nine countries*. Boston, MA: Harvard University Press.

Musashi, T. (1985). *Japanese telecommunications policy*. Cambridge, MA: Program on Information Resources Policy, Harvard University.

Okimoto, D. I., Sugano, T., & Weinstein, F. B. (1984). *Competitive edge: The semi-conductor industry in the U.S. and Japan*. Stanford, CA: Stanford University Press.

Pool, I. de Sola, et al. (1984). *Communication flows: A census in the United States and Japan*. Tokyo: Tokyo University Press.

Salvaggio, J. L. (1983). Information societies and social problems: The Japanese and American experience. *Telecommunications Policy, 7,* 228–42.

Salvaggio, J. L. (1985a). Information technology and social problems: Four international models. In B. D. Ruben (Ed.), *Information and Behavior: Volume 1*. New Brunswick, NJ: Transaction.

Salvaggio, J. L. (1985b). *The Japanese telecom market: A new game plan*. Arlington, VA: Telecom Publishing Group, Capitol Publications.

Salvaggio, J. L. (1987). The trend toward telecommunications reform: A comparison of the divestiture of AT&T and privatization of NTT. *Keio Communication Review, 8,* 55–74.

Salvaggio, J. L., & Steinfield, C. (1985). *An examination of the U.K.'s recent policy shift to a more competitive approach: Implications for a wired nation*. Working paper #1, International Telecommunications Research Institute, School of Communication, University of Houston.

Shimizu, M. (1985). Chronology of events involving new media in Japan (1976–1984). *Studies of Broadcasting, 21* (March), 121–31.

Siegel, L., & Markoff, J. (1985). *The high cost of high tech: The dark side of the chip*. New York: Harper and Row.

Sterling, C. H. (Ed.). (1984). *International telecommunications and information policy*. Washington DC: Communications Press.

Tachikawa, K. (1983). Information network system: New telecommunications converged with computers. *Studies of Broadcasting, 19* (March), 49–69.

Tamura, M. (1987). The information environment around the Japanese people. *Studies of Broadcasting, 23* (March), 7–26.

Telecommunications Act 1984: Chapter 12. London, UK: Her Majesty's Stationary Office.

Telecommunications imports exceeding exports by wide margin (1984). *Telecom Trade Reporter*, September 21, p. 4.

Tomita, T. (1984). Japan's policy on monopoly and competition in telecommunications. *Telecommunications Policy, 8*(1), 44–50.

Tsurumi, Y. (1982). Japan's challenge to the U.S.: Industrial policies and corporate strategies. *Columbia Journal of World Business, 17*(2), 87–95.

U.S. Congress. (1984). *Cable communications policy act of 1984*. 98th Congress, 2d Session, S.66. Washington, DC: Government Printing Office.

U.S. Department of Commerce, National Telecommunications and Information Administration. (1985). *Issues in domestic telecommunications: Directions for national policy* (July). Washington, DC: Government Printing Office. Special Publication 85–16.

Varan, D. (1984). *An analysis of Zaikai influence in Japanese telecommunication liberalization*. Unpublished M.A. thesis, University of Houston.

Yokoi, M. (1982). Agencies and directions of Japanese policy. *Telecommunications Policy, 6*(4), 258–68.

Zeman, Z. P. (1983). The rising challenge of Japan's computer technology. *Canadian Data Systems, 15*, 112–18.

15

University-Industry Technology Transfer in the Information Society

Everett M. Rogers and James W. Dearing

Due partly to increased international competitiveness, university-industry relations are closer in the 1980s than previously. This strengthened relationship is centered around the technology transfer process that occurs between research universities and private industry, with the encouragement of government. Research on university-industry technology transfer processes, although not necessarily cumulative nor systematic, is contributing toward an improved understanding of technology transfer. The present essay considers five questions as they apply to the microelectronics industry and to research universities.

In various attempts to remain competitive in world markets, local, state, and national governments have, since 1980, vigorously pursued policies aimed at increasing technology transfer between research universities and private industry. Technology transfer is important because the exchange of new knowledge among academic, industrial, and government scientists can have a multiplier effect on technological innovation. Such technological innovation is the wellspring of new products and services that provide an economy with increased competitiveness. Such innovations result from applications of theoretical knowledge and basic research. In some cases, national governments are active in sponsoring or in conducting research, and are often scientific partners in tripartite university-industry-government relationships.

The present essay argues that technology transfer, especially in the microelectronics industry, is at the heart of the information society. We shall consider five main questions:

1. Is the research university the key institution in the information society?
2. How does the most effective university-industry technology transfer occur?
3. What is the role of federal, state, and local initiatives in promoting high-technology industry?
4. What are the benefits and the costs of technology transfer for universities, private firms, and government laboratories, for each?
5. What lessons have been learned about promoting high-technology industry in a nation, state, or local area?

The Technology Transfer Process

Technology transfer is the main basis for the new university-industry relationships in a number of information societies and in certain newly informationalizing countries. "Technology transfer" is the communication between people of information that reduces uncertainty in reaching a decision or in achieving a goal. The term "technology" embraces knowledge in the form of either hardware or software and represents any extension of human capabilities. People transfer technology. An example is a biotechnology firm that hires a university biochemistry graduate; this hiring represents technology transfer if the new graduate brings new information (that is, technology) to the firm.

"University-industry" linkages are patterns of communication and exchange over time between people employed in industry and people employed in universities. This definition is very inclusive; it includes informal relationships such as a personnel officer of a microelectronics corporation talking semiregularly over the telephone with an old friend employed in a university library; it also includes more formal, structured relationships such as industry liaison associations, community outreach programs for disadvantaged youths, and the fund-raising efforts of university development offices. Some formal relations are created explicitly for the purpose of transferring technology between a university and surrounding industry. Only those formal relations explicitly created to facilitate technology transfer are considered *formal* university-industry linkages in the present essay. All other patterns of communication and exchange over time between people employed in industry and people employed in a university are considered *informal* university-industry linkages, since the purpose of communication exchange through those interpersonal networks is not primarily technology transfer.

Whether innovations travel through informal or formal linkages, they must be communicated to private firms so that they can be commercialized. *"Commercialization"* is the production, manufacturing, packaging, marketing, and distribution of a new product that embodies an innovation (Rogers, 1983, p. 143). In a number of countries, private companies usually do commercialization, and universities mainly conduct basic research, so a university-to-industry transfer of technology is often involved in the technology transfer process. However, increasingly, academicians and universities own rights to commercial products, and private companies conduct basic research in-house or else join private research consortia. In certain countries, national governments participate in commercialization directly or indirectly.

"Basic research" is defined as original investigations for the advancement of scientific knowledge that do not have the specific objective of applying that knowledge to practical problems. In contrast, "applied research" consists of scientific investigations that are intended to solve practical problems. Applied researchers are the main users of basic research.

"Development" of an innovation is the process of putting a new idea in a form that is expected to meet the needs of potential adopters/buyers. In the case of microelectronics, much of the "D" in R&D is carried out by private industry, and the basic research is mainly conducted by universities, so a university-industry linkage has been involved for some years in the rapid technological advance of the microelectronics industry. What is new in recent years are the major colaborative research centers in microelectronics that are located on university campuses and funded mainly by private firms. The centers are indicators of a recent trend toward closer relationships between research universities and private firms, at least in the United States.

Is the Research University the Key Institution in Information Societies?

Current literature on technology transfer, primarily written by academicians, reflects an unquestioned premise that the university is the key institution in information societies. The theoretical rationale for this assumption is the statement that the growth of an information society rests fundamentally on the rise of knowledge industries that produce and distribute information rather than goods and services (Machlup, 1962). The university produces (1) information as the result of the research that it conducts, especially basic research, and (2) information-producers (individuals with graduate degrees, who are trained to conduct research). The information-producing role is particularly characteristic of the fifty or so research universities in the United States. A *research university* is an institution of higher learning whose main function is to perform research and provide graduate training.

The research university fulfills a role of information societies analogous to that of the factory in industrial societies. It is thought to be the key institution, around which growth occurs, and which determines the direction of that growth. Each of the major high-technology regions in the United States is centered around a research university: Silicon Valley and Stanford University, Route 128 and MIT, Research Triangle and the three main North Carolina universities (Duke, North Carolina State, and the University of North Carolina), and Austin and the University of Texas at Austin, for example.

A *high-technology industry* is characterized by (1) highly educated employees, many of whom are scientists and engineers; (2) a rapid rate of technological innovation; (3) a high ratio of R&D expenditures to sales (typically about 1:10), and (4) a worldwide market for its products. The main high-technology industries today are electronics, aerospace, pharmaceuticals, instrumentation, and biotechnology. Microelectronics, a sub-industry of electronics centering on semiconductor chips and their applications (such as in computers), is usually considered the highest of high technology, because the technology changes more rapidly than in other high-technology industries.

It is particularly microelectronics technology, applied in the form of computers (especially microcomputers) and telecommunications, that is driving nations like the United States, Japan, and several western European countries into becoming information societies. Yet, with industry investing in more basic and collaborative research, as in the United States, does the research university remain the key institution in this information society? Certainly the older centers of high-technology growth have major universities within close proximity. In a 1982 survey of high-technology companies in the United States, nearly 60% of the respondents replied that close proximity to a university was significant or very significant in deciding upon a company location. More respondents, however, listed (1) labor skills/availability, (2) labor costs, and (3) tax climate within the region, as significant or very significant in their location choice. Other factors such as housing costs, environmental quality, cultural attractions, corporate tax rates, and transportation networks are also important.

Not all of the younger high-technology areas share a major university. Sacramento, California, for example, has attracted a significant cadre of microelectronics firms. Basic university research cannot be a factor in this attraction, although a large number of area graduates in engineering combines with a cost of living that is low compared to Silicon Valley (near San Jose, California). Shenzhen Special Economic Zone, in the People's Republic of China, also lacks a research university. The Chinese government is pursuing a strategy of economic development through the attraction of foreign capital and investment in high-technology business, through which the government expects indigenous spin-offs to occur.

In countries where the national government plays a central role in assisting private business, basic research is often conducted in government laboratories, as well as in universities. Japan is an example. Tsukuba, a town in Ibaraki Prefecture, 35 miles north of Tokyo, was designated by the Japanese national government as a primary site for basic and applied research. The area is anchored by a major research university, the University of Tsukuba, which is the pilot institution for a new generation of Japanese universities that emphasize research. The faculty is particularly strong in engineering, basic sciences, and medicine. Twenty-six institutes have been established to carry out advanced research, including the Institute of Biological Sciences, the Institute of Applied Biochemistry, the Institute of Physics, the Institute of Chemistry, the Institute of Applied Physics, the Institute of Materials Science, the Institute of Engineering Mechanics, the Institute of Information Sciences and Electronics, and the Institute of Basic Medical Sciences.

Tsukuba also claims a disproportionately large number of government research laboratories and facilities. For example, in 1985 the Agency of Industrial Science and Technology moved nine of its research units from Tokyo to Tsukuba, which added approximately 2,000 research scientists to the small community. The Tsukuba research facilities now represent one-third of the national research personnel and 50% of the national research and development (R&D) budget. The University of Tsukuba is only one of the key institutions in the emergence of this high-technology area, for the national government not only directed the future of Tsukuba but also added tremendously to the number of scientists and the amount of resources the community now boasts.

The scarcity of major research universities is not stopping communities and national governments from investing in "technopolises." Direct government support of advanced research, coupled with corporate tax incentives and low costs of living are often enough to launch high-technology growth areas. Whether technopolises will fully mature and lead the way to economic development in such Third World countries as Brazil, South Korea, Taiwan, China, and India is yet to be seen. A scarcity of research universities conducting basic research in these areas may relegate them to a second tier of technopolises, as may be the case with certain high-technology areas in Japan and the United States. The problem may not be a shortage of government willingness to invest in research but of scientists trained in basic research. Thus, the worth of research universities in spawning high-tech areas may be more acutely felt in the future, with increasing demand, worldwide, for trained scientists.

How Does the Most Effective University-Industry Technology Transfer Occur?

Relations between U.S. universities and industry historically have followed economic cycles. Linkages have been more robust when economic and technological uncertainty has been high, and have decreased when government research resources for universities have been abundant. According to Baba (1985), new types of university-industry linkages blossomed prior to and during World War I (1900–1916), during the Great Depression (1929–1933), during and after World War II (1943–1954), and over the past two decades (1969–1989).

During the 1980s the federal government cut back severely on funding university research in the United States. Consequently, universities looked to private industry for research funds. The National Science Foundation estimates that industry funding of university research increased fourfold in the past decade, to about $300 million. During the 1980s many state and local governments launched initiatives to encourage the development of high-technology industry in order to create new jobs and to fuel economic growth. Fearful of Japanese competition, many U.S. microelectronics firms formed university-industry collaborative research centers and invested considerable resources in funding these centers.

Largest of the new R&D centers is the Microelectronics and Computer Technology Corporation (MCC), which decided in 1983 to locate on the campus of the University of Texas at Austin. Fifty-six other cities in 27 states competed with Austin for the MCC, with state and local governments offering a variety of incentives. About 300 Texas leaders in state and local governments, universities, and private companies put together approximately $60 million over a 2-month period to win the MCC (Marks, 1983).

Former Arizona governor Bruce Babbitt, whose state was a candidate in the MCC selection process, stated: "Some 60 mayors and 27 governors complained about the unfair advantage of Texas oil money, and promised their constituents a better showing next time" (Babbitt, 1984). Certainly the MCC decision heightened awareness among state and local officials in the United States about the importance of high-technology development, and created a fuller realization of the role of research universities in attracting high-technology firms.

What did the University of Texas, the state of Texas, and the city of Austin get in return for their offer to the MCC? The MCC is supported at $75 million per year by a consortium of 20 U.S. firms that are the giants of the microelectronics industry, plus U.S. government research grants (mainly from the Department of Defense). The MCC presently has a research staff of about 450. During its first two years of operation, the MCC created a boom-town mentality in Austin, and housing prices almost doubled. Fourteen high-technology firms moved all or part of their R&D operations employing 6,100 people to Austin during 1983–84, while in 1982 only four companies with 900 jobs moved to Austin. Several of these newcomers to Austin area microelectronics companies that belong to the MCC and that want to locate nearby in order to facilitate technology transfer.

But the main benefits to Austin of getting the MCC will occur in future years, when a high-technology complex of spin-off microelectronics firms develops in the area. By 1989, only two or three firms had spun off of the MCC although some 40 or 50 new firms had spun off of older microelectronics companies, especially Tracor (which existed for several decades prior to the MCC). So perhaps a high-tech area was beginning in the Austin area. The building boom set off by the 1983 MCC location decision had largely gone bust by 1987, and Austin is presently fighting to attract more high-technology businesses. The world depression of oil markets has affected Texas, and Austin property owners and the local construction industry are reeling from the falling building prices. Shiny new offices, overbuilt during the MCC boom, sit vacant. Residential homes are selling for bargain prices.

Moreover, the losers in the 1983 MCC bidding competition such as Phoenix, Research Triangle, and San Diego, may have become the real winners. For instance, the University of California system has been favored with impressive budget increases since the California governor learned that certain academic deficiencies at the University of California at San Diego were one reason why the MCC decided on Austin. The reaction to losing the MCC to Austin was $85 million in state funding for the Microelectronics Center of North Carolina, an R&D center located in Research Triangle and intended to attract private high-tech firms to the area. The Engineering Excellence Program at Arizona State University is helping boost Phoenix area high-tech industry. So the 1983 MCC decision has had effects not only in Austin.

The MCC is only one of several university-industry research centers in microelectronics. Other examples are (1) the Center for Integrated Systems (CIS) at Stanford University, which was founded in 1981 and is supported by $15 million from 20 U.S. microelectronics firms and $15 million from the U.S. Department of Defense. A new $9 million building houses CIS's 30 faculty, 80 research staff, and 200 graduate students, plus industry R&D workers that are loaned to CIS by sponsoring firms for a 1-year period; and (2) the Microsystems Industrial Group at MIT, sponsored by about a dozen companies, many of them on Route 128.

Today there are over 25 university-industry microelectronics research centers at U.S. universities. Other such collaborative R&D centers have been founded for robotics, biotechnology, and other high-technology fields. In addition, many other technology transfer mechanisms are used by research universities:

- Research parks such as the Research Triangle Park in North Carolina and the Stanford Research Park (the first of its kind, and still the most successful). The late Fred Terman, then vice-president and provost of Stanford University, launched the Stanford Research Park in 1951, as part of his vision for a West Coast electronics complex.
- Industrial liaison programs by universities, which provide a means for private firms to get an early look at research results and to identify promising students to hire as future employees, in exchange for paying an annual membership fee to the university.
- Faculty consulting by university professors. President Carl Taylor Compton of MIT, in the 1930s, not only allowed his faculty to consult for pay one day a week but strongly encouraged them to do so. Compton thought that faculty consulting was one of the most effective means of technology transfer from MIT's research laboratories to for-profit high-technology companies on Route 128. After World War II, the MIT faculty consulting policy spread to Stanford University, and, in recent years, to many other research universities that wish to foster technology transfer.
- Especially in recent years, professors have formed companies of their own, often launching their start-up around a technological idea they bring with them from a university laboratory. In some cases, the faculty entrepreneur who founds a high-technology company then cuts off his/her academic ties. Well-known examples are MIT's Ken Olson, who founded DEC (Digital Equipment Corporation), and, more recently, Nobel laureate biologist Walter Gilbert, who left his Harvard professorship to become board chairman of Biogen, Inc., a biotechnology company. Harvard wants its professors to devote 80% of their time to the university (this is a common "bag limit" on faculty-for-profit activities at many universities today); Gilbert said he was spending 80%–90% of his time in other-than-university responsibilities. The University of California system reviewed 5,000 professors' financial disclosure statements

in 1982–83 and told seven faculty members to modify their industry ties. Some universities require that their faculty cannot serve as president, chairman of the board, or other principal officer in a private firm. At other universities, the faculty are allowed any type of industry role, as long as it does not violate the 20% limit on worktime. At Stanford, the 80-member Department of Medicine in 1980 turned itself into a consulting collective to raise money which is then granted for research by junior faculty in the Department (Culliton, 1982).

These and other novel means of technology transfer are being tried out by professors at research universities today. Unfortunately, little systematic research exists to enable comparative analyses of such industry-university linkages. We do not yet know which types of linkages are most effective for technology transfer. Local, state, and federal governments, as well as industry and universities, are betting millions of dollars on creating formal technology transfer linkages. Some research suggests that linkage types are increasingly complex, that universities are increasingly active in the private sector, and that technology transfer linkages are increasingly centralized and under corporate control. Do these and other trends lead to more effective technology transfer?

One promising theoretical basis upon which technology transfer approaches can be compared is to analyze the formal and informal linkages. Problems with technology transfer are sometimes ascribed to their social organization such as "administrative bureaucracy" (Koenig et al., 1986) or "bureaucratic procedures" (Larsen, Wigand & Rogers, 1987). These studies support the belief that linkage structure is a primary determinant of effective technology transfer.

Rationalization is the tendency for patterns of social interaction to exhibit defined hierarchies of control, task differentiation, and codified procedures. Modern bureaucracies are the classic examples of highly rationalized systems (Gerth & Mills, 1946; Merton, 1968). Rationalization has been hypothesized to affect negatively individual creativity, both within and between organizations, and in geographically bounded scientific communities (Bell, 1973). In science as in art, creativity is the wellspring of innovation (Bronowski, 1956). If rational organization impedes individual creativity, then knowledge generation, a first stage in the technology transfer process, may be inhibited.

Whereas rationalization has been viewed as antithetical to innovation generation, the characteristics of rational organization have been found to be positively related to innovation development and adoption. Commercialization of an innovation, for example, is better accomplished with, not without, organization resources. Rationalization seemingly hinders innovation generation and helps innovation development. How does rationalization affect the middle process of technology transfer? Theoretically, one would expect that the more rationalized a linkage's structure is, the less effective that linkage will be in transferring technology.

Communities may be comprised of overlapping social and task-differentiated communication networks. The same person often belongs to a number of communication networks (Rogers & Kincaid, 1981). Task-differentiated networks exhibit degrees of rationalization in their formal structure. A technology transfer mechanism such as a university-industry liaison office, a business incubator, or a cooperative research laboratory, is typically formalized. Individuals are bound contractually, expected to follow rules, acknowledge hierarchical authority, and work in differentiated tasks. Social networks, on the other hand, exhibit considerably less structure. Despite their informality and lack of visibility, informal networks may be more effective at transmitting technical information than are formal structures. For example, scientists meeting by chance in a restaurant or bar may transfer more technology than a university-industry licensing agreement can achieve in a month (Rogers & Larsen, 1984). Formal, rational boundary-spanning structures may be more ritual than productive (Meyer & Scott, 1983).

The content of information transmitted through formal and informal channels may be different. Despite the participation of scientists, formal linkages may be dominated by information that is largely administrative in content, in accordance with the roles played by the people who use such linkages (Kornhauser, 1962; Merton & Lerner, 1961). Informal networks serve a social function, yet they may also serve to transmit information that is high in intellectual content. An open research question is whether formal technology transfer linkages are more effective than informal communication networks at transferring technology in a high-technology area.

What Is the Role of Federal, State, and Local Initiatives in Promoting High-Technology Industry?

Although young technopolises now typically benefit from direct government support, the most successful, mature high-technology areas arose without much direct government support. Cambridge (England), Route 128, and Silicon Valley are such examples, although indirect government support through military technology contracts contributed to the growth of both Silicon Valley and Route 128.

Many governments are presently eager to support localities and research universities in developing research parks and high-technology zones. In Japan, South Korea, Taiwan, China, India, Brazil, England, and the United

States, governments are undertaking new initiatives to support high-technology industry and university research. The U.S. National Science Foundation (NSF), for example, funds Centers of Engineering Excellence, Cooperative Research Centers, and Innovation Centers. NSF now is concentrating on funding small businesses that are trying to develop innovative high-technology products.

In the United States, federal, state, and local governments directly encourage high-technology development, indirectly seeking that goal through local research universities. The Office of Technology Assessment (1984) identifies the allure of high-technology development: "State and local government leaders are attracted to high-technology industries because of the sector's rapid expansion and presumed job-creating potential. . . . Some critics, however, believe that high-technology job projections are unrealistically high or that the potential for reviving distressed areas has been overstated."

Although state and local governments are far more active than the U.S. federal government in promoting high-technology development (Office of Technology Assessment, 1984), a variety of federal policies and programs encourage high-technology industry to cooperate with research activities. For example, tax credits are allowed for certain corporate R&D expenditures, and for research contracted to universities and to certain other institutions. Further, firms can deduct from their taxes as charitable contributions part of the cost of equipment donated to universities. Federal tax policies have aided the expansion of venture capital; as a result, it has been easier to obtain financing to launch start-up firms (Rogers & Larsen, 1984). One result is an increasing degree of entrepreneurism in starting new microelectronics firms in the United States, especially around Boston and San Francisco/Silicon Valley, where venture capital firms are concentrated.

The recent easing by the federal government of antitrust restrictions on collaborative R&D activities has facilitated closer university-industry relationships. The MCC probably could not have been founded had it not been for a favorable opinion by the U.S. Department of Justice on 28 December 1982. Then, in 1984, federal legislation was passed to remove certain antitrust barriers to collaborative R&D. Since then, about 150 such joint R&D centers have been established in various industries.

State governments have initiated 153 programs with at least some feature directed toward high-technology development, with 38 of these programs in 22 states dedicated to the creation, attraction, or retention of high-technology firms (Office of Technology Assessment, 1984). Research Triangle, for example, has had the strong and continuous support of the state government of North Carolina for over 30 years. Former governor James

B. Hunt devoted about 25% of his time during his eight years in office to recruiting high-technology firms to Research Triangle Park. By about 1970, a critical mass of high-tech firms had accumulated in Research Triangle, and high-tech employment has been growing steadily since then.

The main thrust of recent state programs has been to coordinate the activities of state and local governments, private industry, and universities to facilitate technology transfer between the university and its surrounding high-technology firms (National Governors' Association, 1983; Office of Technology Assessment, 1984). State and local laws also are factors affecting technology transfer and the development of high-technology industry. For example, lack of a state income tax in Texas is cited by some high-tech firms as an important reason why they moved to Austin.

What Are the Benefits and Costs of University-Industry Relationships?

University-industry collaborative research centers in microelectronics represent a new and important force on the university campus, and one that has already generated a great deal of policy controversy. Some observers see this recent development in a very positive light. Babbitt (1984) referred to "a new awareness that the fruits of university research and development activity have little economic value unless they are systematically harvested in the marketplace." The university obviously benefits from the research funds that it receives, and the professors may gain useful experience which they can incorporate into their courses for the benefit of their students.

In general, both the research universities and private industry are pleased with their new, closer relationships. Microelectronics companies feel that their membership fees paid to the collaborative university-industry research centers are one means of dealing with Japanese competition (for example, the MCC publicly justifies its existence as the U.S. response to the Japanese Fifth-Generation Computer Project). In addition, semiconductor companies in Silicon Valley report that they participate in the collaborative centers as a means to identify future employees and faculty consultants from among university students and professors (Larsen, 1984). The several state and local governments promoting high-technology development feel that they are winners as a result of the closer university-industry relationships.

But there are also a variety of problems connected with the industry-sponsored research centers on university campuses. For instance, the priorities accorded by a university to certain disciplines and to certain research problems may be affected by the priorities of private firms that donate research funds, thus causing a feeling of relative deprivation on the part of departments and professors not so favored. The growing emphasis on technology may come at the expense of arts and humanities. University scientists fear that the price of industry collaboration will be a shift from basic research to more product-oriented development.

Problems of inequality also can occur between universities, as well as within a university. When Stanford, Texas, Arizona State, and MIT create university-industry collaborative research centers in microelectronics, are other universities adversely affected? Hancock (1983) noted that in the new era of university-industry relationships, "one trend is apparent; corporate money goes to the academic haves, not the have-nots."

"Concern about the propriety of university-industry relations has been a central theme on the country's research campuses for the past couple of years" (Culliton, 1983). Perhaps one turning point in the recognition of this problem occurred in 1982 when the presidents of five universities met with eleven corporate leaders at Pajaro Dunes (California) to explore such questions as: "How can universities preserve open communication and independence in the direction of basic research while also meeting obligations to industry? Is it acceptable for one corporation to dominate research in an entire [academic] department? Are there adverse consequences in terms of collaboration among faculty in various departments if one group must worry about protecting corporate right to licenses? Will extensive corporate ties erode public confidence in university faculty as disinterested seekers of truth?" (Academic-industry complex, 1982).

The Twentieth-Century Fund Task Force on the Commercialization of Scientific Research (1984) highlighted this conflict-of-interest problem: "Ties between the scientific community and corporations, and between corporations and universities, are not, of course, new. Such ties are one reason for the continued supremacy of American science. But the new relationships differ in magnitude and extent from past relationships, introducing the possibility of conflicts of interest." The general conclusion is that research universities should move carefully into their new partnership relations with private industry.

In summary, there are three main points of potential conflict between the university and private firms in the present era of closer relationships:

1. Restrictions on the communication of research results, where company secrecy policies may conflict with the scientific desire for free communication.
2. The relatively short-term orientation of the private firms vs. the longer-term orientation of university scientists toward basic research.
3. The agenda of priorities for university research may be affected by corporate sponsorship, with emphasis upon scientific fields with a direct potential for commercial payoff.

Clearly the new, closer relationships between industry and the university, often fostered by government initiatives and intended to encourage high-technology development, deserve careful research and analysis. Such investigation has not been mounted to date.

What Are the Lessons Learned about Promoting High-Technology Industry?

Conventional wisdom in recent years indicates that state and local governments in the United States are engaging in a futile activity when they try to attract high-technology firms away from other locales in the United States. Instead, it is usually more effective for a state or city to develop its own high-technology industry. And the seed for starting local entrepreneurial activities is to invest in improving a research university, especially in such academic departments as electrical engineering, computer science, and biotechnology. An investment in improving these university departments is likely to pay off, eventually, in technology transfer to private firms and, still later, to generating an entrepreneurial head of steam in starting up high-tech firms.

A considerable time lag is usually involved from the improvement of a research university to the rise of a local high-technology industry. Clear evidence on this point is provided by the case of Research Triangle in North Carolina. Governor Luther H. Hodges had the original vision of a North Carolina high-technology center back in the 1950s. Hodges followed the Stanford University model of establishing a university research park in order to create a high-technology complex. Only after 20 years of concerted efforts did high-tech firms begin to move to Research Triangle, with a key turning point occurring in 1965, when IBM located an R&D unit there. By 1983, total employment in Research Triangle Park's 40 firms was over 20,000 with annual payroll of $500 million (Rogers & Larsen, 1984, p. 241). But there is not yet much entrepreneurial activity in starting up new firms. Several decades were also necessary for the rise of Silicon Valley in Northern California and for the beginnings of Route 128 around Boston. So high-technology industry does not get under way overnight. On the other hand, the recent Austin takeoff occurred rather rapidly.

The presence of an outstanding research university in a locale does not necessarily cause the development of a high-technology center. Evidence of this point is provided by such excellent universities as Harvard, Columbia, Chicago, Berkeley, and Caltech, none of whom have played a very important role in technology transfer to local firms. Obviously, other factors than just the presence of a local research university are involved in launching a high-technology center; a high quality of life, entrepreneurial spirit, and the presence of venture capital are also important. Even when a research university is present, it must have policies that encourage faculty to assist local firms, or else not much technology transfer will occur. Such favorable policies exist at Stanford, MIT, Texas, Arizona State, the North Carolina universities, and increasingly, at other universities. Harvard, Berkeley, and other outstanding research universities do not particularly encourage technology transfer. And so their potential for encouraging high-technology industry is not fully realized.

Marshalling a united front of support is vital for the development of a high-technology area. In a review of how Austin wooed the MCC, Smilor, Kozmetsky, & Gibson (1987) conceptualized seven categories of persons, groups, or forces important in attracting high-technology firms: (1) a research university; (2) large corporations (*Fortune 500* headquarters/ branches, major sales, and/or research and development); (3) emerging companies (university spin-offs, large company spin-offs, and others); (4) federal government activities like sponsored research and defense spending; (5) state government (e.g., education support); (6) local government (responsible for quality of life, competitive utility rates, and infrastructure); and (7) support groups (business, chamber of commerce, and community). Each of these seven institutional categories and their more specific components are, ideally, tied together by key individuals who "make things happen." The influencers are often charismatic individuals with extensive interpersonal networks. They have access to, and are members of, elite groups at the local, state, and perhaps national level. These leaders unite groups and persons in the seven institutional categories into pursuing a common vision—the development of a technopolis.

A basic characteristic of information societies may be decentralization. Since knowledge is not constrained by the shackles of matter-energy, it lends itself to easy transmission throughout a society via telecommunications, which make distance (spatial constraints) less relevant. However, mature areas of high-technology growth appear to be highly centralized, just as traditional industrial metropolises were. Local support services, including manufacturing plants and distribution outlets, are commonplace in today's technopolises. Rogers and Chen (1987) suggest that information capitals seem to mimic yesterday's industrial capitals because (1) universities are often an initiator of high-technology development, thus they become a logical physical clustering point; (2) interpersonal networks are vital for personal and corporate survival in areas with rapid job turnover and rapid product change such as high-technology areas; (3) entrepreneurs require ease to access to suppliers, financiers, and markets, and advanced telecommunications networks do not yet characterize any nation (although Japan is close); and (4) Silicon Valley and Route 128 provided successful models that have been copied elsewhere. Thus the agglomerated structures of these two older technopolises tend to characterize the newer technopolises as well.

Conclusions

Many research universities in various nations are developing closer linkages with private industry. This trend results in part from pressures to remain competitive in the international marketplace—particularly in such technologies as microelectronics, which change rapidly. Advances in microelectronics are driving the development of information societies in various countries.

Linkages between universities, government research laboratories, and private industry are established to encourage the transfer of technology. Local, state, and national governments hope that scientific knowledge, once transferred to commercial ventures, will result in economic gain and in job creation.

This technology transfer process has not been very systematically studied. Descriptive analyses abound, as do categorizations of linkage types. Many kinds of formal and informal linkages exist. Most R&D agencies and universities have their own versions of linkage models, often formed out of convenience rather than from theoretical knowledge about effective ways to transfer knowledge. The important question of how the technology transfer process is made most effective has not been answered. One promising approach may be to compare all types of linkages by their degree of rationalization.

Technopolises are the generative centers of information societies. To date, these unplanned and planned areas of high-technology growth do not reflect previous theories of how we expect the information society to look. This incongruency may be apparent only because we are currently caught in a transition phase toward an information society.

References

Academic-industry complex. (1982). *Science, 216,* 960–61.
Baba, M. L. (1985). University innovation to promote economic growth and university/industry relations. *Proceedings of the 1985 National Science Foundation Conference on Industrial Science and Technological Innovation,* May 6–8, Albany, New York.
Babbitt, B. (1964). The states and the reindustrialization of America. *Issues in Science and Technology, 1,* 84–93.
Bell, D. (1973). *The coming of post-industrial society.* New York: Basic Books.
Bronowski, J. (1956). *Science and human values.* New York: Harper and Row.
Culliton, B. J. (1982). Stanford doctors try consulting, inc. *Science, 218,* 1122–23.

Culliton, B. J. (1983). Academe and industry debate partnership. *Science, 219,* 150–51.

Gerth, H. H., & Mills, C. Wright. (1946). *From Max Weber: Essays in sociology.* New York: Oxford University Press.

Hancock, E. (1983). Academe meets industry: Charting the bottom line. *Alumni Magazine Consortium, 7,* 1–9.

Koenig, H. E., et al. (1986). *Industry-university cooperation in Michigan: Final report and executive summary.* Report to the National Science Foundation.

Kornhauser, W. (1962). *Scientists in industry: Conflict and accommodation.* Berkeley: University of California Press.

Larsen, J. K. (1984). *Policy alternatives and the semiconductor industry.* Los Altos, CA: Cognos Associates. Report to the National Science Foundation.

Larsen, J. K., Wigand, R. T., & Rogers, E. M. (1987). *Industry-university technology transfer in microelectronics.* Los Altos, CA: Cognos Associates. Report to the National Science Foundation.

Machlup, F. (1962). *The production and distribution of knowledge in the United States.* Princeton, NJ: Princeton University Press.

Marks, D. (1983). Computer dating: the wooing of MCC. *Third Coast,* 32–34.

Merton, R. K. (1968). *Social theory and social structure.* New York: Free Press.

Merton, R. K., & Lerner, D. (1961). Social scientists and research policy. In W. G. Bennis, K. D. Benne, & R. Chin (Eds.), *The planning of change.* New York: Holt, Rinehart and Winston.

Meyer, J. W., & Scott, W. R. (1983). *Organizational environments: Ritual and responsibility.* Newbury Park, CA: Sage.

National Governors' Association. (1983). *Technology and growth: State initiatives in technological innovation.* Washington, D.C.: National Governors' Association Task Force on Technological Innovation. Report to the U.S. Department of Commerce.

Office of Technology Assessment. (1984). *Technology, innovation, and regional economic development: Encouraging high-technology development.* Washington, D.C.: U.S. Government Printing Office, OTA Background Paper 2.

Rogers, E. M. (1983). *Diffusion of innovations* (3d ed.). New York: Free Press.

Rogers, E. M., & Chen, Y-C. A. (1987). *Technology transfer and the technopolis.* Paper presented at the Pan-Pacific Conference IV, Taipei, Taiwan, May 17–20.

Rogers, E. M., & Kincaid, D. L. (1981). *Communication networks: Toward a new paradigm for research.* New York: Free Press.

Rogers, E. M., & Larsen, J. K. (1984). *Silicon Valley fever: Growth of high-technology culture.* New York: Basic Books.

Smilor, R. W., Kozmetsky, G., & Gibson, D. V. (1987). *The Austin/San Antonio corridor: The dynamics of a developing technopolis.* Paper presented at the conference on Technopolis: Emerging Issues in Technology Commercialization and Economic Development. Austin, TX, March 11–13.

Twentieth-Century Fund Task Force on the Commercialization of Scientific Research. (1984). *The science business.* New York: Priority Press.

16

The Communications Revolution Revisited

Frederick Williams

This essay presents a brief review of the changes in information technologies and their uses since The Communications Revolution *was written in 1980–81. The present essay highlights several areas of change that are especially visible such as telephony, electronic leisure, personal computing, and electronic publishing, and offers some generalized social-psychological implications that have resulted from those changes. These implications include (1) demassification of media, (2) increased choice, (3) time displacement, (4) increased mobility, and (5) increased connectivity.*

The Technological Invasion

Much public attention has been given in the last several decades to the invasion of communication technologies into our everyday lives. In their visible form such technologies refer to cable television, videocassettes, audiodisks and videodisks, videogames, new telephones and services, personal computers, electronic mail, and various types of text services. Less apparent to the public are computer time-sharing systems (such as used for airline reservations), new digital switching networks, communications satellites, and broadband optical fiber transmission systems.

On the one hand, simply the increasing visibility and use of these technologies has led to public attention; on the other, the larger concern with their social impacts has been stimulated by books ranging back to McLuhan (1962), Toffler (1970; 1980), or Smith (1981). Along with Williams

(1983), the forecasts were for visible changes in our daily lives. Our occupations were to become more tied to "knowledge work" and our leisure to become more "electronic."

While working on a revision of *The Communications Revolution* (Williams, 1983; the original was written mainly in 1980–81), it has been fascinating to review the changes that have taken place, and perhaps even more intriguing, to examine how they have deviated from forecasts. There is a policy lesson as well in this examination, as we can clearly see the consequences of the United States' turn toward the deregulation of selected computing and telecommunications technologies.

In this brief essay I review several areas of change that are especially visible as the United States approaches a midpoint in a decade that was supposed to introduce the information age (to use one of many labels).

Views of Anticipated Change

Telephony

The largest visible structural change in U.S. communications has been in the telephone business. At the turn of the decade, the American Telephone and Telegraph Company (AT&T) virtually controlled telephony in the United States, having about 80% of all telephone users within its franchises. Affectionately known as "Ma Bell," this company was the world's largest corporation, with assets around $115 billion and over one million employees; daily revenues averaged about $15.5 million daily.

Whatever future the telephone business was to have in the United States was to be a function of the outcome of a long-running antitrust suit pressed by the government against AT&T. That future became abruptly apparent, at least in part, in 1982, when AT&T agreed to divest itself of its 22 regional telephone companies in return for being allowed to engage in such unregulated businesses as data processing and computers, and, after seven years, in electronic publishing. Deregulation was to bring with it a new sense of competition in the telephone business, and thus, in turn, new equipment, services, and a departure from AT&T's sometimes "take it or leave it" attitude.

The mid-1980s presents a confused and volatile picture of telephony in the United States. Fall 1984 statistics indicate that AT&T's record of on-time corporate installations of telephone systems has fallen 20% to 30%, although this is not necessarily a permanent condition. Home telephone users, rather than being enticed by new services, are having to find their way among new practices in purchasing their own phones (if they choose not to pay a new leasing fee), ordering repairs, and choosing among competing long-distance services.

One area of visible growth, due to the new cellular technology rather than deregulation, is in mobile telephone. This extends beyond having more telephones in automobiles and boats, to bringing services to remote and sparsely populated areas. As of this writing, it is not clear if the presumed advantages of open competition will outweigh the confusion of new businesses and business practices in U.S. telephony. To the author's knowledge, no public studies yet show a perception by business or home telephone customers that services or alternatives have improved. On the positive side, there is a steady growth of the lower-priced competing long-distance services that has forced a modest reduction of AT&T's rates. Yet the public seems confused, and if this continues while local rates double or triple, telephone service could become a political issue in this country. One additional note comes from the warning of defense authorities who express anxiety over the reliability of our nation's newly deregulated telephone network in times of national emergency.

Electronic Leisure

From the vantage point of the early 1980s, technologies such as videotape and disk, cable television, and videogames suggested a future of wide-ranging electronic leisure. Cable franchises attracted major investors. Arts and other special channels were introduced. Sales of videotape tape-players were approximately doubled each year. RCA had made a near $0.5 billion dollar commitment to bring an under-$500 disk-player into the home. Warner Communications and American Express had joined forces to develop a fully interactive cable-television system ("Qube") in Colombus, Ohio. Videogame arcades and home videogames were among the nation's faster-growing businesses. High-definition television and direct-broadcast satellite are also on the horizon.

It seemed clear, too, that the penetration of these new services into the American home would be largely shaped by competition in the market-place, as we had already embarked on an era of deregulation. Along with the new technological alternatives presumably would come new varieties of content, thus freeing the public from the "mass taste" domination by the three television networks.

By mid-1980s, only the promise of more time with electronic leisure, not innovations in content, are reflected in market observations. The Nielson summary of the 1983 viewing season indicated that Americans had broken the 6-hour mark in daily average television viewing. Although network offerings had given way a few percentage points to cable and cassette, the bulk of viewing was still a similar mix of light entertainment, news, and sports.

If any type of program has increased in viewership, it is the motion picture, the favorite of cable and cassette viewing. Sophisticated, interactive types of cable offerings have gone unused. Arts channels are rapidly fading into history. Qube has been unprofitable, reflecting the public's disinterest in participating actively in program content. RCA has removed itself from the disk business, not because disks failed to provide movies, but because tape got there first and further allowed a home-recording capability. The videogame business has been dramatic in its near collapse. Direct-broadcast satellite still remains on the horizon. High-definition television is not only still in the wings, but the industry's desire to remain compatible with existing equipment will likely result in more modest goals in the area.

The optimistic premise of public interest advocates of the 1960s and 1970s—that the public would flock to alternative leisure-time content—has fallen flat. The U.S. mass television audience seems to prefer respite and escape rather than stimulation and active involvement. But the growth of videocassette use and cable movies and sports does indicate that even if the type of entertainment remains similar, people are willing to invest in more personal selection to fit both their time schedule as well as individual tastes. I call this phenomenon the "demassification" of media, a trend of our times.

Personal Computing

The 1970s also marked the birth of the microcomputer, and by late in that decade, three companies—Apple, Commodore, Radio Shack—with no history in computers dominated the U.S. market. The 1977 vision was that these machines could grow beyond the electronics-hobbyist market to capture the attention of individuals who might wish to experiment with computing at home. In less than a year, computer stores were opening, orders often exceeded supplies, and the vision was one of using computers in the home for management (e.g., budgeting, electronic checkbooks, education, and recreation videogames).

The small-business market also beckoned, as the 6-digit prices of most minicomputers were out of reach. The idea of bookkeeping, compiling mailing lists, and doing word processing on $5,000 worth of computer equipment was appealing indeed. By the beginning of the 1980s, many thought that the personal computer would change our lives not only in homes and businesses, but in education as well.

The next half decade of the personal computer business has had all of the intrigue of a television soap opera. Giant IBM entered the personal computer market with a quite adequate but not outstanding machine. However, their name and marketing strength led them to dominate a major segment of the market in eighteen months time. This segment was in business applications and the conquest so complete that the major software developers have restricted their development of program innovations to the IBM operating system and a new array of IBM look alikes.

Meanwhile on the home front, Commodore, a vertically integrated manufacturer, was able to reduce its prices so as to drive two companies—Timex, Texas-Instruments—out of the market and seriously threaten a third—Atari. Further adding to the drama has been the ironic twist whereby the founder of Commodore, squeezed out of its corporate structure, has now purchased Atari and is returning to the market with a vengeance. Meanwhile Apple, having restructured itself with more of a marketing orientation, has reemerged as a serious competitor with a moderately priced, highly innovative machine—Macintosh—with sales remarkably exceeding projections.

By the mid-1980s, personal computer use in the United States has divided clearly into two, quite contrasting, levels. Very inexpensive machines, coupled with price wars and discount store marketing, have glutted the home market. Analysts are finding that after the initial novelty of owning a home computer wears thin, the machine is moved to the closet. This, coupled with the dearth of innovative (yet overly expensive) programs, has seriously restricted the earlier visions of the home computer becoming a highly used and common household appliance. The collapse of interest in videogames has further discouraged the purchase of inexpensive computers that can operate them. Moreover, the use of computers for home management has never been a demonstrated advantage. (Of what real advantage is an electronic checkbook anyway?) The prognosis for home computing?—slow growth.

But personal computing continues to grow in business applications, particularly in large corporations where no substantial future was predicted because of the dominance of minicomputer and mainframe systems. Four factors appear to account for this phenomenon. First, the most innovative and productive uses of microcomputers to date have been with programs for business applications—word processing, electronic spreadsheets, and data-base management. Second, the entry of experienced, business-oriented manufacturers (e.g., IBM, Digital Equipment, Hewlet-Packard, and now AT&T) has brought marketing forces to bear in this sector. Third, there is more corporate than personal buying power for this equipment. And fourth, there is a growing compatibility of microcomputers, mainframes, and telecommunications systems, thus providing the smaller machines an integral role in corporate or organizational computing.

Clearly, the investment and growth of microcomputers is strongest in business applications. The current vision is for the arrival of 32-bit machines with all of the power of the older minicomputers, networking capabilities, and mainframe compatibility.

What of microcomputers in education? Recent figures show about one-third of a million microcomputers in use in U.S. schools, which averages out to a ratio of about 1 machine for every 112 students. Relative to a figure of essentially zero in the mid-1970s, this is impressive growth. Yet, there is consensus in today's educational circles that the microcomputer is far from integrated into our schools' educational practices. As we have found in a recent California study (Williams & Williams, 1984; 1985), the problem seems to reflect, first, the lack of truly effective programs that solve curriculum needs, and, second, the lack of teacher motivation and training to promote such applications.

It seems clear that the future of educational computing is still in the balance. No less surprising than visible growth would be the removal of existing computers to join educational television and film equipment on storage shelves.

Electronic Publishing

Another forecast from the 1970s was that we would soon be doing as much of our reading from computer screens as from paper. And if not from screens, we would read from paper with computer-mediated text printed upon our command. For video distribution of text, the image (not unlike PresTel in Great Britain) was one of reading the morning headlines as transmitted via telephone lines or in the vertical blanking interval of television signals to our home television screen. If one wished a paper version of portions of the news, they need only to turn on their printer. Another interesting forecast of the time was that the costs of duplicating books by high-speed computer laser-printing either at a bookshop or library might be eventually more economical than traditional publication and distribution. In evidence, too, in the last decade was that most of the major newspapers were moving to adopt computer-aided editing and typesetting systems.

Whither electronic publishing? Several generalizations are evident. Perhaps taken as a whole, the greatest adoption of new technologies has been by the traditional paper-oriented news publishers to improve the efficiency of their own production facilities. Most such technology is behind the scenes and not visible to the consumer. It includes substantial advances in the aforementioned video-editing and typesetting systems now in use by virtually every major newspaper, including the adoption by reporters of personal computer use for story creation and transmission to their editors.

Advances also include the use of telecommunications networks to transfer edited material for printing and distribution. Most notable in the latter category has been the use of communications satellite networks to distribute copy to regional printing facilities, thus effecting a kind of communications and transportation trade-off in the delivery of products to the consumer. The *Wall Street Journal* and *USA Today* are the most visible examples of national circulation newspapers to benefit from satellite technology. The *New York Times* may not be far behind.

Unlike Great Britain and several other countries, the United States has not seen a national effort at establishing an electronic text network. Instead we have had two types of development. One has been a variety of local or regional trial projects sponsored by companies variously representing entertainment (Columbia Broadcasting System), newspaper (Knight-Ridder) or telecommunications (AT&T) interests. These have represented both the delivery of videotext (telephone lines) or teletext (television broadcasting) materials, but mainly the latter. In these projects, the attempt has been to provide customers with a wide variety of services such as news, features, shopping, civic information, educational materials, theater and transportation schedules. There have been attempts to develop attractive presentation formats, including color and graphics. The more elaborate systems have necessitated use of rather expensive home terminals, which, as it turns out, are a challenge to the commercial viability of such services.

Results of these demonstration projects have been mixed, not encouraging for commercial ventures. In addition to the cost of terminals, another barrier is the lack of consumer interest in having a wide variety of text services available. Variety itself is not a sales strength. Simply put, the transformation of usual magazine or newspaper materials to an electronic delivery service does not appear to be all that commercially attractive in itself. Customers who have desired to continue such services usually use only one or several content options that are important to them and that cannot be as effectively obtained by traditional means; these might be banking or airline schedule services, current stock prices, or classified advertising. Although several companies (e.g., Knight-Ridder, Times-Mirror) have moved formally into electronic text services, others, including Time, Inc., have withdrawn for now.

The other U.S. type of venture into electronic text services is represented in the offerings of companies such as Dow Jones News Service, The Source (owned by Readers Digest), or CompuServe (the H&R Block, a tax consulting firm). These operate via inexpensive telephone network services and do not require any special terminals other than a personal computer or dumb terminal equipped for communications (i.e., connected to the local phone line via an inexpensive modem). Unlike the text experiments described above, these services did not grow out of a plan for electronic publishing but were rather one of extending computer time-sharing services to the public. Because they are restricted to the standard ASCII character format, the screen presentations of these services are unpretentious—mainly the bare text.

In comparison with the publicized text demonstration projects, these new services, only recently widely advertised, have been steadily gaining customers (with each claiming over 100,000 in 1984.) Their apparent success seems to confirm the results of the text studies: people will pay for services that they find important to them and that they cannot obtain as easily elsewhere. Put another way, the path to growth of electronic publishing may be to offer services that take distinct advantage of the computer-telecommunications medium rather than to market a mass medium type service. Such advantages include anything of a data-base nature (e.g., statistical tables, classified advertising), where timeliness is critical (market prices, headlines), and where interactivity is desired (shopping, browsing, mail, conferencing, games).

There is one further factor that may promote the latter type of service—where it is commercially advantageous to the provider. Although figures differ, there is as much as 10:1 cost advantage to a bank when a customer "writes" an electronic check rather than a paper one. As in promoting electronic teller machines, it is to the bank's advantage to have its customers use "on-line" banking services. Marketing campaigns are developing that promote the efficiencies of electronic banking from the customer's point of view (immediacy, 24-hour service, low cost, prestige) but may also offer additional on-line services as premiums. The latter include financial advice, news headlines, market prices, shopping services, and even electronic mail links with other customers.

The new scenario, therefore, for electronic publishing may be for customers to go on line for specific services that are of special advantage to them or to vendors, then eventually to use this same "text-connection" for other, more traditionally published materials. That a consumer has at his/her fingertips a highly personalized selection of information alternatives is another example of the aforementioned demassification.

A Concluding Note

Although the foregoing is but a glimpse into communication changes in the United States, it does provide a bit of the flavor of the mixed consequences of technological advance and deregulation. There are, of course, additional topics that could be added in more detail to the discussion, for example, direct broadcast satellite, fifth generation computers, new wired-city concepts, local area networks, and the entire concept of reindustrialization for a high technology economy, as is found in attempts to replicate California's Silicon Valley phenomenon (Rogers & Larsen, 1985).

Also, there appear to be certain generalizable social-psychological implications of the changes discussed above (Williams, Rice, & Dordick, 1985). Those implications are not all that exclusive or distinct at this point in the development, but they are worthy of consideration. They include the five categories discussed below.

Demassification of media. The proliferation of media channels—for example, as offered by added cable channels or text services—allows for much more personal choice for information and entertainment. Although mass tastes may remain in evidence, there may be much more opportunity for personal choice of exactly how to satisfy that taste.

Increased choice. The need to make choices is not only evident in demassification but also in the many areas where new equipment and services are available. For example, there are virtually hundreds of telephone models on the market as compared with the simple black telephone of several decades ago. What special telephone services (e.g., call waiting), and which long-distance carrier should be chosen; which cable television system or which text services are desired—are a few of the choices to be made.

Time displacement. Especially as evident in the public's use of videocassette players, it is possible now to engage in communications activities more on one's personal schedule than during times imposed by others. This also holds in use of telephone answering machines or in computer-time sharing (as, for example, in an asynchronous teleconference). Time-displacement also interacts with choice, for one now must make new decisions about personal schedules.

Increased mobility. Mobile telephone technologies and portable computers free the user from being in a specific location to obtain the desired services. Increasingly, we are able to carry out our communications activities so long as we can "tap into the network." This makes work at home or "on the road" much easier for some of us, and, like time displacement, imposes further challenges upon choice.

Increased "connectivity." This is a concept that several of my colleagues and I introduced in a recent paper on the social impacts of new technologies. It refers to one's sense of having a wide variety of communications alternatives immediately available, of being in touch, so to speak, with a wide variety of communications alternatives. It is a concept closely tied to the first four, yet deserves attention in itself, for as demassification, time displacement, and mobility vastly increase the immediacy of our personal communications choices, we are perhaps witnessing more than a proliferation of communications alternatives—perhaps it is on the magnitude of an environmental change.

Our and our children's lives will be played out against a context of potentially overwhelming information, entertainment, and personal contact alternatives. Survivors will be those not only with access to these alternatives but with the wisdom to make the wisest choices among them. Granted that this has a McLuhanesque flavor to it; but it may be the broadest conception of how the communications revolution is slowly shaping our information society.

References

McLuhan, M. (1962). *The Gutenberg galaxy*. Toronto: University of Toronto Press.

Rogers, E. M., & Larsen, J. K. (1984). *Silicon Valley Fever*. New York: Basic Books.

Smith, A. (1981). *Goodbye Gutenberg*. Oxford, UK: Oxford University Press.

Toffler, A. (1970). *Future shock*. New York: Random House.

Toffler, A. (1980). *The third wave*. New York: William Morrow.

Williams, F. (1983). *The communications revolution*. New York: New American Library.

Williams, F., Rice, R. E., & Dordick, H. S. (1985). Behavioral impacts in the information age. In B. D. Ruben (Ed.), *Information and Behavior: Volume 1*. New Brunswick, NJ: Transaction.

Williams, F., & Williams, V. (1984). *Microcomputers in elementary education*. New York: Wadsworth.

Williams, F., & Williams, V. (1985). *Success with educational software*. New York: Praeger.

17

The Information Society: Recurring Questions

Rolf T. Wigand

The present essay has two main purposes. First, it provides a synopsis of the Information Societies *Research Forum. Most of the sessions are summarized in detail, with special emphasis on the issues that seemed most important to the participants. Second, it brings some of the issues identified in the 1984 conference up to date, by focusing on themes that have endured in the study of information societies since that time, and by examining the relevant regulatory trends that have evolved in the United States, Japan, and Europe. We therefore begin with brief accounts of the symposium sessions.*

As initially stated, the purpose of the research forum was (1) to review current research on the information society, (2) to explore its policy implications, and (3) to identify useful directions for future research. The information society has been studied by scholars in numerous disciplines (e.g., economics, sociology, communication, technologists), and a unified research paradigm has yet to emerge. Government and private sector policy makers have become seriously concerned with this topic in the last ten years, due to the European/Japanese/U.S. competition in high-technology industries, coupled with issues pertaining to unemployment, job losses, inflation, and a slow economic growth rate. High technology and the information society have become important topics on the public agenda in most advanced, industrialized nations. Information technologies such as computers, integrated circuits, and telecommunications are crucial to

the effective transformation of U.S. and other societies into information
societies.

State and local governments have shown considerable interest in competing for the location of high-technology and information-related industries. In the United States, about 30 of the 50 state governments have
special programs, usually administered by the governor's office, designed
to attract high-technology firms to their states. The decision by the
Microelectronics and Computer Technology Corporation (MCC), as well
as Sematech, to locate in Austin, Texas, for example, may have profound
implications for that region's future economic growth.

The basis of university-industry relationships is also changing in a
fundamental way. A number of U.S. universities such as the University of
Texas at Austin, Arizona State University, Massachusetts Institute of
Technology, the State University of New York at Buffalo, and the three
universities involved in North Carolina's Research Triangle, see their new
role as that of creating and fostering high-technology industries (as did
Massachusetts Institute of Technology and Stanford University in the
cases of Route 128 and Silicon Valley, respectively).

The present essay has two main purposes. First, it provides a synopsis
of the *Information Societies* Research Forum. Most of the sessions are
summarized in detail, with special emphasis on the issues that seemed
most important to the participants. Second, it brings some of the issues
identified in the 1984 conference up to date, by focusing on themes that
have endured in the study of information societies since that time, and by
examining the relevant regulatory trends that have evolved in the United
States, Japan, and Europe. We therefore begin with brief accounts of the
symposium sessions.

Symposium Sessions

*Session: Methodological/Conceptual Issues in Understanding
Information Societies*

Jorge Schement and Leah Lievrouw attempted to respond to the need
to clarify and deepen analytic tools for examining information work in the
so-called information society. Building on the work of Fritz Machlup,
Daniel Bell, and Marc Porat, they nonetheless were critical of what they
regard as a class bias built into Machlup's distinction between knowledge
and non–knowledge producers. They argued that Machlup's class of
knowledge producers tends to be coincidental with white-collar professionals, a classification which "obscures the diffuse pattern of information

workers in all economic sectors." According to Schement and Lievrouw, Machlup also avoids defining the specificity of information work so as to permit its systematic and consistent identification and analysis.

Schement and Lievrouw criticized Daniel Bell on much the same ground. Bell's notion of a knowledge elite exemplified by scientists and engineers ignores the ways in which less-exalted occupational groups also create and operate on information. Schement and Lievrouw did not take issue with the comprehensiveness of Porat's information work classifications or with his documentation of information translations throughout GNP. However, they argued that Porat's analysis "isolated the workforce from its social context," and that Porat's categories are "hard to replicate."

Therefore, instead of asking, "To what extent is GNP composed of information activities?" Schement and Lievrouw offered an alternative analysis based on the question, "To what extent do Americans manipulate information as their principal work activity?" Their categories of information work "focus directly on information manipulation as the principal working behavior." They believe that these categories make it possible to abstract criterion definitions of information behavior, which they prefer to conventional categories that have tended, in their view, to confirm rather than analyze the status quo.

Schement and Lievrouw classified listings in the *Dictionary of Occupational Titles* according to a scheme based on a taxonomy of behavioral outcomes of instruction devised by Bloom et al. (1956). These classifications are (1) information producers defined by the cognitive character of their work rather than by their status as part of a technocratic elite, (2) information recyclers, who move information from one place to another, (3) information maintainers, who store, maintain, and retrieve information, (4) information technology producers, who produce "the first stage of components" for information hardware, and (5) information technology maintainers, who operate, repair, and monitor information technology. According to this scheme, information work is distributed across every economic sector and comprises at least 25% of the occupational titles in each sector. Though industrial occupations still comprise 55% of all occupational titles in this scheme, "the principal finding of the analysis is that information occupations comprise 40% of all the occupations classified." This finding does not, however, explain what percentage of all workers may be said to be involved in information work, according to this set of classificatory categories. This inquiry, according to Schement and Lievrouw, is the next logical step for research, along with charting the historical development of information work by means of these categories.

Session: The Role of Technology in Shaping the Information Society

Frederick Williams emphasized the mixed success of a range of predictions concerning the socio-economic impact of advanced communication technologies and institutional change in the information age. He noted that the largest, most visible structural change in American communication has been the divestiture of AT&T. However, he believed that it was not yet clear whether the presumed advantages of open competition would ultimately outweigh current consumer confusion, decreased telephone efficiency, and increased costs to many consumers. Electronic leisure activities (e.g., videodisk, cable television, and videogames) were cited by Williams as examples of new communication technologies that have not fulfilled the high expectations of product champions and forecasters. In general, Williams stated, the optimistic premise of public interest advocates of the 1960s and 1970s concerning new communication technologies—that the public would flock to alternative leisure time content (e.g., interactive types of cable television offerings)—have fallen flat.

Further emphasizing the difficulty of forecasters, Williams stressed that time and events have dispelled the 1970s' notion that by the 1980s the public would be doing as much of their newspaper and magazine reading from computer screens as from the newspaper. However, he noted two areas where electronic publishing is having a major impact. First, publishers are using new communications technologies to improve the efficiency of their own production facilities. Second, people are using their personal computers to obtain information which they consider important and which they cannot obtain by traditional means.

Despite the confusion as to specific consequences of the "communication revolution," Williams offered five interrelated, generalizable, sociopsychological themes or implications for further consideration. First, he noted that the "demassification" of media (e.g., new cable channels) allows more personal choice in how individuals satisfy their information and entertainment desires. Second, consumers enjoy increased choice concerning new communications equipment and services both at work and at leisure. Third, new communication technologies such as the videotape player and the personal computer allow people to engage in communication activities according to their own personal schedules rather than at times imposed by others. Fourth, mobile telephones and portable computers free individuals from the geographic limitations that have traditionally restricted communication. In conclusion, Williams introduced the concept of "connectivity" to describe the individual's access to a variety of immediately available communicative alternatives, where individuals tend to want or are expected to keep in touch with others.

Mitchell Moss, in his discussion of the emerging information capitals, presented three issues that are especially relevant to understanding the relationship between telecommunications and major metropolitan areas. Moss argued that the emerging telecommunications infrastructure is increasingly based in the large metropolitan centers of the world (e.g., New York, London, Mexico City, Paris, Tokyo). The renaissance of cities as centers of information processing is due, in part, to two factors, says Moss, (1) the importance of face-to-face communication in timely, high-content, sensitive transactions, and (2) the capacity of the information society's technology to improve the flow of information into, through, and out of cities.

This centralization of information-processing activities has reinforced the growth of large cities by restoring their relative position as centers for advanced services such as advertising, law, accounting, finance, and trade. For example, within the United States, international banking is being increasingly concentrated in the Los Angeles and New York metropolitan areas. On the other hand, small- and medium-sized urban communities, which once enjoyed more relative independence with their own economies and local firms, are increasingly becoming service satellites to the few, large metropolitan centers. Moss bases his second major contention on data from phone directories in the New York region, which document the movement of relatively low-paid, routine clerical jobs and other back office activities from Manhattan's central business district to outlying areas. While it may be premature to cite such decentralization of back office activities as a trend, Moss noted that large commercial banks in New York, which initially moved such activities to Long Island, have considered more distant sites in New Jersey, and even offshore locations.

Moss sees such migration as the result of three factors. First, the intense computerization of back office activities, such as insurance and finance, requires very large amounts of energy, space, and personnel for mainframe operation. Such costs are generally less expensive (i.e., more readily available) in suburban areas. Second, the technology of doing these back office jobs is becoming so routine that managerial control does not require face-to-face communciation. Third, increasingly diverse and specialized telecommunication networks are being designed by the private sector.

Next, Moss contended that the private design and implementation of the telecommunications infrastructure is preferred to public intervention. Usually, the public sector responds too slowly to changing technology in a dynamic environment. To illustrate this point, Moss discussed the case of New York's ill-conceived and poorly executed teleport. Several phenomena eventually crippled this venture: to begin with, the regulatory environment changed drastically as a result of AT&T's divestiture. Also, plans were based on a static conception of technology, which was inappropriate in a technologically driven industry. Finally, the public sector underestimated the skill and background required to develop and market such a complex service. Moss concluded that the New York teleport experience represents the casual diffusion of a technology's terminology and the image of success without the proper appreciation for criteria crucial for its successful application.

Judith Larsen discussed the life style of Silicon Valley residents in Northern California as a possible predictor of the norms and values of the information society. Entrepreneurial behavior is an admired characteristic in Silicon Valley; accordingly, a "me"-centered existence revolving around work is the norm for men and increasing numbers of women whether they are spouses, single parents, or have never been married.

Larsen argued that Silicon Valley inhabitants represent the quintessential information society life style: a great percentage of the high-tech workers who live in Silicon Valley, she said, are concerned with product innovation and corporate management. Such concerns require these professionals to be users as well as producers of the high-technology tools of the information society.

Session: Federal, State, and Local Initiatives to Promote High-Technology Industry

Sena Black presented the state programs to encourage high-technology development that are currently underway in South Carolina. In an "underdeveloped" state like South Carolina, a prevailing clash of cultures requires an innovative, realistic response on the part of state and local governments, since the state has none of the obvious resources that support similar efforts in other states: South Carolina has no oil, no major research university, and no research park.

By using a fairly broad definition of high technology and of the information society, there are ways for a state to build an infrastructure that can lead to new jobs, economic opportunity, and technology development. South Carolina is shifting its focus toward the high-technology arena, because national research on small businesses has shown that there are many entrepreneurs who will produce innovative products and who will further an information society if given the tools and the opportunities.

South Carolina has had to force a structural change from an industrial society to an information society. Yet South Carolina has the opportunity to move rapidly into the information society, because the state has not focused on the intermediate economies of product development. Black presented a matrix of the kinds of programs that the state is developing in university recruitment, entrepreneurial development (e.g., through incubators) and industrial revitalization. Significantly, South Carolina has developed one of the nation's best vocational and technical training and continuing education programs.

J. D. Eveland provided several thematic points for discussion as he summarized the issues facing public policy makers concerned with high-technology development. First, a major emphasis seems to be the institutionalization of new concepts and new structures. Second, these activities are creating social innovations, i.e., social organizations as well as scientific enterprises. If they carry out bad science, they will not survive; but if they engage in good science, they still will not survive unless they serve a social function as an organization. Third, these organizations (e.g., MCC) will have to learn how best to operate and go through a social evolution, since there are no real precedents, no existing infrastructure. And fourth, innovative ideas like technology "incubators" need to be adapted to the local environment; accordingly, many divergent models of development should evolve.

Other key points are mostly drawn from a review of a survey of ten National Science Foundation Cooperative Programs. (1) Many of the developments have serious social ramifications (e.g., stratification and the resulting differences in expectations between political or economic groups). In addition, there are differences between institutional and public interests (e.g., McDonald's may create more jobs than high-tech companies but the latter are perceived as more desirable). (2) The interests of faculty members may not be the same as the university's interest. Intellectual property rights are increasingly being held by individuals instead of institutions (i.e., businesses or universities). (3) There is probably very little that governments can do to further many of the high-technology/economic development efforts, despite the several obvious successes. We carry a considerable amount of institutional baggage with us as we move into an information society, and we understand too little of the forces that are driving technological developments.

Session: National Information/Telecommunication Policies Affecting Economic Development

This session provided an overview of some of the international aspects of the U.S. information economy. Bill Burgess of the Bank of America focused on transborder data flow problems faced by industry in conducting corporate business abroad and in selling information services. In his talk, Jerry Salvaggio, of the University of Houston, looked at the economic impact of information technology, namely the differences between a public-utility organizational model for national development (as is generally the case in Europe and Japan) and the commercial model found in the United States.

Bill Sullivan, U.S. Department of Commerce, gave a preview of the situation in international trade in information goods and services, using material that was to be released by the department in February, 1985. His conclusion was: "We're involved in economic warfare. . . . We need to learn from the Japanese and even the Europeans." His discussion underscored the advantage that foreign sellers enjoy in the deregulated U.S. market: while American exporters face mercantilist trade barriers abroad, his figure indicated that U.S. firms are exporting only 7% of total telecommunications equipment production. Twelve firms account for 8% of the market. Part of the problem, therefore, is getting more companies into the export market.

Session: Lessons Learned about Information Societies

To begin this session, Maurice Mitchell, then retiring as director of the Annenberg Washington Program (AWP), referred to AWP's study of the AT&T divestiture, *The Transition of Competition*. He pointed out that the Cable Communications Act of 1984 superimposed federal control over that of states and localities. Local communities are now relatively powerless in governing cable television activities. This move is in the opposite direction of the current trend toward deregulation. Furthermore, new media are not at all new to Mitchell. He has seen several come and stay; media do not replace one another. "It is wise to keep our options open," he said. "The 'Information Age' must be about the twentieth 'age' I've lived through."

Richard Weingarten, head of Communications and Information Section, Office of Technology Assessment (OTA), remarked that the OTA does long-term studies of new technologies on behalf of the U.S. Congress. In the conduct of those studies, Weingarten said, he has come to accept some aspects of the "myth of the information society." Myths are useful, he stated, because they summarize reality and serve as useful guides in making policy decisions. Weingarten stressed that we must explore the corresponding submyths of the information society.

The first submyth is that automation eliminates jobs. Recently, he remarked, the Joint Economic Committee and Senator Benson demanded that the OTA tell them just how many workers robots were going to replace—i.e., how many jobs would be lost. The general view is that automation will be more efficient and eliminate workers through productivity increases. It is also true that technology can bring the costs of products down so low that there is an explosive expansion of the market for those goods. This has happened in the telephone industry, where many new jobs have been created.

People also tend to confuse long-term trends with transitional impacts: some industries are dying while others offer new jobs that do not match the skills of the old workers. The long-term question is—What creates new jobs? If we were to look at events at the turn of the century, Weingarten suggested, we would not be able to tell the head of the Bureau of Labor Statistics what methods he should use to predict the job market of the future. We can only extrapolate from the past, and this has not worked very well.

There have been many failures in information technology industries, for example, Direct Broadcast Satellite (DBS). Technology does not assure success. The United States has a favorable atmosphere for innovation; and there is reason to be optimistic. Occasionally, a government may step in to inhibit industry abuses (e.g., pollution), but most of the time any kind of development is acceptable. There is a considerable amount of experimentation in the United States; in other countries private enterprise often waits for government to take the lead.

Another submyth is that the principal output of an information society is technology, e.g., microchips. To the contrary, Weingarten said, information societies produce services and value-added goods. There is not much intrinsic value in the chip itself. Also, there is the submyth that information is a national good. Technologies are not constrained by national borders, but rather react adversely to attempts at nationalization.

"You can't stop technology" is another submyth. Societies *do* stop technological development when they sense that it is harmful. On the other hand, societies support technologies that offer some benefit and that fulfill societal objectives. The telegraph was not invented to send birthday messages but for more important uses. Policy does not choose between good and evil but rather between competing value systems. The question is—Who wins and who loses?

Christopher Sterling, of George Washington University, remarked that we are in a transition stage in which there are both new and old players, especially old players. One only needs to look at the example of WHOOPS as told in recent *Washington Post* stories. The State of Washington planners were not grossly stupid, they merely followed projections for power needs that seemed to be based on reality. The projections happened to be wrong, which led to the disaster. There is a lesson there for other industries, e.g., the auto industry. Good histories of computing are beginning to appear that illuminate patterns in the development of technology. They may help in making short-term (i.e., 5-year) projections into the future.

The role of government in the dissemination of scientific and technical information is an example of an area that keeps repeating itself. Researchers read the same reports and draw the same conclusions and recommendations, but more diversity of data is needed. The material from the IBM suit and the AT&T case—much of it published in self-defense—could be very valuable. Industry is beginning to publish more and better figures. Studies of who owns what are useful, as are studies of the structure of industries, and of industry shakeouts. Just look at phones, computers, and computer books for forthcoming shakeouts.

And yet, there is a lack of scholarly information. Fritz Machlup died too soon to finish the work on the information economy. Sterling noted that we owe him a great debt and should follow up on Machlup's work. Studies of might-have-been industries (e.g., DBS) would also be useful. The experiences of other countries are helpful, for example, Japan, Brazil, Germany, France as well as some that were not discussed in this symposium such as Canada and Australia. We must reach a broader audience with the issues we discuss here.

Bill Dutton, of the Annenberg School of Communications at the University of Southern California, looked at information technologies from the perspective of political science. He discussed the driving forces and social implications of technologies, as laid out in the Wired Cities Research Forum (also held by the AWP). That forum provided a good example of different approaches to technological implementation.

Dutton questioned Sterling's evaluation of Machlup's work; on the contrary, Dutton said, Machlup's aggregated statistics are not useful for social analysis. The present research forum suggests a different stream of research—one that leads away from the aggregate level of analysis. Dutton proposed three essential questions: (1) What is the information society? (2) Who governs it? (3) Whose interests are served by new technologies? These point the way to different research avenues.

First, what is the information society? Debating about labels is not very useful. The information society, the control revolution, the communications revolution—they each serve a useful purpose but are not rigorous as definitions. They are merely sensitizing concepts that bring us within the range of each other's ideas. The information society label works, but we should not get bogged down in fine-tuning its definition.

Second, who governs the information society? Dutton suggested that it be looked at as an ecology of games. Nobody governs such a society absolutely, but there are banking games, real estate games, community development games, and so on. This research forum itself represents several types of games, including the academic game, the consulting game, the policy game. We understand the rationale of each of those games—the players and strategies. We are headed toward the information society in a very rational way, as a game. It is coordinated by the marketplace, by government policy and by visions of the future. The myth is important, too.

Third, whose interests are served by new technologies? Economic factors are obviously driving things. We have not pointed out the negative impacts of the information society, e.g., who would want to live in Silicon Valley? The cities are spoken of as reservations for the poor—and yet we have Moss's view of New York and Los Angeles as information capitals. In the area of public vs. private sectors, some of the comments here have been oversimplified, for example, misquoting a study of trash collection in order to suggest that the private sector is always more efficient. Finally, Dutton emphasized that the aggregate studies should be implemented by studies at the level of the game, e.g., of industry-university cooperation, and coordinating factors (like images of the future).

John Abel, vice-president for Research and Planning, National Association of Broadcasters, noted that broadcasting is considered a "dinosaur industry," one that grew unbridled from the 1920s. We can consider broadcasting as a model of a technology that grew rapidly and was widely accepted by the public. In the beginning there was little regulation; that is no longer true. There are many people, academics among them, who would like to control these issues, or, as Abel sees it, control the content. There is a whole host of regulations controlling what goes into the home— the Fairness Doctrine, Section 315 of the Communication Act, Equal Time, children's television requirements, advertising controls.

Today it makes perfect sense that television is regulated so heavily. We use this public thing called "the spectrum." If we were not regulated, our stations would interfere with one another. But one can imagine a future time when other technologies are regulated on the grounds of privacy or access. The rationalization would be the same: control of the spectrum. Deregulation did not start with the Reagan administration but rather with Carter's. It has cut across several periods, and probably began in the early 1970s. Yet control of content and the spectrum still exists for television; several rationales still exist by which the government can control content. What can the government do to help information technologies? Tax incentives to those who conduct research or give money to universities, encourage competition, and so on, come to mind. We seem to think that broadcasting is the most powerful medium in the world. Yet advertising is spread across several media, and most is in print. There are many fewer newspapers than television stations.

Research should concentrate on the supply side rather than on the consumption of content. We need more research that compares media to one another, e.g., print media vs. electronic. We ought to look at theories of the marketplace with regards to regulation and deregulation. When does the marketplace begin to break down under the pressure of regulation? We ought to analyze the First Amendment rights of information providers. And we should look at information entrepreneurship, the marketing of information products: What predicts success in this area? There should be more emphasis on the information-providing industries rather than on the consumption of information.

Toward a Framework for Comparative Research: Organizational Differences among Information Societies

Many of the sessions of the Information Societies Symposium provided detailed information and intriguing insights into the information society as a total social phenomenon. The overwhelming complexity of all of the relevant issues prevents them from being presented comprehensively here. However, one issue that seems to weave in and out of many of the authors' remarks is the notion of differences among information societies. Particularly, the notion of *organizational* differences among information societies is a recurring theme that merits more examination in depth.

Larsen's portrayal of Silicon Valley as a prototype of the life styles of workers in the information society can be questioned from several points of view. First, why should Silicon Valley workers characterize the information society any more than the information technology producers working in Singapore, Taiwan, or Hong Kong? On the other hand, Larsen's premise that Silicon Valley residents characterize the forefront of the information society is supported by the point that the great percentage of the high-tech workers who live in Silicon Valley are concerned with product innovation and corporate management, which differentiates them from workers in those other places.

Workers in other industries (e.g., the entertainment industry, and the high-technology aviation and chemical industries) may exhibit the life style characteristics of Silicon Valley residents as well, i.e., high employee turnover, a me-centeredness and centrality of work, high rates of divorce and drug use. Perhaps such characteristics are generally more symptomatic of young and rapidly growing industries rather than being specific to the information society. One might consider alternative forms of organization that also perform the innovative and productive functions of Silicon Valley while enhancing the quality of life of workers. Although the organizational character is clearly mixed for Silicon Valley and perhaps to a lesser extent for Japan, we might engage in the intriguing exercise of comparing these two organizations—Silicon Valley, Inc. and Japan, Inc.—to IBM.

IBM's organizational form can be described as being monarchial with a central staff directing divisions of loyal employees. Silicon Valley, Inc. can be seen to manifest a great deal of head-to-head competition among independent divisions (or firms) that had to contend with a volatile staff. Japan, Inc. can be characterized as independent divisions held together and guided by MITI, the Japanese culture, and an island mentality.

A rough order of magnitude would place the 1983 earnings of IBM and Silicon Valley, Inc. at $40 billion for each organization, and Japan, Inc. (composed of computers and electronic components from Hitachi, NEC, Toshiba, Fujitsu, Matsushita, and Mitsubishi) at about $30 billion. Continuing to use rough estimates to compare these three corporations reveals that IBM has about 370,000 employees, compared with Silicon Valley, Inc.'s 200,000 employees. Barabba indicates that sales are roughly $109,000 per employee for IBM, $200,000 per employee for Silicon Valley, Inc. (where workers commonly work two shifts), and $103,000 per employee for Japan, Inc. Government influence is seen to be indirect for IBM, inconsistent for Silicon Valley, Inc., and significant for Japan, Inc. Both IBM and Japan, Inc. can be characterized as being highly vertically integrated in critical technologies.

Accordingly, IBM's strengths are its size, market share, software, and its being fully integrated. IBM's weaknesses can be considered to be few, with slow market response being the most evident problem. The strengths of Silicon Valley, Inc. are exceptional technological innovation as well as high adaptability and flexibility in response to the market. Its weaknesses, according to this characterization, are the consequences of its independent entities (i.e., companies) being difficult to organize in terms of systems and system software. Japan, Inc.'s strengths are financial, cultural, its ability to bring a product to the market, and the ability to coordinate efforts among the individual entities. The weaknesses of Japan, Inc. include a lack of system software, a focus on components, and the individual entities being slow to react to environmental change.

The typology of three competing organizations could be utilized for encouraging theorists to consider different perspectives when discussing high-technology organizations and life styles that are supposed to characterize the information society. While Larsen characterizes the Silicon Valley as an area exhibiting many extreme social problems, it is worth remembering that within Silicon Valley there also exist corporations that are considered to be among the best the United States has to offer in terms of excellence in management and in encouraging a high quality of community and family life.

As the contributions to this section have suggested, all of these relatively recent developments deserve further analysis and study. Of particular importance is the exploration of their policy implications for national and state governments. A number of such policy issues are addressed in the remainder of this essay.

Policy Trends and Implications

In this section we examine the ways in which selected other nations have developed industrial policies, especially with regard to newer information technologies. By "other nations" we mean non–U.S. nations which have emerged as key nations in the development and marketing of information technology. In recent years many of these nations have pursued government policies designed to encourage private high-technology firms to innovate in the manufacturing of information technologies. These countries seek to gain a competitive edge, and possibly dominance, in specific niches in the world market.

Here we shall consider (1) what difference a national technology policy has made, (2) what it means for a nation to operate without a stated policy, and (3) the relationships of one nation with another, since this reflects aspects of policy as well. The latter concern becomes especially obvious when contrasting the European situation with that of the United States. First, however, a brief description of the Japanese situation is appropriate.

Japan. Since World War II, selected industries have enjoyed government help in the form of tax breaks, subsidies, discount loans, and tariff protection. This has helped Japan to become the leading exporter of steel, cars, machine tools, industrial machinery, color televisions, VCRs, and other electronic appliances. Recently, MITI has begun aiding frontier technologies, e.g., advanced computers (the Fifth Generation Computer Project), new ceramics, nuclear and other non–oil energy development, biotechnology, and laser products. Today, Japan is shifting its strategy away from direct government control of emerging industries toward greater public-private cooperation. For advanced technologies the government aids only research and development (R&D) risks that are too large for private industry alone.

West Germany. The Federal Republic of Germany, i.e., its government, owns the railroads, the PTT, most of Lufthansa Airlines, and part of Volkswagen AG. The government tries to encourage investment in growth industries through its Ministry of Research and Technology, but the money involved is only 1% of the federal budget. Ailing firms are aided on a case-by-case basis by the government, although such assistance is not part of an overall strategy (e.g., the cases of Arbed Saarstahl and AEG-Telefunken).

Great Britain. Steel, coal, gas, railroads, and shipbuilding are nationalized. Prime Minister Thatcher wants to turn back parts of these industries to the private sector, as with British Telecommunications. At the Congress on Integrated Telecommunications, organized by the Muenchner Kreis in Munich in 1984, which was largely concerned with ISDN and related issues, a British Telecom representative informed this writer of the marketing "coup" by Thatcher—the government's television campaign depicting British Telecom as an advanced information technology firm using satellites, fiber optics, and digital communication. This writer was assured that this is not quite the case. The key channel for routing public funds to emerging industry is the British Technology Group, which arranges the financing for promising companies. The Department of Trade and Industry tries to stimulate investment in selected development areas with tax breaks and public grants.

France. The Socialist government of President Francois Miterrand completed the nationalization of the banking, steel, armament, some telecommunications firms (e.g., Thomson), and a number of other major industries in 1982. The French government implements its industrial policy through the banks. For more than two years new industries such as electronics, robotics, and biotechnologies as well as some old industries, have been supported.

France has recently decided to follow Japan's lead. In the past, for example, France insisted that Japanese videotape recorders were imported through an out-of-the-way customs point in Poitiers, France, where one person opened each VCR box by himself, inspected the VCR, attached a seal of approval, closed the box and then sent each box on to the wholesale distributor individually. It would be an understatement to say that this procedure slowed the distribution and sale of Japanese VCRs in France considerably.

France is now anxious to develop much closer ties with Japan; French Prime Minister Fabius thinks that French industry can use Japan as a model for modernization. At the same time, Japanese investments in French industry are booming. Eighteen Japanese-owned plants operate in France, including those owned by Sony, Pioneer, Clarion, and Canon. Japanese firms have created or saved 7,500 jobs in France; accordingly, the government has made development allowances and tax breaks available. The nationalized firm Thomson has a VCR licensing agreement with JVC. Though France is still protectionist when its major industrial interests encounter threats from Japan, such links suggest a change of heart. It appears that one reason for France's warmer welcome of Japan, Inc. is that these firms in France are big exporters. Sony's new cassette plant at Dax in the southwest is due to export 80% of its output. Clarion will sell up to 70% of its car radios outside France, while less than one-half of its components come from Japan.

Western Europe (in general). The political and cultural complexities that exist for western Europe are substantial. The more one looks at the information-technology related policies, practices, market conditions, etc. within the western European context, the more complex and paradoxical this precarious setting becomes.

The paradox in the European setting is that it invented science and is spending twice as much on research and development as Japan, but it is still lagging behind in the high-technology race. Europe's leaders have made significant progress toward economic integration, a feat that seemed almost insurmountable just twenty years ago, but it appears that they would still rather go their paths separately than go together successfully. In this sense, the European Parliament serves as a symbol while national self-interest still largely dominates the European Economic Community (EEC). Twenty-five years after the Treaty of Rome, Jean Monet's vision of a United States of Europe is rarely mentioned.

In fact, western Europe has the human and appropriate technological resources to compete successfully with the United States, Japan, and the Soviet Union, but Europe has not yet accepted the idea of a unified, barrier-free pan-European market. As a consequence, western Europe is exporting its brains and its inventions. Paradoxically, western Europe is quite aware of the New World economic situation and European organizations publish more excellent reports, monographs, and treatises on this subject than anyone else. However, the practical efforts that result seem to reflect piecemeal approaches; European politicians are not keeping up with its scientists. In spite of considerable success in high-technology industries like nuclear energy, biotechnology, computers, aerospace, and certain niches in information technology, most analysts, including western European ones, would acknowledge that western Europe is lagging behind its major industrial competitors. The main reason why Europe is falling into a widening technological gap behind America and Japan is apparently its failure to establish a continent-wide common market. On the other hand, it is not quite fair to speak of western Europe as a single place. Performance in high-tech industry varies widely from one country to another.

The specific worry is Europe's poor performance in the information industry. Western Europe's share of worldwide telecommunications equipment in 1982, for example, was 27%. The general worry is Europe's inability to innovate, i.e., it is sluggish in creating new businesses, whether high or low tech. The telecommunications industry will be Europe's next big test. The market is large and is roughly comparable with the U.S. market. Dataquest estimates that the combined American and European markets for customer equipment alone will have nearly doubled between 1983 and 1988, to some $16.5 billion. The main challenge to Europe's traditional telecommunications habits comes from America's swift and radical deregulation of the telephone system. The result has been an extraordinary flourishing of competition, not only by the companies left after the breakup but among hundreds of new entrepreneurs who make equipment, connect phones to computers, lease and release lines for various communication services.

Western Europe suffers from restraints on innovation even more in telecommunications than it does in other areas of the electronics business, the most serious of which is the division by national markets. A case in point is PBX and public switch makers. It is nearly impossible for one switch producer in one EEC member state to sell their equipment in another, because (1) the markets have been closed off since each country has specified a slightly different standard for equipment; (2) relatively close and unhealthy relationships have developed in some countries between the telecommunication monopoly (PTT) and one or two dominant national equipment suppliers. In West Germany, the supplier is Siemens; in France, the suppliers are CIT, Alcatel, and Thomson; and in Britain, they are GEC, Plessey, and STC.

Similar observations can be made for private telephone equipment makers. If one has to redesign a private office switching system (PBX), this adds 12% to 15% to the products' R&D costs and eight to twelve months of extra development time for each European country where the PBX is introduced. In the United States, anyone who wants to sell a PBX can have it certified in about two months at any registered testing agency. In comparison, the highly successful West German computer firm Nixdorf needed two years to get the Deutsche Bundespost's (PTT) approval for the PBX it wanted to sell to complete with a product from Siemens.

Another important point is that western Europe is very slow in opening competition among business communication services, a competition that is now commonplace in the United States. Japan is moving in this direction as well, and we can see the start of similar movements in Britain and West Germany. It is, however, still illegal for a company to lease lines and resell them to third parties.

Even though Japan, North America, and western Europe are similar-sized markets, a few comparisons of the R&D expenditures for public digital switches speak for themselves: Japan's total R&D expenditures on public digital switches (two companies) is $1.5–2 billion; North America's total R&D expenditures on public digital switches (three companies) is $3 billion; and western Europe's total R&D expenditures on public digital switches (among ten different switching systems) is $10 billion. It has been estimated that western Europe used three times as many engineers as either North America or Japan in developing its switches. European telecommunications firms have fared well with this setup since they could recoup R&D costs for a traditional switch in a single national market the size of Britain, for example. But what will happen now that digital switches have arrived?

Some potentially major deregulatory developments for information technology occurred in 1988 in the Federal Republic of Germany. The policy and regulatory situation in Germany is similar to that of several other western European nations and in this sense serves as a useful case to illustrate prevailing conditions. The Government Commission on Telecommunications met for two years and submitted in September 1988 its 161-page final report (Witte, 1987; Witte Report, 1987) to the cabinet of Chancellor Helmut Kohl. The report lists 40 recommendations and among the major items addressed are:

- Separating the Federal Republic's post office (Deutsche Bundespost) from its telephone-related operations.
- Taking additional initiative in removing the Bundespost's literal monopoly on customer premises equipment.
- Making possible the connection between the public network and private leased-line networks.

The report states that "This will have far-reaching consequences for the whole telecommunications sector and for the competitiveness of the Federal Republic. Everything points to a dramatic increase in the importance of telecommunications for the entire economy." In addition, the drafters are "convinced that only the replacement of the monopoly with competition at all levels can lead to a market capable of withstanding the future."

The meaning of the report can probably best be understood in the context of similar telecommunication restructuring efforts of other industrialized nations. In February 1988 the Commission for the European Communities (CEC) accelerated key portions of its plan to open Europe's telecommunications market to competition by as much as three years. There is some speculation that such a market-opening effort could spread easily also beyond the 12-member European Community (EC) nations, including more than 25 European nations. It could be viewed as the EC's first steps in a campaign to open Europe's heavily regulated telecommunications markets to greater competition. The EC is planning to stick to a strict timetable for the implementation of its proposals:

- There will be full liberalization of the equipment market (telephones, office switchboards, computer modems and most other terminal equipment that connects to phone lines) by 31 December 1990, with a transition period for the first telephone handsets.
- A progressive liberalization of the services market, except for voice telephony services, to start in 1989.
- Full liberalization of receive-only satellite dishes to be achieved by 1989.

In addition, the EC is insisting that tariffs be closely related to costs. If this is not achieved by 1992, the EEC will review the situation. A number of additional provisions covering fair processes for equipment approval throughout Europe, the creation of the European Telecommunications Standards Institute (ETSI) by April 1988, and agreement on the principles of open network provisions (addressing access to leased lines and eventually ISDN) are also included. The commission is also expected to release a directive aimed at opening telecommunications administrations' public procurement in March 1988.

Today, all European countries limit private sales of some of these products, giving the national telephone companies a monopoly or near-monopoly in some segments of the $21 billion European communications equipment market. However, this EC effort leaves the remainder of Europe's $110 billion market for telecommunications services and equipment under strict government controls. Even in the terminal-equipment segment, the target of the order, a thicket of varying technical standards, import restrictions, and other regulations continue to impede competition in most European countries.

One may view the EC effort as the beginning of what is likely to be a noisy, 5-year campaign by the commission to allow more competition in Europe's long-regulated phone markets. The EC will attempt to liberalize broad segments of the phone market, including computer-communications services, telex, satellite services, and switches, cables, and other equipment.

One should also note the generally perceived myth that U.S. deregulation has caused an invasion of the U.S. market by European telecommunications products, with no equivalent opening of the major European markets to the United States. The figures, however, do not support this position. While the EC nations are net exporters of telecommunications equipment, with a total surplus of $1.2 billion in 1986, shipments to the United States totaled $368 million and exports to Japan $39 million. The EC, however, has imported from the United States a total of $988 million and from Japan $724 million of telecommunications equipment.

Even PTT monopolies with the support of their governments are not immune to competitive forces. As the world continues to "shrink" electronically, as business is increasingly globalized, and as international telecommunications traffic increases faster than domestic traffic, PTTs that are unresponsive to user needs may suffer ever more significant competitive inroads into their revenue growth. West Germany may serve as a case in point. In the 1970s, the telex rate structures in West Germany and some other European countries were very expensive compared with some others. For example, sending a telex message from West Germany to Great Britain for forwarding to Hong Kong was less expensive than sending the same telex directly from West Germany to Hong Kong. Consequently, an entirely new business service (telex refiling, a form of arbitrage) was created, taking advantage of this situation. In the long run, European PTTs found it necessary to lower telex prices for long-distance messages which in turn brought telex pricing back in line with underlying costs for providing this service.

A newly published survey of telephone charges in Western nations rates West Germany as the most expensive nation surveyed overall (National Utility Services, 1988), including domestic long-distance calls. Cost trends in Germany have remained stable and expensive over several years. The United States was among the cheapest in all categories (local, long distance, international telephone, including telex). Belgium lost its 1987 position as Europe's most expensive country overall. British Telecommunications PLC's local telephone rates have continued to be the highest of all major Western countries. France reduced local call charges, while most other countries either froze or increased them. Domestic long-distance calls in France also fell by 23.3%. France is now also the cheapest country for international call charges, due to an impressive 41.7% drop in the cost of international telephone calls. Changes in value-added tax laws in France imply that consumers can now reclaim some of their telephone costs.

There are signs that the ultramonopolistic Deutsche Bundespost is opening the West German telecommunications market somewhat (cf. Wigand, 1988). The United States and the European Community countries have been pressing for more access to the German market, the third largest in the world after the United States and Japan. Recently, the German government has given MCI International, Inc., of Rye Brook, New York, the opportunity to establish an independent gateway for telecommunications services to and from the United States in competition with AT&T's international services. A future additional gateway operator, US Sprint International, Inc., of Kansas City, Missouri, is said to be favored by the Germans. Similarly, U.S. trade negotiators and the Commission for the European Communities (CEC) pried loose another finger in the grip of the Deutsche Bundespost in 1986, when the Bundespost agreed to end its monopoly on the provision of modems connected to the public network, although the Bundespost is still the only source for the first telephone terminal a customer attaches to a network (only after the first terminal can private firms provide extensions). Under this ruling the Bundespost now allows stand-alone modems and those incorporated into terminals to be supplied directly by private suppliers. CEC spokespersons have stated that prior to this ruling, users of the public telephone network could not always obtain the type of modem best suited to their needs, and only the market for modems to be used in private networks was open. Perhaps this change is just a symbolic effort on the part of the Bundespost, but it was one of several such efforts pointing to an opening of the German telecommunications market.

Discussions of and reactions to the Witte Report (1987) in the German press do not suggest that significant change in West Germany's telecommunications market is forthcoming. One can expect a small increase in competition, but not a major increase. Most individuals interviewed—especially those with ties to the German telecommunications industry—see the commission's report as a conservative proposal. Many had higher expectations with regard to the Bundespost's opening for competition.

The powerful Deutsche Postgewerkschaft (the Deutsche Bundespost's labor union) has already criticized the recommendations, as this organization views the effort as a threat to the Bundespost's monopolistic position. It is precisely from trade union quarters that the strongest objections are originating. They claim that if the recommendations were implemented, 10,000 of the current 500,000 postal and telecommunications jobs would be lost. The Socialist Party opposes the recommendation to separate the highly profitable telecommunications operation from the Bundespost's unprofitable traditional postal services, as the resulting post office's losses would have to be absorbed by the Finance Ministry. Postal service would have to be reduced or postal rates for services would have to be increased considerably. The various political factions in West Germany reflect the entire spectrum of positions possible in their opinions of the Witte Report: free market and procompetition political factions such as the Free Democratic Party oppose the recommendations for not going far enough. At the other end of the spectrum, politicians from the influential and highly conservative state of Bavaria oppose the Witte Report for going too far. One must expect intense political debate before Chancellor Kohl's cabinet will make a decision whether to accept the commission's recommendations.

West Germany's PTT minister, Mr. Christian Schwartz-Schilling, has stated on several occasions that privatization of the PTT is out of the question. His position may be based on the Deutsche Postgewerkschaft's campaign against selling out the PTT, and on the fact that West Germany's constitution would prohibit a turnabout of the existing state monopoly. As recently as 1986 high Bundespost officials stated that there is no real possibility that the PTT would be split into separate enterprises for post and telecommunications; however, just such a separation is now one recommendation of the Witte Commission. Commenting on the Witte Report's provision that tariffs would be set by the minister of Posts and Telecommunications in conjunction with the Economics Ministry, Mr. Schwartz-Schilling said that he wanted to introduce significant cuts in volume tariffs on lines leased to major customers by the Bundespost. Such tariffs, however, are controversial because they would apply only after the leased line had been used for merely 80 hours a month. It would make leasing lines roughly four times more expensive than in Great Britain.

The Witte Report is presently being analyzed and reviewed by the Ministries of Post, Finance, Economics, Justice, and Interior, which will make recommendations to the cabinet. With subsequent parliamentary debate, deliberations may last well into the future. Actual restructuring of the Deutsche Bundespost, if it occurs, is not likely before 1989.

Conclusion

In this writer's opinion, if Europe does not break its telecommunications monopolies in equipment and business services, European industry will suffer. Europe's worst response to this predicament would be an attempt to resist change by protecting itself from it; there is already talk about the need for protection from American competition in telecommunications. In the past there was a natural protection for a region's industry: the cost of transporting bulky products over long distances. This protection hardly exists for products in the information sector: last year's worldwide production of semiconductors could have been carried in ten Boeing 747s.

When this kind of competition is in information itself, it will be global and instantaneous and we should not try to build walls against the open market this will create. Several general areas of innovation policy that Europe might pursue also apply to other nations:

1. As a market, Europe cannot remain sliced up into a dozen or so semiseparate markets. This is not a technical but a political problem. The solution to this problem will require as much determination as it took to create the Common Market in the first place. This will mean that several big firms will be forced out of the telecommunications market since the market cannot support all of them.
2. The second policy issue concerns information technology itself. In this

sense, Europe needs to adopt the Japanese approach in electronics. One may question the wisdom in trying to catch up with technologies that already exist. A wise strategy would be to acquire and absorb as much Japanese and American technology as they are willing to license, and use the learning to create its own products for the next step in development (again, we have come back to the idea of technology transfer).

3. Immobility of people—job security, minimum wage laws, etc., all surface as market blockers. Government policies in these times of innovative activities should *not* protect old businesses from shrinking or prevent new ones from growing.

4. Capital. America's venture capitalists provide cash and management help to start out firms. In 1983, for example, $2.8 billion in venture capital was committed to start up companies in the United States; this is very different in Europe. Europeans have tended to use government subsidies instead of risk capital from the market to finance young firms. Venture-capital investments in Europe are only at 10%–20% of the American level. With interest rates averaging around 10% in the United States vs. 5% or less in Europe, there is no question where the investment funds will end up.[1]

5. Universities and training. The important role of universities in technology transfer has been addressed by several writers (e.g., Wigand, Larsen, & Rogers, 1988). In his presentation at this symposium, Everett Rogers stressed the importance of research universities in high-technology development; the same point can be made in this context. Europe is behind in its production of engineers and scientists, and it is suffering from a continuing brain drain. For example, Dr. Karl Garris, head of the biotechnology program for the West German chemical giant Hoechst, thought that the company needed a close tie to an academic laboratory. He could not find such a partner at a European university, and he scandalized the German establishment by making a $50 million deal with the Massachusetts General Hospital.

6. Laws. Three types of laws hamper the development of innovative firms:
   a) Income taxes in western Europe are too high. The United States enjoys the tax advantages of the R&D limited partnership and its tax sheltering possibilities by investing in high-risk R&D ventures.
   b) Restrictions on incentives offered to entrepreneurs for going into a startup. The backbone of the American system is the share option that allows the investor to acquire cheap shares in the business; some have become millionaires. In most European countries, this is impossible. It is to some extent possible in Britain, but still too restrictive. Bankruptcy laws are another impediment. Many bankruptcies or failed young businesses are a manifestation of economic health, i.e., they are experiments. There should be laws that allow new entrepreneurs the chance to "dust themselves off" and try again; they should not necessarily be thought of as failures.

c) Mobility inhibitors. Much of the job security legislation in western Europe is now having the effect of destroying jobs. Minimum wage legislation has had some influence in this situation. Furthermore, firms will have to be able to hire and fire people quickly.

When we look at industrial policies around the world we can report mixed findings. Perhaps in the United States we should not feel so bad about not having one. We may have a *de facto* industrial policy after all; some argue that such a policy is imbedded—maybe hidden—in our laws, regulations, and procedures. This writer tends to agree with J. D. Eveland's observation that perhaps there is not all that much that a government can do directly to intervene in the innovation process. Ultimately, the burden will rest with the individual entrepreneur. Government assistance will almost always be temporary.

Similar results were reported as well by a 2-year-long, worldwide study conducted by the Wharton School of the University of Pennsylvania. These researchers ranked Japan's strategy as the most successful. French and Italian policies were rated least effective. They urged policymakers to draw conclusions for American policy from the Japanese experience. They conclude that although Japan's policy has made some difference, no one would argue that its industrial policy is the reason Japan is where it is today, or was the major influence.

Notes

Session summaries in the text were contributed by participants in the conference: Dr. Donald Case, Graduate School of Library and Information Science, University of California, Los Angeles; Mr. James Dearing, Annenberg School of Communications, University of Southern California; Dr. Wilson Dizard, Center for Strategic and International Studies, Georgetown University; Dr. David V. Gibson, Department of General Business, University of Texas at Austin; Dr. Leah Lievrouw, Department of Communication, Rutgers University; Dr. Helena Makinen, Department of Communication, University of Helsinki; Dr. Carolyn Marvin, Annenberg School of Communications, University of Pennsylvania; and Ms. Meg Wilson, Center for Technology Development and Transfer, University of Texas at Austin.

1. A case in point is a West German lawyer who is a friend of mine, who flies to Phoenix every three or four weeks with five or six potential West German investors. Each of these individuals invests a minimum of about $250,000 in the Phoenix area market. My friend informs me that so far no one came to Phoenix without investing his/her money. I am also aware that there are several other similarly organized efforts to invest West German and Swiss capital in the Phoenix area. These are not isolated cases, but are activities that can be observed throughout the United States with investors from many European nations.

References

Bloom, B. S., Engelhart, M. D., Furst, E. J., Hill, W. H. and Krathwohl, D. R. (1956) *Taxonomy of Educational Objectives. Handbook I: Cognitive Domain.* New York: Longman.

National Utility Services. 1988. *The international telecoms price survey.* Croydon, Surrey, UK; Park Ridge, NJ: National Utility Services.

Wigand, R. T. 1988. Integrated services digital networks: concepts, policies, and emerging issues. *Journal of Communication, 38*(1), 29–49.

Wigand, R. T., Larsen, J. K., and Rogers, E. M. 1988. Communication patterns in high-technology development: Industry-university technology transfer. Paper presented to the annual conference of the International Communication Association. New Orleans, LA, May 29–June 2.

Witte, E. 1987. *Neuordnung der Telekommunikation: Bericht der Regierungskommision Fernmeldewesen.* Heidelberg, Germany: R. V. Decker's, G. Schenk.

Witte report: Limited liberalization in West Germany? 1987. *Transnational Data and Communications Report: The International Information Economy Monthly, 10*(10), 5.

Part III
CURRENT REFLECTIONS ON INFORMATION
AND COMMUNICATION THEORY

18

Tropes and Things

Lee Thayer

Most Western scholars who have written about communication—with such exceptions as Vico and Collingwood—have assumed that communication is an individualistic, rational act of will. This essay demonstrates that such an assumption is empirically untenable. People do not learn to take the world into account through their experiences with it, but through the minds they have to do so with. And these minds, of whatever culture, are not a function of the world but of that culture, or subculture. Each of us grasps the world, and each of us is grasped by it, in terms of our capacities for doing so. These capacities are a function of the "epistemic communities" that we represent in our minding of the world. Wherein we stand to "under"stand the world always and everywhere functions as a set of tropisms, and the world we know (as we are capable of attending to it) as the tropes that trigger them. All communication is systemic; and the system is given or closed for humans by the tropisms they can bring to the wrold, and the tropes they encounter or can engender or educe for exciting them into mental existence. Self-reflexivity thus takes on the rather more interesting role of perpetuating an indispensable set of tropisms in the absence of the tropes that constitute one's mental habitat—i.e., the minds of all the others with whom one would communicate or be communicated with.

He could not ope
His mouth, but out there flew a trope.
—Samuel Butler

A *tropism* is the involuntary response of an organism, or of any of its parts, to an external stimulus. Derived from the Greek *tropē* (roughly meaning "a turning"), it is understood from biology and biochemistry (chemotropism, phototropism, thermotropism, etc.) as any automatic reaction to a stimulus.

What turns toward the sun or away from it in nature is a tropism. The closing of lilies at night and their opening in the morning is a tropism. Aversive reactions to noxious substances or odors are tropisms. Exposing the underside of its leaves to the rain is a tropism of the silver maple. The dilation of the pupils of the eyes as light increases or decreases, or as fear or anxiety mount, is a tropism. In the living things of nature the myriad movements toward what is life giving—sunlight, water, food, protection— and away from what is life threatening—an excessively high or low temperature, drought, diminishing nutrition, exposure—are all tropisms. It is a useful term, too long neglected in the study of human communication, and in human behavior in general.

Automatistic Behavior

Most human communication, which is to say, most human behavior, is indeed more automatistic than consciously directed. We do not—typically or in the normal state of affairs—consciously formulate our perceptions of things, our "understandings" of the world, or our responses to it. They come upon us, they arise out of us, as if given—even as if they are a function of the thing perceived, or responded to, or understood. They emerge as if they were inevitable, a part of the flow of things. We "see" them consciously only as or after they occur. They are of us, but rarely under our conscious direction.

If it is something that is said to us, our understanding of what was said— or of what was meant by what was said—is more automatistic than not, more often than not. If we are reading, or watching television or a movie, our reading of what is going on, our tracking of it, its sensibility to us, is quite beyond our willed attention. Like the centipede, if we tried to direct our understanding of what is going on, we could no longer understand it. The musical performance or its reproduction, and our responses to it, seem to go together as if one, or at least mutually to inform each other in some inextricable taken-for-granted way. If we observe something going on, or a problem at work or at play, our reactions—our very awareness of that happening or that problematic event, its almost immediate intelligibility—is something that seems just to happen. Our ways of mentally grasping the world, and of behaving in it, of telling or of listening, of expressing and of comprehending, are not something of our own devising at the moment we are involved in them. We may reflect upon them; we may make them a part of our conscious concerns either before or after they occur; but the process that enables us to participate in the games of social life while engaged in them is a process that is utterly outside our conscious control. Like the astronauts in flight, if we had to contemplate each maneuver consciously, it would already be too late.

We seem to "know" what's funny without thinking about it. We seem to know what's sad, terrible, or wonderful without thinking about it. We seem to know a great deal more than we can say, or even be aware of. We seem to be able to play a wide range of social games without stopping to think how to do so. What accounts for a seemingly spontaneous laugh? Or a seemingly irrepressible tear? Or a pique? Or the good feelings that seem to attend certain sights and sounds, the bad feelings that seem to attend others? How is it that we can understand the world without taking steps to do so? How is it that we can understand things the way we do, without intending to do so?

Not only are our understandings and our reactions to things character- istically automatistic in all of these senses, but so also are our ways of expressing ourselves. The engine and the inertial guidance system for all human behavior are given in how we comprehend the world, in how we take it into account. And they are given in how we express that world, in how we bespeak that world of which we are the witnesses, and thereby have whatever human existence we have in how we give witness to it. Our ways of expressing ourselves—our utterances, gestures, facial expres- sions, our presentations of ourselves in everyday life, and our making of all of our human artifacts—each and all of the ways we have of expressing ourselves and the world we know, whether prompted from within or from without, are also more automatistic than not, more often than not.

If it is something we say to ourselves or to another, how is it that it comes out to be reasonably intelligible, even without our conscious direc- tion of its making? Or how does that other's capacity to understand what we say bear upon how we say what we say, before we ever say it? How can we do all of this without thinking about it, at least without thinking about it while we are doing it? We may be directing what we say in some general sense; but the forms, the structures, the sequences, and the cadences—we are not often consciously engaged in the production of those. They are precast for us, like bricks to the mason, twine to the net maker, rules to the game. We use them without thinking. In fact, we can use them well only by not giving them thought, as every beginning speaker of any language, or as every beginning automobile driver, can testify.

So what is it we do when we produce utterances that others will, in all likelihood, understand? How does a novelist (or a composer, a sculptor, a television broadcaster, or a political cartoonist) "know," without knowing how she knows, that what she is typing on the page will be readable, i.e., intelligible? Or, when we observe something—some happening, event, or problem—how much of the sense that it makes to us, almost immediately, is given in how we can explain it to others, without, in fact, having done so?

What are these mental mechanisms and symbolic devices that do these altogether remarkable things for us, without our conscious heed as to what they are or how they work? And how is it that we know, in spite of that, how to trigger them in ourselves or in others when we want to communicate?

The too-long-neglected partner terms of *tropes* and *tropisms* may go far toward shedding some useful light on this most mysterious, mundane, but absolutely vital characteristic of acting out the role of human being.

Tropisms

If there is something akin to tropisms that functions as the unconscious "performatives" of taking the world into account, of rendering the world of human utterances and human doings of all sorts intelligible, then there must be something akin to tropes that is embedded in, and provide reliable road signs for "reading"—for ensuring the intelligibility of—those human expressions, human artifacts, human doings.

But there still abounds the rather hapless notion that tropes have to do with merely figurative language—with mere embellishments like metaphor, irony, or metonymy: mere figures of speech. This must be anchored in a still more hapless but deeply ingrained prejudice of the Western mind set, which has it that a literal or prosaic way of referring to something is somehow more true to that something than is a figurative or more poetic way of referring to that same thing. Thus, we of the Western episteme feel comfortable with the prospect that a mathematical model of the movement of waves on the ocean's surface is a more adequate and more accurate description of those "things" than is a piece of poetry about them.

Perhaps. Though it appears that those who held to mythic explanations of such "things" lived more or less peaceably and harmoniously with those things of the world and with each other for thousands of years, before the more literal-minded Europeans came along to colonize and to decimate dozens of long-standing cultures and 30 millions of human beings in the name of their "superior" and more scientific way of explaining things. So perhaps a literal way of explaining things is more "accurate." But it may be only different, and in no way superior to any other way of explaining those same things. That we can now, after having tried to do away with every other way of talking about the world but our own, at a flick of one literal switch obliterate the whole planet and all living things on it, may be progress of a sort. But it is not the progress of having gotten by for 40,000 years in cooperation with the "poetry" of the earth, which was the nonliteral achievement of the Australian Aborigines before the Europeans came.

Our literal-mindedness has not only been unfortunate, it has been, and continues to be, in many ways, demonstrably hazardous to the health and welfare of humankind and the planet which we all inhabit. As such, it essentially has eclipsed the emergence of serious conceptual inquiry into the figurative aspects of language, and thus of mind, and thus of human and social behavior in general. Yet it may be only there that such questions as we began with, and which remain with us still, can be answered.

To get a better idea of where we are, which is where we have to start from to get to any place else at all, we may also want to consider the following.

The Literal and the Figurative

This archetype of the Western *mentalité,* this prejudice against the figurative in favor of the literal, perhaps dates from the time when someone occasionally inserted an unauthorized line into the "authorized" liturgy. Being sacrilegious, it was a bold and arrogant business. It also, most significantly, served to challenge the absolute power of the priests, who used the authorized liturgy to subjugate and bilk hundreds of thousands of illiterate peasants. Those who surreptitiously inserted these extra lines— these embellishments—were called "tropists," and the lines they inserted, "tropes."

So our irrational fear of the figurative and our obsession with the literal derives from an ancient anxiety over the loss of authority and thus of the standing order of things. To tamper with the authorized version was no mere play on words; it was a play on power. Those who had the prerogative to say what constituted the authorized version were those who held the power. And to tamper with the authorized version was to tamper with the source of their power.

In Western civilization, if not in all civilizations, the struggle for power is a struggle for who has the prerogative to say what the authorized version—the basic moral law governing all people—is. In our history, that prerogative belonged first to kings and emperors. Their word was law. Then that prerogative was wrested away by the church, and the priest's word was law. Later came the successful challenge of the church's prerogative by science via rationality. And now its word is law, or at least "the truth," which, in our literal-mindedness, we take to be the same thing. And now comes the latest winner in these struggles for the prerogative to dictate the "official" story; now emerging, it appears to be public opinion. We have gone from the tyranny of the almighty emperor to that of the almighty god to that of the almighty fact, and now, to that of the almighty majority.

In transit from there to here we have become even more suspicious of the figurative and more obeisant to the literal. Our idea of what constitutes an adequate description of the world is whatever looks or sounds like a newspaper headline. Anything that is not readily graspable by the mind of an 11-year-old is as readily suspect.

In our way of minding the world, to be literal is to be macho, manly, in charge. To be too figurative is to be sissy, feminine, maybe even queer. It is the poet or the artist who tampers with the authorized version of things. But we keep these latter-day tropists in check: if they cannot entertain us, we simply relegate them to the fringes of society and there largely ignore them. They are either irrelevant or dangerous; the man in the street, who is now in the process of "inheriting the earth," would not have one for a friend.

So our neglect of the concepts of *trope* and *tropism* must be attributed at least in part to our timidity. In wanting to be liked, at least to be relevant, we have surrendered to those hegemonic ways of thought that would relegate such considerations to the intellectual hinterlands. In pursuing the literal, since that is where the mainstream seems to be headed, we not only, faultily, mounted literalistic "theories" and explanations of people. We contributed to the literalizing of things; we imposed a literalism of the very people we were claiming to explain. We contributed to the literalization of things by assuming the literalization of things. In equating truth with literalism, we not only invested monumental effort in constructing largely trivial theories of human nature, but we also aided and abetted the trivialization of all of those lives we could reach with our explanations of things. We failed to notice that it was the tropist who cracked the cosmic egg that made it possible for peasants to become people. And we remain unheedful of the fact that every human mind is born in the figurative and has its life there.

Science as Tropism

What we overlooked was that the "official" story, however concocted and whoever "owned" it, was itself tropistic. The justification for science is no less mythical than is the justification for any other world view. To stand "in" science in order to share the power of the age and thus to diminish others by enhancing oneself is not different in kind from what the high priests did. It is to accede to the prerogative of keeping the official story pure and intact. It is to assume that whatever does not fit the parameters of the official story is thereby a threat to it. It is to preserve the tropes of the official story by making certain that no unauthorized tropes get inserted into it. It is to miss seeing what is most characteristic of humans qua humans. It is to miss seeing that the mind is a tropistic device, and that we are all made of those devices, whatever they may be and however they may be deployed.

To bring those devices to the forefront is not to unearth a theoretical panacea; perhaps they are merely the keys to the Pandora's Box that is the human mind, or merely the stuff of which the box is made. Wherever they may lead us (which is all that any concept ever does), they are the kind of concepts that await our passion to explain people for their own benefit, and not for ours. And perhaps they have been so long awaiting because that is one of the consequences that admitting such concepts into our basic world view would have. To the psychologist—to the behavioral "scientist" in general—there would seem to be two distinct forms of human life: (1) that which is given in their own privileged position as more or less rational finders and keepers of "the truth" about people; and (2) all the rest, referred to as "people," who are not a part of the immunized elite—the properly initiated or anointed—and who are therefore merely victims of whatever stimuli come along. The classical psychologist's argument was that these people of whom he spoke are nothing more than a product of the congeries of stimuli to which they had been exposed. But the psychologist himself, having a mind of his own, could not only exercise his free will in deciding upon the working of his mind and of his doings, but could thereby enable himself to understand those people whether they understood themselves or not. Especially if they pretended or claimed not to understand themselves.

To be such a theorist of human behavior meant being immune to the very cause-and-effect forces which were claimed to account for that behavior. It meant being privileged to account for people and their behavior with explanations from which the explainer was exempt (B. F. Skinner is perhaps our most illustrious—but by no means our only—example). It was the church writ small, being resurrected in the way it was being denounced.

To speculate that minds are primarily tropistic devices, and that our lives and our civilizations are their products, is to call that immunity into question. It is to call into question the subjugation (or the hoodwinking) of people in the name of "truth," or of "facts," or of the opinion of the "expert." It would be to hand back to people the only literacy that counts:

that of being aware of how we are energized and given life and direction by minds not of our own making; and that of being aware of how we are made to be the way we are, and our complicity in all of that, and thus to have a way of grasping the tools of remaking.

The Promise of Human Communication Study

That was the promise of the study of human communication when it came upon the scene. But it is a failed promise, because those who flew that banner were for the most part but reductionists in humanists' clothing. They set about to explain people along the lines of the "official" liturgy— which was by that time scientism/technologism/methodologism. In their pursuit of a place in the scientistic sun, they saw little place for the pervasive and primal presence of the figurative in the life of the mind—of any mind, including their own. So we have to look elsewhere.

The world that Lewis Carroll told—that wonderland—is a great deal more like everyday life as and with humans than are either Hollywood movies or television sitcoms. And those, in turn, are a great deal more like everyday life as and with humans than are the theories of social and behavioral scientists. So the time has come, perhaps, to speak, if not of cabbages and kings, at least of why cabbages appear to be cabbages and kings appear to be kings. Which is to say, of tropes and things.

Tropes and Mental Functioning

So if a cabbage is not a king and a king is not a cabbage; and if a cabbage is not a cabbage until we know what a cabbage is; what then *is* a king before we know what a king is?

To say that the mind is tropistic (or, better, that it tropical) in function is to say first of all that the primal mental function, the primal symbolic function, the one that sets us up for minding the world like a human and sets us off on our human adventure of being a human, is invariably tropical. The first operation of mind is to change what *is* into something that can be thought about because it can be talked about. It is this first operation that *creates* mind, as Helen Keller so eloquently described her own coming into self-conscious existence later in life. To name the world as others name it is to mind the world as others mind it. To call something to mind by its name is to call mind into existence.

But whatever we may call a thing, and whatever language we may use to do so, its name is not the thing. "Whatever we say a thing is," Korzybski put it, "it is not." To create or to use a mental image of something, or to create or to use a mental operation for something, is to change that thing from whatever it is to what we say of it or think of it, to how we see it or use it. In naming something, we transform it. In naming something, whether that something exists independently of our naming or not, we transform ourselves. We transform it from whatever it was (literally) to what it is (figuratively) in our way of minding it. And we transform ourselves from whatever we were (literally) to whatever we (figuratively) do in our minding of the world. We cease to live in the world as it is, and come to self-awareness in authoring the world as we tell it. The ecstatic moments of the birth of Helen Keller's mind came not from brushing up against the things of the world but from a sudden realization—which comes to the rest of us slowly and unnoticeably—that the world in which humans live is not the world of things but the world of the names of things.

Every human mind comes to life in a uniquely human world by grasping the humanly given names of the things of that world. And that name— whether for an object or an event, a relationship or a condition—is always a figurative name. It is always tropical; it is always a turning-away from whatever it is to whatever we say it is. The drawings of the "bison" on the cave walls at Lascaux, and the drawings of "crocodiles" on the cliff walls at Kakadu: such ways of speaking of bison and of crocodile are not themselves bison or crocodile. They are ways of creating and maintaining minds by creating and maintaining a way of minding the world. A culture, whatever its language or its languages, is a way of minding the world. A mind is a way of minding the world which recapitulates that culture. One does not learn from one's experiences. One learns from one's interpretations of one's experiences. And the parameters for all such interpretations are given only in the habitation of human minds, which is to say, in human cultures.

Thus, any culturally legitimated way of describing or depicting anything whatsoever, in whatever form and for whatever purpose, is metaphoric. It is metaphoric in the sense that any such description or depiction is taken for the thing described or depicted. To re-cognize something, to recognize something, is to be able to call upon the words that might be necessary or adequate to describe that thing to oneself or to another. To real-ize something, to realize something, is to arrive at a way of describing or accounting for that thing in some language that another would comprehend and real-ize therein. The intelligibility of something is a measure of the familiarity of its description or depiction. Whatever is known that is not widely known is to that same degree unintelligible. We give life to the mind by mastering the cultural intelligibility of things, by learning how to bespeak the world that can be known only in terms of what can be said of it.

We know what cabbages are. And we know what kings are. And we know that the one is not the other because the category of things we know as cabbages excludes those things we know as kings, and vice versa.

Cabbages may be things of a sort before we know that they are cabbages. We might sit on those things or bind a bunch of them together to make a raft. But to know them as cabbages is to accede to the prescriptions and the proscriptions for their use given in the concept of "cabbage" to which the word refers. For words do not refer to things; they refer to concepts of things.

It—this thing we call "cabbage"—may have been many things before we knew it as a cabbage. But once we know it as a cabbage, it can no longer be anything we want it to be, or imagine it to be. Its "cabbageness" is something that we give to it in our minding of it, just as it is the "chairness" of a chair that constrains us from burning it up in the fireplace or hanging it on the wall. It might occur to us to use it to fend off an attacking tiger (because we have seen that done in the movies), or as a weapon in a barroom brawl (because we have seen that done in the movies, too). But its chairness, like the cabbageness of a cabbage, is not a property of the chair, or of the cabbage, but of our way of minding the one and the other, our way of behaving toward them or with them. Cabbages are something we may talk about in terms of "liking" or not. But people do not often say, "I don't like chairs." So a chair is not a "chair" until we know what "chairs" are. And a cabbage is not a "cabbage" until we know what "cabbages" are. Chairs, like cabbages, are categories of things. Genres.

So what *is* a king before we know what a king is? There cannot be *one* of anything until there is a category—a conceptual category—of things of same nature. Without the concept of king there can be none. A king before we know what "kings" are may be something else. Something of some other sort—a chief, perhaps, or an elder, or a guru, the guy in charge, the son of heaven, or perhaps just the one who can beat the tar out of anyone else in the tribe.

But the "kingness" of kings—that is wholly in our way of minding the world. A king can be in the world we mind because we have a concept of "kings." But not otherwise. Whatever the "kingness" of kings may be said to be, it is not *in* the person we so address and defer to any more than the "chairness" of chairs is in the object.

Hence, when Lewis Carroll says it is "time to speak of many things . . . of cabbages and kings," he is asking us to put together two things for which we do not have an aggregating concept. What are the two together to be called?

It is precisely the absence of such a concept of the two together that puzzles and intrigues us, or frustrates and irritates us. We do not know what he is talking about because we do not have a category for conceiving of and thus making sense of the two together. We have no ready conceptual category for cabbages and kings.

Lewis Carroll takes us to the edge of our own capacity for minding the world. We know what cabbages are, and we know what kings are—without thinking about it. But cabbages *and* kings? Without an inclusive category for the two together, we are left either to invent a new category of things or to pass it off as non-sense. That is the option Carroll gives us. And Wittgenstein, who asked us if it were not, all of it, a form of play. Human civilization is a play on words. And the mind is the device for making moves, for having a part in it, for helping to author it or to "explain" it.

What is non-sense to us is merely that for which we have no working metaphor, no tropical way of grasping, of re-cognizing. What is sensical is merely that for which we do. It is not the world that makes sense. It is only we who make sense or do not—we tellers of the world, knowers of the world—to ourselves, to one another. What we can make "make sense" to us is what we can fit into a culturally given category of things. That is why it "makes sense" to others who bring to bear the same sets of categories as we do. There is nothing which in itself makes sense. The "sense" it makes to us is given in the culturally given concept with which we grasp it, into which we fit it.

The Error of Communication and Information Theorists

We grasp the world with whatever capacity we have to grasp it. The world grasps us with whatever capacity we have to be "grasped" by it. This is why Herman Melville could say that no great wonder of the world could be wonderful to us unless we could rise up to meet it with an equal wonder. And this is where the communication and the information theorists go awry, and the structuralists and the semioticians, for that matter.

They would have us believe that there are self-evident things in the world, and that when one calls these things by some name, one is referring to those things and not to the culturally given concepts from which we apprehend and speak of those things. More than this, they would have us believe that all things are more or less equally tellable, and that all things are more or less equally comprehensible—that is to say, that we people are more or less interchangeable with respect to those things and the names for those things. They would have us believe that the meaning of things is something to be discovered rather than invented.

They would have us believe that the world is a given, and that the purpose of words or pictures or formulae is merely to produce an ever-more veridical picture or rendering of that given world. They would have us believe that their perspective on the world is merely "objective"—that, with the proper scientific indoctrination and posture, one can be enabled to see the world as it is, unconstrained by any a prioris, unconstrained by any concepts taken *to* an observation of the world. They would have us believe that anything that does not make sense to the rest of us simply has not been explained well enough, or that we simply have not tried hard enough. Some of them would have us believe that love is something that happens to us, not us as something that happens to love. Some of them would have us believe that a scientific description of something is superior, because "truer," than a poem or a painting of that same thing.

They would have us believe that a theory of something is built up out of "facts" about that thing, even though Einstein himself understood that one needs a theory in order to know what facts to look for, or even what a relevant fact would look like. They would have us believe that people, themselves included, understand the world by their capacity to abstract facts from it, rather than their capacity to give facts to it. They would have us believe that the world informs us, rather than that we inform the world. They would have us believe that facts themselves are properties of the world rather than of the minds that would take those worlds into account. They would have us believe that the words and the numbers we may use to describe the world are a reasonable substitute for that world, rather than for ourselves.

In all of this, they are the tropists who embellish on the original text (nature itself, if that is what they purport to be describing). If "nature" or "human nature" are the authorized liturgies, then theirs is the surreptitious insertion or translation. We cannot in any wise create and nurture human minds except tropically.

To ask, as Warren McCulloch did—What is a number, that a human may know it? And what is a human that he may know a number?—is to suggest that a number is what it is because of the way we know it, and that we are the way we are because of the way we know a number. The one informs the other by how the one and the other have been "in-formed" to be informed. The thing and whatever sense we make of it are the same. The one *is* what it is because the other *is* what it is.

Systems of Knowing

A human tropism is an immediate and effortless "recognition" of something. To "re-cognize" something is to be a part of the system in which it is "some-thing." To be someone is to be able to play those games in which things are some-things. That which is known defines the knower in the same measure as the knower defines the thing known, as Dewey said.

What directs the mind is not the world, but the capacity of mind to meet the world, wonder for wonder, wonder with wonder. What we grasp with mind is a function of that which we have to grasp it with. The more complex the mind that would grasp the world, the more complex the world; the simpler the mind that would grasp the world, the simpler the world. Sadness is not something that is caused by the world; it is merely something that can be had, like all else, because it can be explained to other minds. It *is* only because it makes sense to those who would grasp it. The world we know is the world we can explain. And the life we have is a function of the world we can explain. One arises out of one's explanations of things.

A sign means whatever we read into it, not what it says. What is obligatory to mind is not the structure of the world but the structures of mind with which we would grasp it, with which we would explain it. What thought comes or goes unpackaged—dressed in other than the clothes one can provide for it? The world is naked. We clothe it with our words, numbers, renderings, our images of it. We know it only as it is clothed. And what we bring to clothe it with is the stuff of the mind.

Civilization progresses, Whitehead once wrote, not by increasing its conscious control over the world, but by increasing the number of operations it can perform without being conscious of them. It is the same with the development of mind. Learning to drive a car, to speak a second language, or to play the piano—any complex human competence—proceeds very slowly from small actions consciously and laboriously directed to larger and more complex performances, possible only because the smaller actions of which they are composed have been routinized out of conscious awareness. The professional tennis player concentrates on the game, leaving it to what has been built into her muscles, sinews, nerves, feet, and glances—leaving it to what her body knows—to do all the rest. As does the reader.

What we can do consciously is very limited. Or, put another way, what we learn to do unconsciously permits us to do other things consciously. Where, exactly, *is* the story in the words we read on a page? Where, exactly, *is* the theme in the splashes of color we observe on the canvas?

We can consciously attend a word. But not the meaning of a sentence. Try it. We achieve the larger meaning of something only in virtue of not having to attend consciously to its parts. A story, for example, is more than the sum of the words used to tell it, or the words sighted to read it; it requires these, and more, but it is more than these. It is what is possible for mind when all of these smaller operations can be integrated into an unconscious routine. The more one has to concern oneself with the parts, the less of the whole one can grasp.

To read a story—to "get" a story out of a series of marks on a page—is an achievement comparable to the achievement of a civilization in the Whiteheadian sense. It requires nested hierarchies of complex operations that have been routinized, which form the infrastructure for what we call "reading," and which are not only unconscious but cannot be made conscious without the loss of the virtuosity required to "get" the story.

One must know the language without knowing or directing how one knows it. One must know what stories are. And one must know how they are told. Stories are not told as research reports are "told." If one does not know the difference, one will be unable to read either one. And one must know one's role as reader. Learning how to "be" a reader is no less demanding than learning how to "be" a writer; it is just less romantic. And that's why people may say, "I want to be a writer," but not, "I want to be a reader."

The one is presumed to require practice, perhaps a certain competence, maybe even a little talent. But this is merely a cultural bias. One does not extract the story from the marks on the page. If that were all there were to it, we would all be equally good at it. One does not in fact get the message of a television commercial. One must be able to *give to it* whatever message one gets out of it.

To read the world in any of its forms, whether human made or natural, is a high-level competency. That it is a commonplace and mundane one should not blind us to the considerable skills and virtuosities involved. It is certainly a competency that far surpasses that of playing tennis. But we do not say that the message telling the player what to do or how to think is *in* the approaching ball. The ball is a part of the game as are the racket, the court, the net, the rules, and one's "psychological" state—and the opposing player. But it is the player who is or is not competent to play the game. It is the strategies he can bring to bear, the tactics that he may have developed; it is the state of his body and his mind on that day, at that moment; it is his experience—given, for better or for worse, in what his body knows; it is all of these that make a difference. And there is still the opponent. There is still the unexpected. It is the player's capacity to read the dynamics of the game at any instant that determines its history. It is certainly not the game itself that makes it interesting, or exciting, or challenging. And surely not the ball itself. It is the player, and what that player brings to the game.

In the same way, what makes a story, or an incident, or an image of something interesting, or exciting, or even meaningful in some humanly communicable way is not its existence. It is one's ability to "play the game." It is one's ability to be a player in the game. And it varies with one's proficiencies and sensibilities as a player of that game.

The point is that no amount of information that the ball is—by some observer—purported to carry makes any difference if the person on the court does not know how to play the game. One's play in the game is no better than one's reading of the moment-to-moment concatenation of all the elements of the game. And this ongoing reading of what is going on is not a conscious or a rational (or even a cognitive) activity. It depends upon all of those unconscious, routinized programs that one has built into oneself over time for reading the momentary state of things in the game and for responding to it in some more or less intelligent way, without thinking.

It is what we know without knowing how we know it that makes all such higher-order games—like tennis, reading stories or watching television, knowing one's next moves in what is going on around one socially, deciding whether or not you like someone, or knowing what to say next— possible. No amount of conscious effort will in itself make of one an accomplished pianist, or a newspaper reader. Nor will any way of packaging information get a message across to a person who cannot impute that message to the sights or sounds to which she may be exposed. Information is no more than one's ability to "read" it "rightly"—to impute an appropriate meaning or relevance to something—in a game in which such information is an element.

What we all learn more or less well is how to play the myriad games of social life: how to present oneself, how to pow-wow or gossip, how or when to be embarrassed, shocked, amused, or grieved; how to explain things; how to read an advertisement; how to carry on a conversation; how to know when and how to take your leave of a cocktail party; how to recreate and certify social reality; and so on ad infinitum.

Knowing how to play is not a matter of information. Rather, information is a matter of knowing how to play the game—the game of love, science, politics, business, schooling, the arts, commuting, hanging around, shopping—all of them.

One learns to be a player in a conversation—which is what human societies are made of—in much the same way that one learns to be a tennis player. In neither case is the reading self-evident in the form of the things that are moved in the play—balls or words. And in neither case can one generate that reading consciously. There is neither the time nor the capacity to do so. How one knows what is going on is not a function of what is going on but of one's capacity for reading the situation.

What's critical in either case are the reader's reflexes *in* the game, as the game is going on. What's critical is how one is given to make immediate sense of what one is observing without giving thought to how one does so. What's critical are the developed reflexes one can bring to bear for making sense of something going on in one's purview.

The Value of the "Tropism" Concept

Because all language is metaphorical, we need not ask of some way of talking about something—Is it true, this way of talking about that? We need only ask of the language—Is it useful, will it get us where we want to go?

Let us refer to those congeries of reflexes that enable us to read something in some more or less appropriate or intelligent way as *tropisms*. Just as certain amoeba may "know" to turn toward or away from certain chemicals in response to their presence, certain people may "know" how to respond to certain messages or certain situations just by recognizing their presence. Whether such tropisms may ultimately be judged as intelligent or not depends not upon how well those aspects of one's environment have been read (which is often how human intelligence is defined), but upon what the consequences of those responses turn out to be. One may indeed be able to gyrate or otherwise groove on the sounds of one's favorite rock group played at high volume on one's headset. But if one has some eventual hearing loss as a consequence, this appreciative response may turn out to be something other than intelligent. One may be able to read the cigarette ads quite as intended, but if one suffers lung cancer as a consequence, we would not want to say that one's reading of that ad was an intelligent one.

And let us refer to all of those thus readable signs as may be taken to account for such reflexes of perception as *tropes*. Tropes are neither good nor bad, right nor wrong, intelligent or not. They either "work" or they do not. A trope that works is merely one that triggers a tropism, for which there *is* a tropism. The more people there are who have perceptual/ conceptual reflexes susceptible to certain tropes, the more powerful and universal those tropes are. And the less obvious, for if everyone is reflexing to the same tropes, those reflexes will be interpreted as natural and not learned or arbitrary. If only one person can read something, he's thereby a nut, and the stuff he claims to understand or appreciate is for all the others nonsensical drivel, perhaps even dangerous. If "everyone" can read or appreciate something (the newspaper headlines, say) they are thereby "normal," because what they are reading is thereby "true."

What it comes down to is the ease with which one can "understand" the world one lives in. The comfortableness of one's understandings of one's world is a function of how universal those understandings seem to be (among those others, at least, who count). And the ease with which those understandings are produced is a function of how readily and imperturbably one's reflexes work on the world. It takes little or no effort to understand the familiar, the ritualized, the repetitive. We may resist or even be incapable of understanding anything that is much outside the familiar. So we seek the one and avoid the other. We assume that what is familiar or readily understandable *is* the world, or at least is all of the world that counts, which explains why we see alien cultures as being inferior cultures.

What we cannot grasp easily with the reflexes that provide our window on the world we either ignore or belittle. Thus, the teenage rock consumer's disdain of "long-hair" music. If we do come across something that is unfamiliar but that we may want to understand, we do so by translating it into familiar terms—as in: "Oh, that sounds (looks, smells, tastes) just like ——— (this or that familiar category)."

We Live by Tropes

We live by tropes. We "sight-read" the world by the tropes that trigger our reflexive understandings of it.

Rock music, for example, is amplified, has a heavy beat, a mundane, highly-repetitive lyric. Its performers wear garish costumes, provide garish images. Classical music is not amplified, is not usually driven by a heavy beat, and if there is a lyric, it usually tells a fairly complex story. Its performers wear dressy costumes and provide conservative images. And we know, as members of the audiences, how to act (differently indeed) in witnessing the one or the other.

If you see a "boom box" on the beach or in a park, you will predict what the music will be without hearing it. If you hear "classical" music, you will predict the age of the listeners without seeing them. Yet, whether rock or classic, we will understand the music because of the tropes of its construction and its progressions, although we will not as readily and with as much comfort understand Eastern music, which is produced out of an expanded scale of notes, with different progressions, less regularity, etc.

We can immediately recognize the front end or the back end of a car, and we know whether a person is coming or going without taking account of any movement. We know when most kinds of music and most kinds of movies are about to end, but most of us would not know how we know this. The evening news makes sense to us regardless of how alien the location, how extraordinary the event, or how complex the issues. We can easily understand it all, because of how the familiar tropes are employed— the camera angles, the transitions, the confident smiles, the easy banter, the "newsy" music themes, the hair styles and the on-camera posturing, the temporal and visual structures of the whole and of each of the parts of the program (its semiotics), the human interest twist to the most incredible stories, the dramatic plotting, the opening and closing quips, the stage design itself (how much do the settings and the props from which the "talking heads" perform the news vary around the world, even from East to West?).

Most Americans, apparently, cannot remember what the specific news stories were even thirty minutes later. This is because it is not the content we read, but the tropistic nature of its packaging. If that is familiar enough, and easily readable, we come away with the feeling that everything is right in the world yet another day—at least as we expected, in spite of the horrors of some of the reports.

Romance fiction, which accounts for more than one-half of all the sales of mass market paperbacks in the United States is, like most other genres—whether in science, politics, or art—formulaic. Thus, in a romance, the heroine is (usually) blonde, full-bodied, and "ripe," but virginal, for complex psychological reasons which make her unable to love, and destined for a dull and meaningless, but (usually) very well-to-do life. Onto the scene comes the tall, dark stranger—the hero. She resists him; there is something ominous about him and his manner. He eventually "rapes" her, although not necessarily by force, and she therein and thereafter learns the "real" meaning of love, and gives herself to him eagerly (almost always depicted on the cover). And they, like their fairy tale predecessors, "live happily ever after."

We "like" television sitcoms, in the same way that we like the top 40 tunes of the week, not in spite of knowing what's coming, but *because* we do. We know the next words and we know what's going to happen next; all the tropes are there for those who can read them; and that is indeed what happens. If what we expect to happen does not, and this is too often, we change channels and take up another favorite program. What is funny or what is sad is what is supposed to be funny or sad, and what we can easily anticipate—be set up for. When in doubt about what is funny, there is a "laugh track." When in doubt about what is sad, the performers will appear to be crying. Something novel, on the other hand, is simply ambiguous: we do not know whether to laugh or cry, and if after awhile we cannot figure this out easily and reliably, we simply change channels.

How do certain bits of business, certain actions, certain clothing, makeup, or countenances, certain expressions, colors, settings, certain kinds of music, and all the rest become tropes? Because they "work." And the more they work, the more they are worked.

Although things are sometimes reversed and still work, why does the hero wear a white hat or ride a white horse? Why are his guns pearl-handled? Why is he clean-shaven and apparently bathes, but the villain is not? Why does he get the girl (as in the Bond movies), but the villain does not? Why does he appear to be better educated and more "gentlemanly" (Paladin even quoted Shakespeare)?

How can we "tell" just by listening to the music what is going on, or what kind of movie we are about to see? Why are the covers of the more so-called serious novels sort of artsy, and those of mass market novels more representative—more literal? We signal a genre by its proprietary tropes. So there is "romantic" music, "spook" music, "space" music, and "chase" music, to signal a genre of movie, television show, and even television commercial. Whether it is dandruff or ring around the collar, the music on a 10-second commercial is first "problem" music, which is displaced by happy or "solution" music when the product arrives on the scene (what Tony Swartz calls "the responsive chord"). There is essentially nothing in a modern advertisement—from the setting to the sounds, to the color, to the casting, to the props (as in the use of carefully arranged plastic ice-cubes in a drink glass, since they photograph as more real than "real" ones)—which is not carefully calculated to have "tropic" power of some sort for some set of people.

How did blue get to be a trope for certain "down" moods, and red a trope for a ready-for-life woman? Why is black for funerals in our society, and white for weddings? (The tropic power of something depends upon the certainty and the universality of the appropriate tropisms or reflexes among an identifiable set of people or an audience.) Why would it be difficult, maybe impossible, to sell hand cream that is brown, even though that product worked better than white cream? Or, similarly, lipstick that is the color of well-cooked pork? And why do we buy and buy into things not on the basis of whether they are good for us in their long-range consequences, but on the basis of the familiarity and the appeal of the tropes by which they are packaged? How did a voluptuous, swimsuit clad female get to be the most ubiquitous "testimonial" ever used to sell everything from automobile brake pads to fishing poles and sparkling water? How did we come to make a fetish (a kind of trope) of the female breast, whereas another culture made a fetish of the female foot? This could surely not have been caused by the object itself.

Further, the more harmful the product, it would seem, the "healthier" the tropes employed to package it or background it—e.g., clean mountain air for cigarettes, happy and harmonious interpersonal relations for beer, wealth and power for booze. Why do toilet tissue and sanitary napkin packages have flowers on them? And why do rich people not need Mr. Tidy Bowl or springflower-scented room deodorants?

All advertising, all propaganda—in fact, all attempts made to influence others' thoughts or actions, whether grand or everyday and mundane—are more like a game than anything else. It is a game in which the one tries to figure out what the other's perceptual-conceptual reflexes (tropisms) are, and then design a set of tropes to trigger them in the desired direction. Thus, all communication is, in this sense, "subliminal"; most of our reactions and attentions to, and recognitions of, the world around us are reflexive—they occur automatically, out of our control. The game for one is to couch one's purposes (e.g., a political ideology) or one's products (e.g., oneself or a mouthwash) in the kinds of tropes the other will attend to without realizing it, and may thereby be well disposed toward. The game for the other is to avoid tropelessness, or ambiguous or uncertain tropes that would require thought or conceptual effort to decipher, and to navigate the world by using familiar and reliable tropes as the markers.

It is a game which everybody wins, even though both or all may lose. For there is communication "pleasure" and communication "pain." One seeks the one and hopes to avoid the other, without regard for the consequences. Once on the track, a neurotic is difficult to derail, because that which ratifies and endorses his neuroticism has become communication pleasure, while all ways of "understanding" the world that might return him to "normal" are now communication pain. The consumer of any kind of communication artifact seeks communication pleasure—the repetition of universal and reliable tropes—and avoids those that may bring communication pain, that is, those which are unfamiliar or novel. Like all communication, this is collaborative in nature and in spirit, else it does not work. What the one expects and is capable of understanding is always a constraint on what the other may say and on how he may package what he has to say. And what the other may have to say and how the other is capable of packaging what he has to say is always a constraint on what the one, and how the one, may understand the world.

Tropes Are Clichés

All tropes are, in a sense, clichés. There are clichés of all sorts. Political rhetoric, like everyday conversation, is ridden with clichés. But so are architecture (Tom Wolfe's *Bauhaus*), clothing (jeans, lapels), adornment (earrings but not nose rings, eye makeup but not ear makeup), faces (standardized makeup patterns which are fashionable), countenances and postures (the teenage pout, the old man's shuffle), home decoration, automobiles, hotels and fast-food places, text-book formatting, genres of book covers and record jackets, genres of food packages, mealtime rituals, disk jockey banter, tourist brochures and tour-guide commentaries, publicity posters, ads, amateur snap-shots, musicals, art genres of all sorts, subculture paraphernalia, and so on.

It is as if the only way people can understand the world is in clichés. Yesterday's novelty, if it catches on—and of course only a minor few do catch on—becomes today's cliché. Art objects are reproduced or used as icons and made into kitsch. Until about 1930, for a female to be "sexy" meant, among other tropes, having white (untanned, thus unseen) skin.

From that time on, it has been the other way. Tan = "beautiful" (no matter the skin damage involved). You and I have never seen an "underdeveloped" female in *Playboy,* or one with bad skin (we have our stereotypes, as Lippmann called them). Nor have we seen an overweight model on the cover of *Cosmopolitan,* the editor's feminism notwithstanding: she knows what sells magazines. Thin = glamorous. Attractive = smart, but beautiful and blonde = dumb (thanks to the Marilyn Monroes of the film world and their directors). Tall = the obvious "take-charge" type. Makeup = that "natural" look. Rich = good looking (how many ugly people have there been on "Dynasty"?).

These are all clichés, and all "readable" without giving thought to them. And all usable tropes, whether in personal life (why *is* it the rich guys seem to get the prettiest women?), in political life (where American governors have come to look more and more alike, and to act as if they were taking lessons from Jack F. Kennedy's drama coach), in commercial life (where the only rule for success seems to be: if something works, imitate it), in sports (where the camera angles and the replays and the announcer's commentary are all calculated to heighten the "drama" of the conflict), in tourism and travel (not only are the hotel rooms clichés, but most of us could identify the tourist by his or her dress, exclamations, and accoutrements), and so on throughout every aspect of our lives, large or small.

If it seems that the only way we can understand the world is in clichés, perhaps that is because that is the case. What is not a cliché we typically do not understand, or do not want to trouble ourselves to try. What *is,* in our eyes, is sufficient: the world we see *is* the world. And the more standardized our perceptions can be because the more standardized the packaging of the thing perceived, the surer we can be that the world we see *is* the world.

One might think that the world of science is the one exception to all this. But a "scientific" paper is not merely a neutral device for storing or conveying information. As a genre, scientific papers are as clichéd as a television soap opera, ads for body products, or "the news." They are highly formulaic, their plots, themes, and structures as standardized as those of any other genre. Posture and voice are highly dissanctionable matters of custom: one would refrain from using the active voice, as in "I did this and then I did that," in favor of the passive voice, as in, "It was observed that". One does not presume to be speaking on behalf of oneself, but on behalf of the establishment or of the "facts"; one's conclusions follow more or less inevitable from the works of others, cited to legitimate one's own and to provide the appropriate seeming humility and dispensability. One must make it appear that the facts compel the conclusion, rather than admitting that one started with it. And there are paraphernalia like charts and tables to give it all a more "scientific" and objective appearance. As a genre, so-called scientific papers are no less concocted than "60 Minutes," which is the most heavily edited news show on television.

Once initiated, one accepts and "understands" what is there because one has learned to read the tropes. The subject and even the findings may be trivial or irrelevant, but they contribute to what scientists understand to be the building-toward-truth that is going on, as pieces are reported and used as building blocks. Further, one can always enhance one's own standing in the field by citing the high and mighty in that field, the field's celebrities (while claiming to be influenced only by the facts)—a sort of glory by association, which as a process is not at all unlike what goes on in commercial advertisements, using celebrities as product endorsers.

So prevalent is all of this that the parody of the *Journal of Irreproducible Results* has become quite popular. The interesting thing is that one cannot be sure when the writer is serious; if all the tropes, all of the jargon, all of the "scientese" is employed, it seems to make good sense to those of us who have the appropriate reflexes even though the methods reported are absurd, or the conclusions reached inane.

What enables understanding is not information as such, but rather tropes. Sir Peter Medawar once commented that it was no wonder that young scientists could not do research. After some years of reading published research reports, they come to assume that research is done the way it is reported in the journals, that it is as tidy, as lockstep, and as rational as the formulaic way of reporting would make it seem. So they are disabled from doing any worthwhile research.

We do not understand the world, nor even seek to do so. All of us are like bundles of tropisms, of perceptual-conceptual reflexes, wandering around awaiting a trope or two to capture our attention, and thus to lead us down those paths that we have a capacity, due to our reflexes, to be led.

Tropes Are Shorthand

We should not imagine that all of this is deplorable because it is avoidable. It is not. The more we want to be able to take into account, the more efficient must be our means of categorizing and indexing things. The volume of our knowledge may have grown, but the equipment we have for comprehending it has not.

Our everyday language is characteristically synecdochical or metonymical in nature: the part of something becomes a trope for the whole, or an attribute of something becomes a trope for the thing. We abbreviate, clip, use all kinds of "shorthand" for grasping all of that we want to take into account, for all that we wish to express. When the whole goes beyond our capacity to comprehend, we break up into smaller and smaller groups, having a jargon and a style of communicating all our own. The pieces grow and grow, and fragment again. It is a matter of quantity. No one even knows how complex systems (like the power supply to the Eastern seaboard) works. It is enough for most of us that we can find someone to talk to—which is to say, someone whose reflexes are much like our own, and who reads the world in terms of the same tropes we do.

Tropes and Change

Not all of us are made of clichés, however. There are those who would break the mold, who would come up with something novel—a novel way of seeing something, or a novel way of expressing something. These few are often called "artists," but they are more like *bricoleurs*. Most of us are brokers of the familiar, the well- and widely used ways of seeing and of saying. Our ideal is to see what everyone else sees, to know what everyone else knows, to feel like everyone else feels, to express ourselves like everyone else does, to work at what "everyone" else works at, to play at and where "everyone" else (who counts) plays—and to do so while singing, as if we had written it, "Doing It My Way." We think that being able to say things like others do, or to see things like others do, is to understand those things. But occasionally there is the one who would see or say the world differently, on-behalf-of herself. She is the *bricoleur*—the one who takes the same raw material as is available to everyone else—the same 88 piano keys, paints and canvases, the dictionary full of words, the same set of surgical instruments—and does something idiosyncratic with them.

If the rest of us are the reliable, predictable synapses of the social machinery, they are the misfires. If their way of seeing or saying becomes the clichéd way of seeing or of saying in some epistemic community—some subculture—we may idolize them (as we did Michael Jackson or Albert Einstein). Or we may, to avoid the discomfort of change in our ways of seeing and of saying, eliminate them or simply ignore them.

The *bricoleur* uses whatever tools there may be at hand to fashion a "custom-made" conception or expression of something. The rest of us deal in ready-mades: off the rack conceptions and expressions. What is information to the one is not what is information to the other. And what comprises communication for the one is not what comprises communication for the other. The differences are remarkable, and bear upon how we define such terms as "communication" and "information."

Conclusion

So what should we conclude from all of this?

First, that the world we inhabit—all of us—is not *the* world, but the communicated world, the communicable world. We confuse ourselves because we posit the world and then concern ourselves mainly with the truthfulness of this or that interpretation of it. The human world *is* the interpreted, the interpretable, world.

Therefore, our main target of inquiry should be how people do that, and what the consequences have been, and might be. If we did so, we would be struck by the fact that all communication—which is to say, all ways of taking the world into account and of expressing oneself in it—is systemic in nature. For the most part, a way of taking the world into account requires a way of expressing it, and vice versa. It also implies that these systems of perception and comprehension are sufficient unto themselves, and are not, except for our Western bias, necessarily to be measured against the truth of the matter—which is in any case merely another way of perceiving and of expressing the world.

The world that people come to see is the world that they are capable of expressing; and what they are capable of expressing is not enabled and constrained by what *is*, but by what others are capable of comprehending. So a tropism defines a trope, and vice versa. We are not moved to enlightenment by "facts," or by information, or even by the "truth." The only world that counts is the one which others see by what they say, and what I may see by what I can say. That I must rely upon automatisms both to "see" the world that is spoken of, and to express the world that is thus seen, is no more than the nature of the beast. We humans cannot do it any other way.

So the logic of how we actually communicate one with another; and the logic of how we inform ourselves, or even of the nature of information in a given society—these are not the logics of our theorizing about such matters to date. We skipped square one. Perhaps we should not have.

Second, we conclude from our discussion that tropes and things constitute all of the metacommunication in social life, without which no communication of any sort could occur. They comprise the unexamined place where we all stand in order to examine the world. They constitute Polanyi's "tacit knowledge," the heart of the matter.

Third, we conclude that all communication—all instances of informing oneself of the world, about the world—is typically of one of two sorts. It is either automatistic, occurring instantaneously without our conscious attention or direction—which is why such metaphors as tropism and trope may be useful. Or it is problematic: How does one know when or whether to move one's head in or over, or to close one's eyes or adjust one's lips, for the first kiss? Such ways as we might have of navigating the intricacies of everyday life are either automatic or problematic.

They are not, as we have studied thus far, somewhere in between.

Note

This essay was prepared during the early fall of 1986, when I was Distinguished Visiting Professor at Kuring-gai College of Advanced Education, just outside of Sydney, Australia. I am grateful to my colleagues there not only for their fine hospitality and graciousness, but for the intellectual stimulation they provided. Ka pai.

19

Resonance and the Energy of Intelligence

Gordon L. Miller

In the spirit of general systems theory, this essay focuses on the concept of resonance as a way of highlighting isomorphisms in a large variety of systems. Resonance is essentially an acoustical concept, but its use as a metaphor in the fields of physics, chemistry, biology, medicine, psychology, and communication is examined here. The connection between the notions of resonance and intelligence is drawn out by analyzing the nature of order, or structure. Following the suggestion of David Bohm that the apprehension of order lies in the ability to perceive similarities and differences, and that this ability is an essential attribute of intelligence, the concept of resonance—a phenomenon based on the special relationship that exists between similar structures—is proposed as a useful way to describe and to unify our understanding of intelligent activity in various sorts of systems.

> *Were the eye not attuned to the Sun,*
> *The Sun could never be seen by it.*
> —Goethe

Introduction

In this age of professional specialization and intellectual fragmentation, the perception and elaboration of a general principle that crosses conceptual and disciplinary boundaries can have a much-needed integrating and healing effect. Such healing is the avowed purpose of Bertalanffy's (1968)

349

theory of general systems as "a general science of wholeness." In that book, *General System Theory*, Bertalanffy develops the notion of isomorphism, or structural similarity, as an essential element of the systems view of the world. He sees the subject matter of general systems theory as "the formulation and derivation of those principles which are valid for 'systems' in general" (p. 32), regardless of the particular kind of entities involved. In the process-oriented paradigm of self-organization represented by Bohm (1980), Jantsch (1980), Haken (1983), and Prigogine (1984), these systems similarities could perhaps more appropriately be called "isodynamics."

Bertalanffy (1968) proposes that a general system theory could be "a useful tool providing, on the one hand, models that can be used in, and transferred to, different fields, and safeguarding, on the other hand, from vague analogies which often have marred the progress in these fields" (p. 34). In this regard, Bertalanffy suggests that the perception and investigation of similarities in various systems should be guided not by "vague analogies" but by more strict and logically sound "homologies" (pp. 84–85). The concept of resonance holds some interesting descriptive and explanatory possibilities with regard to various sorts of systems. In this essay we examine some of these possibilities, particularly the possibilities this concept presents for describing these system isodynamics as a form of intelligent activity.

The Nature of Resonance

The concept of resonance is fundamentally an acoustical concept—literally the term means "a re-sounding." When a sound wave of one frequency strikes a body that will vibrate naturally at the same frequency, the vibration of the body is called "sympathetic vibration," and resonance refers to the resultant reinforcement of sound. In this essay the term "resonance" refers to this process as a whole, i.e., to the amplification of energy and to the sympathetic vibration upon which this amplification is based.

If a tuning fork of a particular frequency is struck in the presence of an entire set of tuning forks representing each note of a musical scale, the fork in the set corresponding to the frequency of the solitary fork will begin to vibrate automatically, or sympathetically (along with some of the other forks to a much lesser degree). This resonance response rests upon the natural similarity of structure of the two forks. The selective nature of resonance activity is further demonstrated in radio and television tuning, in which the frequency of the oscillating or resonating circuit in the receiver is adjusted so that it resonates with, and therefore selects, a particular frequency and program from out of the larger set of possible programs.

There are, of course, innumerable variations of this basic principle, and resonance does not require strictly identical structures. Some form and degree of matching must exist, however, if resonance, and the implied amplification of energy, is to occur. Following is a survey of some of the contexts outside the realm of acoustics in which the concept of resonance has been utilized as a metaphor to aid in the understanding and description of various sorts of systems.

The Modulation of the Metaphor

Physics.   The notion of resonance appears in physics in several places. The selective response of atoms or atomic nuclei to the presence of certain magnetic fields is called magnetic resonance. At the subatomic level the concept is employed in connection with the reaction channels of colliding subatomic particles. These channels represent the flow of energy in various patterns and frequencies and the probability of interaction of various channels is described on the basis of resonance principles. When appropriate frequencies come into contact, the channels begin to resonate and a resonance particle is formed. These particles are so extremely unstable and ephemeral that they do not qualify as particles or "objects" in the sense of classical physics, and could just as easily be described as "events."

Chemistry.   Linus Pauling (1948) has made the concept of resonance the cornerstone of his very influential theory of chemical bonding. Pauling integrated findings from quantum mechanics into his chemical investigations and thus interpreted electrons as spread out wave forms which often contain several frequencies that will resonate in the presence of other similarly structured electrons. This resonance response results in a fairly stabilized interaction between the electrons so that the atoms involved are bonded into a particular compound.

Biology.   In a recent and controversial theory of biological morphogenesis, Rupert Sheldrake (1981) has proposed that the emergence of biological forms is guided by a process he calls "morphic resonance." He suggests that developing embryos of a particular species are attuned to spatial structures called morphogenetic fields, which are analogous to magnetic fields in being invisible but nevertheless physically influential. These fields are set up and sustained through the repetition of specific biological forms throughout the history of a species. The development of a newly emerging organism is then influenced through its morphic resonance with an appropriate, i.e., similarly structured, set of morphogenetic fields.

Medicine. In a medical context, the concept of resonance has been invoked to describe the central process in the art and science of homoeopathic medicine, as developed by Hahnemann (1921), and Vithoulkas (1980). Extending the basic Pythagorean doctrine that "like knows like," homoeopathic medicine's fundamental principle is "like *cures* like." This idea is called the Law of Similars and states that "any substance which can produce a totality of symptoms in a healthy human being can cure that totality of symptoms in a sick human being" (Vithoulkas, 1980, p. 98). A state of resonance is therefore set up between the similar disease patterns in the patient and in the therapeutic substance. The ensuing amplification of energy helps the patient to overcome the disorder.

Psychology. Considering the acoustical origins of the concept of resonance, it is quite understandable that the concept apparently found its first and fullest psychological application in the study of hearing. Gaspard Bauhin, a Swiss anatomist, proposed a resonance theory of hearing in 1605, followed, in 1683, by the much more sophisticated theory of the French anatomist Joseph Guichard Du Verney. While these seventeenth-century theories presaged important later developments in auditory theory, they were based on a rather limited knowledge of the finer structure of the inner ear (Stevens & Warshofsky, 1965, pp. 53–54). But developments in otological anatomy were forthcoming in the nineteenth century, largely due to improved microscopic instruments and techniques. These developments were integrated into the physiological psychology of the nineteenth-century scientific virtuoso Hermann von Helmholtz. In his resonance or "place" theory of auditory perception, proposed in 1863, he described the basilar membrane in the ear as a resonator which vibrates, at different rates in different places, to a range of sound wave frequencies (Helmholtz, 1863).

The major twentieth-century version of a place theory is Georg von Bekesy's (1949; 1953) "traveling wave" theory. This theory suggests that a sound impulse sends a wave sweeping across the basilar membrane, which resonates selectively at certain places to particular frequencies. Bekesy also extended this idea to the study of skin perception, showing that the sensitivity of the human skin may also be a function of selective responses to the frequencies of traveling waves (Bekesy, 1955). Bekesy, though trained as a physicist and employed originally as a communication engineer, received the 1961 Nobel Prize in physiology and medicine for his investigations of the inner ear.

Resonance-type theories have also been proposed by the brain scientist Karl Lashley (1950) in his influential studies on memory and his unsuccessful "search for the engram" or neurological memory trace, and by Donald Hebb (1949) with his theory of cortical reverberation. More recently James J. Gibson has introduced the concept of resonance in a critique of the idea that the nervous system lends structure or organization to environmental information, and he extends this theme into a discussion of the role of recognizing and remembering in the establishment of perceptual meaning. In his book *The Senses Considered as Perceptual Systems,* Gibson (1966) says that "instead of postulating that the brain constructs information from the input of a sensory nerve, we can suppose that the centers of the nervous system, including the brain, resonate to information" (p. 267). Gibson's approach to perception has given great impetus to the ecological movement in contemporary psychology, the fundamental belief that human beings mirror the structure of the natural world. References to resonance as an explanatory principle can be found in various places in the writings of these psychologists (see also Gibson, 1979; Michaels & Carello, 1981; Shaw & Bransford, 1977).

In the past two decades the concept of resonance has been employed in quite precise and technical ways in the study of perception. Cornsweet (1970) uses the term to describe the interaction, or "fittedness," of certain wavelengths of light with the visual pigment in the retina. The concept has also become associated with the techniques of Fourier analysis and Fourier synthesis—mathematical functions for alternatively selecting out and building up complex patterns or wave forms from smaller component waves—which are now commonly used in the investigation of a variety of perceptual processes. Karl Pribram (1971; 1979; 1984) has built his holographic theory of memory and perception around the suggestion that the brain can be understood as a "wave form analyzer" that resonates to, and therefore recognizes, patterns in the environment. In Pribram's words:

> We are always constructing our own reality out of a great deal of what ordinarily seems like noise. But it is a structured noise: We have ears like radio tuners, and eyes like television tuners that pick out particular programs. (1984, p. 178)

Similarly, Grossberg (1982) develops the idea of "adaptive resonance" as a way of understanding the basic act of recognizing something. He suggests that

> the functional unit of perception and cognition is a state of resonant activity within the system as a whole. Only the resonant state enters consciousness. Only the resonant state can drive adaptive changes in system structure, such as learned changes. The resonant state is therefore called an *adaptive resonance.* (P. 1; see also Grossberg, 1980, 1984)

The general idea in these theories is that an organism is selectively tuned to respond to certain aspects of its environment and not others.

With regard to parapsychological phenomena, Jantsch (1980) has pointed out that subconscious influences (manifested in a variety of physiological responses) between persons in remote locations, but in states of particular sensitivity, can be described in terms of resonance. He says that the experimental arrangement used in such studies at the Stanford Research Institute has succeeded in making such phenomena reproducible.

Communication.   While the concept of resonance does not appear to have been developed explicitly in the history of communication theory, it is contained rather implicitly in much of this theorizing. A particularly good example is Schramm's (1954) model of communication in which he employs the notion of "field of experience" and emphasizes the importance of similar "tuning" of sender and receiver as the essence of communication. More recently Ruben (1984, pp. 60–62) has proposed a general model that describes communication as the process through which organisms establish "commonness" with their environments and fellow creatures.

Certain communication theorists have made direct reference to the idea of resonance in their work. Marshall McLuhan's (1974) concept of a "global theater" emphasizes the increasing interdependence of human events as a result of the revolutions in electronics and communication technology that followed the launch of Sputnik in 1957. He says that that event stimulated the emergence of "ecological thinking," and he describes the situation as follows:

> Ecological thinking and planning have always been native to preliterate man, since he lived not visually but acoustically. Instead of having external goals and objectives, he sought to maintain an equilibrium among the components of his environment in order to ensure survival. Paradoxically, electronic man shares much of the outlook of preliterate man, because he lives in a world of simultaneous information, which is to say, a world of resonance in which all data influence other data. (P. 49)

Gerbner et al. (1980) present a much stronger application of the resonance concept in their study of the ways in which television contributes to the cultivation of certain conceptions of reality in its viewers. They identify two basic processes involved in the dynamics of such cultivation—"mainstreaming" and "resonance." Mainstreaming refers to "the cultivation of general concepts of social reality"; resonance denotes "the amplification of issues particularly salient to certain groups of viewers" (p. 10). These two processes are thought to account for the differences between groups of television viewers, specifically with regard to the connection between the television world and the real life world:

> The relationship of real life experience to television's cultivation of conceptions of reality entails not only this generalized notion of "mainstreaming" but also special cases of particular salience to specific issues. This is what we call "resonance." When what people see on television is most congruent with everyday reality (or even *perceived* reality), the combination may result in a coherent and powerful "double dose" of the television message and significantly boost cultivation. Thus, the congruence of the television world and real-life circumstances may "resonate" and lead to markedly amplified cultivation patterns. (Gerbner, et al., 1980, p. 15)

The perceived commonness of the two worlds thus forms the basis for an intensified embracing of a particular view of reality.

Implications

Having thus reviewed some of the evidence for the presence of resonance-type activity in a variety of contexts, we must inquire into the nature of this apparent similarity of structure and function across systems. To say that something special happens when similar structures coincide is to say nothing truly analogical or metaphorical. To call this something special *resonance,* however, is indeed metaphorical, since one is carrying the meaning of the term beyond its original acoustical context and applying it in other contexts which exhibit an apparent similarity. The crucial element in the concept of resonance is that with it we can describe the way in which certain structures are selected and stabilized from out of a larger ensemble of possibilities, regardless of the particular kind of entities or systems involved.

An influential forerunner of both general systems theory and the self-organization approach is Whitehead's organismic philosophy. Whitehead (1925) has attempted to do justice to the essential integration or wholeness of reality with his proposal that the most fundamental category, more fundamental than the category of material things, is that of *organism*. A basic tenet of Whitehead's philosophy is that the qualities and characteristics of things arise from an underlying matrix of intricate internal relations, and that a change in the nature of these relations makes for a change in the nature of the substances involved. Whitehead thought that the natural world is thoroughly organismic (and therefore alive), and said that "biology is the study of the larger organisms; whereas physics is the study of the smaller organisms" (1925, p. 103).

The concept of resonance is related to Whitehead's notion of organism by virtue of the fact that Whitehead saw organisms as essentially periodic, or vibratory, phenomena. In his view, "each primordial element will be an organized system of vibratory streaming of energy . . . [and] apart from being a periodic system, such an element would have no existence" (1925, pp. 35–36). One of the primary benefits of the resonance metaphor is the possibility it presents for understanding this basic organizing activity, which makes things what they are, as a manifestation of a universal intelligence.

Resonance and Intelligence

The nature of intelligence is a hotly debated topic, but perhaps we can gain a clue into this mystery by examining the essentially equivalent term "rationality." The root of rationality is "ratio," and ratio implies the relationship of one thing to something else—the ratio of the sides of a triangle, the ratio of hydrogen atoms to oxygen atoms in a molecule of water, the ratio of professors to students in a university or of city folk to country folk in a society. To go one step further, ratios are indications of the structure of things—of triangles, molecules, universities, and societies. And to understand the nature of structure is to understand something very fundamental, something closely tied to rationality or intelligence. We will therefore consider briefly the nature of structure in an effort to reveal the link between the concepts of resonance and intelligence.

The Concept of Structure

Structure is such a fundamental and pervasive aspect of experience that it defies definition. This is because structure, or order, is actually implied in every definition since any intelligible definition necessarily involves some sensible (i.e., orderly) language or symbol system. The existence of structure is therefore a prerequisite for the development and intelligibility of any system of symbols (from poetry and mythology to mathematics) or indeed for any intelligible experience at all. Since linguistic definitions of the concept of structure fail to reach the root of the issue, we must resort to the more ostensive method of pointing out examples of it in a variety of contexts if we are to convey the meaning of this fundamental feature of reality. Bohm (1980) suggests that the key to a general way of apprehending order in various contexts is *"to give attention to similar differences and different similarities"* (pp. 115–16).

Bohm explains this proposal:

> Let us illustrate these notions in terms of a geometric curve. To simplify the example, we shall approximate the curve by a series of straight-line segments of equal length.

FIGURE 19.1
The Concept of Structure

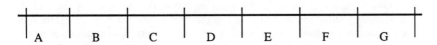

Source: Bohm, 1980.

We begin with a straight line. As shown in Figure 19.1, the segments in a straight line all have the same direction, so that their only difference is in the position. The difference between segment A and segment B is thus a space displacement which is similar to the difference between B and C, and so on. We may therefore write

A:B::B:C::C:D::D:E.

This expression of "ratio" or "reason" may be said to define a curve of *first class,* i.e., a curve having only one independent difference. (P. 116)

Bohm then considers the structure of circles and helixes, which display curves of second class and third class respectively, as well as of other more complicated structures that involve not only similar differences but also different similarities of those differences:

By thus introducing what is in effect the beginning of a hierarchy of similarities and differences, we can go on to curves of arbitrarily high degrees of order. As the degrees become indefinitely high, we are able to describe what have commonly been called "random" curves—such as those encountered in Brownian motion. This kind of curve is not determined by any finite number of steps. Nevertheless, it would not be appropriate to call it "disordered," i.e., *having no order whatsoever.* Rather, it has a certain kind of order which is of an indefinitely high degree.

In this way, we are led to make an important change in the general language of description. We no longer use the term "disorder" but instead we distinguish between different degrees of order (so that, for example, there is an unbroken gradation of curves, beginning with those of first degree, and going on step by step to those that have generally been called "random." (Pp. 116–17)

But since Bohm, echoing Whitehead's organismic views, believes that all structures or objects are actually "events," he introduces the term "structation" in order to shift attention from the relatively static appearance of "structures" to the underlying active process that produces such structures:

Structation thus implies a *harmoniously organized* totality of order and measures, which is both *hierarchic* (i.e., built on many levels) and *extensive* (i.e., "spreading out" on each level). The Greek root of the word "organize" is "ergon" which is based on a verb meaning "to work." So one may think of all aspects of a structure as "working together" in a coherent way. . . . Here it is important to emphasize the *essentially dynamic* nature of structation, in inanimate nature, in living beings, in society, in human communication, etc. (e.g., consider the structure of a language, which is an organized totality of everflowing movement).

The kinds of structures that can evolve, grow or be built are evidently limited by their underlying order and measure. New order and measure make possible the consideration of new kinds of structure (p. 120).

Structure implies integration and wholeness, and structation implies "flowing wholeness"—integrated and evolving patterns of differences and similarities. Structural differences that make a meaningful difference in a particular context or system constitute information in that context. Differences that do not make a difference imply missing information, and therefore constitute the entropy of the system.

Ratio and Rationality

In our discussion of order as involving sets of differences, we saw that the relationship between the parts of a structure can be expressed in terms of ratios. For a very simple and symmetrical structure such as a square, the relationship between the sides could be expressed by saying that as side *A* is to side *B*, so side *B* is to side *C*, and so on. Stated more concisely, this relationship would be A:B::B:C, etc.

The relationship between different structures can, of course, also be expressed in terms of ratios. If we had three squares *A*, *B*, and *C*, each successive one of which enclosed twice the area of the former, as illustrated below,

FIGURE 19.2
Ratio and Rationality

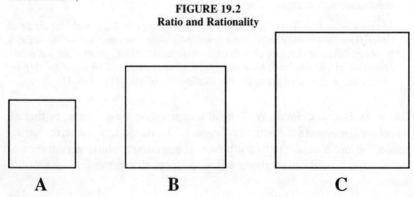

A   B   C

we could express the relationship of the area of each square to the next by a ratio of the same form as the one above: A:B::B:C. It would also be a rather simple matter to imagine, or to draw in an approximate way, what the next square in this series would look like if we were certain that the progression would continue in a regular way so that B:C::C:D.

As a further consideration, if after having been confronted with squares A, B, and C above we were confronted at a later time with three triangles displaying a similar relationship between their areas, we might have noticed that, though the objects involved are different, the relationship between them is the same. In a much more general sense, this is the essential structure of the analogical and metaphorical operations upon which much of the pattern and texture of mental life are based. Thus the analogical movement of thought expressed in the statement "the snow blankets the ground" could be analyzed into the following parts: as a blanket is to a bed, so the snow is to the ground. The formulation of this expression rests on the discernment of a similarity of relationship between the two components in these different situations.

The utilization of analogy or metaphor also plays an indispensable role in scientific discovery and explanation. Bohm (1980) has used the example of Newton's insight concerning the law of universal gravitation to illustrate this point. He says that the essence of what Newton noticed as he saw the apple fall from the tree can be expressed as follows: "As with the order of movement in the fall of an apple, so with that of the Moon, and so with *all*" (p. 114). Newton's formulation of the inverse square law to explain how the proposed gravitational force diminishes as the distance between the bodies increases also developed on the basis of essentially analogical reasoning (see Bohm, 1979; Bronowski, 1978).

The metaphorical basis of many, and perhaps all, cognitive processes has been emphasized by many thinkers (e.g., Black, 1962; Lakoff & Johnson, 1980a, 1980b; Ortony, 1979; Wheelwright, 1962). Jaynes (1976) even proposes that consciousness originated, and is sustained, on the basis of metaphor, and that "understanding a thing is to arrive at a metaphor for that thing by substituting something more familiar to us. And the feeling of familiarity is the feeling of understanding" (p. 52).

The present inquiry is concerned primarily with the proposal that a key characteristic of intelligence in general, and of the intelligence of perception in particular, is the operation of discerning similarities in different contexts, and that this operation may thus be described as a resonance process. Various theorists who have emphasized the thoughtlike quality of perception emphasize the importance of that operation (e.g., Arnheim, 1969; Bruner, 1957a, 1957b; Gregory, 1970; Helmholtz, 1867), and a leading exponent of artificial intelligence also suggests that the apprehension of "sameness-in-differentness" and the question "When are two things the same?" are deeply connected with the nature of intelligence, whether in human or machine manifestations (Hofstadter, 1979, p. 148).

Human intelligence can be seen as a manifestation of a larger intelligence, rationality, or self-organizing activity inherent in things, an activity that mediates the meaningful interaction of all types of structures. The process by which certain structural differences come to make a significant difference in a particular context, and the particular sensitivity existing between sets of similar differences, can be described in terms of resonance. The concept of resonance is therefore a valuable metaphor for describing and emphasizing intelligent operations in a wide variety of systems.

Conclusion

In focusing on the notion of resonance, we find ourselves in sympathy with one of the earliest "systems theorists" in the history of Western thought. Pythagoras enunciated the basic idea of the concept of resonance in his principle that "like is known by like" (Guthrie, 1962, pp. 206–212). The entire Pythagorean approach to thought and life was based on the belief in a universal kinship or sympathy among things, and the justification for studying philosophy (i.e., the investigation and contemplation of the orderly structure of the cosmos) was that through such study one could become identified with or attuned to the cosmos. A person would become a sort of miniature cosmos, or microcosm, by providing the conditions under which the harmonious structure of the wider cosmos, or macrocosm, could become manifest in him. If one were fully successful in this quest, as Pythagoras purportedly was, one could actually hear the music of the spheres.

Wherever resonance occurs there is an instance, in some form and degree, of like knowing like. Resonance implies that knowing is a form of identifying, because when any two things resonate, this resonance is based on some measure of identical structure in the two things. Whether the entities involved are lower organisms such as atoms and molecules, or higher organisms such as animals and human beings, their ways of knowing always imply ways of being, a point emphasized by philosophers for centuries, and in this century by physicists and other scientists as well.

To resonate means that two aspects of the world's immense structural richness have established commonness, that they have found a way of fitting together. The notion of resonance highlights the fact that were we not well fitted to our environments, whether natural or artificial, we could experience no meaningful relations—perceptual, interpersonal, or whatever—no sense of belongingness. The challenge is to provide the conditions under which such relations can be deepened and enhanced, the conditions under which intelligence can manifest itself—for a deeply meaningful life is evidence of a deeply active intelligence. We can devote time and effort to our attunement and to the attunement of others through education and other forms of discipline. But the occurrence of resonance, which gives us the experience of apprehending meaningful patterns, of gaining insight into how things fit together, is always a gift bestowed upon us from moment to moment.

Being a gift, this experience cannot be aggressively achieved; it can only be effortlessly received. And as with all resonance events, the experience of meaning implies an amplification of energy. We have all experienced the spark of a newly realized possibility, the illuminating effect of gaining an insight, or the excitement of discovering a fitting metaphor or analogy that opens up new ways of thinking. Perhaps an amplification of energy is just what is needed for the implementation of a unifying perspective and for the healing of conflict and fragmentation. Such is the task of a general science of wholeness—to envision a cosmos in which we feel at home, and to engender a world in which human beings can become whole.

References

Arnheim, R. (1969). *Visual thinking*. Berkeley, CA: University of California Press.

Bekesy, G. von. (1949). On the resonance curve and the decay period at various points on the cochlear partition. *Journal of the Acoustical Society of America, 21*(3), 245–49.

Bekesy, G. von. (1953). Description of some mechanical properties of the organ of Corti. *Journal of the Acoustical Society of America, 25*(4), 770–85.

Bekesy, G. von. (1955). Human skin perception of traveling waves similar to those on the cochlea. *Journal of the Acoustical Society of America, 27*(5), 830–41.

Bertalanffy, L. von. (1968). *General system theory: Foundations, development, applications*. New York: Braziller.

Black, M. (1962). *Models and metaphors*. Ithaca, NY: Cornell University Press.

Bohm, D. (1979). On insight and its significance, for science, education, and values. *Teachers College Record, 80*(3), 403–418.

Bohm, D. (1980). *Wholeness and the implicate order*. London: Routledge & Kegan Paul.

Bronowski, J. (1978). *The origins of knowledge and imagination*. New Haven, CT: Yale University Press.

Bruner, J.S. (1957a). Going beyond the information given. In *Contemporary approaches to cognition*. Cambridge, MA: Harvard University Press. (Reprinted in Bruner, J.S. *Beyond the information given*. New York: W. W. Norton, 1973.)

Bruner, J.S. (1957b). On perceptual readiness. *Psychological Review, 64*, 123–52. (Reprinted in Bruner, J.S. *Beyond the information given*. New York: W. W. Norton, 1973.)

Cornsweet, T.N. (1970). *Visual perception*. New York: Academic Press.

Gerbner, G., Gross, L., Morgan, M., & Sigmorielli, N. (1980). The "mainstreaming" of America: Violence profile no. 11. *Journal of Communication, 30*(3), 10–29.

Gibson, J.J. (1966). *The senses considered as perceptual systems.* Prospect Heights, IL: Waveland Press.

Gibson, J.J. (1979). *The ecological approach to visual perception.* Boston: Houghton Mifflin.

Gregory, R.L. (1970). *The intelligent eye.* New York: McGraw-Hill.

Grossberg, S. (1980). Direct perception or adaptive resonance? *Behavioral and Brain Sciences, 3,* 385–86.

Grossberg, S. (1982). *Studies of mind and brain.* Dordrecht, Holland: D. Reidel.

Grossberg, S. (1984). Some psychophysiological and pharmacological correlates of a developmental, cognitive and motivational theory. In R. Karrer, J. Cohen, & P. Tueting (Eds.), *Brain and information: Event-related potentials.* New York: New York Academy of Sciences.

Guthrie, W.K.C. (1962). *A history of Greek philosophy* (Vol. I: *The earlier presocratics and the Pythagoreans*). Cambridge: Cambridge University Press.

Hahnemann, S. (1921). *Organon of medicine:* Reprint 1982. Los Angeles: J.P. Tarcher.

Haken, H. (1983). *Synergetics: Nonequilibrium phase transitions and self-organization in physics, chemistry, and biology* (3d rev. & enlarged ed.). Berlin: Springer-Verlag.

Hebb. D.O. (1949). *The organization of behavior.* New York: Wiley.

Helmholtz, H. von. (1863). *On the sensations of tone.* 3d English ed. Trans. from the 4th German ed. by Alexander J. Ellis. 1895. London: Longmans, Green. (Rep. 1895)

Helmholtz, H. von. (1867). *Treatise on physiological optics* (Vol. 3). (Trans. from the 3d German ed.). J.P.C. Southall (Ed.). New York: Dover, 1962.

Hofstadter, D.R. (1979). *Godel, Escher, Bach: An eternal golden braid.* New York: Vintage.

Jantsch, E. (1980). *The self-organizing universe.* Oxford: Pergamon.

Jaynes. J. (1976). *The origin of consciousness in the breakdown of the bicameral mind.* Boston: Houghton Mifflin.

Lakoff, G., & Johnson, M. (1980a). The metaphorical structure of the human conceptual system. *Cognitive Science, 4,* 195–208.

Lakoff, G., & Johnson, M. (1980b). *Metaphors we live by.* Chicago: University of Chicago Press.

Lashley, K.S. (1950). In search of the engram. In *Physiological mechanisms in animal behavior* (symposium no. 4, *Soc. Exper. Biol.*). New York: Academic Press.

McLuhan, M. (1974). At the moment of Sputnik the planet became a global theater in which there are no spectators, but only actors. *Journal of Communication, 24*(1), Winter, 48–58.

Michaels, C.F., & Carello, C. (1981). *Direct perception.* Englewood Cliffs, NJ: Prentice-Hall.

Ortony, A. (Ed.). (1979). *Metaphor and thought.* Cambridge: Cambridge University Press.

Pauling, L. (1948). *The nature of the chemical bond.* 2d ed. Ithaca, NY: Cornell University Press.

Pribram, K.H. (1971). *Languages of the brain: Experimental paradoxes and principles in neuropsychology.* New York: Brandon House.

Pribam, K.H. (1979). Holographic memory. *Psychology Today, 12*(9), February, 71–84.

Pribram, K.H. (1984). The Holographic hypothesis of brain function: A meeting of minds. In S. Grof (Ed.), *Ancient wisdom and modern science.* Albany, NY: State University of New York Press.

Pribram, K.H., Nuwer, M., & Baron, R.J. (1974). The holographic hypothesis of memory structure in brain function and perception. In D.H. Krantz, R.C. Atkinson, R.D. Luce, & P. Suppes (Eds.), *Contemporary developments in mathematical psychology: Vol. II—Measurement, psychophysics, and neural information processing.* San Francisco: W.H. Freeman.

Prigogine, I., & Stengers. (1984). *Order out of chaos: Man's new dialogue with nature.* New York: Bantam.

Ruben, B.D. (1984). *Communication and human behavior.* New York: Macmillan.

Schramm, W. (1954). How communication works. In W. Schramm (Ed.), *The process and effects of mass communication.* Urbana, IL: University of Illinois Press.

Shaw, R., & Bransford, J. (Eds.). (1977). *Perceiving, acting, and knowing: Toward an ecological psychology.* Hillsdale, NJ: Lawrence Erlbaum.

Sheldrake, R. (1981). *A new science of life.* Los Angeles: J.P. Tarcher.

Stevens, S.S., Warshofsky, F., & the Editors of *Life.* (1965). *Sound and hearing.* New York: Time.

Vithoulkas, G. (1980). *The science of homeopathy.* New York: Grove.

Wheelwright, P. (1962). *Metaphor and reality.* Bloomington, IN: Indiana University Press.

Whitehead, A.N. (1925). *Science and the modern world.* Reprint 1953. New York: Macmillan.

Whitehead, A.N. (1929). *Process and reality.* Corrected ed., D.R. Griffin & D.W. Sherburne, (Eds.). 1978. New York: The Free Press.

20

Thinking in Museums: Reflections among Masks

David Carr

This essay describes the museum as a setting for thought and reflection, an environment where the museum user carries and explores personal contexts in order to learn. These contexts include knowledge, memory, and the continuous everyday experiences that configurate individual lives. Informed by these contexts, museum learners engage in encounters with objects, information, other people; above all, they encounter ideas. Such encounters involve subtle, invisible, and largely private behaviors, leading to the active construction of knowledge. Much of this knowledge has to do with an awareness of pattern and order in the museum's objects and experiences. The learner reveals these awarenesses by using language to express questions, to communicate with companions, and to capture the information in the museum setting that leads the learner on. Museum use also involves participation in a community of knowing, and in thinking that exemplifies Polanyi's concepts of "indwelling" and "personal knowledge."

At the Field Museum in Chicago, in the rooms devoted to Maritime Peoples of the Arctic and Northwest Coast, one finds behind a wall of glass a wall of masks. Each face is similar, yet no two are the same. Eye- and mouth-holes are fixed and empty. Wooden, painted, some marked with ivory, they are elemental, powerful faces. Seemingly startled, angry, and amused, they are ceremonial images; once they looked into other civilizations and beyond them, to spirit worlds. The museum user observes these masks; looks back and forth, comparing; makes notes; sketches several faces in a notebook; steps back. And stepping back, another face appears among the false faces of the Inuit, reflected in the glass: almost as wooden, and similarly startled, it is his own.

The user's living face among the masks of the museum reminds us that the user's presence among these objects brings another unspoken fabric to the museum, part history and memory, part feeling and response. The power of these masks, out of time and under glass, is transformed by the museum and given to the museum user—to the mind in the museum—for use among all his other experiences and thoughts. For the scholar who has attended to museums and their objects over time, these thoughts have led to notebook after notebook of reflections on the thinking—the scholar calls it "cognitive management"—that characterizes museum experiences.

Among masks and paintings, observing natural specimens and dioramas, counting the ribs of prehistoric skeletons, admiring the artifacts of other times and cultures, the museum user thinks. Thinking of museums, thinking in museums, sometimes lost in silent rooms, the user asks naive, occasionally bewildered questions about where she is, or what happens as he sees into the worlds captured there. There is a scientific side to this naiveté; the questions that move the museum user rarely change, replicating the unknowns that open the museum and its objects to vision, memory, and comprehension: What has been brought here? What am I looking at? What am I looking for? What can I find in this? What is happening to me here? What is expected of me?

These questions help to organize our ignorances. They are particularly useful in the museum, where our tendency is to present ourselves (perhaps out of discomfort among the passionate visions of artists or the rich complexity of other cultures) as "knowing" and full of data about what we see (Morris, 1965). Naive questions might best be thought of as essentially contemplative statements that show a light touch, in contrast to the intensity of more purposeful inquiries—questions in the strong grip of certain themes, traditions, or methods (Krantz & Bacon, 1977). Naive inquiries are exploratory and responsive to an invitation to ask; they neither tell nor know too much, though their simplicity may belie a more complex agenda. Such questions are particularly fitting for the nurturant, uncoercive museum, the most exploratory and least hortatory of cultural institutions.

In thoughtful museum experiences, the user creates a frame for the encounter. One looks and writes, photographs where not restricted, speaks softly to a companion or a tape recorder, makes notes, thinks some more, moves away, looks elsewhere, goes back again for another look.

Yet, in every museum, even after a challenging day of documenting the visible, the most important matter at hand is what cannot be seen or described, something suppressed or unexpressed in the place.

Museums hold objects that speak about more than themselves, objects that, in the words of Paul Valéry in "Man and the Sea Shell" (1964), "stand out from the common disorder of perceptible things" (p. 7). The museum user is drawn by these objects. They resonate with implications, stories about processes and passages. They invite witnesses, encounters, conversations, invisible transactions, inaudible dialogues. Such encounters amuse us, renew us, help us to think and see differently. As we are first drawn to museums by the objects kept there, we are also and perhaps more powerfully drawn by what they promise: to move us beyond the frames of mind we are in at the moment we enter. The museum is magnetic, inviting the user to subtle moments of becoming, moments of moving forward, or of growing up.

Stephen Weil (1983), deputy director of the Hirshhorn Collection, lists a slough of museum roles. Though this list is generated with the art museum in mind, it is widely applicable to museums of other kinds. Some of these roles are familiar: (1) preservation, (2) display, (3) ownership in the name of the public mass, who can use the museum for (4) recreation, and (5) education—as (6) a "temple of contemplation," or (7) a center for scholarship. Weil also sees the museum as (8) a journalist, reporting to the public about what is new; (9) a connoisseur or arbiter of what is good or great; (10) a patron or advocate of difficult or neglected ideas or work.

The less familiar roles Weil lists are worth counting, too. Consider the museum as (11) a symbol of power, wealth, cultural elitism; (12) an influence on the migration of objects; (13) part of a national museum network; (14) an agent of social change; (15) a center for the romantic image of the artist ("The more mythic the artist, the greater will be the public response. Van Gogh packs them in every time" [p. 51].); and finally (16) the museum as a monastery—in Weil's words: "The museum as a community of people committed to the truth that the visual is a separate, vital, and important part of human experience" (p. 51).

Weil sees this last role—the exaltation and separation of the visual—as a unifying image, the museum role that adds coherence to all other roles. "To see well," he says, "is to live richly, and the museum can be a school for seeing, a place where seeing is celebrated" (p. 51). This visual celebration pervades virtually all museums; they are places for all senses, but especially for vision. What one remembers is what one sees. And yet, as Weil murmurs praise for the visual, the learner's naive questions must be asked. And one thinks of John Cotton Dana, founder of the Newark Museum, who in *The Gloom of the Museum* (1917) derided museums built as "gazing temples" set aside in parks where their remoteness could breed an aristocracy—the acerbic Dana called them "high priests of a peculiar cult" (p. 17). In contrast, when Dana described his vision of "the new museum," he asked: "What shall the new museum collect?" and answered himself: "First of all, ideas" (p. 35).

The ideational processes of the museum involve objects in contexts suffused with information and rich with meaning. Thinking in museums, the user thinks of objects surrounded by ideas. Despite Weil's advocacy for the visual, the museum role that subsumes all others is conceptual and informative: the museum informs the user's ways of knowing and changing, ways of transforming experiences, memories, and responses to meanings. While the museum and its objects are formative in these responses, a museum's power as an informing institution rests not on its objects alone but on its human contents as well—those persons who use the museum, their conversations, and engagements. The passive object informs the user's perceptions, stimulates vision and thought, and nurtures the meanings that move through the active mind in the museum.

The conspicuous roles and functions Weil describes cluster around the notion that museums are truly about the objects they contain. An alternative view, intended to supplement Weil's emphasis on the visible, is that it is more likely that museums are about mutual nurturance between museums and the societies that keep them, the communities that support them, and the persons who use them. In contrast to the museum as a monastery devoted to the exaltation of the visible, the museum is more emphatically about the *in*visible. Its purpose may be not what meets the eye, but what meets the sensibility—the capacity for thought and feeling— of the human being. Literally, the museum is an objective environment; we bring our naturally intense subjectivity to it. Thoughtful experiences there are blends of private, unspoken meanings brought to bear on public encounters with objects.

The museum is an evocative text, a private mnemonic environment that summons a range of memories, thoughts, and meanings—images like those we find surviving in diaries and letters, in accumulated snapshots of enduring experiences, in fragments and allusions. The user carries permanent, evolving texts and an array of private captivities: visions, dreams, encounters without language. In the presence of objects we go beyond objects to recognize our continuous histories. Out of these continuities we articulate silent hypotheses, and as we gain new information, we alter them. Each new encounter in the museum means the revision of one life: new understandings, even drastic or unexpected reorganizations expand the bursting backpack we carry.

The museum is a place for the dreamer to see private dreams in public places, deep memories framed anew. The content of the museum has to do with choices and desires, with things that please the senses, satisfy values, and explore human fears. In museums we are living examples of Jerome Bruner's idea that "perceiving takes place in a tuned organism" (1973, p. 92). The museum evokes those strands of experience and memory that human beings use to attune themselves, to remember themselves as actors framed by the continuities in their lives.

The museum is a public space for private feelings. The intensity of such privacy indicates the power of the museum to isolate its users in contemplation, to allow them to engage with an object and its surrounding, and beyond that, to explore its meanings. "Theoretical concepts are not handled in empty space," Rudolf Arnheim (1969, p. 111) writes. Whatever the museum or collection of objects at hand, museum encounters are acts of the imagination, and privacy is the necessary condition for these explorations. Looking at objects in museums is active, not passive, a process of construction and reconstruction. In museums we are led by objects to imagine; in Valéry's (1964) words, we "substitute our own machinations for the gaps in our knowledge" (p. 20). Valéry remarks that explanations and acts of interpretation are ways to *remake* objects in thought. In the museum, the life of the user may be seen as a closed referential field containing past and present, real world and dream world. Across this field, the mind moves its meanings.

Bruner (1973) describes the most characteristic thing about our mental life as the tendency constantly to go beyond the information given. How well does the museum assist this, or make it happen, in us? How does the environment assist the user to make well-informed (coherent, logical, fulfilling) choices? How well does the museum invite us to go beyond the objects it contains, to contemplate their conceptual dimensions, their origins, their social meanings?

Every museum stimulates in the user a form of "indwelling," to use Polanyi's (1958) concept, which means an interiorization or a surrender to contemplated objects: "This is neither to observe nor to handle them, but to live in them" (p. 196).

Contemplation dissolves the screen, stops our movement through experience and pours us straight into experience; we cease to handle things and become immersed in them. Contemplation has no ulterior intention or ulterior meaning; in it we cease to deal with things and become absorbed in the inherent quality of our own experience, for its own sake. And as we lose ourselves in contemplation, we take on an impersonal life in the objects of our contemplation; while these objects themselves are suffused by a visionary gleam which lends them a new vivid and yet dreamlike reality. (P. 197)

Such forms of personal knowing move one toward understanding what it is to be a maker, a source of evolution, pattern, invention, design—how the life and decisions of the author dwell within the made object. Valéry's (1964) naive questions about the sea shell are useful—Who *made* this? of *what?* and *why?* The indweller lives through the maker's eye and hand, the better to see fine order and curious accidents, this blend of colors or forms, that aberration or surprise.

In this way the museum user can construct knowledge of creativity and its patterns, and can come to understand the acts of generative lives. Knowledge of objects and the courage or skill to make them appears here in intimate terms—the maker held this in her hands; now it is here. In the object, one might think, there is a part of the life I could have led, the vision I could have had, the adventure I could not risk. Embedded in this romance is the need to grasp and understand the nature of handmade life, and the object as a handmade piece: unique, capturing the moment of mutual possession shared by the thing and its maker. This identification with the artist may be just one of the many "inner images" (to use Jung's term) one brings to museums, and it may be suggestive of new creative choices open to the life of the user.

And where is "handmade life" in the museum of technology? It is often visible in the inventor's crude prototype or cookbook demonstration, but it is also invisibly present in the idea of change and growth, of altering the narratives of everyday life by following a path of innovation and risk. Consider the flint axe and its meanings for the persons who first chipped such tools into existence in the palms of their hands. Such an axe in the hand means power and skill, an end to life controlled by accidents. The same axe in the museum implies technology, transformation, and revolution in human capability. Such axes lead to thinking about the human as the creator of his own handmade future.

There is similar power in the museum of natural history, especially among images of balance and form in the universe, in its exquisite patterns, and in the architectures of evolution, and the emergence of human mentality. To comprehend the sweep of time and the combined effects of innovation, industry, and the design that impose order on chaos is to contemplate an intellectual problem of inspiring dimensions. It is even more striking to contemplate the chaotic unknowns that remain. As Valéry (1964) writes: "We yearn for a profound geometry" (p. 6).

Everywhere one finds connections between technology and domestic human welfare. In one Philadelphia Museum, for example, a museum user finds a surprising display documenting the evolution of the city through the history of its water and gas supply systems, its police and fire departments. In another corner of the same museum is a room of maps, from deerskin to Exxon, tracing the history of the community as it filled a geographic space and created a network of roads and a system of civic technologies. These are innovations that have transformed and expanded lives. The museum is about this particular kind of remembering that is also an ordering, a bringing of the unreachable concept (the expanding dimensions of a city) into touching distance.

Even so, displayed and explained, museum objects hide themselves, and astonish our thinking. Here, in the most empirical of institutions, experience offers its continuous ultimatum. Yet in search of pattern and order, one finds the most powerful objects are those that break the rules, addressing us with their brilliant disorder. Speaking of "a crystal, a flower, a sea shell," Valéry (1964) writes:

> They present us with a strange union of ideas: order and fantasy, invention and necessity, law and exception. In their appearance we find a kind of *intention* and *action* that seem to have fashioned them rather as man might have done, but at the same time we find evidence of methods forbidden and inaccessible to us. . . . The shell which I hold and turn between my fingers, and which offers me a combined development of the simple themes of the helix and the spiral, involves me in a degree of astonishment and concentration that leads where it may: to superficial remarks and observations, naive questions, "poetic" comparisons, beginnings of reckless "theories." . . . And my mind vaguely anticipates the entire innate treasure of responses that rise within me in the presence of a thing that arrests and questions me. (Pp. 7–8)

Arrested and questioned by visible objects, we search for invisible actions and meanings, to give them words. Especially in the museum, we strive to understand the existence of an object, its similarities and differences among other objects. Our struggle is to understand the ineffable process of formation that caused it to be. "Although we ourselves were formed by imperceptible growth," Valéry (1964) reminds us, "we do not know how to create anything in that way" (p. 8).

The museum is about order and continuity of several kinds, those nearly timeless landmarks of adult knowledge that remain important and useful to us as we assemble our understanding. Some are memories, the private meanings and remembrances of early years. Some are private, familiar objects, motifs, themes, forms. Some are concepts of faith, transcendence, images of our personal gods and goddesses. Some continuous concepts inform our thinking: society, history, family; so do some disciplines: biology, astronomy. Grasp any of these strands and it can lead from everyday to the cosmos.

Everywhere one finds formative continuities or awarenesses carried from day to day: how to do one's tasks, ease aggressions, make choices, act on values, ask questions, respond to others. These daily continuities can be brought to the museum for new kinds of contemplation. Because the informing museum touches thoughts, and influences values and choices, it can change the design of one life, especially the possible future of one's own interior life. The museum reaches into the past as well, through the legacy that links the living to the dead. This is the continuity one of my students named as she described the photographed faces of Ellis Island as having "symbolic immortality." Continuities appear in the faces and objects we recognize from our own histories.

In the museum there is also the more immediate social continuity of the visitor who shares the same space with others, gazes at the same objects, contemplates the same enclosed world. No matter how diverse the actors, this continuity may range from a simple, accidental copresence to a more complex tacit or overt relationship with another person, a relationship in which museum users can find in each other models of sensitivity and response. Museum conversations are especially important to museum thinking. Objects often require dialogue because they suggest stories that must be told or messages that need a voice. Martin Nystrand (1977) describes language as a heuristic tool:

> One of the fundamental assumptions of my conception of language is that language, like intelligence, is an instrument of adaptation. . . . Language plays an instrumental role in facilitating the individual's entry into new experience. It does this by serving to construct and maintain new meanings. (P. 99)

The museum thinker needs language, and a listener. It is a hollow moment, to stand before a Breughel painting with words to speak and no one to listen. Alone at times, one must write. In one notebook are three words which were written in the presence of a carved wooden figure from the South Seas, its maker unknown: "continuity overcomes futility." Continuities include those parts of the museum that are nouns but not objects: patterns, forms, passages, inimitable acts. The museum contains and displays these continuities; the witness reaches to possess them.

When a person enters a museum, she does not withdraw from other communities she participates in; she carries them with her. As we may read fiction for the kinds of intensely felt knowing that lends vision to our own lives, we may also use the museum for knowing that is applicable in the contiguous world waiting outside the door. Museum insights are founded on broad transpersonal experiences that, crossing time and space, give visions into private, obscure, disappeared or disappearing worlds. (It is appropriate here to think of the windows so often seen in paintings by Bonnard. One may imaginatively gaze through them to find what Bonnard saw. Like the museum, Bonnard's windows invite the viewer to look beyond the room, to move out into the garden that is there.)

In every museum, there is a story, something to be told or written, allegory or history or speculation, some narrative that waits seamlessly behind the objects given. Often one must stay in one place for a while, for hours sometimes, to know or capture this story wholly. Entire collections can confer this sense of entity: how it must have been to be in a particular time or place. Again, we may find in our museums the same kinds of touching narratives experienced in novels—scenes that tell us what it must have been like to see the light at Giverny or enter the court of Henry VIII. In this way, too, one might come to see the collective power of objects in so-called primitive art collections—their strengths heightened and made coherent by concentration and juxtaposition—as messages capturing invisible unities of an ancient time and place, shared streams of belief, hope, or common dreaming.

At these moments, distances are nothing. One can share a distant horizon of constructs, images, and information. One can also see a culture's way of being powerful, of transcending smallness and isolation; its ways of having magic, of participating in the local universe. For the museum user, this is ecstasy because it implies thoughts beyond intellect or aesthetics, toward grasping directly the energy captured in objects or icons. Such moments are wonderful by their apparent immediacy to another world or another view of the world, one that can, however briefly, be possessed for oneself. Yet such passionate moments are rare in museums, because the intellect intrudes. Recall the masks behind the wall of glass.

All museums hold images, tools, and passages in the public memory, there to touch everyone, whatever their capacity to be touched. By "images" I mean the obvious things—masks, costumes, portraits, illustrations, dioramas—whatever tells or shows us how things, people, or environments appeared. "Image" is also used to evoke Kenneth Boulding's (1956) sense: as a subjective summary of our knowledge, a network of informing streams of messages, our evolving picture of the world and our place in it. It is also useful to acknowledge the importance of Jung's idea of the archetype here. The myth-creating level of mind that operates across cultures is concentrated especially in images of great faith and great love, omnipresent death, evanescent fear and joy in a threatening world. We see these archetypes in museum artifacts constantly. The enormous task of the museum user is to integrate them into individual experiences.

"Tools" here means the instruments, technologies, and techniques that imply methodological innovations or critical changes in the skills or powers of entire civilizations. These often are summarized by transforming inventions or more progressive, evolving innovations that change not only how humans do things, but how we know, think about, or capture images of things as well. Every tool or tool-like object, in this sense, is the solution to a problem. Consider the button, the camera, the calculator, the manned satellite. Over time, the innovative power of such tools is lost in the common society, where it is difficult to imagine a world without buttons. In some cases commonplace objects, tools, or instruments are artifacts themselves—musical instruments, furniture, ceramic ware, timepieces. Though such common tools may inform our lives, they become invisible, except to those who witness their evolution and the passage they imply. Museums permit us to be those witnesses.

"Passages" has two meanings here. The first suggests historic time as a line or continuum, from prehistory to some unknown future. The second kind occurs to us when we think of our personal evolutions through the labyrinthine situations of one life: crises, influences, fascinations, confusions, disorders, impenetrable mysteries. One way of evaluating a museum might be to consider its opportunities for both kinds of passage. What is the depth and complexity of the historic passage it displays? How might the museum be used to advance one's own passage? How great is the trouble it causes to our thinking? What kinds of remembering does the museum evoke? How does it resonate within the contexts of cultural and individual life? What is the scope of the world to which the museum refers? How fully does it disturb our sleep, or our sleepwalking?

To proceed thoughtfully through one life is to carry a set of constant unknowns—topics, passions, questions—that resist closure. In museums one attends to such unknowns almost unknowingly; they lead the learner to revise his working models of the world. Over time, such thinking makes lines in a nonlinear field—draws a web of continuous strands touching technology, ecology, the social memory, the family, the history of relationships.

Such thinking in museums is not extraordinary, but it is also not routine. One thinks of the scope of a museum collection, its time and topic, its *edges*. Contemplating an object, reading the thing and its written texts in search of explanations about contexts, origins, and functions, the learner also thinks of its unwritten texts, as nearly as they can be imagined: social meanings and customs, aesthetic pleasures, connections to distant lives. Noticing one's own participation and response in the museum, it is possible as well to consider the thinking of others. Some new questions appear. The questioner seeks help, more texts to read, a human explainer. All of this leads to what one needs to know next, the critical moment of museum thinking, and perhaps the essential part of any intellectual life.

Acts of thought are necessarily acts of language as well: unless a question is given words, we have no way to document its passage. Unless my companion and I speak, we teach each other nothing. When given language, these questions are like the sounds of a bat; they seek informing resonance. Knowledge here arrives through articulating our unknowns, then matching our experiences of museum things with those of recollection, reverie and anticipation. Contemplating unknowns, looking for the next question, groping, turning and tuning one's attention, defining classes and categories, projecting one bit of information onto another realm, the learner is captured by captive objects.

In the museum we are voluntary members of a transient group. Present in the presence of others, we remain private. All of us there may undergo similar, but far from identical, experiences; we may see familiar images, perhaps even travel along similar passages, and emerge into lives more alike than different. But our intensely subjective lives are certainly different in the ways and things we have come to know through thinking in museums. We can leave the museum and yet continue to inhabit it; or better, it continues to inhabit us and our knowing. We carry away our everchanging histories, newly informed by further encounters with objects. We examine what the museum contains, and are, for the moment, also among the museum's contents, temporary inhabitants of an invisible city, reconvened every day with different citizens. And then we leave, just as Valéry (1964) abandons the contemplation of the sea shell: "This sea shell has *served* me, suggesting by turns what I am, what I know, and what I do not know" (p. 29).

If this is a community, it is one whose cohesion lies in the forms of participation and knowing it offers to its population: a community of people engaged in like interior processes. We hold in common this place at this time. We think and respond and for the moment we are alive here. This cohesion may have to do with our ways of investment in museum thinking—the ways we strive to change, to become, by designing our experiences here. What we do and think in museums—classifying and fantasizing, projecting and contemplating—make us different. These events of resonance and devotion, possession and captivity that occur to us confirm that the museum is about acts of changing, becoming, knowing. It presents us with extraordinary images of the possible, and by these we nurture our growth, our maturity.

To exist, every museum must support a community of knowing, or a community of knowers, people engaged in acts of cognizance or intelligence, learners devoted to understanding images, instruments, and passages, actors participating in a range of personal and cultural continuities and patterns. These intelligent engagements are not always overt or even specific, but they are no less passionate or committed than other kinds of formative knowing. They are examples of what Michael Polanyi (1958) calls "personal knowledge": an original and indescribable "act of groping" by which we "feel our way forward" toward knowing that is both coherent and integral with the other intellectual commitments of our lives (p. 61–63).

The image of the museum as an invisible city leads one to Italo Calvino's (1974) novel *Invisible Cities* for a metaphor to counter Weil's (1983) image of the museum as a monastery. But to choose among Calvino's cities is difficult. There is the city of Tamara, covered by a "thick coating of signs." That is like a museum—messages everywhere. There is Zaira, where the dimensions of the city are based on the events of the past. For good or ill, that is the choice most museums make as well. There is Maurilia, where "the traveler is invited to visit the city and, at the same time, to examine some old post cards that show it as it used to be"— precisely what happens at any historical society. There is Euphemia, where travelers trade their memories—close to what companions exchange in museums. And there is Valdrada, comprising both itself, built above a lake, and its mirror image below. This is almost exactly right: near but untouchable reflections of our own faces, fears, and relationships.

Throughout all of these journeys, recounted in Calvino's novel by Marco Polo to the aged Kublai Khan, there is the idea of the traveler reimagining not only the cities he visits, but reinventing himself as well:

> What he sought was always something lying ahead, and even if it was a matter of the past it was a past that changed gradually as he advanced on his journey, because the traveler's past changes according to the route he has followed: not the immediate past, that is, to which each day that goes by adds a day, but the more remote past. Arriving at each new city, the traveler finds again a past of his that he did not know he had: the foreignness of what you no longer are or no longer possess lies in wait for you in foreign, unpossessed places.(P. 28–29)

Thinking of these tissues and integuments of the past, at once waiting for us and carried within, one is transported finally to the most museumlike of these invisible cities, Ersilia. Here:

> to establish the relationships that sustain the city's life, the inhabitants stretch strings from the corners of the houses, white or black or gray or black-and-white according to whether they mark a relationship of blood, of trade, authority, agency. (P. 76)

In this invisible city, even after the buildings and people disappear, the labyrinth of string remains to mark the evanescent community: "spiderwebs of intricate relationships seeking a form." Thinking in museums, one must encounter the articulate web of meaning—the phrase is Vygotsky's (1962, p. 100)—that is spun out of one life, present and past, and entangled invisibly with the transparent strands of other vanishing lives.

Note

A grant from the Rutgers University Research Council has been useful in the preparation of this work.

References

Arnheim, R. (1969). *Visual thinking*. Berkeley: University of California.
Boulding, K. (1956). *The image: Knowledge in life and society*. Ann Arbor: University of Michigan.
Bruner, J.S. (1973). *Beyond the information given*. New York: W.W. Norton.
Calvino, I. (1974). *Invisible cities*. New York, NY: Harcourt Brace Jovanovich.
Dana, J.C. (1917). *The gloom of the museum*. Woodstock, Vermont: Elm Tree Press.
Krantz, D.L., & Bacon, P. (1977). On being a naive questioner. *Human Development, 20*, 141–59.
Morris, R.E. (1965). The art museum as a communication center. *Museum News,* January, *43*(5), 26–31.
Nystrand, M. (1977). Language as discovery and exploration: Heuristic and explicative uses of language. In M. Nystrand (Ed.), *Language as a way of knowing*. Ontario: Ontario Institute for Studies in Education.
Polanyi, M. (1958). *Personal knowledge*. Chicago: University of Chicago Press.
Valéry, P. (1964). Man and the seashell. In *Aesthetics* (Trans. R. Manheim), Bollingen Series XLV, 13 (pp. 3–30). New York: Pantheon.
Vygotsky, L.S. (1962). *Thought and language* (trans. E. Hanfmann & G. Vakar), Cambridge, MA: MIT Press.
Weil, S.E. (1983). An inventory of art museum roles. In *Beauty and the beasts*. Washington, D.C.: Smithsonian Institution Press.

21

Information as an Economic Good: A Reevaluation of Theoretical Approaches

Benjamin J. Bates

Information has proved to be a problematic concept for economic theory. In particular, scholars have noted that the distinctive nature of information as a good has given rise to a series of externalities that have hampered its treatment and consideration as an economic good under traditional approaches, and that have led to a number of seeming paradoxes. Some have argued, in fact, that information should not *be treated in economic or other analyses as an economic good on theoretical grounds. This study reviews the considerations of information that have lead to this view, and finds that such conclusions are based on a limited, traditional approach to information goods. Specifically, it is suggested that an extended and redefined conceptualization of the value and costs of information goods can internalize the perceived externalities and allow the consideration of such goods as regular economic goods. The concept of the value and cost of information is extended here to a consideration of three aspects of information goods traditionally seen as problematic in economic theory.*

> The exercise of determining the quality and definition of information is one that has to be survived and gotten over, rather than resolved.
> —George Gerbner

The question of information and its economic nature is one that has plagued social scientists for decades. Due to its ubiquitous and pervasive nature, information has, by and large, defied attempts at precise definition, much less quantification. While attempts have been made to measure concretely the flow (cf. Edelstein, 1982; Ito, 1981; Pool, 1984; Takasaki and Ozawa, 1983) and value (cf. Machlup, 1962; Porat, 1978; Fukushima, 1986) of information, these have tended to aggregate only external ramifications of information rather than address the more fundamental concerns over the role of information in economics and/or the economy. As a result, these studies have tended to raise more theoretical questions than they address. In the absence of consensus on what information is (much less how it can be measured), the concept of information as an economic good has remained largely theoretical.

Yet even in theory information has remained a problematic concept in economics. That has hampered considerations of the question of the value, and/or the economics, of information in its various forms in other disciplines. The goal of this essay is to examine the problematic nature of information and to propose an extension of economic theory that may help to resolve some of the quandaries and apparent paradoxes which currently hamper economic considerations of information in the field of communication.

Information and Economics

From the beginnings of the field of economics in the eighteenth century, information has played a dual role in economic theory. First, information (as a discrete entity) can be considered as a commodity or good, and thus a subject of economic theory. Information—as a state of awareness—however, has also been one of the primary assumptions of any economic theory. Second, this reflects the ubiquitous, somewhat heterogeneous nature of information that has been noted in both economic (Black & Marchand, 1982; Hirshleifer, 1973) and noneconomic (Dervin, 1976; Korobeinikov, 1980) studies. Because this second aspect of information in economics is a feature of theory rather than the object of theory, it will be disregarded in favor of considering information as a distinctive good.

Information as an Economic Good

In economics, the concept of a good is generally defined quite broadly. Ferguson (1972), for example, defines economic goods as the ends through which the goals of economic actors are achieved. Marshall (1930, p. 54) was equally general when he used the term "goods" to "represent all desirable things, or things that satisfy human wants." Goods may be material or nonmaterial, transferable or not, free or costly. Only some of these goods, however, fall within the scope of economic science, and these are termed "commodities," or economic goods.

There has been some doubt raised in the field as to whether information can even be considered as an economic good or commodity. Krippendorf (1984) stated that information (albeit conservatively defined) was in fact not a good, although his definition of information can be made to fit his definition of a good. Economists, as a rule, have failed to make this extreme statement, although they have noted often that information violates some features generally attributed to consumer goods (Arrow, 1962; Boulding, 1966; Hall, 1981; Hirshleifer, 1973).

It is clear, though, that information is something which (1) can be transferred, (2) has some utility and (3) is capable of having a value attached to it. Therefore, despite its distinctive, problematic nature, information can be considered to be an economic good. This consideration of information as an economic good, however, has led to three basic quandaries in the economic treatment of information.

First, there is the problem of whether information is truly a public or a private good. Some economists (Boulding, 1966; Demsetz, 1967; Marshall, 1974; Stigler, 1983) have argued that information, in particular additional information about a market, creates economic value through its use, and has thus entered the realm of theory as a private good. Others, led principally by Samuelson (1954; 1958), have argued that certain features of information, notably that the consumption of information by one consumer does not affect the availability of that good to other potential users, earmarks information as a public good.

Second, there is the quandary of advertising. As Stigler (1983, p. 171) quipped: "One of the information-producing industries, advertising, is treated with a hostility that economists normally reserve for tariffs or monopolists." While recognizing that advertising may have value as information, and may be socially desirable through the reduction of market imperfections, the general argument has been that most advertising content is persuasive and misleading (therefore of little informational value) and that the supply of advertising is excessive, since it is supplied at zero price to consumers.[1] While objections have been expressed to these sentiments (e.g., Doyle, 1968), advertising is generally perceived as being economically inefficient and nonoptimal.

A third problem area exists in the suggestion that information goods inherently fail to meet the conditions of social efficiency (Arrow, 1962; Hall, 1981). This problem arises from the unique nature and features of information as a good. In particular, the problem is traced to the same features of information that make consideration of the value of information problematic; uncertainty of the precise outcome of production or exchange of information goods, the infinite reproducibility of information, and that the transfer of information goods to another does not diminish the stock of information held by the first holder.

It is primarily the last feature—when combined with the fact that information is reproducible essentially at no cost (although there may well be costs associated with the distribution of that information)—that has made economic analysis of information problematic. This situation arises from the perceived failure of information to satisfy one of modern economic theory's most basic optimality and efficiency criteria: that the marginal cost of a good equal the marginal revenue gained from the exchange of the good.[2] This problem is linked to the issue posed by the first feature of information as a good mentioned above—the difficulty of ascertaining the value of information.

We begin with an examination and consideration of the economic value of information. The resulting definition of the source and nature of value for information and information goods is then applied to the three potential paradoxes, in order to clarify and resolve any problematic aspects of information as an economic good.

The Value of Information Goods

There are two basic sources, or types, of economic value for goods recognized in economic theory. "Exchange value" is defined as the value of the good used as a medium of exchange, in trade, for other goods. "Utility (or use) value" is defined in terms of the good's usefulness to the ultimate consumer of the good. While much of economic theory has focused on exchange value as a more determinate and standardized measure, that is where information is most problematic. The best goods for exchange purposes are uniform in nature and attributes, relatively scarce, with clearly recognizable and determinable value. Information is clearly not standardized, not terribly scarce, and difficult to be given a concrete value. It would thus seem to be more appropriate to focus on the utility value of information rather than its exchange value.

There have been many considerations of the value of information, across several disciplines, mostly focusing on utility value. A conclusion reached by nearly all is that the value of a piece of information is not fixed. Hirshleifer (1973), for example, noted five general attributes affecting the value of information: certainty, diffusion, applicability, content, and decision relevance. Black and Marchand (1982) added to this by stating that the value of information is related to its mode of use as well as to structural and political factors. These, of course, are in addition to the more traditional factors affecting the value of a good such as opportunity costs and the costs associated with production and/or distribution.

While these attributes and factors may be seen as influencing the value of information, they provide little insight into the question of determining the value of information. The beginnings of such an insight may be found in Arrow (1962), who noted that the full value of information could not be known in certainty until after it had been consumed and put to use. That insight was developed and extended by Stigler (1983), Marshall (1974), and Hirshleifer (1971), who concurred in finding that the value of information arises from its use.

A further step in addressing the problem can be made by formally taking the step from a deterministic to a probabilistic framework of analysis. From the above beginnings, it is known that value is uncertain but arises from the use of the good. The development of decision theory and decision analysis has provided a theoretical framework to deal with uncertainty through probabilistic analysis. Thus, the problem of uncertain value is handled through the concept of expected value, essentially an averaging of the possible value outcomes weighted by their likelihoods.

The value of an information good, X, can then be expressed as the expected value to be gained from the use of that information good, or expressed as

$$\text{Value of } X = E[\text{use}(X)].$$

The use of expected value enables the analyst to treat the value of information goods as fixed. There is still a degree of variability inherent in this conceptualization of value in that the value of the information good X is still dependent upon context and the differing tastes or preferences of the parties involved. This, however, is not that different from more traditional goods, whose utility value to the consumer has long been considered variable in precisely the same manner, although it has not always been treated as such in economic analysis.[3] Only the concept of exchange value (for the producer) has been regarded as fixed, and for all intents and purposes considered to be the same as price.

Thus, as suggested by Coase (1974), it would seem that information goods can be treated in economic analyses in much the same manner as traditional goods: subject to the same criteria, laws, and manipulation. It should therefore be expected that information should be subject to the same optimality and efficiency criterion as traditional economic goods, namely, that the marginal cost of information goods be equal to the marginal revenue that the transfer of the goods brings about (i.e., the price of the information good).[4] Why, then, have information goods been perceived generally as failing to satisfy this basic criteria?

While the use of expected value and probabilistic analysis provides a framework for the resolution of one of the problematic aspects of information as a good, there remains a second problem in the consideration of the value of information; specifically, that there may be several sources of value that contribute to the total (or net) value of a good. The peculiar nature of information would seem to make these other potential sources of value, which are often ignored in theoretical analyses, of greater import for information goods than for more traditional economic goods.

Minasian (1967), for example, argued that traditional theory ignored some aspects of costs that rendered such theory deficient as an analytical tool. More generally, Demsetz (1967), Lee (1982), and Leff (1984) have noted that the failure of theory to incorporate important aspects of information is a source of the problematic status of information in economic theory. The present study will attempt to demonstrate that this perception is largely rooted in the failure to consider all the sources of information value, through an examination of the effects on value of the transfer of information between users.

The Full Costs of Information Transfer

As noted above, information is a distinctive good. Its unique features are evident even in typical cost considerations. The production of information for distribution is characterized by a high fixed cost (the cost of acquiring or developing the information in question) and essentially a zero variable cost. This zero variable cost reflects information's distinctive characteristics of being nonmaterial and infinitely reproducible. Physical distribution of information, it should be noted, may contribute additional fixed and variable costs, depending upon the medium used.

Ignoring, for the time being, distribution costs, the marginal cost of production for economic goods would typically be seen as being equal to the fixed cost of production for the first transfer of the good, and equal to the variable cost for any subsequent production. For information, that would suggest an initial high marginal cost, but one which, after the first transfer, would be essentially zero. For all intents and purposes, then, the marginal cost of production for information goods was treated as being zero. Even when including the cost of physical distribution, the marginal cost may be zero, and thus requires for efficiency and optimality a price, or exchange value, of zero. If the marginal cost for the mode of distribution is not zero, then the price of the information good (i.e., of the physical means of distribution and the information embedded in it) would be equal, under optimal conditions, to the marginal cost of the distribution channel.

This is where traditional considerations have led: the paradox where the economic (exchange) value of information is linked to the medium of distribution rather than the quality or utility of the information itself. This improper focus on the physical manifestations of information rather than on the information itself has been cited by several scholars as the source of many of the perceived problems with information as a good. This is because any consumer's demand for information goods (and thus its price-given supply) is linked to the utility value of the good, and thus to its quality and potential usefulness, rather than to any inherent value in the product containing the information. That is, under the more traditional considerations of the past, different aspects of information goods have determined cost and price; price by the usefulness of information, and cost largely by the mode of distribution. With costs not necessarily based on the same aspects of the good as price, it was conceivable, perhaps even likely, that problems might arise with the application of traditional economic analysis.

Information, however, is not a typical good. With the typical economic good, transfer entails loss of the good and the rights to it. Thus, the loss in value to the producer (seller) of the transfer of the good is the cost of producing and transferring the good, called the marginal cost of production for that good. This has led to the general perception that the marginal cost of the good to be exchanged was simply its cost of production. With information, though, transfer does not necessarily entail the loss of the information good and the rights to its use. Thus, the loss to the producer (seller) from the transfer of information goods is not only the marginal costs associated with that good's production and transfer (distribution), but also the expected loss of value resulting from any future use of that information by the producer resulting from that transfer.

In other words, as the producer of the information retains the information as well as exchanges it and the value of information lies in its future usefulness, then if the exchange of the information affects that information's future usefulness to the producer, that impact should be reflected in any cost computations for that good. Thus, a loss in what may be termed the stock value of information is an appropriate component of the cost of information production and transfer, and therefore should be considered in marginal cost considerations.[5] This returns the consideration of cost to be based on the utility, or usefulness, of the information itself, rather than solely on the mode of transmission.

There are other potential sources of value that can and should be considered in the marketplace for information. Not only does ancillary private value exist, but social value exists as well. The exchange and/or use of information may create value beyond the immediate participants in the exchange. The spread of information on prices and availabilities, for example, is held to make markets operate more efficiently and to increase total social welfare. Information on candidates and their positions on issues allows voters to make better choices and thus contributes to public welfare. Information, therefore, can be seen as having, in addition to basic utility value, what could be called ancillary private and social value.[6]

It would therefore seem that the perceived quandaries in the economics of information result from the exclusion of what is likely to be vital, if not necessarily major, components of marginal cost from traditional analysis. The following sections reconsider these perceived difficulties in light of the oversight of what may be important and sizable sources of value.

The Public Good/Private Good Debate

Previous considerations in the public vs. private good debate have tended to focus on different aspects of information as a good. Supporters of the notion that information is a private good have largely focused on information as market information and the reduction of uncertainty. Within this approach lies information with definite economic value, value that accrues to those who control the information and its use. This consideration was bolstered by the recognition of property rights to information (Boulding, 1966; Demsetz, 1967), and Marshall's (1974) arguments that information which was public was valueless.

On the other hand, supporters of the notion of information as public goods have largely focused on information goods such as television and radio broadcasts (Samuelson, 1954; 1958). Such goods clearly fit the proffered definition of public goods as those whose consumption by one individual did not affect that good's availability for any other consumer. It is little wonder that with no common basis for argument, the debate over whether information was essentially a public or a private good remained unresolved.

At first glance, it would seem that information as a good would be inherently public in nature. With the feature of infinite reproducibility at zero cost, any level of consumption still leaves an infinite potential supply. It would therefore seem that consumption of information by any one consumer would not affect that information's availability to other potential users. There are, however, two basic problems with this argument.

First, there is what Demsetz (1969) referred to as the fallacies inherent in the "nirvana approach." In this approach, efficiency and optimality are judged against some ideal state. There is a world of difference between the theoretical "ideal," and reality. In the real world of markets, information will not be made available unless the return from the supply of those goods is at least as great as their real cost, at least in the long run. While such returns need not be directly linked to the transfer, the costs must be met in some form, suggesting that the good will not be supplied unless some minimum level of consumption is expected. There is also the potential problem of "congestion" when the (over)use of the good by enough consumers reduces the utility of the good for all.[7] Thus, while in theory availability may be unaffected by consumption, in practice it is quite likely that the availability of any information good, whether by public or private agents, will depend upon certain minimum and maximum levels of consumption.

Second, this approach fails to consider the possibility of the impact of consumption of information goods upon their stock value or utility. One implication of the commonly accepted definition of public goods is that the marginal cost of such goods is zero; but as argued above, full marginal cost considerations must include the impact of the marginal transfer upon the stock value of the good. In some cases, such as market information, the value of the information good is clearly dependent upon the degree of diffusion of the information; with each additional transfer of information the potential gain to the supplier of the information from his or her subsequent use of the information is decreased. On the other hand, there is other information, such as entertainment or advertising, where the marginal impact of distribution would have no impact on the stock value of the information, or might even increase the stock value.

Therefore, at least for those information goods whose "consumption" has a negative impact on the stock value of that good for the producer, the consumption of the information good by one may well have an impact on that good's future availability. There may well be information goods that are not public, because considerations of the impact of consumption upon the producer's stock value in the good would act to restrict supply and availability. However, there may well be information goods whose distribution and consumption does not decrease the producer's stock value, and may even enhance it. In the first case, one would expect no change in supply due to consumption: such goods would clearly be true public goods. In the second case, consumption might even be encouraged, thus explaining the private production of public information goods such as radio and television programming.

While this expansion does not resolve the question whether information goods are public or private, it does provide theoretical justification for arguing that information goods, like other goods (Davis & Whinston, 1967; Head & Shoup, 1969), may be either public or private, depending on features of the good itself and its means of production and distribution. In this sense, both sides of the debate may have been correct in viewing their particular examples of information goods as either inherently public or private, depending upon criteria other than their particular nature as information goods.

Information Goods and Social Efficiency

Modern economic theory has yielded—via the theory of welfare economics—the concepts of social efficiency and welfare maximization. Such theory has further yielded the result that under the conditions of perfect competition, social efficiency and welfare are optimized. Thus, in one sense, optimality can be traced to the basic condition that marginal costs equate with marginal revenues within all markets for goods, a condition known as "marginal-cost pricing." Information goods have been held to violate this condition in two basic ways.

The first manner in which information is held to violate efficiency conditions derives from a seminal paper by Kenneth J. Arrow (1962). Arrow argues that free enterprise, or perfect competition, does not lead to the ideal allocation of resources to the production of knowledge, due to information's properties as a good. In effect, Arrow claims that information will be underproduced, because economic returns are not fully appropriable: that the producer does not receive the full value of the information from its transfer. This can be construed as suggesting that, within free markets, marginal revenue is less than it should be for information goods. Under marginal-cost pricing, this suggests that marginal costs are understated.

Other economists have argued the reverse: that some forms of information would be overproduced, because it is priced at less than marginal cost. Advertising is the prime example given (Telser, 1966), although Hirshleifer (1971) argues that foreknowledge also tends to be overproduced in private markets. Provided at a zero price to the consumer, advertising is said to violate marginal-cost pricing, because marginal costs can not be negative. However, it could also result from true marginal-cost pricing if the perceived marginal costs were overstated.

In other words, if one assumes the validity of the marginal-cost pricing condition, which results from the producer's profit-maximizing behavior, both results could be explained by the statement that the marginal costs of information goods as generally perceived by the theorists are not true reflections of the real marginal cost of such goods. In the first case, marginal costs are understated; in the second, they are overstated. As was noted above, traditional considerations of marginal cost for information have omitted consideration of a prime factor of the cost of information goods exchange: the changes in stock value. This heretofore largely ignored component of marginal cost may explain how such misstatement of cost occurred.

Consider Arrow's (1962) example of invention and research. Real costs are assumed in its production, and real returns may be expected by the producer in her future use of that information, be it from personal use or the sale of that information. Such (expected) returns may be seen as the initial stock value of that good. The problem of the "inappropriateness" of information reduces to the argument that others may gain revenues from the use of information: that the producer may lose future revenues by other's use of that information.[8] In other words, the stock value of information may be reduced through other's actions.

The likelihood of such actions is clearly linked with the degree to which the information in question is disseminated, as well as the system of property rights and enforcement of such rights within a society. Taking such systems as given suggests that the loss in stock value is truly marginal: that there is a positive loss in the stock value with each additional transfer or use of that information good. For such information, this can clearly be considered a positive marginal cost of production and transfer.

To the degree that such marginal costs are disregarded (by the producer as well as by the theorist), the attempt of the producer to maximize profits by equating marginal costs with marginal revenues will result in the setting of prices below the true optimum, thereby yielding Arrow's (1962) finding of suboptimal allocation. It is perhaps only in the ethereal world of economic theory that this factor of marginal cost is ignored: the actions of information producers in protecting and conserving the value of such information would seem to indicate that producers are indeed aware of this component of marginal cost, and would likely include this factor in their calculations and actions.

Advertising as a Special Case

Advertising is one form of information good that has long been viewed as contrary to economic optimality and social welfare. In part, this is due to the argument that the persuasive nature of advertising distorts the market allocation process by getting consumers to purchase goods they neither need nor desire. A second perceived difficulty is that since advertising is delivered free to the consumer, it is likely to be oversupplied. The first argument lays outside of the purview of this paper, and so will not be addressed here. The second, however, is a problem of a presumed violation of the marginal-cost pricing condition for efficiency and welfare maximization.

Advertising is produced and delivered to the consumer free of charge. In fact, in some circumstances, the advertising subsidizes the production and distribution of related goods. In the first case, the price of advertising as an information good is zero. In the second, one can see that the effective price of the advertising good is actually negative: the presence of advertising reduces the actual price of the related good. On the other hand, there are positive marginal costs associated with the distribution of advertising.

According to the traditional theory, then, the marginal cost of advertising is strictly positive (i.e., nonzero), while the price of advertising is strictly nonpositive. It is thus seen as being impossible for the marginal pricing condition to be obtained by advertising as a good. Advertising is thus judged to be inherently inefficient. Yet if one considers the contribution of changes in the stock value of information goods in the determination of "true" marginal cost, this dilemma may be resolved.

Advertising is a peculiar form of information: one with a particular purpose. This purpose is to inform or persuade consumers of certain features, attributes, or values of other goods. Specifically, advertising as an information good is used to increase the consumption of other (target) goods, or at least to prevent a decrease of consumption. Thus, the value of the advertisement to the producer of the target good is the likelihood of the message's effect upon consumption, multiplied by the economic value of that effect, i.e., the expected value of the (added) consumption of the target good. Further, this value is clearly marginal: the degree of distribution of advertising (as an information good) will affect both the likelihood of, and expected return from, changes in consumption.

Assuming that the producer of the target good is also the producer of the information good (advertising), the producer can thus be seen to accrue economic value with each additional transfer (consumption) of the information good.[9] Structurally, this can be seen as a change (increase) in the stock value of the information good, and thus as a (negative) component in the marginal cost computations for that good. The nature of advertising is such that the presumed change in its stock value through dissemination is positive. This implies that the contribution of the marginal cost component is in fact negative—that it can be said to reduce the costs of transfer, and perhaps even to render the net marginal cost for this form of information good to be negative over some range of quantity.

The concept of zero, or negative, marginal cost carries with it some interesting implications, primarily when subject to the marginal-cost pricing condition. Under such conditions, for advertising to be socially efficient and contribute to welfare maximization, such information goods would have to be supplied free, in the case of zero net marginal cost, or with a payoff to the consumer, either directly or through the subsidization of another good, should the net marginal cost be negative. And, indeed, such are the conditions under which advertising is produced. Therefore, with the inclusion of stock value considerations, there is no a priori reason for advertising, as an information good, to be considered as socially inefficient or to lead to suboptimal conditions.

Summary

Information is clearly a peculiar economic good. Its distinctive nature and features have contributed to its problematic treatment in economic theory. These problems appear to arise from the treatment of information as a traditional good, with an extensive set of affiliated externalities. In fact, the problems that traditional economic theory has evidenced with information are attributed to these externalities resulting from the peculiar nature of information.

This essay argues that rather than treat information traditionally as a problematic good rife with externalities, economic treatment (analysis) of information should be expanded so as to account effectively for the distinctive nature of information within the structure of traditional economic analysis, thereby precluding any resort to externalities lying "outside the sphere of analysis." That is, that one expand one's concept of value and cost and related constructs and theories, incorporating the notion of information as a regular economic good subject to the same analysis and conditions as other goods.

To this end, two concepts have been advanced. First, that the value of information is probabilistic, rather than deterministic, and depends on the returns from the (future) use of that information. The expected value of information at any particular point, so defined, was called its "stock value." Second, that the stock value of information may be affected by the transfer of the information to others, thus making such changes in stock value a valid component of marginal cost considerations of the exchange of information goods.

With the use of these concepts, it was shown that there need be no paradoxes raised in the economic consideration of information. While the development of these concepts do not preclude such problems nor definitively resolve those addressed, treatment of information goods in such a manner does demonstrate that information goods are not necessarily problematic: that they are neither necessarily public or private in nature, nor that they are necessarily socially inefficient. In short, that within

392   Mediation, Information, and Communication

properly structured conceptualizations and analyses, information can be treated as any other economic good.

Notes

1. It has been argued that consumers do, in fact, pay for advertising through increased prices for other products (e.g., Lees & Yang, 1966). This can not be considered to be a direct price, however, as it is not associated with the acquisition or consumption of the good itself. That is, such costs are accrued independent of the consumption of the information good—advertising.
2. This criteria is actually valid only in competitive markets, although it also forms a first-order condition for equilibrium in monopoly markets as well. In other cases, equilibrium is also affected by marginal cost considerations, both directly and through its impact on average cost (Ferguson, 1972). Thus, it is useful to focus on the impact of marginal cost.
3. To illustrate, the value of a gallon of water is recognized as being higher for a person dying of thirst in a desert than for another person sitting beside a freshwater spring, having drunk his fill. Most economic analyses, however, focus on the exchange value of goods rather than on their utility value.
4. Again, strictly speaking, this is valid only under competition, although the concepts are extendable to other market situations.
5. As an example, suppose that an individual knows that a merger will soon be announced that will double the price of a certain stock. Clearly, the value of such information to that individual is the expected returns from being able to use that information, i.e., the profit to be made from purchasing that stock. If that individual should transfer that information to others, who then also purchase that stock, the increased demand will cause the stock's price to rise, reducing the amount of gain to be made from the individual's future use of that information, which is what has been defined as the stock value.
6. A further discussion of ancillary private and social value, and its implications for the economics of information, can be found in Bates (1988).
7. As an illustrative example, consider bridges. Many communities located on rivers find that they have use for more bridges than they presently have; the demand for bridges is present. However, in many cases that demand is considered to be insufficient for the costs involved; as was the case with one city that, upon being denied funding for a bridge, applied to foreign governments for aid. On the other hand, many are aware of the impact of congestion on bridges; a bridge that is clogged with traffic is of much less value than one that is not.
8. Although outside the traditional definition of research and invention, a prime example of the question of appropriateness may be seen in the current controversy over the "pirating" of recorded entertainment material. Producers of such material argue that the copying of such material reduces the opportunity (likelihood) of future sales of that material, and thus their overall revenues from the production of that information good.
9. In cases where there is an intermediary, value can be seen as flowing through such an intermediary, through the provision of intermediate goods or services.

References

Arrow, K.J. (1962). Economic welfare and the allocation of resources for invention. In *The rate and direction of economic activity: Economic and social factors.*

Princeton: Universities-National Bureau for Economic Research Conference series.

Bates, B.J. (1988). Information as an economic good: Sources of individual and social value. In V. Mosco, & J. Wasko (Eds.), *The political economy of information*. Madison, WI: University of Wisconsin Press.

Black, S.H., & Marchand, D.A. (1982). Assessing the value of information in organizations: A challenge for the 1980s. *Information Society, 1*(3), 191–225.

Boulding, K.E. (1966). The economics of knowledge and the knowledge of economics. *American Economic Review, 56*(2), 1–13.

Coase, R.H. (1974). The market for goods and the market for ideas. *American Economic Review, 64*(2), 384–91.

Davis, O.A., & Whinston, A.B. (1967). On the distinction between public and private goods. *American Economic Review, 59*(2) 360–73.

Demsetz, H. (1967). Toward a theory of property rights. *American Economic Review, 59*(2), 347–59.

Demsetz, H. (1969). Information and efficiency: Another viewpoint. *Journal of Law and Economics, 12*(1), 1–22.

Dervin, B. (1976). Strategies for dealing with human information needs. *Journal of Broadcasting, 20*(3), 324–33.

Doyle, P. (1968). Economic aspects of advertising: A survey. *The Economic Journal, 78:* (September), 570–602.

Edelstein, A.S. (1982). *Comparative communication research*. Beverly Hills, CA: Sage.

Ferguson, C.E. (1972). *Microeconomic theory*. 3d ed. Homewood, IL: R.D. Irwin.

Fukushima, A. (1986) Electronic info-communication indicator (EICI): The national accounts of information. Paper presented at the 36th annual conference of the International Communication Association, Chicago, IL. (May).

Hall, K. (1981). The economic nature of information. *Information Society, 1*(2), 143–66.

Head, J.G., & Shoup, C.S. (1969). Public goods, private goods, and ambiguous goods. *The Economic Journal, 79*, 567–72.

Hirshleifer, J. (1971). The private and social value of information and the reward to inventive activity. *American Economic Review, 61*(4) 561–74.

Hirshleifer, J. (1973). Where are we in the theory of information. *American Economic Review, 63*(2), 31–39.

Ito, Y. (1981). The "johoka shakai" approach to the study of communication in Japan. In B.C. Wilhoit, & H. de Bock (Eds.), *Mass Communication Review Yearbook, Vol. 2*. Beverly Hills, CA: Sage.

Korobeinikov, V.S. (1980). Conflicts of media in modern industrial society. *International Social Science Journal, 32*(2), 238–46.

Krippendorf, K. (1984). Information, information society and some Marxian propositions. Unpublished paper presented at 34th Annual International Communication Association Conference, San Francisco, CA (May).

Lee, D.R. (1982). On the pricing of public goods. *Southern Economic Journal, 49*(1) 99–105.

Lees, F.A., & Yang, C.Y. (1966). The redistributional effect of television advertising. *The Economic Journal, 76*, 328–36.

Leff, N.H. (1984). Externalities, information costs, and social benefit-cost analysis for economic development: An example from telecommunications. *Economic Development and Cultural Change, 32*(2), 255–76.

Machlup, F. (1962). *The production and distribution of knowledge in the United States*. Princeton: Princeton University Press.

Marshall, A. (1930). *Principles of economics*. 8th Ed. London: Macmillan.

Marshall, J.M. (1974). Private incentives and public information. *American Economic Review, 64*(3), 373–90.

Minasian, J.R. (1967). Public goods in theory and practice revisited. *Journal of Law and Economics, 10*, 205–7.

Pool, I. de S. (1984). Tracking the flow of information. *Science, 221* (12 August) 609–13.

Porat, M.U. (1978). Global implications of an information society. *Journal of Communication, 28*(1), 70–80.

Samuelson, P.A. (1954). The pure theory of public expenditures. *Review of Economics and Statistics, 36*(4), 387–89.

Samuelson, P.A. (1958). Aspects of public expenditure theories. *Review of Economics and Statistics, 40*(4), 332–38.

Stigler, G. (1983). *The Organization of Industry*. (Chapter: The economics of information.) Chicago: University of Chicago Press.

Takasaki, N., & Ozawa, T. (1983). Analysis of information flow in Japan. *Information Economics and Policy, 1*(2), 177–93.

Telser, L.G. (1966). Supply and demand for advertising messages. *American Economic Review. 56*(2) 457–66.

22

A Time-Line of Information Technology

Jorge Reina Schement and Daniel A. Stout, Jr.

This time-line illustrates the evolution of information technology by identifying developments along three axes and two dimensions. The axes to be considered are: 1) contributions to conceptual developments, 2) information acquisition devices: and 3) information manipulation devices. The two dimensions to be considered are: 1) technologies of symbol manipulation; and 2) technologies of sensory extension. The time-line demonstrates how technologies build on previous discoveries by synthesizing basic features of two or more devices. Also, by overlaying the dimensions of symbol manipulation and sensory extension, the time-line identifies the periods of convergence that have punctuated the course of technological change.

Introduction

The purpose of this time-line is to illustrate the growth of information technology as a complex interplay between conceptual and material invention, and to place this growth within a chronological framework. In creating this time-line we seek to meet three goals.

First, we identify the order of appearance of material information technologies such as the clock, the telescope, and the book. Second, we include a selected chronology of conceptual and social technologies that created the knowledge foundation for material invention; the phonetic alphabet, decimal counting, the library at Nineveh, and the university of Paris are examples of this class of innovations. Third, the interplay of functions is traced through a scheme of symbol notations, in order to demonstrate the alphabetical[1] and mathematical bases, as well as the audial and visual utilities of information technologies. In addition, the symbol scheme illustrates how specific information technologies are built upon previous innovations, by synthesizing the features of earlier technologies. Thus, the computer, which can be visual or aural, and can manipulate mathematical or alphabetical symbols, demonstrates the convergence of previous print and electronic innovations. By establishing the interplay of functions it is possible to identify patterns of convergence that have punctuated the course of technological change.

We propose a broad definition of "information technology" as the hardware, software, organizational structures, and social values by which information is recorded, stored, processed and/or transmitted. "Information" refers to the telling of something, or the something that is told. Thus, the concept of information used here is that developed by Machlup (1983).[2] In this sense, communication technology represents a subset of information technology.

The broad definition chosen here avoids the mistake of assuming that only mechanical or electronic devices constitute information technology. For example, a conceptual technology, such as the decimal system, contributed to so many later inventions that it is easy to overlook the contribution of those early mathematicians who developed it. Like the decimal system, many earlier technologies are represented in later inventions. Thus, the invention of the camera depended on the synthesis of two earlier information technologies, the decimal system as applied to calibration, and lenses. To ignore either conceptual and social technologies or the influence of previous inventions imposes a false picture on the history of information technology, giving the impression that each device sprang full blown from the head of its inventor.

Our time-line is an attempt not only to answer the question of which device came first but also to shed some light on the chain of ideas and events that contributed to the ferment of invention. The list presented here is not exhaustive. While we have attempted to identify important inventions, we have surely overlooked others of equal value.

The organization for the time-line is rooted in Mumford's (1963) list of inventions, which he constructed as a supplement to *Technics and Civilization*. He included ideas and institutions as technologies representing the social processes that underlay the family lineages of inventions. Our "conceptual and social technologies" category follows his lead. Furthermore, of all machines in Mumford's list, 20% fall within our definition of information technology. When these are added to the conceptual and social information technologies in his list, the total equals one-half of all inventions. Indeed, information technologies can be seen as an important cause of "machine civilization," which, according to Mumford, began with the invention of the clock as a device to communicate the recording of regularly measured time. Mumford discusses "communication" only in the context of the electronic media, and paper. "Information" is never mentioned. Though Mumford went beyond previous time-lines, the long history of inventions to acquire, store, manipulate, or transmit information remains masked within his one-dimensional list.

The multidimensional aspect of the time-line reflects Grun's *The Time-tables of History* (1975). Grun employed a chronological method in which time-lines of achievement in history and politics, literature and theater, religion and philosophy, visual arts, music, science and technology, and daily life are juxtaposed in vertical columns. His goal in creating this historical representation was to communicate the "many-sidedness of past experience."

We adopt Grun's basic approach, but while his "many-sided" format provides a sense of events occurring contemporaneously, the items in any single column are treated as a simple time-line. Thus, it is helpful to find out, for example, that two years before Morse demonstrated the telegraph in 1837, Bennet helped create the Penny Press by publishing the first edition of the *New York Herald;* use of the telegraph would boost the power of the newspaper. So Grun's time-line presents a broader framework within which to understand technological change, but technology is still treated as a list of entries, each independent of the others. In other words, what Grun did was to create seven lists, following Mumford's (1963) list, and place them side by side. To go beyond such a format requires the functional categorization of information technologies.

Can we learn more about technological growth if we identify information technologies by function? For example, both the telescope and the computer are devices that can be labeled as information technologies. The telescope's primary function is to extend the sense of sight, while the computer aids the senses in more complex ways through symbol manipulation. Both devices are quite different in use of information. Yet this distinction is lost in a simple list of inventions. To gain greater insight into the growth of information technologies by function, all of the devices in the time-line are grouped as technologies of acquisition and storage, or processing and transmission.

A second deficiency of earlier time-lines has to do with their inability to present the evolution of information technologies as a process. Although Mumford (1963) includes some conceptual innovations in his list, the one-dimensional nature of the representation makes it difficult to distinguish conceptual and social technologies from material ones. What, therefore, can be found of the relationship between knowledge growth and invention in a time-line?

Such a question suggests the need for a historical chronology that specifically identifies the development of ideas and their institutional manifestations. For example, the inventions of the alphabet and of mathematics represent monumental advances in human knowledge that continue to be felt through their application to all subsequent inventions. Thus, the lead pencil, and block printing, furthered the conceptual technology of the alphabet, while the development of precision instruments such as the microscope, and the wristwatch, depended upon the application of mathematics. Furthermore, once these conceptual technologies were accepted, their increasing use demanded the invention of social technologies, e.g., the university, to insure their transmission to succeeding generations.[3]

To demonstrate the relationship between "idea" and "thing," the time-line column labeled "conceptual and institutional developments" presents a selective list of ideas and institutions that contributed to the invention of material information technology. In addition, the role of the alphabet and of mathematics can be traced by the symbol placed next to each entry.

The chronology presented here is complex and can be read along several dimensions, since each one sheds some light on an aspect of technological growth. Taken as a whole, the time-line of information technology illustrates the long and continuing human effort to extend the reach of the senses and the power of the brain.

Procedures

Design of the Time-Line

Historical events are presented in three axial columns: conceptual and institutional developments; information acquisition and storage devices; and, information processing and transmission devices. In addition, each entry is identified as a technology of symbol manipulation (alphabetical or mathematical), and/or as a technology of sensory extension (audio or optical-visual).

To follow better the concurrence of significant developments, the time-line links the three categories of information technology by year. In this way, the reader may see which events occurred during the same period by reading across (although no time-line can do more than hint at the complexity of interplay between conceptual developments and inventions).[4]

The following definitions determined whether an event would be included in the time-line:

1. *Conceptual and institutional developments:* Conceptual developments include fundamental theories, principles, ideas, and techniques underlying the development of information technologies. Institutional developments include libraries, schools, universities, and observatories, that is, social structures through which conceptual developments are disseminated.
2. *Information acquisition and storage devices:* Information acquisition devices assist human information processing by directly expanding the capacities of the eye and the ear. Storage devices aid in the manipulation of information by recording, copying, logging, and/or preserving symbols for the primary purpose of allowing access or retrieval at a later time.
3. *Information processing and transmission devices:* Information processing devices aid in the manipulation of information by performing distinct operations, modifications, or conversions of symbols. Transmission devices communicate, transport, or distribute symbols across space.

The particular pairing of functions chosen here is a response to space constraints. While it makes sense for most of the history covered in this chronology, it forces splitting hairs, especially during the computer era. Indeed, the nature of information means that information technology do not fit neatly into categories.[5] We appreciate any corrections and additions.

Symbol Notation

The scheme of circles and squares denotes the functions of symbol manipulation or sensory extension. A combination of figures demonstrates how technologies build on previous discoveries by synthesizing basic features of two or more devices. For example, the computer can be visual or aural and can manipulate mathematical or alphabetical symbols.[6]

◯ *Alphabet technologies:* manipulate symbols to form words according to a phonology and/or morphology of language, having both syntactical and semantic dimensions.

● *Mathematical technologies:* manipulate symbols for the purpose of counting, or for clarifying relationships between phenomena through quantification.

◑ refers to a combination of alphabetical and mathematical technologies.

▢ *Audio technologies:* extend the sense of hearing.

■ *Optical/visual technologies:* extend the sense of seeing.

■ refers to a combination of audio and optical/visual technologies.

Various forms of convergence are illustrated by the following combinations: □○, □●, ■○, ■●, ■○, ■●, ■●.

By overlaying the dimensions of symbol manipulation and sensory extension on the columns, the time-line identifies the periods of convergence that have punctuated the course of technological change.

Discussion

When the growth of information technology is viewed from the perspective of the time-line, several themes stand out.

First, until the sixth century B.C., all efforts focused on inventing systems of writing, counting, or representing time. Their profound significance is evident when one considers the break with tradition required by such levels of abstraction as the map and the calendar. Furthermore, early farmers considered the counting of the seasons of such importance that calendars were invented at numerous places and times, representing the first direct application of mathematics. These earliest information technologies formed the basis for all that follows. The Sumerians stand out as inventors of the library and of the library catalog. In terms of information technology, they were the first to experience the necessity for a social institution devoted to storing information, and for a technology of retrieval. Such inventions imply the complexity of their civilization.

Second, throughout the time-line, there are consistent efforts aimed at extending the advantages of writing. While the pace of technological invention seems slow from the position of the twentieth century, nearly every century contains a contribution to written communication.

Third, capitalism and the industrial revolution spawned intense development of all information technologies. Industrial organization incorporated earlier knowledge systems such as science, while capitalism offered rewards for inventing new devices and improving on existing ones. Though antecedents can be detected in the time-line as early as the sixteenth century, this period intensified at the turn of the nineteenth century and continues to the present at a rapid pace.

Fourth, the second half of the twentieth century contains a series of inventions that defy easy categorization. They consist of a convergence of functions, a synthesis of symbol manipulation, and the simultaneous extension of the eye and the ear. Moreover, the ease with which complex technologies (e.g. television) can be combined with other complex technologies (e.g., the calculator and the telephone) to produce even more complex technologies (e.g., computer networks or cable television) illustrates how recent information technologies operate more as components of universal machines than as free-standing developments.

Finally, the time-line illustrates how consistent have been human desires to sharpen vision, improve hearing, communicate over distances, record time, speed up calculations, and expand knowledge.

Notes

The authors wish to acknowledge the contributions of James Anderson and Leah A. Lievrouw of Rutgers University. Donald O. Case of the University of California, Los Angeles, and Loy A. Singleton of the University of Alabama.

1. "Alphabet" and "alphabetical" are used here in their broad sense to indicate symbol systems for the representation of language, thus including syllabic, pictographic, and morphemic systems as well as the use of "alphabetic" in the narrow sense of phonemic systems.
2. The overall definition of "information technology" is partly derived from Rogers (1986, p. 1).
3. The invention of literacy brought profound social conflict to ancient Greece and was not universally accepted as a positive influence on Greek civilization, as Havelock (1976) has noted.
4. B.C./A.D. notation is used in the time-line because it is commonly accepted.
5. In addition, some technologies in the time-line cross over category boundaries, especially in the twentieth century. They are marked by an asterisk (*).
6. Not all entries in the time-line are technologies. Those entries lacking a symbol notation do not qualify as a technology.

Selected Bibliography

Mumford's and Grun's contributions and biases already have been mentioned. Because Mumford's time-line begins in the year 1000 and ends in 1934, Grun was especially helpful in filling the period before 1000. Calder's *Timescale: An Atlas of the Fourth Dimension* provided specific information about the early uses of symbols and language. Dilke, *Reading the Past: Mathematics and Measurement,* generated dates for devices of measurement, including early calendars and clocks. Other sources listed below were used to cross-check specific entries.

Calder, N. (1983). *Timescale: An atlas of the fourth dimension*. New York: Viking.
Communication. (1961). *Oxford English dictionary*. Vol. II, C. Clarendon Press, 699–700.
Dalby, A. (1986). The Sumerian catalogs. *The Journal of Library History, 21*(3), 875–87.
Dilke, O.A.W. (1987). *Reading the past: Mathematics and measurement*. London: British Museum.

Grun, B. (1975). *The timetables of history: A horizontal linkage of people and events*. New York: Simon & Schuster.

Havelock, E.A. (1976). *Origins of Western literacy*. Toronto, Ontario: The Ontario Institute for Studies in Education.

Havelock, E.A. (1986). *The Muse learns to write*. New Haven, CT: Yale University Press.

Information. (1961). *Oxford English dictionary*. Vol. V, H-K, Clarendon Press, 274.

Machlup, F. (1983). Semantic quirks in studies of information. In F. Machlup, & U. Mansfield (Eds.), *The study of information: Interdisciplinary messages*. New York: John Wiley & Sons, 641–71.

Mumford, L. (1963). *Technics and civilization*. New York: Harcourt, Brace, & World, 437–46.

Rogers, E.M. (1986). *Communication technology: The new media in society*. New York: Free Press.

Ruben, B.D. (1988). *Communication and human behavior*, 2d. ed. New York: Macmillan.

Time-Line

	Conceptual &/or Institutional Developments	Information Acquisition &/or Storage Devices	Information Manipulation &/or Transmission Devices

Pre-Tenth Century B.C.

■ Cave paintings introduce symbolic representation [c. 20,000 B.C.]

■● Egyptian calender [5,000 - 4,000 B.C.]

■ Pictographs on clay tablets [c. 3,500 B.C.]

■● Jewish calender [4,000 - 3,5000 B.C.]

● Egyptian number system [3,500 - 3,000 B.C.]

◒ Egyptian hieroglyphics as symbol system [c. 3,000 B.C.]

● Numerical system in Sumeria [3,000 - 2,500 B.C.]

■ Metal mirrors in Egypt [3,000 - 2,500 B.C.]

● Concept of 365-day year in Eqypt [3,000 - 2,500 B.C.]

● System of solar-lunar year in China [2,500 - 2,000 B.C.]

■ Papyrus used by Egyptians [2,500 - 2,000 B.C.]

	Conceptual &/or Institutional Developments	Information Acquisition &/or Storage Devices	Information Manipulation &/or Transmission Devices
Pre-Tenth Century B.C.		■ Map of Babylon [2,500 - 2,000 B.C.]	
	● Decimal system used in Crete [2,000 - 1,500 B.C.]	■ ○ Catalogs of written clay tablets [2,000 B.C.]	
	○ Alphabet in use among Semitic people [c. 1,800 B.C.]	☐ Hearing aid or "ear trumpet" [c. 1,600 B.C.]	
Tenth Century B.C.			● Water-filled cube to measure time, weight [1,000 - 900 B.C.]
Ninth Century B.C.			
Eighth Century B.C.	○ Phonetic alphabet in use among Greeks [c. 700 B.C.]	■ ● Calenders in Babylon [800 - 700 B.C.]	
Seventh Century B.C.	■ ○ Library at Nineveh [700 - 600 B.C.]		
Sixth Century B.C.			■ ● Sundial in China [600 - 500 B.C.]
	● Length of Roman lunar year has 10 months [c. 500 B.C.]		■ Regular courier service in Persia [c. 500 B.C.] Cyrus

	Conceptual &/or Institutional Developments	Information Acquisition &/or Storage Devices	Information Manipulation &/or Transmission Devices
Sixth Century B.C.	● Length of lunar month determined [c. 500 B.C.]		
Fifth Century B.C.			■ Carrier pigeons in Greece [c. 425 B.C.]
Fourth Century B.C.	● East-west line introduced as map division [320 B.C.]		
	■○ Library at Alexendria [307 B.C.] Ptolemy Soter		
Third Century B.C.		■ Parchment produced in Pergamum [c. 250 B.C.]	■● Sophisticated sundial used in Rome [c. 263 B.C.]
	● Leap year in Egyptian calendar [c. 240 B.C.]		
	● Chinese weights and measures standardized [c. 220 B.C.]		

	Conceptual &/or Institutional Developments	Information Acquisition &/or Storage Devices	Information Manipulation &/or Transmission Devices
Second Century B.C.	● Dividing lines of inhabited world measured [c. 194 B.C.] Eratosthenes	■ World globe [c. 140 B.C.] Crates of Mallus	■● Clepsydra water clock in Rome [c. 159 B.C.]
	College of Technology at Alexandria [c. 105 B.C.] Heron		
First Century B.C.	○ Shorthand invented [c. 63 B.C.] Mareus Tullius Tiro		■ Handwritten news sheet in Rome [59 B.C.]
			■● Julian calender adopted with leap year [c. 45 B.C.]
First Century			
Second Century	■● Systematic map drawing [c. 170] Ptolemy	■ Paper invented [105] China	
Third Century		■◒ Early compass in China [c. 270]	

	Conceptual &/or Institutional Developments	Information Acquisition &/or Storage Devices	Information Manipulation &/or Transmission Devices
Fourth Century			■● Jewish calender reformed [338]
Fifth Century			■ Block printing in Asia [450]
Sixth Century			● Abacus [c. 500] Eurasia
	● Method of dating by years of the Christian Era [c. 525] Exiguus		
Seventh Century	● Decimal Counting in India [c. 600]		■○ Book printing [c. 600] China
	● Modern numerals introduced with zero and place value [c. 680]		
Eighth Century	● B.C.-A.D. Notation [c. 730] Venerable Bede		
	Arts and sciences studied [c. 750] Han Lin Academy China	■ Paper making introduced to Arabs from China [751]	■○ Printed newspaper in Peking [c. 750]

	Conceptual &/or Institutional Developments	Information Acquisition &/or Storage Devices	Information Manipulation &/or Transmission Devices
Eighth Century	⬣ "Arabic" numerals introduced to Baghdad from India [c. 760]		◼ Pictorial book printing in Japan [c. 765]
Ninth Century	⬣ Algebra [810] Muhammed ibn Musa Formal study of astronomy [813] Baghdad Library founded at St. Gallen [816] Gosbert Cyrillic alphabet invented [c. 863] Cyrus and Methodius	◼● Arabs perfect astrolabe [c. 850]	◼ Calibrated candles as time recorders in England [870]
Tenth Century	⬤ Arithmetic notation brought to Europe by Arabs [c. 975]	◼ Paper manufactured in Cairo [c. 900]	◼ Regular postal service [c. 942] Caliph's empire ◼● Water clock [c. 950]

	Conceptual &/or Institutional Developments	Information Acquisition &/or Storage Devices	Information Manipulation &/or Transmission Devices
Eleventh Century	Decimal System [1080] Azachel	■ Real lenses [1050] Alhazen Astrolabes introduced to Europe [1050]	■ Movable type [1041 - 1049] Pisheng
Twelvth Century	● University of Paris founded [1150] forerunner of modern university "Geography" [1154] Mohammed al-Idrisi	■ Paper manufactured [c. 1150] Arabic Spain ■◒ Magnetic compass mentioned in English literature [1195]	■ Use of woodcuts for capital letters [1147] Monastery at Engleberg
Thirteenth Century	● Introduction of Arabic Numerals to Europe [1202] "liber abaci" Fibonacci Treatise on Lenses [1270] Vitello	■◒ Pivoted magnetic compass [1269] Petrus Peregrinus ■ Compound lenses [1270] Bacon	

	Conceptual &/or Institutional Developments	Information Acquisition &/or Storage Devices	Information Manipulation &/or Transmission Devices
Thirteenth Century		■ Glass mirror [1278] ■ Eye glasses [1290]	■ Block printing [1289] Ravenna
Fourteenth Century	● Division of Hours and Minutes into Sixties [1345] First written use of the word "communication" in English [1382] First written use of the word "information" in English [1387]		■ Wooden type [1300] Turkestan ■ ○ Mechanical clock [1354] Stasbourg cathedral ■ ○ Mechanical clock development [1370] Van Wyck ■ Metal type [1390] Korea
Fifteenth Century	"Yung Lo Ta Tien" encyclopedia [1403] China	■ Book printed using movable type [1409] Korea ■ Observatory at Samarkand [1420]	■ Oil painting [1402] Bros Van Eyck ■ Wood engraving [1418] ■ Woodcuts in Europe [1423]

	Conceptual &/or Institutional Developments	Information Acquisition &/or Storage Devices	Information Manipulation &/or Transmission Devices
Fifteenth Century	◒ Scientific Cartography [1436] Banco		
			■ Modern printing [1440 - 1460] Gutenberg and Schoeffer
	Laws of Perspective [1440] Alberti		
			■ Copper plate engraving [1446]
		42-line "Mazarin" bible at Mainz [1453 - 1455] Gutenberg and Fust	■ Metal plates used in printing [1453]
	● Foundations of Trigonometry [1470] Muller		
	◒ Ship's Log [1472-1519]	■ Observatory in Nürnberg [1472] Bernard Walther	■ Copper etching [1483] Wenceslaus von Olnutz
	Profession of Book Publisher established [1492]	■● Terrestrial globe constructed [1492] Behaim	
Sixteenth Century			■○ Regular postal service between Vienna and Brussels [c. 1500]
			■● Portable watch with iron main-spring [1500]

Conceptual &/or Institutional Developments	Information Acquisition &/or Storage Devices	Information Manipulation &/or Transmission Devices

Sixteenth Century

◼● Intricate cathedral clocks developed [c. 1500 - 1650]

◼ Multicolored woodcut [1508]

◼ Eye glasses for shortsightedness [1518]

● Reinvention of taxi meter for coaches [1528]

Theory suggesting longitude can be computed from differences in time [1530] Regnier Gemma Frisius

Manual of production of paints and inks [1533]

◼ Astronomical map [1539] Alesandro Piccolomini

◼ First map of Flanders [1540] Gerardus Mercator

"Index Librorum Prohibitorum [1543] Pope Paul III

"Cosmographia Universalis" [1544] Sebastian Münster

	Conceptual &/or Institutional Developments	Information Acquisition &/or Storage Devices	Information Manipulation &/or Transmission Devices

Sixteenth Century

● Elaboration of algebraic symbols [1544] Stifel

"Biblioteca Universalis" [1549] Konrad von Gesner

■ Camera with lense and stop for diaphragm [1558] Daniello Barbaro

Academia Scerotorum Naturae at Naples [1560] The first scientific society

■ Lead pencil [1565] Gesner

● Use of triangulation system in surveying [1581-1626] Willebrord snell van Roijen

■● Gregorian calender revision [1582]

● Decimal system [1585] Simon Stevin

■ Compound microscope [1590] Jansen

■ Revolving theater stage [1597]

Seventeenth Century

Treatise on terrestrial magnetism and electricity [1600] Gilbert

	Conceptual &/or Institutional Developments	Information Acquisition &/or Storage Devices	Information Manipulation &/or Transmission Devices
Seventeenth Century	Academia dei lincei at Rome [1603]		
		■ Telescope [1608] Lippersheim	
	First law of motion [1609] Galileo		
	● Discovery of logarithms [1614] John Napier		
	● First logarithm table [1617] Henry Briggs		
	● Infinitesimal calculus [1636] Fermat	■ Periscope [1637] Hevel, Danzig	■ Fountain pen [1636] Schwenter
		● Barometer [1643] Torricelli	
	Calculation of focuses on all forms of lenses [1647]		
			● Calculating machine [1650] Pascal
	● Law of probability [1654] Pascal		▭● Pendulum clock [1657] Huygens
	● Law of probability tied to insurance [1660] Jan de Witt		
		■ Mirror-telescope [1666] Newton	
		■ Paris observatory [1667]	

Conceptual &/or Institutional Developments	Information Acquisition &/or Storage Devices	Information Manipulation &/or Transmission Devices

Seventeenth Century

⬜ Speaking tube [1671] Morland

⬤ First determination of speed of light [1675] Roemer

⬛ Greenwich observatory [1675]

⬤ Differential calculus [1680] Liebnitz

Newton's "Principia" [1687]

Eighteenth Century

⬛⬤ Physicians' pulse watch with second hand [1707] Floger

⬛ Stereotype [1710] Van der Mey and Müller

⬤ Mercury thermometer [1714] Fahrenheit

⬛⚪ Typewriter [1714] Henry Mill

⬛ Three color printing from copper plate [1719] Le Blond

⬛ Stereotype [1727] Ged

⬛ Light images with silver nitrate [1727] Schulze

	Conceptual &/or Institutional Developments	Information Acquisition &/or Storage Devices	Information Manipulation &/or Transmission Devices
Eighteenth Century		■ Stereotyping process [1730] Goldsmith	● Accurate chronometer [1736] Harrison
	Calculation of water resistence to ships [1749]		● Modern type chronometer [1763] Le Roy
	Description of ball-bearing [1772]		□ Signal telegraph [1793] Claude Chappe
	Ecole Polytechnique founded [1794]		■ Lithography [1796] Senefelder
	Conservatoire Nationale des Arts et Métiers [1799] Paris		
Nineteenth Century			■ Kymograph, recording of continuous movement [1807] Young
			Steam printing press [1814] Koenig
	Principle of motor [1823] Faraday	□ Stethoscope [1818] Loennic	

	Conceptual &/or Institutional Developments	Information Acquisition &/or Storage Devices	Information Manipulation &/or Transmission Devices
			● Calculating machines [1823 - 1843] Babbage
			■ Chromo-lithography [1827] Zahn
Nineteenth Century	Ohm's law [1830] determining flow of electricity through a con ductor, G. S. Ohm	■ Paper matrix stereotype [1829] Genoux	
	Laws of Electrolysis [1833]		□ Magnetic telegraph [1833] Gauss and Weber
	● Application of statistical method to social phenomena [1835]		□ Needle telegraph [1837] Wheatstone
			□ Electromagnetic telegraph [1837] Morse
		■ Daguerrotype [1839] Daguerre and Niepce	■ Electrotype [1839] Jacobi
			■ Callotype [1839] Talbot
	Electromagnetism [1840] conversion of mechanical energy to electrical energy, Faraday	■ Microphotography [1840] Donne	
		■ Paper positives in photography [1841] Talbot	
	● Spectrum analysis [1843] Miller		■○ Typewriter [1843] Thurber

Conceptual &/or Institutional Developments	Information Acquisition &/or Storage Devices	Information Manipulation &/or Transmission Devices
■■		
Nineteenth Century	Electric arc patented [1845] Wright	
		■ ○ Rotating cylinder press [1846] Hoe
	■ Opthalmoscope [1850]	■ ● Electromagnetic clock [1851] Shepherd
	■ ● Mechanical ship's log [1853] Semens	□ Multiple telegraph on a single wire [1853] Gintl
		□ ○ Automatic telegraph messge recorder [1854] Hughes
	■ Color photographs [1856]	□ Phonautograph [1858] Scott
Theory of light and electricity [1864] Clerk-Maxwell	■ Moving pictures [1864] Ducos	
Electromagnetic wave theory [1870] Maxwell		■ ○ Typewriter [1867] Scholes
		□ Electric telephone [1876] Bell
		□ Microphone [1877] Edison
		□ Phonograph [1877] Edison

	Conceptual &/or Institutional Developments	Information Acquisition &/or Storage Devices	Information Manipulation &/or Transmission Devices

Nineteenth Century

Radio waves [1880] Hertz

◼ Motion picture camera [1882] Marley

◼ ○ Linotype [1884] Mergenthaler

◼ Hand camera [1886] Eastman

▢ Automatic telephone [1887]

◼ ○ Monotype [1887] Leviston

◼ ● Recording adding machine [1888] Burroughs

▢ Hard Rubber Phonograph records [1889]

◼ Motion picture camera [1889] Edison

▢ Radio-telegraph [1896] Marconi

▢ Loading coil for long distance telegraphy and telephony [1899] Pupin

	Conceptual &/or Institutional Developments	Information Acquisition &/or Storage Devices	Information Manipulation &/or Transmission Devices
Twentieth Century	Quantum theory [1900] Planck		☐ Transmission of human speech via radio waves [1900] Fessenden
		■ Ultramicroscope [1903] Zsigmondy	☐ Radio-telephone [1903]
		■● Electrocardiograph [1903] Einthoven	☐ Thermionic tube used to send radio waves [1904]
	Theory of relativity [1905] Einstein		
		■ Three-color screen photography [1907] Lumiere	
		■ Television-photograph [1907]	
		■● Gyrocompass [1910] Sperry	
		■ Reflecting telescope [1917]	Vacuum tube [1912] de Forest
		■ Space photography in discovery of asteroids [1920]	
			■● Self-winding wristwatch [1922] Harwood

Conceptual &/or Institutional Developments	Information Acquisition &/or Storage Devices	Information Manipulation &/or Transmission Devices

Twentieth Century

■ Sound-motion pictures [1923] de Forest

■ Iconoscope [1924] Zworkin

■ Television transmission of recognizable human images [1925] Baird

□ Electrola [1926]

■ Color motion picture demonstrated [1928] Eastman

■ Color television [1928] Baird

■ Coma-free mirror telescope [1930]

■ Radar [1935] Watson

□ Frequency modulation [1939] Armstrong

■ Electron microscope demonstrated [1940] Radio Corporation of America

■● "Electronic brain", automatic computer in U.S. [1942]

Idea of communications satellite proposed [1945] Clarke

	Conceptual &/or Institutional Developments	Information Acquisition &/or Storage Devices	Information Manipulation &/or Transmission Devices *20*

			■● Electronic digital computer [1946] University of Pennsylvania
Twentieth Century			
			Transistor [1947 Bell laboratory
	Mathematical Theory of Communication [1948] Shannon, Weaver	☐ Long-playing record [1948] Goldmark	
		■ Port radar system [1948]	
			▬ Cable television [1950]
		■ Optical scanners developed [1954]	
			▬ Ultra high frequency radio waves generated [1955] MIT
		■ Ion microscope [1956] Müller	☐ Transatlantic cable telephone [1956]
			▬ Visual telephone [1956] Bell Labs
			☐ Stereophonic recordings in common use [1958]
			■● "Second generation" computers [1958]*

Conceptual &/or Institutional Developments	Information Acquisition &/or Storage Devices	Information Manipulation &/or Transmission Devices

Twentieth Century

■ Weather satellite transmitting cloud cover images [1960]

▭ Radio-reflector satellite [1960]

☐ Experimental communications satellite [1960] NASA

■ TIROS I weather satellite transmitting Television images [1960]

▭◉ "Third generation" computers using integrated circuits [1965]*

■ 150-inch reflecting telescope [1970]

Microprocessor or semi-conductor chip [1971]

▭◉ Experimental coast-to-coast computer network in U.S. [1972]

▭ Video cassette recorder [1975]

▭ Cable TV integrated with TV satellite transmissions [1975]

▭ Fiber optics [1975]

■○ Teletext in Britain [1976]

Conceptual &/or Institutional Developments	Information Acquisition &/or Storage Devices	Information Manipulation &/or Transmission Devices

■ ○ QUBE interactive cable television in U.S. [1977]

Twentieth Century

☐ Cellular telephone [1977] AT&T

■ ○ Videotext [1979] British Telephone Authority

▬ ◖ 16K microcomputer [1980]

▬ ◖ 256K microcomputer [1986]

* = Also used for information storage.

About the Contributors

Benjamin J. Bates is a visiting assistant professor in telecommunications at Michigan State University. His studies focus on examining the evolution and development of communication systems through a consideration of the sources of, and influences on, value in those systems.

Robert Cathcart is professor in the Department of Communication Arts and Sciences at Queens College of the City University of New York. He coedited, with Gary Gumpert, three editions of *Inter/Media: Interpersonal Communication in a Media World* and coauthored, with Gary Gumpert, "Media Grammars, Generations, and Media Gaps," which appeared in *Critical Studies in Mass Communication,* and "I am a Camera: The Mediated Self," which appeared in *Communication Quarterly.*

David Carr is an associate professor of library and information studies at Rutgers University. His primary research interest is the cognitive management of cultural institutions—libraries, museums, public broadcasting, and similar settings for thought and learning. He has recently written essays entitled "The Situation of the Adult Learner in the Museum" and "The Situation of the Adult Learner in the Library." He serves as a consultant to the W.K. Kellogg Foundation, and will develop content for its conference, The Educative Museum, to be held in 1989. His book devoted to this topic is under preparation for Jossey-Bass.

James W. Dearing is a doctoral student at the Annenberg School of Communications, University of Southern California. He is currently investigating, along with Everett M. Rogers, the role of governments, universities, and private business in creating and managing areas of high-technology growth. Dearing is conducting his Ph.D. dissertation research on Tsukuba Science City in Japan.

T. Andrew Finn is a research associate at AT&T Bell Laboratories, Lincroft, NJ, and an associate member of the Ph.D. Program in Communication, Information, and Library Studies at Rutgers University. He is involved in the implementation and evaluation of new communication technologies and he has authored papers on the dynamics and organizational effects of voice and electronic messaging, computer conferencing, and organizational videotext.

Luis Fonseca is the Secretary for Manpower at the Ministry of Labour, Brazil.

Gary Gumpert is chairperson and professor in the Department of Communication Arts and Sciences at Queens College of the City University of New York. He coedited, with Robert Cathcart, three editions of *Inter/ Media: Interpersonal Communication in a Media World* and coauthored, with Robert Cathcart, "Mediated Interpersonal Communication: Toward a New Communication Typology," which appeared in the *Quarterly Journal of Speech,* and "Stereotyping: Images of the Foreigner," in *Intercultural Communication: A Reader.* He is the author of *Talking Tombstones and Other Tales of the Media Age.*

Michael Krippendorf is a doctoral Candidate in Communications at Temple University.

Judith K. Larsen is president and senior research scientist of Cognos Associates, a nonprofit research firm located in Silicon Valley, CA. She has directed research studies dealing with information use and the information society. Her research at Cognos Associates has focused on the impact of technology, and on public policy affecting the microelectronics industry.

Leah A. Lievrouw is an assistant professor in the Department of Communication at Rutgers University. She received her Ph.D. in Communication Theory and Research from the Annenberg School of Communications at the University of Southern California, and is a former research associate of the Institute for Communication Research at Stanford University. She is the editor, with Jorge Reina Schement, of *Competing Visions, Complex Realities: Social Aspects of the Information Society* (Ablex, 1988). Her research interests include scientific and scholarly communication and the social impacts of new communication technologies.

Quentin W. Lindsey is director of organized research in the College of Humanities and Social Sciences, North Carolina State University, Raleigh, and director of research and interdepartmental programs, North Carolina Central University, Durham. He has served as Science and Public Policy Advisor to James B. Hunt Jr., governor of North Carolina, and has directed various programs associated with the Research Triangle Institute.

Joshua Meyrowitz is professor of communication at the University of New Hampshire. His research areas have included instructional technology, Euripidean tragedy, role theory, news, and the impact of media on conceptions of childhood and adulthood, gender roles, and politics. Meyrowitz is the author of *No Sense of Place: The Impact of Electronic Media on Social Behavior* (Oxford University Press, 1985). His scholarly articles have appeared in various anthologies and in such journals as *Daedalus, Et cetera, The Educational Forum, American Theatre,* and *The Psychoanalytic Review.*

Gordon L. Miller received his Ph.D. from the School of Communication, Information, and Library Studies, Rutgers University, and a M.Phil in the History of Science from Cambridge University, England. His present research interests lie primarily in the social history of communication and information technologies, especially writing, printing, and computers. He was formerly assistant editor of *Information and Behavior* and is currently coediting, with Brent D. Ruben, a book entitled *Information, Communication, and the Unity of Life: General Systems Theory and Beyond.*

Mitchell Moss is an associate professor in the Graduate School of Public Administration at New York University.

Richard A. Nelson was formerly an associate director at the International Telecommunications Research Institute at the University of Houston.

Ryuzo Ogasawara is the executive managing director of Satellite Channels Incorporated of Tokyo, Japan. He worked as a senior writer for the *Asahi Shimbun,* covering government policies and business activities in telecommunications and broadcasting for 17 years. He is the author of many books and articles, including *Between Newspaper and Broadcasting, A Reader on Communications, Telecommunications,* and *Broadcasting Satellite.*

Gary P. Radford is a doctoral candidate in the School of Communication, Information, and Library Studies at Rutgers University. His research is involved with a cultural and textual examination of the discourses surrounding the concept of "the subliminal." He was assistant editor of *Information and Behavior: Volume Two* and is currently assistant editor of *Information and Behavior: Volume Three*.

Sheizaf Rafaeli is an assistant professor at the Hebrew University of Jerusalem, Israel. His areas of interest are the new technologies of interactive communication as well as political communication. His most recent article, "Interactivity: From New Media to Communication," appeared in *Advancing Communication Science: Merging Mass and Interpersonal Processes* (Sage, 1988).

Kathleen Kelley Reardon is an associate professor of business communication and preventative medicine in the School of Business Administration, University of Southern California. She was formerly research associate professor at the Health Behavior Research Institute, University of Southern California. She received her Ph.D. in interpersonal communication and persuasion from the University of Massachusetts. Her research interests include persuasion and its application to health, particularly cancer and AIDS.

Everett M. Rogers is Walter H. Annenberg Professor of Communications at the University of Southern California. He is currently investigating, along with James W. Dearing, the role of governments, universities, and private business in creating and managing areas of high-technology growth. He is author, with Arvind Singhal, of the forthcoming book *India's Information Revolution* (Sage, in press).

Jerry Salvaggio is the chief information officer for Whataburger, Inc., in Houston. He was formerly an associate professor and director of the International Telecommunications Research Institute at the University of Houston. He is author of *Telecommunications: Issues and Choices* (1983) and *Broadcast Communications Technology* (1985).

Jorge Reina Schement is an associate professor in the Department of Communication at Rutgers University. He received his Ph.D. from the Institute for Communication Research at Stanford University. He is coeditor of the *Telecommunications Policy Handbook* (Praeger, 1982). His research interests include theories of the information society, information policy, international communications, and minorities and communication issues.

Daniel A. Stout Jr. is a doctoral candidate in the School of Communication, Information, and Library Studies, Rutgers University, and a faculty member in the Department of Communication at Brigham Young University. He has published articles which focus on advertising and the social impacts of mass media in *Southern Speech Communication Journal* and the *Newspaper Research Journal*.

Lee Thayer is professor of communication and director of the honors program at the University of Wisconsin - Parkside. His most recent books are *On Communication: Essays in Understanding,* and *Talk and the Life of the Mind.* He has served as visiting professor in many universities in the United States and abroad.

Sari Thomas is the director of the Institute of Culture and Communication, and an associate professor of radio, television, and film, at Temple University. She received her Ph.D. from the Annenberg School of Communications at the University of Pennsylvania. Her research interests focus on the relationship between communication behavior, media, and culture.

Joseph Turow is an associate professor at the University of Pennsylvania's Annenberg School of Communications. A former head of the Speech Communication Association's Mass Communication Division, he is a member of the editorial boards of *Critical Studies in Mass Communication, Journal of Communication,* and the *Sage Annual Review of Communication Research.* His most recent book is *Playing Doctor: Television, Storytelling, and Medical Power* (Oxford University Press, 1989).

Rolf Wigand is a professor of communication and public affairs at Arizona State University. He has published nationally and internationally in the areas of organizational communication and behavior, social and policy issues of satellite broadcasting, telecommunication issues, and the impacts of office automation on the work environment.

Frederick Williams is professor and director of the Center for Research in Communication Technology and Society at the University of Texas at Austin. He is author of *The Communications Revolution, The Executive's Guide to Information Technology* (with H. Dordick: Wiley, 1984) and *Growing up with Computers* (with V. Williams: Morrow, 1984). Williams also served as a major consultant to the Walt Disney organization in the design of "Spaceship Earth," a pavillion at Disney's EPCOT Center near Orlando, Florida, that portrays highlights in the history of human communication.

Subject & Citation Index

Gary P. Radford and James D. Anderson

This index was created using the NEPHIS (Nested Phrase Indexing System), developed by Timothy C. Craven, as implemented in the IOTA (Information Organization through Textual Analysis) textual database management system.

References

Anderson, James D.; Radford, Gary (1988). "Back-of-the-book Indexing with the Nested Phrase Indexing System (NEPHIS)." *The Indexer* 16(2): 79–84; October 1988.

Anderson, James D. (1988). "IOTA: Information Organization based on Textual Analysis." In *The Library Microcomputer Environment: Management Issues,* edited by Sheila S. Intner and Jane Anne Hannigan. Phoenix: Oryx Press. pp. 145–168.

Craven, Timothy C. (1986). *String Indexing.* Orlando, FL: Academic Press. 246 p.

Abel (J.)
  Reference on Role of Broadcasting in Information Societies : 305
Abel (J.D.) : 129
Access to Information
  See Information Access
Adaptation
  and Mediation : 31
Adoption
  of Information Technology and Ideology : 255
  of Information Technology and Information Infrastructure : 255
Adoption Studies
  and Communication Technology : 48

Advertising
  and Information : 381
  ProblematicNature in Economic Theory : 389–391
  Role of Tropisms : 341
Agarwala-Rogers (R.) : 48
AIDS Prevention
  and Communication Theory : 96, 109–110
  and Language : 111
  and Mass Communication.
    —Reference to Williams (L.S.) : 111
  and Minority Groups.
    —Reference to Williams (L.S.) : 111–112

AIDS Prevention *(continued)*
and Persuasion Strategies : 108
—Reference to Reardon (K.K.) : 107
and Self-Perception : 110
Alwin (D.F.) : 142
American Cancer Society : 111
American Society for Information Science :
45
American Telephone and Telegraph Com-
pany
See AT&T
Analogy
Role in Science : 360
—Reference to Bohm (D.) : 39
Anderson (J.D.) : 401
Apple Computers : 196
Applied Research
versus Basic Research : 269
Argyle (M.) : 69, 71, 72
Aristotle : 109
Arnheim (R.) : 359, 369
Aronson (S.H.) : 123
Arrow (K.J.) : 381, 383, 389
Arrow (K.J.)
Reference on Social Efficiency of Infor-
mation as Problematic Concept :
388
Asher (H.B.) : 174
Asynchronous Nature
of Communication Technology : 190
AT&T : 61, 73
AT&T
Deregulation Communications Revolu-
tion : 286–287
Atkin (C.) : 90
Atkin (C.K.) : 110
Atkin (C.K.)
Reference on Sociability and Mass Me-
dia Use : 133
Auditory Perception
Traveling Wave Theory
—Reference to Bekesy (G. von) : 352
Automatistic Nature
of Human Communication : 324–326
—Role of Tropisms : 326
of Self-Expression : 325
of Understanding : 325
Automobile Industry
in Brazil : 220
Avery (R.K.) : 131

Baba (M.L.) : 272
Babbitt (Bruce) : 272, 278
Babe (R.E.) : 263
Bacon (Francis) : 118, 122
Bacon (P.) : 366

Badzinski (D.M.) : 99
Ball-Rokeach (S.J.) : 5, 47, 96, 104, 128
Ball-Rokeach (S.J.)
Reference on Media Dependency The-
ory : 104–105
Ball-Rokeach (S.J.) and DeFleur (M.L.)
Reference on Dependency Model of
Mass Communication : 24
Bandura (A.) : 103
Bank of America : 194
Banking and Financing Industry
in Brazil : 224
Banks (C.) : 70
Barefoot (J.) : 48
Barker (R.G.) : 71
Barker (R.G.)
Reference on Role of Social Situations in
Human Behavior : 70
Barron (J.A.) : 130
Barthes (Roland)
Reference on Mass Communication and
Literacy : 29
Basic Research
versus Applied Research : 269
Bates (B.J.) : 392
Bauer (C.) : 47, 50
Bauer (R.A.) : 130
Bauhin (Gaspard) : 352
Beat Generation : 120, 122
Beat Generation Poets : 118
Becker (L.) : 152
Behavior
See also Human Behavior
and Communication : 40, 49
and Context : 68, 74, 77
and Mediated Encounters.
—Reference to Schleflen (A.E.) : 75–
76
and Physical Location : 76
in Children and Peer Groups : 102
Behavioral Psychologists
View of Human Life : 329
Bekesy (G. von)
Reference on Traveling Wave Theory of
Auditory Perception : 352
Bell (D.) : 185, 191, 275, 297
Bell (D.)
Class Bias.
—Reference to Schement (J.R.) and
Leivrouw (L.A.) : 297
Reference on Information Societies ver-
sus Industrial Societies : 187
Beniger (J.) : 191
Beniger (J.R.) : 3, 126, 171
Bentsen (Senator Lloyd) : 302
Berelson (B.) : 13, 132, 133

Bertalanffy (L. von)
  Reference to Transdisciplinary Nature of
    General Systems Theory : 349, 350
Bierig (J.) : 131
Biology
  Role of Resonance Concept : 351
Biotechnological Explanation
  of Mediation : 31
Biotechnology
  See also North Carolina Biotechnology
    Center
Black (M.) : 359
Black (S.)
  Reference on Promotion of High Tech-
    nology Industries in South Carolina :
    300–301
Black (S.H.) : 380, 382
Blank (A.) : 104
Bloom (B.S.) : 297
Bloom (J.L.) : 263
Bloomsbury Circle : 118, 120
Blos (P.)
  Reference to—on Knowledge of Health
    of Children : 97
Blumberg (H.H.) : 107
Blumer (H.)
  Reference on Crowds versus Public : 14
Blumler (J.G.) : 132, 134
Bogart (L.) : 133
Bohm (D.) : 350
Bohm (D.)
  Reference on Concept of Structure : 356,
    357
  Reference on Role of Analogy in Science :
    359
  Reference on Structure and Order : 357
  Reference on Structure and Organization :
    358
Bohn (T.W.) : 73
Bolling (G.H.) : 260
Bolter (W.G.) : 257
Bond (James) : 340
Bonnard : 372
Boorstin (D.J.) : 120–121
Bostian (L.R.) : 133
Boulding (K.) : 373
Boulding (K.E.) : 381, 386
Bowes (J.E.) : 188
Bradley (H.) : 47, 62
Bransford (J.) : 353
Braudy (L.) : 120
Brazil
  Adoption of New Technology : 218–219
  Automobile Industry : 220
  Banking and Financing Industry : 224
  Computer Industry : 220

Development of Industry : 217
Government Policy and Communication
  Technology : 221–225
Growth and Modernization : 218
Level of Employment : 218
Military Weapons Industry : 220
Pharmaceutical Industry : 220
Technological Development.
  —Reference to Castro (C. de M.) :
    220–221
Unemployment and Technological De-
  velopment : 223–224
Vocational Education : 217
Broadcasting
  Role in Information Societies.
    —Reference to Abel (J.) : 305
Brody (R.) : 129, 130
Bronowski (J.) : 275, 359
Brooks (J.) : 123
Brown (J.D.) : 107, 108, 110, 112
Brown (J.R.) : 132, 134
Brown (R.V.) : 130
Brown (T.R.) : 129–130
Browning (E.) : 242
Bruner (J.S.) : 359, 369
Buarque (S.) : 224
Budd (R.W.) : 6
Buell (E.H. Jr.) : 129, 130, 152
Bullet Theory
  of Mass Communication : 4
Bullfinch Mythology : 22
Burgess (Bill) : 301
Butler (Samuel) : 323

Cable and Broadcasting Act
  in Great Britain : 262
Cable Communications Act : 302
Calvino (I.) : 376
Calvino (I.)
  Reference on Invisible City Metaphor of
    Museum Experience : 376
Campbell (J.)
  Reference on Information as Unifying
    Concept : 191
Cantril (H.) : 13
La Capra (D.) : 123
Carello (C.) : 353
Carey (J.) : 48
Carey (J.)
  Reference on Innis-McLuhan Perspec-
    tive of Mass Communication : 23
Carlin (J.C.) : 131
Carlson (F.) : 47
Caroll (Lewis) : 330, 332–333
Carroll (S.) : 69
Carter (President Jimmy) : 305

Case (D.) : 48
Case (D.O.) : 401
Castro (C. de M.) : 212, 222
Castro (C. de M.)
  Reference on Communication Technol-
    ogy and Third World Countries :
    214–215
  Reference on Technological Develop-
    ment in Brazil : 220–221
Cathcart (R.) : 3, 4, 5, 25, 28
Cathcart (R.) and Gumpert (G.)
  Reference on Photography and Self-Im-
    age : 29
Central Countries
  and Communication Technology : 212
Chaffee (S.) : 15
Chaffee (S.H.) : 95, 132, 133, 134, 135, 175
Chaffee (S.R.) : 101
Chanowitz (B.) : 104
Charters (W.W.) : 13
Chassin (L.A.) : 102
Chemistry
  Role of Resonance Concept : 351
Chen (Y-C.A.) : 281
Chesebro (J.W.) : 25
Children
  Behavior Peer Groups : 102
  Knowledge of Health : 96–97
    —Reference to Blos (P.) : 97
    —Reference to Gochman (D.) : 97
    —Reference to Lewis (C.E.) and
      Lewis (M.A.) : 97
    —Reference to Nagy (M.H.) : 97
Childs (Julia) : 136
Choice
  and the Communications Revolution :
    293
Christie (B.) : 47, 50, 171
Chu (G.C.) : 129
Chu (L.L.) : 129
Class Bias
  in work of Bell (D.).
    —Reference to Schement (J.R.) and
      Leivrouw (L.A.) : 297
  in work of Machlup (F.).
    —Reference to Schement (J.R.) and
      Leivrouw (L.A.) : 296
Clausen (A.R.) : 129–130
Cliches
  and Tropes : 342–343
Coase (R.H.) : 383
Cohen (R.B.) : 240
Collins (L.M.) : 102
Columbia University
  Mass Communication Research : 13

Commercialization
  and Technological Innovation : 269
Common Carriers
  Regulation : 60–61
Communication
  and Behavior : 40, 49
  and Control : 50
  and Involvement : 50
  and Mediation : 4, 28, 41, 42
  and Social Context : 54, 55, 57
  and Temporality : 49–50
  Common Dimensions : 49–55
  Convergence Model : 40, 190
  Coordinated Management of Meaning
    Theory : 41
  Human—*See* Human Communication
  Interpersonal—*See* Interpersonal Com-
    munication
  Roman Systems : 32
  Sense-Making Theory : 41
  Shannon and Weaver's Model : 190
  University-Industry—.
    —Definition : 268
Communication Monopolies
  Reference to Innis (H.A.) : 33
Communication Networks
  and University-Industry Technology
    Transfer : 276
Communication Patterns
  Failure of the Objective Perspective :
    333–334
  Role of Resonance Concept : 354–355
Communication Policy
  and Communications Systems Model :
    60–61
Communication Research
  Role of Interactivity in— : 171
Communication Systems Model : 37–61
Communication Systems Model
  and General Systems Theory : 39
  and Group Processes : 59–60
  and Media Effects : 56–57
  and Media Uses and Gratifications : 58
  and Uses and Gratifications Theory : 59
  Underlying Assumptions : 38–41
Communication Technology
  and Adoption Studies : 48
  and Central Countries : 212
  and Everyday Life : 285
  and Global Markets : 214
  and Government Policy in Brazil : 221–
    225
  and Implications for Communication Re-
    search : 190
  and Information Societies : 193
  and Intellectual History : 121

Communication Technology *(continued)*
and Interactivity : 125–126
and Literary Circles : 121
and New Media : 45
and Production Patterns.
—Reference to Coriat (B.) : 212
and Sociability : 171
and Social Structure : 48
and Third World Countries.
—Reference to Castro (C. de M.) :
214–215
Asynchronous Nature : 190
Demassified Nature : 190
Deregulation in West Germany : 312
Interactive Nature : 190
Role in Information Societies : 189, 190,
298, 299, 300
Role in Organizations.
—Reference to Kling (R.) : 48
Communication Technology Policy
in France : 309–310
in Great Britain : 309
in Japan : 308
in West Germany : 308
in Western Europe : 310–313
of European Economic Community
(EEC) : 312–317
Communication Theory
and AIDS Prevention : 96, 109, 110
and New Media.
—Reference to Rice (R.E.) and associates : 45
—Reference to Steinfield (C.) and
Fulk (J.) : 46
Communications Revolution
and Choice : 293
and Connectivity : 293
and Demassification of Media : 293
and Deregulation of AT&T : 286–287
and Electronic Leisure : 287–288
and Electronic Publishing : 290–292
and Mobility : 293
and Personal Computing : 288–290
and Telephony : 286–287
and Time Displacement : 293
Social-Psychological Implications.
—Reference to Williams (F.), Rice
(R.E.), and Dordick (H.S.) : 293
Communications Revolution (Book by F.
Williams) : 286
Communications Systems Model
and Communication Policy : 60–61
Communist-Totalitarian Model
of Technological Innovation : 255–256
Community
Role in Museum Experience : 375

Competitive Model
of Technological Innovation *See* Market-
place Model of Technological Inno-
vation
Complexity
and Mediation : 31
Compte (Auguste) : 11, 35
Computer Conferencing Systems
and Group Processes : 59
Computer Industry
in Brazil : 220
Computer Users
and Sociability : 171
Computer-Mediated Communication
and Sociability.
—Reference to Kiesler (S.), Siegel
(J.), and McGuire (T.W.) : 171
Computers
Fifth Generation—in Japan : 228
Computing
See also Personal Computing
Conceptual Categories
Role in Understanding : 332–333
Conflicts of Interest
and University-Industry Technology
Transfer : 279
Connectivity
and the Communications Revolution :
293
Consciousness
Priority of Unconsciousness : 335
Constructivist Approach
to Social Behavior : 40
Content Analysis
and Para-Social Interaction : 137
Context
and Behavior : 68, 74, 77
and Information Systems : 74, 76
and Mass Communication : 26, 76, 77
and Media Use : 78–84
and Roles : 86
and Situation : 67–68
Control
and Communication : 50
Convergence Model
of Communication : 40, 190
Conversation
Role in Museum Experience : 372
Conversational Technologies
and Mass Communication : 38
Converse (P.E.) : 129–130
Cook (T.D.) : 103
Cooley (C.H.) : 74, 84
Cooley (Charles Horton) : 12

Coordinated Management of Meaning Theory
  of Communication : 41
Coriat (B.)
  Reference on Communication Technology and Production Patterns : 212
Cornsweet (T.N.) : 353
Costs
  Marginal—of Information : 384
  of Information as Problematic Concept : 384–386
Coulombe (J.) : 47
Courville (L.) : 263
Cowling (M.) : 129
Craik (F.I.M.) : 104
Crawford (M.H.) : 256
Creativity
  Role of Tropes : 345
Crisis
  and Technology : 212
Crittenden (J.) : 131
Cronen (V.E.) : 41, 50
Cronkite (Walter) : 138, 176
Crowds
  versus Public.
    —Reference to Blumer (H.) : 14
Culliton (B.J.) : 275, 279
Culture
  and Mind : 331
Cunha (P.) : 218
Czitrom (D.) : 12–13

Dana (J.C.) : 367–368
Dannefer (W.D.) : 131
Davis (H.) : 130, 172
Davis (O.A.) : 387
Davis (W.)
  Reference on Information Exchange in Silicon Valley : 198
Dearing (J.) : 106
Decentralization
  and Information Societies : 281
  Role in Information Societies.
    —Reference to Moss (M.L.) : 299
  and Family Units.
    —Reference to McLeod (J.M.) and Chaffee (S.R.) : 101
    —Reference to Wood (B.) : 99–100
  and Peer Groups.
    —Reference to Sussman (S.) : 102
Decentralization of Production and Decision Making Operations
  Role of Telecommunications : 240
Decision Theory
  and Information : 383
Deetz (S.A.) : 62

DeFleur (M.L.) : 24, 35, 47
Degler (C.N.) : 86
Demassification
  of Media and Electronic Leisure : 288
  of Media and the Communications Revolution : 293
Demassified Nature
  of Communication Technology : 190
Demsetz (H.) : 381, 384, 386
Department of Health and Human Services : 110
Dependency Model
  of Mass Communication.
    —Reference to Ball-Rokeach (S.J.) and DeFleur (M.L.) : 24
Deregulation
  of Communication Technology in West Germany : 312
Dervin (B.) : 41, 380
Description
  Metaphoric Nature : 331
Dewey (John) : 12, 334
Dictionary of Occupational Titles : 297
Dimmick (J.) : 131
Direct Broadcast Satellite Systems (DBS)
  in Japan : 230
Direct Sources
  of Documentation : 119
Disorder
  Role in Museum Experience.
    —Reference to Valery (P.) : 371
Documentation
  Direct Sources : 119
  Personal Sources : 119
Donohew (L.) : 133, 136
Donohew (L.)
  Reference on Sociability and Mass Media Use : 134
Dordick (H.) : 45, 47, 62
Dordick (H.S.) : 293
Doyle (P.) : 381
Dubrovsky (V.) : 48
Duke University : 206
Duncan (H.D.) : 74, 84, 87
Duncan (H.D.)
  Reference on Social Identity and Physical Location : 85
Dungeons and Dragons Game : 176
Dunwoody (S.) : 152
Dutton (W.) : 47
Dutton (W.)
  Reference on Ecology of Games Perspective of Information Societies : 304–305
  Reference on Information Societies and Political Science : 304

Eastern Communication Association : 9
Eckland (B.K.) : 107
Ecological Thinking
and Resonance Concept.
—Reference to McLuhan (M.H.) : 354
Ecology of Games Perspective
of Information Societies.
—Reference to Dutton (W.) : 304–305
Economic Competition
United States-Japan : 186
Economic Good
Information : 380–385
Economic Success
and Technological Innovation : 263
Economic Theory
Problematic Nature of Advertising : 389–
391
Problematic Nature of Information : 379,
380, 382
Role of Information : 380
Economics of Information Technology
as an Area of Study : 254
Edelstein (A.S.) : 380
Edgar (P.) : 257
Education
and Personal Computing : 290
Einstein (Albert) : 334–345
Eisenstein (E.L.) : 87
Electronic Leisure
and Demassification of Media : 288
and the Communications Revolution :
287–288
Electronic Publishing
and the Communications Revolution :
290–292
Electronic Text Services
in United States : 291–292
Ellis (D.G.) : 131
Ellis Island : 372
Ellul (J.)
Reference on Media Determinism : 23–
24
Energy Amplification
and Resonance : 350
Engel's Ratio : 188
Entrepreneural Boldness
and Marketplace Model of Technological
Innovation : 260
Entrepreneurism
and Silicon Valley : 195–199
Environment
and Mediation : 32
Episteme
Western-.
—Literalizing Nature : 328

Western—of Referential Language :
326–327
Escape
and Mass Media Use.
—Reference to Katz (E.) and Foulkes
(D.) : 135
Europe
See also Western Europe
European Economic Community (EEC)
Communication Technology Policy :
312–317
European Information Industries
Poor performance : 310, 311
Evans (J.) : 262
Eveland (J.D.)
Reference on Policy Making Organiza-
tions and Technological Innovation :
301
Everyday Life
and Communication Technology : 285
Evolution
Two-Sided—Mediation : 32
Eward (R.) : 257
Exchange Value
of Information : 383
Eyal (C.) : 130
Eysenck (H.J.) : 138
Eysenck (S.G.B.) : 138

Facts
Objective Nature : 334
Faculty Consulting
and University-Industry Technology
Transfer : 274
Faculty Entrepreneurs
and University-Industry Technology
Transfer : 274–275
Fame
See also Sociology of Fame
Family Units
and Communication Patterns; Reference
to
—Reference to McLeod (J.M.) and
Chaffee (S.R.) : 101
—Reference to Wood (B.) : 99–100
and Health Attitudes.
—Reference to Mechanic (D.) : 98, 99
Fashion Genres
Role of Tropisms : 341
Federal Communication Commission : 60–
61
Feedback
and Self-Perception : 107
Fei (X.) : 106
Ferguson (C.E.) : 380, 392
Ferment in the Field : 46

Fibre Optics
  See Optical Fibre Systems
Field Museum of Chicago : 365
Fielding (G.) : 62
Fifth Generation Computers
  in Japan : 228, 260
Figurative Language
  versus Literal Language : 327–328
Financial Markets
  Growth.
    —Telecommunications Reference to
      Germany (J.D.) and Morton (J.E.) :
      241
    —Telecommunications Reference to
      Kindleberger (C.P.) : 241
  Growth in the Pacific Rim : 242
  Growth Optical Fibre Systems : 243–244
Financial Times Media Intelligence Unit :
  261
Finn (T.A.) : 4, 44, 48, 55
Fiske (S.T.) : 107
Fitzpatrick (M.A.) : 99
Flay (B.R.) : 102, 110
Flay (B.R.)
  Reference on Mass Communication and
    Health Attitudes : 103
Forgas (J.P.) : 71
Forsythe (S.A.) : 130
Foulkes (D.) : 135, 136, 137, 175
Fourier Analysis
  and Resonance Concept : 353
France
  Communication Technology Policy :
    309–310
France (Raoul) : 35–36
Fredericksen (N.) : 71
Friedson (E.) : 14
Fukushima (A.) : 380
Fulk (J.) : 48
Fuller (W.E.) : 122
Furnham (A.) : 69, 71, 72
Furstenberg (F.F.) : 102

Games
  Role in Understanding : 336–337
Garfinkel (H.) : 70
Garris (Karl) : 317
Gaudet (H.) : 13, 132, 133
Geiger (K.) : 130
Geller (V.) : 47
Gemeinschaft : 11–12
Gender
  and Roles : 86
General Systems Theory
  and the Communication Systems Model :
    39

Transdisciplinary Nature.
  —Reference to Bertalanffy (L. von) :
    349, 350
Genres
  Fashion—.
    —Role of Tropisms : 341
  Literary—.
    —Role of Tropisms : 340
  Musical—.
    —Role of Tropisms : 341
  Television—.
    —Role of Tropisms : 340
Gerbner (G.) : 15, 379
Gerbner (G.)
  Reference on Resonance Concept and
    Mainstreaming : 354–355
Germany (J.D.) : 241
Germany (J.D.) and Morton (J.E.)
  Reference on Telecommunications and
    Growth of Financial Markets : 241
Gerson (E.M.) : 48
Gerth (H.H.) : 275
Gibbs (B.) : 48
Gibson (D.V.) : 281
Gibson (J.J.)
  Reference on Resonance Concept and
    Perceptual Meaning : 353
Gilbert (Walter) : 274
Giles (H.) : 69
Gilfillan (D.) : 123
Gill (C.) : 199
Gitlin (T.)
  Reference on Television and Information
    Access : 87
Global City
  London.
    —Reference to Hewlett (N.) and Topo-
      rowski (J.) : 240
Global Markets
  and Communication Technology : 214
Glover (T.W.) : 131
Gochman (D.)
  Reference on Knowledge of Health of
    Children : 97
Goffman (E.) : 71, 72, 74, 79, 84, 87
Goffman (E.)
  Reference on Role of Social Situations in
    Human Behavior : 68
Goldman (Albert) : 121
Gottlieb (B.H.) : 102
Gouldner (A.) : 11
Gove (W.R.) : 92
Government Policy
  and Communication Technology in Bra-
    zil : 221–225
  and Information Societies : 191

Government Support of University-Industry
—Technology Transfer : 276
—Technology Transfer in Research Triangle of North Carolina : 277–278
—Technology Transfer in United States : 277
Granovetter (M.) : 102
Gray (P.) : 47
Great Britain
    Cable and Broadcasting Act : 262
    Communication Technology Policy : 309
    Public Utility Model of Technological Innovation : 262
    Telecommunications Act : 262
Greenberg (S.R.) : 133
Gregory (M.) : 69
Gregory (R.L.) : 359
Grey (D.L.) : 129–130
Gross (L.) : 15
Grossberg (S.)
    Reference on Resonance Concept and Perception : 353
Group of Thirty : 241
Group Processes
    and Communication Systems Model : 59–60
    and Computer Conferencing Systems : 59
Grube (J.W.) : 104
Grun (B.) : 397
Guest (Romeo) : 206
Guichard Du Verney (Joseph) : 352
Gumpert (G.) : 3, 4, 5, 25, 28, 34
Guthrie (W.K.C.) : 360
Gwilliam (K.M.) : 123

Hahnemann (S.) : 352
Hakansson (P.A.) : 137
Haken (H.) : 350
Hall (A.) : 102
Hall (E.) : 79
Hall (K.) : 381
Hancock (E.) : 279
Haney (C.) : 70
Hanneman (G.) : 47
Hansen (W.B.) : 102
Harre (R.) : 70
Hauser (R.M.) : 142
Hawkins (R.P.) : 3
Head (J.G.) : 387
Health Attitudes
    and Family Units.
        —Reference to Mechanic (D.) : 98–99
    and Mass Communication.
        —Reference to Flay (B.R.) : 103

Hebb (D.O.) : 353
Helmholtz (H. von) : 352, 359
Henry VII : 373
Hershleifer (J.) : 382–383
Hewlett (N.) : 240–241
Hewlett (N.) and Toporowski (J.)
    Reference on London as a Global City : 240
Hewlett-Packard : 196
Hiebert (R.E.) : 73
High Definition Television (HDTV)
    in Japan : 229–230
High Technology Companies
    Factors which Determine Location.
        —Reference to Smilor (R.W.), Kozmetsky (G.), and Gibson (D.V.) : 281
High Technology Industries
    Promotion in South Carolina.
        —Reference to Black (S.) : 300–301
Hill (C.T.) : 107
Hill (D.B.) : 129
Hiltz (S.R.) : 47, 48, 59, 60, 171
Hirshhorn Collection : 367
Hirshleifer (J.) : 380, 381, 388
Historical Chronologies
    and Knowledge : 398
History
    Intellectual—See Intellectual History
Hodges (Governor Luther) : 205, 206, 207, 280
Hofstadter (D.R.) : 360
Holographic Theory
    of Memory and Resonance Concept.
        —Reference to Pribram (K.H.) : 353
Home Shopping Networks
    and Information Network Systems (ISDN) : 228
Homet (R.) : 258
Horton (D.) : 73, 136, 137
Horton (D.) and Wohl (R.R.)
    Reference on Mass Communication and Para-Social Interaction : 136–137
Hot Rod Magazine : 31
Houlberg (R.) : 137–138
Hovland (C.) : 13
Howitt (D.) : 90
Hughes (M.) : 92
Human Behavior
    and Personality : 69
    Role of Social Situations. Reference to
        —Barker (R.G.) : 70
        —Goffman (E.) on— : 68
        —Milgram (S.) : 68–69
Human Communication
    and Information Societies : 187
    and Mediation : 22

Human Communication (continued)
  and Rationality : 40
  Automatistic Nature : 324–326
    —Role of Tropisms : 326
  Role of Tropisms : 338
  Subliminal Nature : 341
Human Communication Theory
  Conceptual Failure : 330
Human Experience
  and Museums.
    —Reference to Weil (S.E.) : 367
Humphrey (Hubert) : 80
Hunt (Governor James) : 207, 278
Hunter (L.) : 38
Hymes (D.) : 69
Hypodermic Model
  See Bullet Theory

IBM
  and Silicon Valley.
    —Organizational Differences : 307
Ideas
  Role in Museum Experience : 368
Identification
  Role in Museum Experience : 370
Ideology
  and Adoption of Information Technology :
    255
Ikeda (K.) : 262
Imagination
  Role in Museum Experience : 369
Independent Commission for Worldwide
    Telecommunications Development :
    248
Individual Psychology
  and Mass Communication : 13
Industrial Liaison Programs
  and University-Industry Techology
    Transfer : 274
Industrial Societies
  versus Information Societies : 194
    —Reference to Bell (D.) : 187
    —Reference to Porat (M.U.) : 187
Industrialized Nature
  of Mass Communication : 16, 17, 26
Industry-University Technology Transfer
  See University-Industry Technology
    Transfer
Indwelling
  Role in Museum Experience.
    —Reference to Polanyi (M.) : 369
Information
  and Advertising : 381
  and Decision Theory : 383
  and Social Efficiency : 388–389
  as Economic Good : 380–385

as Private Good versus Information as
    Public Good : 386–388
  as Unifying Concept.
    —Reference to Campbell (J.) : 191
  Costs as Problematic Concept : 384–386
  Exchange Value : 383
  Marginal Costs : 384
  Problematic Nature in Economic Theory :
    379, 380, 382
  Public versus Private Nature : 381
  Role in Economic Theory : 380
  Role in Understanding : 337
  Social Efficiency as Problematic Con-
    cept.
    —Reference to Arrow (K.J.) : 388
  Utility Value : 382
  Value as Problematic Concept : 382–384
Information Access
  and Information Systems : 88–89
  and Literacy : 89
  and Roles : 87–88
  and Television.
    —Reference to Gitlin (T.) : 87
Information Age
  See Information Societies
Information Capitals
  Growth.
    —Reference to Moss (M.L.) : 299
Information Exchange
  in Silicon Valley.
    —Reference to Davis (W.) : 198
Information Infrastructure
  and Adoption of Information Technology :
    255
Information Needs
  versus Information Delivery : 3
Information Network Systems (ISDN)
  and Home Shopping Networks : 228
  Evaluation in Japan : 229
  in Japan : 228
Information Overload
  Reference to Pool (I. de Sola) : 188
Information Societies
  Alternative Classifications.
    —Reference to Schement (J.R.) and
      Leivrouw (L.A.) : 297
  and Communication Technology : 193
  and Decentralization : 281
  and Government Policy : 191
  and Human Communication : 187
  and Personal Relationships : 198
  and Policy Issues : 308–316
  and Political Science.
    —Reference to Dutton (W.) : 304
  and Regulation.
    —Reference to Mitchell (M.) : 302

Information Societies *(continued)*
and Social Problems : 189
and University-Industry Technology
Transfer : 268
and Values : 209–210
Areas of Academic Concern : 295–297
Characteristics.
—Reference to Rogers (E.M.) and
Chen (Y-C. A.) : 281
Current Research : 185
Definitions : 187
Development of Analytical Tools.
—Reference to Schement (J.R.) and
Leivrouw (L.A.) : 296–297
Ecology of Games Perspective.
—Reference to Dutton (W.) : 304–305
in States of Transition.
—Reference to Sterling (C.) : 303–304
Japanese Perspective : 187–188
Methodological and Conceptual Issues :
296–297
Myths.
—Reference to Weingarten (R.) : 302–
303
Nature of Technological Innovation : 208
Organizational Differences : 306–307
Problems of Prediction.
—Reference to Williams (F.) : 298
Role of Broadcasting.
—Reference to Abel (J.) : 305
Role of Communication Technology :
189, 190, 298, 299, 300
Role of Decentralization.
—Reference to Moss (M.L.) : 299
Social-Psychological Implications.
—Reference to Williams (F.) : 298
University-Industry Relations : 296
versus Industrial Societies : 194
—Reference to Bell (D.) : 187
—Reference to Porat (M.U.) : 187
Work Ethic : 195
Information Systems
See also Meta-Information Systems
and Context : 74, 76
and Information Access : 88–89
nd Meta-Information Systems : 89
Nationalization Public Utility Model of
Technological Innovation : 261
Information Technology
See also Communication Technology
Adoption and Ideology : 255
Adoption and Information Infrastructure :
255
and National Economies : 254
Definition : 396

Time-Line : 403–423
—Design : 398–400
—Intellectual Themes : 400–401
Information Theory
Failure of the Objective Perspective :
333–334
Inkeles (A.) : 130
Innis (H.A.) : 23, 35, 78
Innis (H.A.)
Reference on Communication Monopo-
lies : 33
Innis-McLuhan Perspective
of Mass Communication.
—Reference to Carey (J.) : 23
Innovation
See also Technological Innovation
Intel : 196
Intellectual History
and Communication Technology : 121
and Literary Circles : 118–123
Intelligence
and Rationality : 356
and Resonance : 356–360
Interaction
Para-Social—*See* Para-Social Interaction
Interactive Nature
of Communication Technology : 190
Interactive Use
of Mass Communication : 126
Interactivity : 4, 5
Interactivity
and Communication Technology : 125–
126
and Interpersonal Communication : 172
and Letters to the Editor : 128
and Mass Communication : 127
and Mass Media Use : 172
Definition : 127
functionality : 173
Implications for Further Research : 174–
176
Methodological Weaknesses : 173, 174
Role in Communication Research : 171
International Communication Association :
45
International Trade
and Marketplace Model of Technological
Innovation : 261
and Public Utility Model of Technological Innovation : 261
Interpersonal Communication
and Interactivity : 172
and Organizational Communication : 44
and Place : 72
as Face-to-Face Communication : 43

Interpersonal Communication Theory
versus Mass Communication Theory : 3,
4, 5, 6, 41, 42, 43, 73, 95, 96, 126,
128, 132
Interpersonal Encounters
versus Mediated Encounters : 75–76
Interpersonal Relationships
and Mass Communication.
—Reference to Thayer (L.) : 25–26
Interpersonal Values
in Silicon Valley : 201
Interpretation
Role in Understanding : 331, 335
Invisible City Metaphor
of Museum Experience.
—Reference to Calvino (I.) : 376
Invisible Meanings
Role in Museum Experience : 371
Involvement
and Communication : 50
and Social Presence : 50
Ito (Y.) : 188, 263, 380
Ito (Y.)
Reference on Johoka Shakai : 187

Jackson (Michael) : 345
James (Henry) : 122
Janis (I.) : 13
Jantsch (E.) : 350, 354
Japan
Communication Technology Policy : 308
Direct Broadcast Satellite Systems
(DBS) : 230
Evaluation of Information Network Systems (ISDN) : 229
Fifth Generation Computers : 228, 260
High Definition Television (HDTV) :
229, 230
Intormation Network Systems (ISDN) :
228
Public Utility Model of Technological Innovation : 262
Research and Development of Microelectronics : 228
Satellite Technology Development : 232
Space Development : 231–232
Telecommunications Industry : 231
Telecommunications Market : 232–233
—Effect of Bureaucracy : 233–237
University-Industry Technology Transfer :
271
Japan Model
of Technological Innovation versus
United States Model of Technological Innovation.
—Reference to Tomita (T.) : 263

Japanese Ministry of Posts and Telecommunications : 229
Jaynes (J.) : 359
Jensen (J.) : 6
Johansen (R.) : 47, 59
Johnson (B.M.) : 48
Johnson (K.) : 48
Johnson (M.) : 359
Johnsson-Smaragdi (U.) : 137
Johnstone (J.W.C.)
Reference on Sociability and Mass Media Use : 134
Johoka Shakai : 188, 263
Johoka Shakai
Reference to Ito (Y.) : 187
Journal of Irreproducible Results : 344
Jowett (G.) : 12
Jung (Carl) : 370, 373

Katz (E.) : 132, 135, 136, 137, 138, 148, 175
Katz (E.) and Foulkes (D.)
Reference on Mass Media Use and Escape : 135
Kefauver (E.) : 130
Keller (Helen) : 330–331
Kelley (H.) : 13
Kennedy (President John F.) : 343
Kerlinger (F.N.) : 173–174
Kerlinger (F.N.)
Reference on Nature of a Theory of Mediation : 34
Kerouac (Jack) : 120
Kiesler (S.) : 47, 48, 50, 59, 171
Kiesler (S.), Siegel (J.), and McGuire
(T.W.)
Reference on Sociability and Computer-Mediated Communication : 171
Kincaid (D.L.) : 190, 276
Kincaid (L.) : 5, 40
Kindleberger (C.P.)
Reference on Telecommunications and
Growth of Financial Markets : 241
Kirby (S.) : 242, 245
Klein (F. G.) : 133
Klempner (A.) : 129
Kling (R.) : 62
Kling (R.)
Reference on Role of Communication
Technology in Organizations : 48
Knorr-Cetina (K.D.) : 40
Knowledge
and Historical Chronologies : 398
Knowledge of Health
of Children: 96–97
—Reference to Blos (P.) : 97
—Reference to Gochman (D.) : 97

Knowledge of Health *(continued)*
—Reference to Lewis (C.E.) and
Lewis (M.A.) : 97
—Reference to Nagy (M.H.) : 97
Koenig (H.E.) : 275
Kohl (Helmut) : 312
Kornhauser (W.) : 276
Korobeinikov (V.S.) : 380
Korzenny (F.) : 47, 50
Korzybski (Alfred) : 330
Kozmetsky (G.) : 281
Krantz (D.L.) : 366
Krasnow (E.G.) : 62
Krippendorf (K.) : 381
Kubla Khan : 376
Kuroda (Y.) : 133

Lakoff (G.) : 359
Lander (B.G.) : 130
Langer (E.J.) : 104
Language
and AIDS Prevention : 111
and Power : 327
and Reality : 330
Figurative—versus Literal Language :
327–328
Literal—Figurative Language : 327–328
Referential—.
—Western Episteme : 326–327
Role in Museum Experience.
—Reference to Nystrand (M.) : 372
Role in Understanding : 335–336
Scientific—and Power : 327
Scientific—and Truth : 328
Larkin (J.P.) : 130
Larsen (J.K.) : 186, 196, 199, 200, 275,
276, 277, 278, 280, 293, 307, 317
Larsen (J.K.)
Reference on Life-Styles in Silicon Val-
ley : 300, 306
Lashley (K.S.) : 352
Lazarsfeld (P.F.) : 13, 132, 133, 138, 148
Lazarsfeld (P.F.), Berelson (B.), and Gau-
det (H.)
Reference on Role of Opinion Leaders in
Mass Communication : 132
Le Bon (Gustav) : 12
Le Bon (Gustav)
Reference on Mass Audience Concept :
11
Lee (D.R.) : 384
Lees (F.A.) : 392
Leff (N.H.) : 263, 384
Leisure
See also Electronic Leisure

Lemert (J.B.) : 130
Lerner (D.) : 276
Leroy (D.J.) : 131
Letters to the Editor
and Interactivity : 128
Demographics : 129
Reasons for Writing : 130
Levin (J.) : 130
Levinson (P.) : 75
Levy (M.R.) : 135, 137, 138, 139, 147, 154
Lewis (A.) : 129
Lewis (C.E.) : 97
Lewis (C.E.) and Lewis (M.A.)
Reference on Knowledge of Health of
Children : 97
Lewis (M.A.) : 97
Lewis (R.W.B.) : 120
Lewis-Beck (M.S.) : 174
Lievrouw (L.A.) : 4, 47, 296, 401
Life-Styles
in Silicon Valley.
—Reference to Larsen (J.K.) : 306
Life-Styles
in Silicon Valley.
—Reference to Larsen (J.K.) : 300
Linguistic Analysis
and Mediation : 30
Linguistic Signs
and Tropes : 338
Linguistic Variables
and Social Situations : 69
Lippmann (Walter) : 343
Literacy
and Information Access : 89
and Mass Communication.
—Reference to Barthes (Roland) : 29
and Roles : 87
Literal Language
versus Figurative Language : 327–328
Literalizing Nature
of Western Episteme : 328
Literary Circles
and Communication Technology : 121
and Intellectual History : 118–123
and Reference Citations : 119
Literary Genres
Role of Tropisms : 340
Little (B.R.) : 69
Lockhart (P.) : 104
Lodge (G.C.) : 255
Loesberg (J.) : 123
Loevinger (L.) : 30
Logue (T.) : 245
Lohr (S.) : 241

London
  as a Global City.
    —Reference to Hewlett (N.) and Topo-
      rowski (J.) : 240
Longley (L.D.) : 62
Longshore (D.L.) : 110
Loughlin (J.) : 40
Lowery (C.R.) : 107
Lum (P.) : 47, 58
Lyle (J.) : 133, 134, 136, 161, 169

Machlup (F.) : 185, 195, 269, 296, 304, 380,
      396
Machlup (F.)
  Class Bias.
    —Reference to Schement (J.R.) and
      Leivrouw (L.A.) : 296
Mainstreaming
  and Resonance Concept.
    —Reference to Gerbner (G.) : 354–355
Maitland Commission : 248
Mandeville (T.) : 248
Manufacturing Automation Commission of
      the Special Secretariat of Informat-
      ics of Brazil : 211
Marchand (D.A.) : 380, 382
Marginal Costs
  of Information : 384
Margolis (S.) : 120–121
MarketModel
  of Technological Innovation and Profit
      Motive : 260
Marketplace Model
  of Technological Innovation : 255
  of Technological Innovation and Entre-
      preneurial Boldness : 260
  of Technological Innovation and Interna-
      tional Trade : 261
  of Technological Innovation and Policy-
      Making Organizations : 256–258
  of Technological Innovation in the
      United States : 256–258
  of Technological Innovation.
    —Disadvantages : 260
    —Role of National Government : 257
  versus Public Utility Model : 258, 264
Markoff (J.) : 260
Marks (D.) : 272
Marshall (A.) : 380, 381, 383, 386
Marvin (C.) : 131
Marx (Karl) : 11, 15
Marxist Perspective
  of Mass Communication : 14
Mass Audience
  versus Public.
    —Reference to Park (Robert E.) : 13

Mass Audience Concept
  Reference to Le Bon (Gustav) : 11
Mass Communication
  and AIDS Prevention.
    —Reference to Williams (L.S.) : 111
  and Context : 26, 76, 77
  and Conversational Technologies : 38
  and Health Attitudes.
    —Reference to Flay (B.R.) : 103
  and Individual Psychology : 13
  and Interactivity : 127
  and Interpersonal Relationships.
    —Reference to Thayer (L.) : 25–26
  and Literacy.
    —Reference to Barthes (Roland) : 29
  and Para-Social Interaction.
    —Reference to Horton (D.) and Wohl
      (R.R.) : 136–137
  and Persuasion Strategies.
    —Reference to Reardon (K.K.) : 106
  and Place : 72
  and Self-Perception.
    —Reference to Solomon (G.) : 104
  and Social Realities : 30
  and Social Situations : 81
  and Society : 12, 13
  and Stereotyped Images : 15
  as a Problematic Term : 9–18
  as Extension of Human Psychological
      Processes : 27–28
  Bullet Theory : 4
  Contextual Characteristics : 77–78
  Dependency Model.
    —Reference to Ball-Rokeach (S.J.)
      and DeFleur (M.L.) : 24
  Extrinsic Factors : 25
  Industrialized Nature : 16, 17, 26
  Innis-McLuhan Perspective.
    —Reference to Carey (J.) : 23
  Interactive Use : 126
  Marxist Perspective : 14
  Paine Studies : 5
  Role of Opinion Leaders in—.
    —Reference to Lazarsfeld (P.F.), Ber-
      elson (B.), and Gaudet (H.) : 132
  Uses and Gratifications Theory : 4, 132
Mass Communication Concept
  Contemporary Significance : 15–18
  History : 11–15
Mass Communication Research
  at Columbia University : 13
  at Ohio State University : 13
  at Princeton University : 13
  at University of Chicago : 12
  at Yale University : 13

Mass Communication Theory
   versus Interpersonal Communication
      Theory : 3–6, 41, 42, 43, 73, 95, 96,
      126, 128, 132
Mass Media
   See also Mass Communication
Mass Media Use
   and Escape.
      —Reference to Katz (E.) and Foulkes
      (D.) : 135
   and Interactivity : 172
   and Para-Social Interaction : 138
   and Rationality : 136
   and Sociability : 131–136
      —Reference to Atkin (C.K.) : 133
      —Reference to Donohew (L.) : 134
      —Reference to Johnstone (J.W.C.) :
      134
McCain (T.A.) : 131
McCulloch (Warren) : 334
McEachern (M.) : 131
McGuire (B.) : 131
McGuire (T.W.) : 47, 48, 171
McGuire (W.J.) : 110
McLeod (J.M.) : 101
McLeod (J.M.) and Chaffee (S.R.)
   Reference on Family Units and Commu-
      nication Patterns : 101
McLuhan (M.H.) : 23, 27, 47, 57, 285
McLuhan (M.H.)
   Reference on Resonance Concept and
      Ecological Thinking : 354
McMurray (S.) : 242
McQuail (D.) : 132, 134
Mead (G.H.) : 84
Mechanic (D.)
   Reference on Health Attitudes and Fam-
      ily Units : 98–99
Medawar (Sir Peter) : 344
Media
   Demassification Communications Revo-
      lution : 293
   Demassification Electronic Leisure : 288
Media Characteristics
   Reference to Schramm (W.) : 47
Media Dependency Theory
   Reference to Ball-Rokeach (S.J.) : 104–
      105
Media Determinism
   Reference to Ellul (J.) : 23–24
Media Effects
   and Communication Systems Model: 56–
      57
Media Grammar : 29
Media Institutions
   and Mediation : 26–27

Media Use
   and Context : 78–84
Media Uses and Gratifications
   and Communication Systems Model : 58
Mediated Encounters
   and Behavior.
      —Reference to Schleflen (A.E.) : 75–
      76
   versus Interpersonal Encounters : 75–76
Mediated Sensory Experience
   and Television : 90
Mediation
   and Adaptation : 31
   and Communication : 4, 28, 41, 42
   and Complexity : 31
   and Environment : 32
   and Human Communication : 22
   and Linguistic Analysis : 30
   and Media Institutions : 26–27
   and Projection : 30
   and Reflection : 30
   and Specialization : 31
   and Symbiosis : 33–34
   and Two-Sided Evolution : 32
   Biotechnological Explanation : 31
   Theory : 22–36
Medicine
   Role of Resonance Concept : 352
Mehrabian (A.) : 50
Melville (Herman) : 333
Memory
   Holographic Theory Resonance Con-
      cept.
      —Reference to Pribram (K.H.) : 353
Merton (R.K.) : 275–276
Meta-Information Systems
   and Information Systems : 89
   and Roles : 86
Metacommunication
   and Tropisms : 346
Metaphoric Nature
   of Description : 331
Meyer (J.W.) : 276
Meyrowitz (J.) : 3, 5, 72, 73, 75, 82, 86, 87,
      90
Michaels (C.F.) : 353
Microelectronics
   Research and Development in Japan :
      228
Microelectronics and Computer Technol-
      ogy Corporation (MCC) : 186
Microelectronics and Computer Technol-
      ogy Corporation (MCC)
   Location at University of Texas at Aus-
      tin : 272–273
   and Spin-off Microelectronics firms : 273

Microelectronics Center of North Carolina
   History and Description : 206
Microelectronics Research
   Role of Universities : 274
Milgram (S.) : 70
Milgram (S.)
   Reference on Role of Social Situations in
      Human Behavior : 68–69
Military Weapons Industry
   in Brazil : 220
Miller (A.H.) : 147
Miller (G.R.) : 3
Miller (W.) : 129–130
Miller (W.E.) : 147
Miller Thomas (Alan) : 35
Mills (C. Wright) : 275
Minasian (J.R.) : 384
Mind
   and Culture : 331
   and Tropisms : 330–331
Ministry of International Trade and Indus-
   try (MITI) : 189, 230, 260
Ministry of Posts and Telecommunications
   (MPT) : 189
Minority Groups
   and AIDS Prevention.
      —Reference to Williams (L.S.) : 111–
      112
Mischel (W.) : 69
Mitchell (M.)
   Reference on Regulation and Informa-
      tion Societies : 302
Miterrand (President Francois) : 309
Mobility
   and the Communications Revolution :
      293
Moholy-Nagy (Laszlo) : 36
Monet (Jean) : 310
Monologic Communication
   versus Telelogic Communication : 47
Monroe (Marilyn) : 343
Moore (K.A.) : 102
Morgan (M.) : 15
Morris (R.E.) : 366
Morton (J.E.) : 241
Moses (A.M.) : 47
Moss (M.L) : 244, 249
Moss (M.L.)
   Reference on Growth of Information
      Capitals : 299
   Reference on Private versus Public Man-
      agement of Telecommunications
      Systems : 299–300
   Reference on Role of Decentralization in
      Information Societies : 299

Multinational Corporations
   Growth.
      —Role of Telecommunications : 240
Mumford (L.) : 396–397
Murray (T.J.) : 197
Musashi (T.) : 263
Museum Experience
   Invisible City Metaphor.
      —Reference to Calvino (I.) : 376
   Role of Community : 375
      —Conversation : 372
      —Disorder : Reference to Valery (P.) :
      371
      —Ideas : 368
      —Identification : 370
      —Imagination : 369
      —Indwelling: Reference to Polanyi
      (M.) : 369
      —Invisible Meanings : 371
      —Language: Reference to Nystrand
      (M.) : 372
      —Observer : 366
      —Passages : 374
      —Personal Knowledge : 376
      —Questions : 366
      —Resonance : 367
      —Stories : 373
Museum Roles
   Reference to Weil (S.E.) : 367
Museums
   and Human Experience.
      —Reference to Weil (S.E.) : 367
   and Texts : 368
   Thinking : 365–377
Musical Genres
   Role of Tropisms : 341
Mutz (D.C.) : 95
Myths
   of Information Societies.
      —Reference to Weingarten (R.) : 302–
      303

Nadel (I.B.) : 120, 122, 123
Nagy (M.H.)
   Reference on Knowledge of Health of
      Children : 97
Nanus (B.) : 47, 62
Narcissus
   as Metaphor for Process of Mediation :
      22
National Commercial Training Service
   (SENAC) : 217
National Council of Informatics and Auto-
   mation (CONIN) : 221
National Economies
   and Information Technology : 254

National Government
  Role in Marketplace Model of Techno-
    logical Innovation : 257
National Governors Association : 278
National Industrial Training Service
  (SENAI) : 217
Nationalization
  of Information Systems and Public Util-
    ity Model of Technological Innova-
    tion : 261
New Media
  and Communication Technology : 45
  and Communication Theory.
    —Reference to Rice (R.E.) and associ-
      ates : 45
    —Reference to Steinfield (C.) and
      Fulk (J.) : 46
  versus Old Media : 46
New York
  New Jersey Teleport : 186
New York Times : 291
Newark Museum : 367
Newly Industrialized Country (NIC) Model
  of Technological Innovation : 255–
    256
Newton (Sir Issac) : 359
Nielsen (A.C.) : 73, 90
Nightingale (V.) : 48
Nilles (J.) : 47
Nisbett (R.E.) : 107
Nixon (Richard) : 77
Noelle-Neumann (E.) : 15, 132
Nordlund (J.E.) : 135, 137, 138, 139
North Carolina
  See also Research Triangle of North Car-
    olina
North Carolina Biotechnology Center : 207
North Carolina State University at Raleigh :
  206
Noyelle (T.J.) : 240
Nystrand (M.)
  Reference in Role of Language in Mu-
    seum Experience : 372

Objective Nature
  of Facts : 334
Observer
  Role in Museum Experience : 366
Odum (Howard W.) : 206
Office of Technology Assessment : 277,
  278, 302
Ogburn (W.F.) : 123
Ohio State University
  Mass Communication Research : 13
Okimoto (D.I.) : 260

Old Media
  versus New Media : 46
Olson (Ken) : 274
Ong (W.J.) : 23, 26
Opinion Leaders
  Role in Mass Communication.
    —Reference to Lazarsfeld (P.F.), Ber-
      elson (B.), and Gaudet (H.) : 132
Optical Fibre Systems
  and Growth of Financial Markets : 243–
    244
  and Satellite Communication Systems :
    245
  in the Pacific Rim : 245–248
  in the United States : 244
Order
  and Structure.
    —Reference to Bohm (D.) : 357
Organism Concept
  and Resonance Concept.
    —Reference to Whitehead (A.N.) :
      355–356
Organization
  and Structure.
    —Reference to Bohm (D.) : 358
Organizational Communication
  and Interpersonal Communication : 44
Organizational Differences
  among Information Societies : 306–307
  between IBM and Silicon Valley : 307
Organizations
  Role of Communication Technology.
    —Reference to Kling (R.) : 48
Ortony (A.) : 359
Ownership
  of Telecommunications Systems : 248–
    250
Ozawa (T.) : 380

Pacific Rim
  Growth of Financial Markets : 242
  Optical Fibre Systems : 245–248
Paine Studies
  of Mass Communication : 5
Paisley (W.J.) : 129
Paladin : 340
Para-Social Interaction : 5
Para-Social Interaction
  and Content Analysis : 137
  and Mass Communication.
    —Reference to Horton (D.) and Wohl
      (R.R.) : 136–137
  and Mass Media Use : 138
  and Real Interaction : 144–145
  and Sociability : 139
  and Social Interaction : 139

Para-Social Interaction *(continued)*
  Definition : 136
  Difference from Previous Approaches :
      170
  Empirical Testing : 146–170
  Measures : 137–138
  Research Questions : 143–146
  Statistical Tests : 140, 144, 155, 157
  Theoretical Model : 138–143
Parducci (A.) : 107
Park (Robert E.) : 12, 14, 15
Park (Robert E.)
  Reference on Public versus Mass Audi-
      ence : 13
Parker (E.B.) : 133, 134, 136, 161, 169
Partridge (D.) : 123
Passages
  Role in Museum Experience : 374
Pasternack (S.) : 130
Pauling (L.) : 351
Pearce (W.B.) : 41, 50
Pedhazur (K.) : 173–174
Peer Groups
  and Behavior in Children : 102
  and Communication Patterns.
      —Reference to Sussman (S.) : 102
Peliano (J.C.P.) : 223
Peplay (L.A.) : 107
Perception
  and Resonance Concept.
      —Reference to Grossberg (S.) : 353
Perceptual Meaning
  and Resonance Concept.
      —Reference to Gibson (J.J.) : 353
Personal Computing
  and Education : 290
  and the Communications Revolution :
      288–290
  Business Applications : 289
  Home Use : 289
  in United States : 289
Personal Knowledge
  Reference to Polanyi (M.) : 376
  Role in Museum Experience : 376
Personal Relationships
  and Information Societies : 198
Personal Sources
  of Documentation : 119
Personality
  and Human Behavior : 69
Persuasion Strategies
  and AIDS Prevention : 108
      —Reference to Reardon (K.K.) : 107
  and Mass Communication.
      —Reference to Reardon (K.K.) : 106
  and Rationality : 106

Pervin (L.A.) : 71
Peterson (J.L.) : 102
Pharmaceutical Industry
  in Brazil : 220
Philadelphia Museum : 370
Phillips (A.) : 47, 58
Photography
  and Self-Image.
      —Reference to Cathcart (R.) and
          Gumpert (G.) : 29
Physical Location
  See also Place
  and Behavior : 76
  and Social Identity.
      —Reference to Duncan (H.D.) : 85
  and Social Situations : 71
  and Status: : 85
Physics
  Role of Resonance Concept : 351
Pierce (J.R.) : 123
Pingree (S.) : 3
Place
  See also Context
  and Interpersonal Communication : 72
  and Mass Communication : 72
Plato : 68
Plenge (G.) : 48
Polanyi (M.) : 346
Polanyi (M.)
  Reference on Personal Knowledge : 376
  Reference on Role of Indwelling in Mu-
      seum Experience : 369
Policy Issues
  and Information Societies : 308–316
Policy Making Organizations
  and Technological Innovation.
      —Reference to Eveland (J.D.) : 301
Policy-Making Organizations
  and Marketplace Model of Technological
      Innovation : 256–258
  and Public Utility Model of Technologi-
      cal Innovation : 258
Political Science
  and Information Societies.
      —Reference to Dutton (W.) : 304
Polo (Marco) : 376
Pool (I. de Sola) : 62, 263, 380
Pool (I. de Sola)
  Reference on Information Overload : 188
Porat (M.U.) : 185, 195, 297, 380
Porat (M.U.)
  Reference on Information Societies ver-
      sus Industrial Societies : 187
Postindustrial Societies
  See Information Societies
Poushinsky (N.) : 131

Power
  and Language : 327
  and Scientific Language : 327
Powesland (P.F.) : 69
Pribram (K.H.)
  Reference on Resonance Concept and
    Holographic Theory of Memory :
    353
Prigogine (I.) : 350
Princeton University
  Mass Communication Research : 13
Private Good
  Information versus Information as Pub-
    lic Good : 386–388
Private Sector
  and Telecommunications Systems : 249–
    250
Privileged Nature
  of Scientific Knowledge : 329
Production Patterns
  and Communication Technology.
    —Reference to Coriat (B.) : 212
Profit Motive
  and MarketModel of Technological Inno-
    vation : 260
Projection
  and Mediation : 30
Psychology
  See also Individual Psychology
  Role of Resonance Concept : 352–354
Public
  versus Crowds.
    —Reference to Blumer (H.) : 14
  versus Mass Audience.
    —Reference to Park (Robert E.) : 13
Public Good
  Information as Private Good : 386–388
Public Utility Model
  of Technological Innovation : 255, 258,
    259:
    —and International Trade : 261
    —and Nationalization of Information
      Systems : 261
    —and Policy-Making Organizations :
      258
    —in Great Britain : 262
    —in Japan : 262
  versus Marketplace Model : 258, 264
Publishing
  See also Electronic Publishing
Pythagoras : 360

Quality of Life
  in Silicon Valley : 201–202
QUBE Interactive Television System : 190

Questions
  Role in Museum Experience : 366

Rafaeli (S.) : 3, 4, 5, 126, 152
Rahim (S.) : 257
Rarick (G.) : 130, 172
Rationality
  and Human Communication : 40
  and Intelligence : 356
  and Mass Media Use : 136
  and Persuasion Strategies : 106
  and Structure : 358–359
Rationalization
  and University-Industry Technology
    Transfer : 275–276
Rattner (H.) : 213, 215
Rattner (H.)
  Reference on Technological Nationalism :
    216
Rayfield (G.E.) : 131
Reagan (President Ronald) : 305
Real Interaction
  and Para-Social Interaction : 144–145
Reality
  and Language : 330
  and Self-Perception.
    —Reference to Taylor (S.E.) and
      Brown (J.D.) : 107
Reardon (K.K.) : 4, 5, 47, 95, 96, 102, 105,
    109, 110, 128
Reardon (K.K.)
  Reference on Mass Communication and
    Persuasion Strategies : 106
  Reference on Persuasion Strategies and
    AIDS Prevention : 107
Reference Citations
  and Literary Circles : 119
Referential Language
  Western Episteme : 326–327
Reflection
  and Mediation : 30
Regulation
  and Information Societies.
    —Reference to Mitchell (M.) : 302
Renfro (P.C.) : 130
Research and Development
  of Microelectronics in Japan : 228
Research Triangle of North Carolina
  and Silicon Valley : 208
  History and Description : 206–208
  University-Industry Technology Transfer :
    270, 274, 280
    —Government Support : 277–278
Resonance
  and Energy Amplification : 350
  and Intelligence : 356–360

Resonance *(continued)*
  as Like Knowing Like : 360
  Definition : 350
  Role in Museum Experience : 367
Resonance Concept
  and Ecological Thinking.
    —Reference to McLuhan (M.H.) : 354
  and Fourier Analysis : 353
  and Holographic Theory of Memory.
    —Reference to Pribram (K.H.) : 353
  and Mainstreaming.
    —Reference to Gerbner (G.) : 354–355
  and Organism Concept.
    —Reference to Whitehead (A.N.) :
      355–356
  and Perception.
    —Reference to Grossberg (S.) : 353
  and Perceptual Meaning.
    —Reference to Gibson (J.J.) : 353
  Role in
    —Biology : 351
    —Chemistry : 351
    —Communication Theory : 354, 355
    —Medicine : 352
    —Physics : 351
    —Psychology : 352–354
  Transdisciplinary Nature : 360, 361
Restivo (S.) : 40
Rice (R.E.) : 47, 48, 171, 190, 293
Rice (R.E.) and associates
  Reference on Communication Theory
    and New Media : 45
Rice (S.A.) : 123
Richardson (J.L.) : 105
Riley (J.W.) : 133, 134, 136, 175
Riley (M.W.) : 133, 134, 136, 175
Roberts (D.) : 47
Roberts (D.F.) : 129
Robinson (H.) : 121, 122
Rogers (E.M.) : 5, 23, 35, 39, 40, 48, 95,
    106, 125, 132, 152, 186, 190, 196,
    208, 269, 275, 276, 277, 280, 281,
    293, 317, 401
Rogers (E.M.) and Chen (Y-C. A.)
  Reference on Characteristics of Informa-
    tion Societies : 281
Rokeach (M.) : 104, 148
Roles
  and Context : 96
  and Gender : 86
  and Information Access : 87–88
  and Literacy : 87
  and Meta-Information Systems : 86
  and Social Identity : 84
Roman Systems
  of Communication : 32

Romantic Poets : 118
Rosen (S.) : 107
Rosenau (J.N.) : 129
Rosenberg (J.E.) : 107
Rosengren (K.E.) : 135, 137, 138, 139
Rosenthal (R.) : 70
Rosnow (R.L.) : 70, 71
Ross (J.E.) : 133
Ross (L.) : 107
Rowley (A.) : 242
Ruben (B.D.) : 3, 5, 6, 41, 62, 354
Rubin (Z.) : 107
Ruchinskas (J.) : 47
Rules
  and Social Situations : 70

Salvaggio (J.L.) : 189, 255, 262, 301
Samuelson (P.A.) : 381, 386
San Jose Mercury : 199
Satellite Communication Systems
  and Optical Fibre Systems : 245
Satellite Technology Development
  in Japan : 232
Saturday Evening Post Magazine : 31
Scacchi (W.) : 48
Schement (J.R.) : 62, 296
Schement (J.R.) and Leivrouw (L.A.)
  Reference on Alternative Classifications
    of Information Societies : 297
  Reference on Class Bias in work of Bell
    (D.) : 297
  Reference on Class Bias in work of
    Machlup (F.) : 296
  Reference on Development of Analytical
    Tools in Information Societies :
    296–297
Schickle (R.) : 120
Schleflen (A.E.) : 71
Schleflen (A.E.)
  Reference on Mediated Encounters and
    Behavior : 75–76
Schmieder (R.) : 196
Schneider (Pierre) : 36
Schramm (W.) : 133, 134, 136, 161, 169,
    354
Schramm (W.)
  Reference on Media Characteristics : 47
Schultze (Q.J.) : 131
Schwartz-Schilling (Christian) : 315–316
Science
  and Tropisms : 328–329
  Role of Analogy : 360
    —Reference to Bohm (D.) : 359
  Role of Tropes : 343–344
Scientific Knowledge
  Privileged Nature : 329

Scientific Language
  and Power : 327
  and Truth : 328
Scott (W.R.) : 276
Secord (P.F.) : 70
Self-Expression
  Automatistic Nature : 325
Self-Image
  and Photography.
    —Reference to Cathcart (R.) and
      Gumpert (G.) : 29
Self-Perception
  and AIDS Prevention : 110
  and Mass Communication.
    —Reference to Solomon (G.) : 104
  and Reality.
    —Reference to Taylor (S.E.) and
      Brown (J.D.) : 107
Self-Perception
  and Feedback : 107
Semiconductor Industry Association : 198
Semiconductors
  and Silicon Valley : 194–195
Sense-Making Theory
  of Communication : 41
Shakespeare (William) : 118, 120, 340
Shannon (C.E.) : 190–191
Shannon and Weaver's Model
  of Communication : 190
Shaw (R.) : 353
Sheldrake (R.) : 351
Shenkel (R.J.) : 107
Shimizu (M.) : 262
Shirts (R.G.) : 47
Shore (M.F.) : 123
Short (J.) : 47, 50, 171
Shoup (C.S.) : 387
Shrauger (J.S.) : 107
Siegel (J.) : 47, 48, 171
Siegel (L.) : 260
Signiorelli (N.) : 15
Sikorski (L.A.) : 129
Silicon Valley
  and Entrepreneurism : 195–199
  and IBM.
    —Organizational Differences : 307
  and Research Triangle of North Carolina :
      208
  and Semiconductors : 194–195
  Description : 194
  Effects on Family Life : 199–200
  Information Exchange.
    —Reference to Davis (W.) : 198
  Interpersonal Values : 201

Life-Styles.
  —Reference to Larsen (J.K.) : 300,
    306
Nature of Work Force : 195
Quality of Life : 201–202
Social Impacts : 186
Social Problems : 199
Traditional Values : 202
University-Industry Technology Transfer :
    270
Work Ethic : 195, 200, 201
Singer (B.D.) : 129–130
Singletary (M.W.) : 129–130
Singleton (L.A.) : 401
Situation
  and Context : 67–68
Skinner (B.F.) : 329
Smell-O-Vision : 32
Smilor (R.W.) : 281
Smilor (R.W.), Kozmetsky (G.), and Gib-
    son (D.V.)
  Reference on Factors which Determine
      Location of High Technology Com-
      panies : 281
Smith (A.) : 285
Snyder (C.R.) : 107
Sociability
  and Communication Technology : 171
  and Computer Users : 171
  and Computer-Mediated Communica-
      tion.
    —Reference to Kiesler (S.), Siegel
      (J.), and McGuire (T.W.) : 171
  and Mass Media Use : 131–136
    —Reference to Atkin (C.K.) : 133
    —Reference to Donohew (L.) : 134
    —Reference to Johnstone (J.W.C.) :
      134
Sociability
  and Para-Social Interaction : 139
Social Behavior
  Constructivist Approach : 40
Social Context
  and Communication : 54, 55, 57
Social Efficiency
  and Information : 388–389
  of Information as Problematic Concept.
    —Reference to Arrow (K.J.) : 388
Social Identity
  and Physical Location.
    —Reference to Duncan (H.D.) : 85
  and Roles : 84
Social Interaction
  and Para-Social Interaction : 139
Social Presence
  and Involvement : 50

Social Problems
  and Information Societies : 189
Social Realities
  and Mass Communication : 30
Social Situations
  and Experimentation in Social Psychol-
    ogy : 70
  and Linguistic Variables : 69
  and Mass Communication : 81
  and Physical Location : 71
  and Rules : 70
  Problematic Nature : 71
  Role in Human Behavior.
    —Reference to Barker (R.G.) : 70
    —Reference to Goffman (E.) on— : 68
    —Reference to Milgram (S.) : 68–69
Social Structure
  and Communication Technology : 48
Social-Psychological Implications
  of Information Societies.
    —Reference to Williams (F.) : 298
  of the Communications Revolution.
    —Reference to Williams (F.), Rice
      (R.E.), and Dordick (H.S.) : 293
Society
  and Mass Communication : 12–13
Sociology of Fame : 120
Solomon (G.) : 105
Solomon (G.)
  Reference on Mass Communication and
    Self-Perception : 104
South Carolina
  Promotion of High Technology Indus-
    tries.
    —Reference to Black (S.) : 300–301
Space Development
  in Japan : 231–232
Spangler (K.) : 47, 59
Speaking Behavior
  on Telephones : 75
Special Commission on Manufacturing Au-
    tomation : 219
Specialization
  and Mediation : 31
Speech
  Role of Tropes : 344–345
Spencer (Herbert) : 35
Spin-off Microelectronics firms
  and Microelectronics and Computer
    Technology Corporation (MCC) :
    273
Sproull (L.S.) : 47, 48, 50, 59
Staff (F.) : 122
Stanbach (T.M. Jr.) : 240

Stanford Research Park
  University-Industry Technology Transfer :
    274
Status
  and Physical Location : 85
Steinfield (C.) : 48, 262
Steinfield (C.) and Fulk (J.)
  Reference on Communication Theory
    and New Media : 46
Sterling (C
  Reference) : 303–304
Sterling (C.H.) : 257
Stevens (S.S.) : 352
Stewart (C.M.) : 48, 55
Stigler (G.) : 381, 383
Stories
  Role in Museum Experience : 373
Strickland (D.E.) : 44
Strickland (L.) : 48
Structure
  and Order.
    —Reference to Bohm (D.) : 357
  and Organization.
    —Reference to Bohm (D.) : 358
  and Rationality : 358–359
  Concept.
    —Reference to Bohm (D.) : 356–357
Subliminal Nature
  of Human Communication : 341
Sugano (T.) : 260
Sullivan (Bill) : 302
Sussman (L.) : 129
Sussman (S.) : 110
Sussman (S.)
  Reference on Peer Groups and Commu-
    nication Patterns : 102
Svenning (L.) : 47
Symbiosis
  and Mediation : 33–34

Tachikawa (K.) : 262
Takasaki (N.) : 380
Tamke (F.) : 123
Tamura (M.) : 255
Tarrant (W.D.) : 129
Tauile (J.R.) : 223
Taylor (S.E.) : 107, 108, 110, 112
Taylor (S.E.) and Brown (J.D.)
  Reference on Self-Perception and Reality :
    107
Taylor Compton (Carl) : 274
Technological Development
  and Unemployment in Brazil : 233–224
  in Brazil.
    —Reference to Castro (C. de M.) :
      220–221

Technological Innovation
and Commercialization : 269
and Distribution of Economic Benefits :
213
and Economic Success : 263
and Policy-Making Organizations.
—Reference to Eveland (J.D.) : 301
and University-Industry Technology
Transfer : 267
Communist-Totalitarian Model : 255–256
Competitive Model *See* Marketplace
Model of Technological Innovation
MarketModel and Profit Motive : 260
Marketplace Model : 255
—Disadvantages : 260
—Role of National Government : 257
Marketplace Model and Entrepreneurial
Boldness : 260
Marketplace Model and International
Trade : 261
Marketplace Model and Policy-Making
Organizations : 256–258
Marketplace Model in the United States :
256–258
Nature in Information Societies : 208
Newly Industrialized Country (NIC)
Model : 255–256
Public Utility Model : 255, 258, 259
—and International Trade : 261
—and Nationalization of Information
Systems : 261
—and Policy-Making Organizations :
258
—in Great Britain : 262
—in Japan : 262
Role of Universities in— : 270
Theoretical Models : 255
United States Model versus Japan Model
of Technological Innovation Refer-
ence to Tomita (T.) : 263
Technological Nationalism
Reference to Rattner (H.) : 216
Technology
and Crisis : 212
Technology Transfer
Definition : 268
University-Industry—.
—Benefits and Costs : 278–279
—Government Support : 276
—Lack of Research : 275
—Role of Universities : 269, 270, 280,
281
—and Communication Networks : 276
—and Conflicts of Interest : 279
—and Faculty Consulting : 274

—and Faculty Entrepreneurs : 274–
275
—and Industrial Liaison Programs :
274
—and Information Societies : 268
—and Rationalization : 275–276
—in Japan : 271
—in Research Triangle of North Carolina : 270, 274, 280: Government
Support : 277–278
—in Silicon Valley : 270
—in Stanford Research Park : 274
—in United States. Government Support : 277; History : 272
—Technological Innovation : 267
Telecommunications
and Growth of Financial Markets and
Reference to Germany (J.D.) and
Morton (J.E.) : 241
and Growth of Financial Markets and
Reference to Kindleberger (C.P.) :
241
Role in Decentralization of Production
and Decision-Making Operations :
240
Role in Growth of Multinational Corpo-
rations : 240
Telecommunications Act
in Great Britain : 262
Telecommunications Industry
in Japan : 231
Telecommunications Market
in Japan : 232–233
—Effect of Bureaucracy : 233–237
Telecommunications Systems
and the Private Sector : 249–250
and Urban Development : 250
Ownership : 248–250
Private versus Public Management.
—Reference to Moss (M.L.) : 299–300
Telelogic Communication
versus Monologic Communication : 47
Telephones
Speaking Behavior : 75
Telephony
and the Communications Revolution :
286–287
Television
See also High Definition Television
(HDTV) and Information Access.
—Reference to Gitlin (T.) : 87
and Mediated Sensory Experience : 90
Television Genres
Role of Tropisms : 340
Television News
Role of Tropisms : 339–340

Telser (L.G.) : 388
Temporality
   and Communication : 49–50
Terman (Fred) : 274
Terry (H.A.) : 62
Tesser (A.) : 107
Texts
   and Museums : 368
Thatcher (Prime Minister Margaret) : 309
Thayer (L.) : 3
Thayer (L.)
   Reference on Interpersonal Relation-
      ships and Mass Communication :
      25–26
Theory
   of Mediation : 22–36
Theory of Mediation
   Nature.
      —Reference to Kerlinger (F.N.) : 34
Thinking
   in Museums : 365–377
Third World Countries
   and Communication Technology.
      —Reference to Castro (C. de M.) :
      214–215
Thomas (S.) : 4, 6
Thomas (W.I.) : 12
Thomas (William I.) : 67
Thornton (L.R.) : 129
Three Dimensional Movies : 32
Time Displacement
   and the Communications Revolution :
      293
Time-Line
   of Information Technology : 403–423
      —Design : 398–400
      —Intellectual Themes : 400–401
Toffler (A.) : 285
Tomita (T.)
   Reference on United States Model of
      Technological Innovation versus Ja-
      pan Model of Technological Innova-
      tion : 263
Tonnies (Ferdinand) : 11
Toporowski (J.) : 240–241
Traditional Values
   in Silicon Valley : 202
Transdisciplinary Nature
   of General Systems Theory.
      —Reference to Bertalanffy (L. von) :
      349–350
   of Resonance Concept : 360–361
Traveling Wave Theory
   of Auditory Perception.
      —Reference to Bekesy (G. von) : 352

Tropes
   and Clichés : 342–343
   and Linguistic Signs : 338
   Role in Creativity : 345
   Role in Science : 343–344
   Role in Speech : 344–345
Tropisms
   and Metacommunication : 346
   and Mind : 330–331
   and Science : 328–329
   Definition : 324
   Implications for Communication Re-
      search : 346
   Role in
      —Advertising : 341
      —Automatistic Nature of Human
         Communication : 326
      —Fashion Genres : 341
      —Human Communication : 338
      —Literary Genres : 340
      —Musical Genres : 341
      —Television Genres : 340
      —Television News : 339–340
      —Understanding : 334, 338, 339, 340,
         341, 342
Truth
   and Scientific Language : 328
Tsurumi (Y.) : 263
Tulving (E.) : 104
Turoff (M.) : 47, 59, 60, 171
Turow (J.) : 4, 5, 6, 17, 18, 131
Twentieth-Century Fund Task Force on the
      Commercialization of Scientific Re-
      search : 279
Two-Sided Evolution
   and Mediation : 32

U.S. Bureau of the Census : 83
Unconsciousness
   Priority over Consciousness : 335
Understanding
   Automatistic Nature : 325
   Role of
      —Conceptual Categories : 332–333
      —Games : 336–337
      —Information : 337
      —Interpretation : 331, 335
      —Language : 335–336
      —Tropisms : 334, 338, 339, 340, 341,
         342
Unemployment
   in Brazil and Technological Development :
      223–224
Ungurait (D.F.) : 73
United States
   Electronic Text Services : 291–292

United States *(continued)*
  Marketplace Model of Technological In-
    novation : 256–257, 258
  Optical Fibre Systems : 244
  Personal Computing : 289
  University-Industry Technology Trans-
    fer.
    —Government Support : 277
    —History : 272
United States Model
  of Technological Innovation versus Ja-
    pan Model of Technological Innova-
    tion.
    —Reference to Tomita (T.) : 263
United States-Japan
  and Economic Competition : 186
Universities
  Role in
    —Microelectronics Research : 274
    —Technological Innovation : 270
    —University-Industry Technology
      Transfer : 269, 270, 280
    —in University-Industry Technology
      Transfer : 281
University of Chicago
  Mass Communication Research : 12
University of North Carolina at Chapel
    Hill : 206
University of Texas at Austin
  Location of Microelectronics and Com-
    puter Technology Corporation
    (MCC) : 272–273
University-Industry Communication
  Definition : 268
University-Industry Relations
  in Information Societies : 296
University-Industry Technology Transfer
  and Communication Networks : 276
  and Conflicts of Interest : 279
  and Faculty Consulting : 274
  and Faculty Entrepreneurs : 274–275
  and Industrial Liaison Programs : 274
  and Information Societies : 268
  and Rationalization : 275–276
  and Technological Innovation : 267
  Benefits and Costs : 278–279
  Government Support : 276
  in Japan : 271
  in Research Triangle of North Carolina :
    270, 274, 280
    —Government Support : 277–278
  in Silicon Valley : 270
  in Stanford Research Park : 274
  in United States.
    —Government Support : 277
    —History : 272

Lack of Research : 275
Role of Universities : 269, 270, 280, 281
Urban Development
  and Telecommunications Systems : 250
US Cable Communications Policy Act :
    263
US Congress : 263
US Department of Commerce : 257
USA Today : 291
Uses and Gratifications Theory
  and Communication Systems Model : 59
  of Mass Communication : 4, 132
Utility Value
  of Information : 382

Vacin (G.) : 129–130
Valery (P.) : 367, 369, 370, 375
Valery (P.)
  Reference on Role of Disorder in Mu-
    seum Experience : 371
Vallee (J.) : 47, 48, 59
Value
  of Information as Problematic Concept:
    382–384
Values
  See also Interpersonal Values
  See also Traditional Values
  and Information Societies : 209–210
Van Gennep (A.) : 83, 85
Van Gogh (Vincent) : 367
Varan (D.) : 263
Verba (S.) : 129–130
Vithoulkas (G.) : 352
Vocational Education
  in Brazil : 217
Vogel (E.F.) : 255
Volgy (T.J.) : 129–130
Vygotsky (L.S.) : 377

Wall Street Journal : 136, 291
Warner (E.) : 103
Warshofsky (F.) : 352
Watergate : 121
Watson (A.) : 199
Weaver (W.) : 190
Weber (D.) : 243
Weber (Max) : 15
Webster (I.) : 48
Weil (S.E.) : 368, 376
Weil (S.E.)
  Reference on Museum Roles : 367
  Reference on Museums and Human Ex-
    perience : 367
Weingarten (R.)
  Reference on Myths of Information So-
    cieties : 302–303

Weinstein (F.B.) : 260
Wellman (B.) : 102
West Germany
    Communication Technology Policy : 308
    Deregulation of Communication Tech-
        nology : 312
Western Episteme
    Liberalizing Nature : 328
    of Referential Language: 326–327
Western Europe
    Communication Technology Policy: 310–
        313
Wharton (Edith) : 120–121
Wharton Circle : 118, 120
Wheelwright (P.) : 359
Whinston (A.B.) : 387
Whitehead (A.N.) : 335, 357
Whitehead (A.N.)
    Reference on Resonance Concept and
        Organism Concept : 355, 356
Wiemann (J.M.) : 3
Wigand (R.T.) : 275, 314, 317
Wilcox (W.) : 130
Wilkins (H.) : 48
Willey (M.M.) : 123
Williams (E.) : 47, 50, 171
Williams (F.) : 47, 58, 285, 286, 290, 293
Williams (F.)
    Reference on Problems of Prediction in
        Information Societies : 298
    Reference on Social-Psychological Im-
        plications of Information Societies :
        298
Williams (F.), Rice (R.E.), and Dordick
        (H.S.)
    Reference on Social-Psychological Im-
        plications of the Communications
        Revolution : 293

Williams (L.S.)
    Reference on AIDS Prevention and Mass
        Communication : 111
    Reference on AIDS Prevention and Mi-
        nority Groups : 111–112
Williams (R.) : 11
Williams (V.) : 290
Wilmot (W.W.) : 43
Wilson (L.R.) : 206
Windahl (S.) : 135, 137, 138, 139
Winick (C.) : 131
Witte Report : 312, 315, 316
Wittgenstein (Ludwig) : 333
Wohl (R.R.) : 73, 136, 137
Wolfe (Tom) : 342
Wood (B.)
    Reference on Family Units and Commu-
        nication Patterns : 99, 100
Woodward (Bob) : 121
Woolf (Virginia) : 120
Woolgar (S.) : 40
Work Ethic
    in Information Societies : 195
    in Silicon Valley : 200–201
Work Ethic in Silicon Valley— : 195
Worthington (G.M.) : 110

Yale University
    Mass Communication Research : 13
Yang (C.Y.) : 392
Yokoi (M.) : 262

Zaniecki (Florence) : 12
Zeman (Z.P.) : 263
Zimbardo (P.) : 70
Zubrow (D.) : 47
Zwibelman (B.B.) : 131